NEW GRE® PRIME 2017

FREE LIVE SUPPORT

At Argo Brothers, we want students to succeed and achieve the score they want by using our book. To further support your exam preparation, we have introduced a free Live Support feature. If you need further explanation of problems or concepts presented in this text, you may submit a help ticket and one of our expert tutors will contact you to assist you with your issue. This service is **100% FREE** to those who have purchased our text. We respond via e-mail and provide detailed video explanations to your questions. To submit a ticket request, please visit our website at: ***www.einstein-academy.com/GRE***

TABLE OF CONTENTS

Chapter 1: Introduction 7
Chapter 2: GRE Exam Structure 15
Chapter 3: Introduction to Analytical Writing 25
Chapter 4: How to Prepare: Analytical Writing 33
Chapter 5: The Analyze an Issue Prompt 41
Chapter 6: The Analyze an Argument Prompt 51
Chapter 7: Introduction to Verbal Reasoning 65
Chapter 8: Reading Comprehension Questions 71
Chapter 9: Text Completion & Sentence Equivalence Questions 87
Chapter 10: Introduction to Quantitative Reasoning 97
Chapter 11: Math Primer 105
Chapter 12: Algebra: The Basics 121
Chapter 13: Geometry: The Basics 141
Chapter 14: Practice Problem Set 157
Chapter 15: Quantitative Comparison 177
Chapter 16: Problem-Solving & Data Interpretation 189
Chapter 17: Writing on The GRE 201
Chapter 18: Analyze an Issue: Model Essay 213
Chapter 19: Analyze an Argument: Model Essay 217
GRE Practice Tests 221
GRE Practice Test 1 223
  Practice Test 1 (Answer Explanations) 246
GRE Practice Test 2 255
  Practice Test 2 (Answer Explanations) 275
GRE Practice Test 3 285
  Practice Test 3 (Answer Explanations) 306
GRE Practice Test 4 315
  Practice Test 4 (Answer Explanations) 334
GRE Practice Test 5 343
  Practice Test 5 (Answer Explanations) 362
GRE Practice Test 6 371
  Practice Test (Answer Explanations) 391
Vocabulary 401
Prefixes & Suffixes 411

ARGO
BROTHERS

I | INTRODUCTION

About the GRE

The GRE® Revised General Test (GRE) is the most commonly accepted exam for many graduate programs. While the exam typically is required for many Master's and Ph.D. programs, many business schools are now starting to accept GRE scores in place of GMAT scores. The exam measures your aptitude for advanced graduate study using three core assessment areas: Verbal Reasoning, Quantitative Reasoning, and Analytical Writing. Each year, admissions committees receive applications from thousands of candidates with diverse educational backgrounds; the GRE provides a standard measure of candidates' educational qualifications that transcripts and other application materials are often unable to provide.

As the name of the exam itself implies, the GRE® Revised General Test is a general exam and tests your overall knowledge of reading comprehension, high school-level math, and critical writing. In addition to the general exam, there are also subject-specific exams. Depending on the program and institution you are applying to, the subject exams may be required in addition to, or in place of, the general exam.

The GRE is offered in more than 150 countries in two formats: computer-adaptive and paper-administered. In most locations, you can register to take the computer-administered exam any time during the year. In locations where the paper-administered exam is available, it is typically only offered three times a year. The GRE is administered by Educational Testing Service (ETS), the same organization that administers other standardized tests such as the TOEFL exam. The latest updates about the GRE Revised General Exam are available on the ETS GRE website at: www.ets.org/gre.

Computer-Adaptive Testing

The GRE is administered most often on a computer, though a paper-administered exam is available. There is often much confusion about the differences between the computer-administered exam and the traditional paper exam. Test-takers are often unsure of their options and which route might be best for them. The overhaul of the GRE in 2011 helped reduce some of this confusion by narrowing the options available to test-takers. Let's explore the characteristics of each of the exams.

Computer-Adaptive Exam vs. Paper Exam

- The **computer-adaptive exam** is the most common version of the exam and is the only option available in most of the more than 150 countries where it is offered. The exam is administered via computer and offered continuously throughout the year at testing centers around the world. The computer-adaptive exam requires you to input your answers into a computer and to type your Analytical Reasoning essay using a basic word processor; the exam has adaptive scoring based on your performance on the first sections of Verbal Reasoning and Quantitative Reasoning. We will dive into adaptive testing shortly.

- The **paper exam** is only available to those testing in an area where the computer-adaptive exam is not available; not many testing locations fall into this category. The paper exam differs from the computer-adaptive exam in a number of ways. Of course, the exam is taken on paper as opposed to the computer. Because of this, adaptive testing is not possible. So, regardless of your performance on the first sections of Verbal Reasoning and Quantitative Reasoning, your second section will not change. Instead of the on-screen calculator, you will receive a calculator at the testing site for you to use during the Quantitative Analysis section.

More about the Computer-Adaptive Exam

The computer-adaptive exam has several advantages over the paper exam. Perhaps the biggest advantage those who take the computer-adaptive exam have over those who take the paper exam is the time frame for receiving scores. With the computer-adaptive exam, you will receive your unofficial scores at the end of the exam. The score will be an unofficial assessment of your Verbal and Quantitative Reasoning sections and will not include your Analytical Writing score. Your official scores are available 10-15 days after the exam. With the paper exam, you will not receive an unofficial score report at the end of the exam, and you may have to wait 5-6 weeks before receiving your score.

The GRE Revised General Test is section-adaptive, not question-adaptive. This means that your performance on the first Verbal Reasoning and Quantitative Reasoning sections determines the difficulty of the questions you will receive in the second section.

Your performance in one assessment area is not linked to the other. So, it is possible to receive more difficult questions for the second Quantitative Reasoning section and not the Verbal Reasoning section. Test-takers who receive less difficult questions on the second section will encounter a scoring ceiling that can make it difficult to reach the top percentile ranks.

Only the Verbal Reasoning and Quantitative Reasoning sections are adaptive. Your performance on the first sections of both Verbal Reasoning and Quantitative Reasoning is assessed in real-time using a proprietary algorithm created by ETS. The Analytical Writing section is not adaptive; your response on the first prompt will not influence which prompt you receive for the second essay.

The computer-adaptive exam is meant to be test-taker friendly, allowing you to test how you feel most comfortable. So, you can skip questions and come back to them later, work within the section in any order you feel comfortable with, and mark questions for review so you can revisit them. You are also always free to change your answers within the allotted time for each section. Even with the adjustments of adaptive testing, it is best to not worry too much about whether or not the questions have increased in difficulty. Just try your best on each of the questions to try to optimize your score.

Testing Instruments for Computer-Adaptive Testing

The computer-adaptive exam has several on-screen tools to help you navigate the exam with ease. You will be able to click through all of the questions for each section and approach them in any order you see fit. In each section, you will be able to scan the entire section, mark questions for later review, and change your answers within the given time period.

For the Quantitative Reasoning section, you also have an on-screen calculator available to assist you with computations. The calculator has basic functionalities and is not nearly as robust as a typical graphing calculator. Since the calculator only has the basic operation functions and a square root key, it is important to hone your understanding of concepts like exponent rules and simplifying expressions to better position yourself to calculate values.

> **Prep Fact:** Because a vast majority of the test-takers who register for the GRE will take the computer-adaptive exam, this text will focus primarily on the preparation for the computer-adaptive exam instead of the more rarely administered paper exam.

How to Register for the Exam

The computer-adaptive exam is offered continuously throughout the year in more than 800 locations worldwide. You can register for the exam by visiting the ETS website at www.ets.com/gre. You can also register via phone. In some areas, the computer-adaptive exam is not offered on a continuous basis, and test-takers must select one of the test administrations offered, which is usually twice per month.

Test-takers in areas where the computer exam is not available can still register online, via phone, or by mail in most locations. The options for test dates are more limited, however, with paper exams only being administered several times per year, usually in February, October, and November. For up-to-date information about the exam, including how to register and current fees, test-takers should consult the official ETS website at ww.ets.com/gre.

Changing your Exam Date or Canceling your Registration

If after you schedule your exam, you need to cancel, reschedule, or change your testing location, you must do so at least four days prior to the exam depending on your location. If you do not make the necessary changes within the allowable time window, you may forfeit your testing fees.

Taking the Exam Multiple Times

You are allowed to take the computer-adaptive GRE once every 21 days; it is important to note that you can only sit for the exam five times in any 12- month period. If you register for the paper exam, you are eligible to take it whenever it is offered without any restrictions.

Test-Takers with Disabilities

ETS provides additional resources for test-takers with documented disabilities. Special accommodations can be made for test-takers who need:

- Additional testing time or extended breaks
- Special medical or computer equipment at the testing site
- Recording devices
- Sign language interpreters
- Other special services or requests

In addition to arranging special accommodations, ETS also has its online study materials available in accessible formats. Test-takers requiring special accommodations should refer to the Bulletin Supplement for Test Takers with Disabilities, available as a download on www.ets.org. Review of submitted documents could take several weeks; so be sure to submit all of the required forms and information well in advance of your test date.

Test Day Expectations

Obviously, the most important thing on test day is to be prepared to tackle the three core assessment areas. But, you also want to make sure that you have a clear understanding of what to expect on test day.

Registration on Test Day

- Be sure to arrive early to allow yourself time to find parking and the precise location. It is a good idea to do a test run prior to the exam to find the location and determine how long it will take you to get there, particularly if you're unfamiliar with the location.
- Make sure that you have the proper identification. Your ID should be valid, be signed, and be issued by a government agency. Examples of proper identification include a valid driver's license, a passport, or a student ID with a signature and expiration date.
- At some testing sites you can expect to be fingerprinted; refusal to comply may impact your ability to take the exam, and you may not receive a refund for your fees.
- If you're taking the computer-adaptive exam, be sure to bring the required admissions documents sent to you by ETS.
- Prior to the start of the exam, you will be required to complete a confidentiality agreement. Failure to completely write out the confidentiality statement will void your registration and you will not be able to sit for the exam. In this event, your fees will not be refunded.

Test Center Regulations

- Food and beverages are not allowed in the testing center. If you have a medical issue that requires you to bring food or beverages into the testing center, accommodations will need to be arranged ahead of time using the resources outlined on the ETS website for testing accommodations.
- Smoking is not allowed in the testing center.
- Aside from your identification and registration materials, no other items may be brought into the testing center. It is best to arrive with as few things as possible. The testing center assumes no responsibility for your personal items that may need to be left outside of the testing area while you sit for the exam.
- Some testing centers have video surveillance equipment to monitor the administration of the exam.
- Personal calculators nor watch calculators are permitted to be used during the exam. Some test sites may ask that you leave your watch outside of the testing area.
- Cell phones and other electronic devices are not allowed in the testing area.
- At most test centers, you will be assigned a seat.
- Prior to the exam, you will be given scratch paper for use on each of the sections at your discretion. If you need more scratch paper you can obtain it from your test administrator. You're not allowed to bring your own scrap paper into the test center or take scratch paper out of of the test center.
- Be sure to dress in layers. The temperatures in the testing centers can vary widely. By dressing in layers, you have more control over your comfort level while taking the exam.

Breaks

- At the completion of each section, there is a one-minute break before the next section begins. After the third section, there is a 10-minute break. This break is optional; you may choose to continue working if you would like.
- If you need a break outside of those provided, you may raise your hand and get the attention of the test administrator. Additional breaks other than those allotted will not stop the testing timer.
- Depending on your test site, you may be required to sign in and out whenever you leave the testing room.

ETS Exam Resources and Services Powerprep® II Software

Taking an exam on the computer can be awkward, especially if you have not had previous practice using the testing software. To help test-takers better prepare for the computer-adaptive testing environment, ETS has made available the PowerPrep® II Software. The software, which is Mac and PC compatible, allows test-takers to:

- Practice answering real test questions using all the options available on the actual exam
- Get accustomed to navigating the calculator and word processing functions
- Take timed exams to simulate actual testing conditions

The software can be downloaded from the ETS website and includes two full-length practice exams.

GRE Search Service®

ETS also offers the GRE Search Service to help graduate schools find students who fit the criteria they are looking for in a qualified candidate. When you register for the exam, you can opt-in to being included in the registry. You can also change your mind and register or hide your profile at any time by changing your preferences on your online applicant profile. Graduate schools and fellowship programs peruse the profiles of those who have registered, and may reach out to test-takers directly to introduce their programs. While this service is used primarily as a recruitment tool for schools and fellowship programs, there are many benefits for the test-taker. By registering, test-takers may become aware of programs and scholarship opportunities they were otherwise not aware were available and have the opportunity to make connections with those directly involved in the admissions process.

GRE Subject Exams

The GRE is a general exam. It measures your understanding of broad concepts and your ability to reason logically. ETS does, however, administer GRE Subject Exams that test your in-depth knowledge in a particular subject area. These exams are meant for students with an extensive knowledge in a particular field, and scores can be used to supplement the General Exam scores. While some programs require the GRE Subject Exams in addition to the General Exam, other programs may only require the Subject Exam. Similar to the GRE General Exam, you can take the subject exam multiple times. Unlike the General computer-adaptive exam, however, the Subject Exams are only offered three times a year in September, October, and April. These exams are not adaptive and are only administered in paper format. All subject exams are scored on a 200-990 scale.

Available GRE Subject Exams

Biochemistry, Cell and Molecular Biology: 170 multiple-choice questions. Focused primarily on biochemistry, cell biology, molecular biology, and genetics.

Biology: 200 multiple-choice questions. Focused primarily on cellular, organismal and molecular biology, and ecology.

Chemistry: 130 multiple-choice questions. Focused primarily on analytical, inorganic, organic, and physical chemistry.

Literature in English: 230 multiple-choice questions. Focused primarily on literary analysis, literary criticism, literary history, and identification of key literary periods, authors and works.

Mathematics: 66 multiple-choice questions. Heavily focused on calculus while a significantly smaller portion of the exam tests knowledge of algebra, real and discrete analysis, and statistics.

Physics: 100 multiple-choice questions. Broadly focused on key physics concepts such as classical and quantum mechanics, optics and wave phenomena, relativity, laboratory methods, and thermodynamics, to name a few.

Psycology: 205 multiple-choice questions. Focused primarily on development, learning, abnormal and clinical psychology, and psychometrics and research design.

About this Book

This book is your comprehensive guide to tackling the GRE. Studying for the GRE can be a daunting task. Figuring out where to start, what to study, and how to track your progress, adds additional stress. The goal of this book is to eliminate that stress and provide you with a proven study outline and plenty of exercises and examples to help you build your proficiency in the core assessment areas. In addition to the chapters that provide you with an in-depth look at the content of the exam in each section, this book also includes a multitude of additional resources to help you:

- Understand the format and core assessment areas of the exam
- Identify your areas for improvement and work toward addressing them
- Refresh your math and vocabulary proficiency
- Simulate real testing conditions using full-length GRE practice exams

Managing your Time

Time is a critical aspect of the GRE. It is important to monitor your time closely so that you are able to work through the section efficiently and attempt as many questions as possible. When taking the computer-adaptive exam, you will have an on-screen clock that shows how much time has elapsed and how much time you have remaining. While this can be a daunting tool, the on-screen clock allows you to track your pace and manage your time.

While time is an important aspect, your primary focus when beginning to study for the GRE should be solidifying your strategy and approach to each of the core assessment areas. First, get comfortable with your approach for each of the sections, then incorporate timing into your study plan.

Preparation Resources in this Book

Diagnostic Exam: There are 6 full-length exams included in this book and 2 full-length exams online. We strongly recommend to take one practice test as a Diagnostic Test before starting this book to help you ascertain your starting point and general understanding of the core assessment areas on the GRE. Don't take your score too personally, especially if the score falls below the score you're hoping to earn. Instead, use this exam as a guide to identify areas you may need to pay more attention to and to measure your progress as you become more familiar with the exam and complete other practice tests.

Math Primer: The Math Primer will help you dig up all that high school math you thought you'd never use. From angles to fractions to algebra, this refresher will prepare you to navigate your way through the Quantitative Analysis section of the exam.

Writing Primer: The Analytical Writing section is usually the section students prepare for the least. But, since graduate programs are keenly interested in your writing ability, it's best to spend some time preparing for this section. The Writing Primer will walk you through common writing mistakes and discuss the key characteristics of good, logically sound writing that essay graders are looking for in your essays.

Extensive Vocabulary Study List: Having a strong vocabulary is key for the verbal section and plays a critical role in the Analytical Writing Section as well. The vocabulary list provides you with commonly used words on the exams as well as an overview of prefixes, suffixes, and roots to help you better understand words you may not know.

Sample Analytical Writing Prompts and Essays: When it comes to the Analytical Writing section, practice is key. In this text, you'll not only find essay prompts to practice with, but you will also find example essays that model what a good essay looks like.

Practice Exams: Monitoring your progress is a critical component of optimizing your performance on the exam. The practice exams will help you keep track of your progress and identify areas for improvement.

ARGO
BROTHERS

2 | GRE EXAM STRUCTURE

For the GRE Exam Overview video you may use this QR Code or visit us at:
www.einstein-academy.com/GRE

Exam Structure

The GRE is comprised of three core assessment areas:

- Analytical Writing
- Verbal Reasoning
- Quantitative Reasoning

These areas are designed to measure your aptitude for critical reasoning and quantitative analysis, and to assess your ability to write coherent, well-supported arguments based on provided evidence and instructions.

The core assessment areas are spread out across the exam in five scored sections: one analytical reasoning section, two verbal reasoning sections, and two quantitative reasoning sections. You will have 30 minutes to complete each Analytical Writing prompt and Verbal Reasoning section, and 35 minutes for each Quantitative Reasoning section. The exam can take anywhere from 3½ - 4 hours depending on the version of the exam administered, unscored sections that we will address later, and the amount of time you spend on the exam orientation tutorial.

The exam orientation tutorial is an untimed introduction to the computer system used to administer the GRE. Only those taking the computer exam will need to complete this tutorial. During the tutorial, you will walk through and familiarize yourself with the various functionalities of the system including the calculator and word processing functions.

It is important to take your time during this tutorial and make sure you are clear on how to operate the system to optimize navigation and avoid issues that could impact your score. You must demonstrate your ability to navigate the testing platform before being allowed to move on to the timed exam. Each section of the exam is scored and timed separately. You can only work on one section at a time.

GRE Core Assessment Areas

Analytical Writing

In this section, you will be asked to write well-reasoned and supported responses to two separate topics chosen at random from the database of available questions. This assessment area is designed to test your analytical and critical thinking skills as well as your ability to both formulate and critique arguments.

Your exam will consist of **one** scored Analytical Writing section that includes **two** prompts:

1. ***Analyze an Issue prompt***

   The Analyze an Issue prompt will present you with specific instructions on how to analyze a given topic. The topic lends itself to multiple perspectives, and there is no correct answer. What is important is that you construct a well-reasoned, cohesive argument that both supports your stance on the issue and closely follows the instructions given in the prompt.

2. ***Analyze an Argument prompt***

   The Analyze an Argument prompt will present you with an argument and ask you to evaluate its merits and logical soundness. Unlike the Analyze an Issue prompt, you will not choose a side for this prompt. Instead, you will write a critical assessment of the argument presented.

The Analytical Writing section will always appear first on the exam. You will have 30 minutes to complete each prompt. The prompts are separately timed, and you can only work on one prompt at a time. The section is scored on a scale of 0-6, in half-point increments. A "6" is the highest possible score. The score reflects your combined Analytical Writing performance; you will not receive a separate score for each prompt.

Verbal Reasoning

In the two Verbal Reasoning sections, you will be asked to read and synthesize information presented in various forms from short sentences to multi-paragraph passages. This assessment area is designed to test your ability to comprehend and evaluate written material. The Verbal Reasoning sections also measures your understanding of sentence structure, punctuation, and proper use of vocabulary.

Your exam will consist of **two** scored Verbal Reasoning sections that include the following question types:

Reading Comprehension

Reading Comprehension questions require you to read the given passages and select the answer choice that best completes the question task. Content of the passages can come from a wide-range of subject matters, and there is often more than one question that corresponds to each passage.

Text Completion

Text Completion questions require you to identify the appropriate term (or terms) that best completes a given sentence. Text Completions can have anywhere from one to three terms that need to be identified. A strong vocabulary and the ability to understand context clues are both essential in this section.

Sentence Equivalence

Sentence Equivalence questions require you to identify two terms for a single blank in a sentence that will create two similar sentences that express the same main idea. Similar to the Text Completion questions, this section requires a strong vocabulary and command of context clues.

The Verbal Reasoning sections can appear in any order on the exam following the Analytical Writing section. You will have 30 minutes to complete each section. Each section on the computer-adapted test consists of 20 questions. The sections are separately timed, and you can only work on one section at a time. The section is scored on a scale of 130-170, in one-point increments. A 170 is the highest possible score. The score reflects your combined Verbal Reasoning performance; you will not receive a separate score for each verbal section.

Quantitative Reasoning

In this section, you will be asked to solve mathematical problems drawn from the subject areas of arithmetic, geometry, algebra, and data analysis. This section tests your ability to solve quantitative problems, understand real-world applications of mathematical principles, and interpret statistical data from charts and graphs.

Your exam will consist of **two** scored Quantitative Reasoning sections that include the following question types:

Quantitative Comparisons

Quantitative Comparison questions require you to analyze the relationship between two given quantities and select the answer choice that best describes the relationship. These questions focus more on understanding mathematical relationships and less on actual mathematical calculations.

Mathematical Problem-Solving

Mathematical Problem-Solving questions require you to use various mathematical formulas and processes to solve for the correct answer to the given problems. These are multiple-choice questions that can have either one or multiple correct answers. These questions may also require you to input your own answer without being provided any answer choices to select from.

Data Interpretation

Data interpretation questions require you to interpret data from charts and graphs in order to solve for the correct answer. These questions are a sub-set of the Mathematical Problem-Solving questions and occur as part of a set where you will use one chart or graph to answer multiple questions.

The Quantitative Reasoning sections can appear in any order on the exam following the Analytical Writing section. You will have 35 minutes to complete each section. Each section on the computer-adapted test consists of 20 questions. The sections are separately timed, and you can only work on one section at a time. The section is scored on a scale of 130-170, in one point increments. A 170 is the highest possible score. The score reflects your combined Quantitative Reasoning performance; you will not receive a separate score for each quantitative section.

Unscored Research and Experimental Sections

Your exam may also include one or two unscored sections. The unscored sections can either be an unidentified experimental section, an identified research unscored research section, or in rare instances, both. The unscored experimental section can occur at any point after the Analytical Writing section, and will be either a Verbal Reasoning or Quantitative Reasoning section. The research section will always be identified as such and will always occur last. Both these sections are used by Educational Testing Services (ETS) to assess the current test methods and to try out new question types and material.

It is important to approach every section as if it is a scored section. Don't try to outsmart the test by figuring out which section, if you have one, is an unscored section. A miscalculation can seriously impact your overall score.

Let's Recap!

The **computer-adaptive exam** consists of three core assessment areas:

Verbal Reasoning: Two 30-minute sections; 20 questions per section.

Quantitative Reasoning: Two 35-minute sections; 20 questions per section.

Analytical Writing: One section with two 30-minute essay tasks: Analyze an Issue and Analyze an Argument.

The assessment areas are tested over five scored sections. Your exam may also include additional unscored experimental and/or research sections.

Core Assessment Area	Sections/Questions	Time Allotted
Analytical Writing	One Section Two Essay Tasks	30 minutes per essay task
Verbal Reasoning	Two Sections 20 questions each section	30 minutes per section
Quantitative Reasoning	Two Sections 20 questions each section	35 minutes per section
Unscored Experimental and Research Sections	Varies	Varies

GRE Scores and Score Reporting

As we've already touched on, the GRE test is divided into three core assessment areas: Verbal Reasoning, Quantitative Reasoning and Analytical Writing. The score range for the Verbal and Quantitative Reasoning sections is 130-170 points, in one-point increments. The score range for the Analytical Writing is 0.0-6.0, in half-point increments. Your official score report will reflect three separate scores:

Score	Score Range
Cumulative Verbal Reasoning	• 130-140 in one-point increments • Sections where no responses are recorded will be notated "No Score (NS)"
Cumulative Quantitative Reasoning	• 130-140 in one-point increments • Sections where no responses are recorded will be notated "No Score (NS)"
Cumulative Analytical Reasoning	• 0.0-6.0 in half-point increments • Prompts that are off-topic or in a language other than English may receive a score of "0"

The maximum score you can receive on the Verbal and Quantitative Reasoning sections combined is a 340. For the Analytical Writing section, the maximum score you can receive is a 6.0. If you fail to enter any responses for any of the Verbal or Quantitative sections, you will not receive a score. If you fail to submit a response for an essay prompt, you will not receive a score. If your essay is off-topic or in a language other than English, you may receive a "0" for that prompt.

Raw Scores and Scaled Scores

For the Verbal and Quantitative Reasoning sections, your raw score is simply the number of correct responses you entered. Your raw score on these sections is converted into a scaled score that takes into account the difficulty of your second section based on the adaptive nature of the exam. The calculation of the scaled score ensures that the scores reflect your performance in comparison to all test-takers and provides an accurate picture of your overall performance.

Guessing on the Exam

Oftentimes students are confused about how guessing might impact their score. When you take exams in school, wrong answers often detract from your overall score.

Good news! There is **no penalty for guessing** on the GRE. You will not be penalized for incorrect answers; your raw and scaled score are solely based on the number of correct responses you submit. However, even though there is no penalty for guessing, you should do your best to try to make an educated guess, especially in the first sections of Verbal Reasoning and Quantitative Reasoning given the adaptive nature of the exam and the impact your overall first section performance has on your second section question difficulty. Try to eliminate 2-3 incorrect answer choices if possible before making a guess.

Unofficial and Official Test Scores

Those taking the computer-adaptive exam will receive their unofficial Verbal and Quantitative Reasoning scores at the completion of the exam. These scores may not be your final score. Official scores are typically available 10-15 days after the test administration. You can log in to your online account where you registered for the exam to view your scores. Your Analytical Writing score will be reflected on your official score report. If you take the paper exam, you will not receive an unofficial score report. Instead your official scores will be available within 5-6 weeks of your test date.

Score Validity

GRE scores are only valid for five years. If you are applying to graduate schools and/or fellowships and your scores are more than five years old, they may not be accepted and you may need to sit for the exam again.

Sending your Scores to Institutions

Your exam registration allows you to send your official GRE scores to four institutions at no additional cost. At the testing center, after you have completed the exam and reviewed your unofficial scores, you can select the institutions you would like to receive your scores. Scores will be received by the institutions within 10-15 days of your test date. If you need to send additional score reports, you can do so by logging in to your online account and selecting the institutions you would like to receive a score report. Score reports above the four included reports incur an additional fee. If you take the paper exam, you can select your institutions when you register or when you submit your admissions ticket at your test site.

ScoreSelect® Service

ScoreSelect® is an additional service offered by the ETS, the administrators of the GRE, that allows you more flexibility in how you report your scores to institutions. This is an optional service that carries an additional fee. With ScoreSelect®, you decide which scores you send to which institutions. After your test administration, you can decide to send institutions your most recent scores, all of your scores, and any single exam score earned within the past five years. Regardless of which scores you choose to report, it is important to remember that your scores on all three sections for any single test administration will be reported. This means you cannot mix and match scores from different exams or elect to exclude a score on a particular section on an exam while including another. ScoreSelect® is available for both the General and Subject Exams and only allows you to select from valid scores reported within the past five years.

Canceling Your Scores

At the end of the exam, you will be given the option to cancel your scores. You will be prompted to cancel your score before the unofficial score is displayed on the screen. Once you view your scores at a computer-delivered exam, you cannot cancel them.

Canceling your score ensures the score is not reported to any institution and does not become a part of your testing record. When you cancel your score, you cancel all section scores for the entire exam. It is not possible to cancel a score from a particular section while keeping the others. Although you will not receive a score for the exam and the exam will not appear on your test record, you are not entitled to a refund for a cancelled score.

With available options like ScoreSelect® that allow you to report more control over your score reports, and the option to have your scores sent only to you, you should strongly consider whether or not you want to cancel your score.

Score Reinstatement

If you cancel your scores and later decide you want to have them reported, you can request your scores to be reinstated up to 60 days from the date of your exam. All requests must be submitted via fax or mail and require a $50 reinstatement fee. When you request a reinstatement of scores, you can request to have the scores sent to up to four score recipients, the same option that would have been available on test day had you not cancelled your scores. You are still eligible to use ScoreSelect® once your score is reinstated.

Once a reinstatement is requested, it can take up to 14 days for scores to be reported. If you have selected institutions to receive your scores, your scores will be sent shortly after they are reported to you.

Chapter Overview

At the end of each chapter, you will find a recap of the key concepts presented. The Chapter Overview is a great way to review the material and serves as a good reference guide for quick questions about material covered in a particular chapter.

Key Chapter Concepts

In this chapter, we have covered the basics of the GRE format and scoring, as well as information on how to register for the exam and manage the distribution of your scores.

Core Assessment Areas and Scoring

The **computer-adaptive** exam consists of three core assessment areas:

Verbal Reasoning: Two 30-minute sections; 20 questions per section.

Quantitative Reasoning: Two 35-minute sections; 20 questions per section.

Analytical Writing: One section with two 30-minute essay tasks: Analyze an Issue and Analyze an Argument.

Core Assessment Area	Sections/Questions	Time Allotted	Score Range
Analytical Writing	One Section Two Essay Tasks	30 minutes per essay task	0.0-6.0
Verbal Reasoning	Two Sections 20 questions each section	30 minutes per section	130-140
Quantitative Reasoning	Two Sections 20 questions each section	35 minutes per section	130-140
Unscored Experimental and Research Sections	Varies	Varies	Unscored

Computer Adaptive Testing

Only the Verbal Reasoning and Quantitative Reasoning sections are adaptive. The Analytical Writing section is not adaptive; your response on the first prompt will not influence which prompt you receive for the second essay.

Your performance on the first sections of both Verbal Reasoning and Quantitative Reasoning is assessed in real-time using a proprietary algorithm created by ETS. The GRE Revised General Test is **section**-adaptive, not **question**-adaptive. This means your performance on the first Verbal Reasoning and Quantitative Reasoning sections determines the difficulty of the questions you will receive in the second section. Your performance in one assessment area is not linked to the other. So, it is possible to receive more difficult questions for the second Quantitative Reasoning section and not the Verbal Reasoning section.

Score Reporting

At the conclusion of the exam, you can choose to have your scores reported or you can elect to cancel them. If you cancel your scores, you will not receive a report of them and they will not appear on your testing record. If you change your mind after canceling your scores, you have 60 days to submit a request for your scores to be reinstated.

For those taking the computer-adaptive exam, unofficial scores for all sections except that Analytical Writing section are presented at the end of the exam. Official scores for both the paper and computer-adaptive exams are reported to the test-taker and your selected institutions usually within 10-14 days.

ETS Resources

ETS Resources	Benefits
GRE® Search Service	GRE® Search Service helps graduate schools and fellowships programs find students who fit the criteria they are looking for in a qualified candidate. When you register for the exam, you can opt-in to being included in the registry. Graduate schools and fellowship programs peruse the profiles of those who have registered and may reach out to test-takers directly.
PowerPrep® II Software	The software, which is Mac and PC compatible, allows test-takers to practice answering real test questions using all the options available on the actual exam, get accustomed to navigating the calculator and word processing functions, and take timed exams to simulate actual testing conditions.
ScoreSelect®	With ScoreSelect®, you decide which scores you send to which institutions. After your test administration, you can decide to send institutions your most recent scores, all of your scores, and any single score earned within the past five years.

Resources in this Book

This book is your comprehensive guide to tackling the GRE. A number of resources are included to help you better prepare for the exam and optimize your score. More specifically, the available resources can prepare you to:

- Understand the format and core assessment areas of the exam
- Identify your areas for improvement and work toward addressing them
- Refresh your math and vocabulary proficiency
- Simulate real testing conditions using full-length GRE practice exams

Resources in this Book	Benefits
Diagnostic Exam	We strongly recommend to take one practice test as a Diagnostic Test before starting this book to help you ascertain your starting point and general understanding of the core assessment areas on the GRE.
Math and Writing Primers	The Math Primer will help you dig up all that high school math you thought you'd never use and prepare you for the content you will encounter on the Quantitative section. The Writing Primer will walk you through common writing mistakes and discuss the key characteristics of good, logically sound writing essay graders are looking for in your essays.
Vocabulary List	The vocabulary list provides you with commonly used words on the exams as well as an overview of prefixes, suffixes, and roots to help you better understand words you may not know.
Practice Exams	Monitoring your progress is a critical component to optimizing your performance on the exam. The practice exams will help you keep track of your progress and identify areas for improvement.

UP NEXT: The next chapter will introduce the Analytical Writing section of the exam and provide you with an overview of the section scoring and the characteristics of a good essay.

ARGO
BROTHERS

3 INTRODUCTION TO ANALYTICAL WRITING

Analytical Writing: The Basics

The Analytical Writing section is designed to test your ability to think critically and formulate cohesive, analytical arguments on a given topic. This section will always appear first on the exam. Each essay prompt is presented separately, and you will not be able to switch between the two or use remaining time from one essay for the other. You will have 30 minutes to complete each essay. For those taking the computer-adaptive exam, responses are typed using basic word processing software. While basic functions like cut and paste are available, common features like spelling and grammar check are not.

Do I Really Need to Prepare for the Analytical Writing Section?

The Analytical Writing section is of particular importance to graduate and business schools. It was introduced specifically to ascertain the writing skills of candidates and their ability to meet the often writing-intensive curriculum characteristic of a majority of graduate school programs. Across the board, test-takers spend less time preparing for the Analytical Writing section than the other sections on the exam. In many cases, students are underprepared for this section, relying on their perceived writing ability and feeling like they can easily master the essays with little preparation. However, it is important to familiarize yourself with the specific essay tasks and understand what GRE essay reviewers are looking for in a top-rated essay.

Even if you are a strong writer, you should still devote some time to preparing for the Analytical Writing portion of the exam. This chapter will discuss the Analytical Writing section in general and explore the key strategies for approaching the section, distinguishing the fundamental difference between the two prompts, and writing a logically sound essay that scores well.

In the Analytical Writing section, you will be presented with two essay tasks and given 30 minutes for each task:

Analyze an Issue: The Analyze an Issue prompt will present you with specific instructions on how to analyze a given topic. The topic lends itself to multiple perspectives, and there is no "correct" answer. What is important is that you construct a well-reasoned, cohesive argument that both supports your stance on the issue and closely follows the instructions given in the prompt.

Analyze an Argument: The Analyze an Argument prompt will present you with an argument and ask you to evaluate its merits and logical soundness. Unlike the Analyze an Issue prompt, you will not choose a side for this prompt. Instead, you will write a critical assessment of the arguments presented.

About the Prompts

The prompts for the Analytical Writing section are drawn from a wide range of subject areas. You can expect to see topics from the social sciences, humanities, and physical sciences, for example. While the prompts are drawn from a broad pool of subjects, no content knowledge is expected. So, if you encounter a physical science prompt on the exam, rest assured you will not need to be a science expert in order to write a well-reasoned response.

Sample Analyze an Issue Prompt

Colleges and universities should require students to study a foreign language for at least two semesters.

Write a response in which you discuss your views on the policy and explain your reasoning for your position. As you develop your position and your supporting evidence, consider and address the possible consequences of implementing the policy and explain how these possible outcomes affect your position.

Sample Analyze an Argument Prompt

A recent sales study found that consumption of beef dishes in New York City dine-in restaurants has increased by 20 percent during the past three years. But, there are currently no operating city restaurants whose specialty is beef. Moreover, the majority of families in New York City are dual-income, and a nation-wide study has shown that such families eat significantly fewer home-cooked meals than they did five years ago, though they are more concerned about healthy eating.

Therefore, the new Moo-town Steakhouse restaurant that specializes in premium beef should be quite popular and profitable in New York City.

Discuss the questions that need to be asked about the argument to determine if the proposed outcome is likely. In your response, explain how these answers will aid in evaluating the argument.

Prompts on the ETS Website

Unlike other exams you have taken, all of the possible Analytical Writing essay prompts are provided for you ahead of time to review. The ETS makes available all the possible topics you can have for each prompt on the exam. This is an excellent resource and opportunity to practice with real essay questions. You can view the prompts on the ETS website, or you can request a copy by mail. There are lots of possible prompts with no real way to determine which ones you might have on your exam. But, with the prompts available, at least you have the opportunity to work with real exam material and get a clear idea of the phrasing of questions and their accompanying instructions. Even though you have access to all the prompts, that doesn't mean you need to work through all of them. Working through all the prompts would be a huge undertaking, and your time could be better used honing your writing skills or spending time reviewing the Writing Primer or the Vocabulary List. The subsequent chapters will outline some key strategies to help you make the most of practicing with the available prompts and developing an effective approach to the essay tasks.

Plagiarism

It is important to remember that the work you submit for each essay is your own work. ETS uses proprietary software to scan submitted essays for similarities to other published print and electronic material. The software also detects similarities between essays submitted by other test-takers. If ETS determines your work is too similar to other submitted essays or published material, they may cancel your score. If your score is canceled because similarities are detected, you will not receive a refund of fees paid. Under certain circumstances, you may file an appeal with ETS by contacting them directly.

Prep Tip: You can find the prompts for the exam on the ETS GRE Website at:
https://www.ets.org/gre/revised_general/prepare/analytical_writing/

How Essays Are Scored

Essays are scored based on your demonstrated ability to logically construct an argument from the provided evidence, use appropriate examples, and adequately defend your position. Only one score, scaled from 0-6 in half-point increments, is assigned to reflect your combined performance on both essays; you will not receive a separate score for each essay task. Essays that are off-topic or written in a language other than English, will receive a score of "0."

Two reviewers will evaluate each of your prompts. Essay reviewers are typically faculty members at colleges and universities with a broad range of specialties. Each reviewer will assign you a score of 0-6 based on your demonstrated ability to formulate a logical argument and appropriately respond to the essay task.

To arrive at your cumulative section score, the scores assigned by both reviewers for each essay are averaged, then the average of those figures is taken to arrive at your cumulative score.

For example, if your Analyze an Issue essay receives a score of a "3" from one reader and a score of "4" from the other, your final score for the Analyze an Issue essay would be "3.5." Then, let's suppose that for your Analyze an Argument essay, you receive a score of "4" from one reader and a score of "5" from the other reader, your final score for the Analyze an Argument essay would be "4.5." To arrive at your cumulative section score, you would simply average the final scores for each essay, in this case, "3.5" and "4.5." So the cumulative section score in this example would be calculated using the equation: 4.5 + 3.5/2. This leaves us with a final cumulative score of "4."

Scoring Discrepancies

If the two reviewers assign you scores that differ by more than one point, a third reviewer will review your essay. In this case, the third reviewer, who is typically a more senior and experienced reviewer, will simply assign your essay a score. No averaging will happen for that particular prompt. The score assigned by the third reviewer will be averaged with the score from your other essay task to derive your cumulative section score.

Score Reporting

Only one score, the average of your scores for each essay task, will be reported on your official score report. Unlike for the Verbal and Quantitative Reasoning sections, you will not receive an unofficial Analytical Writing score at the end of your test administration. Your Analytical Writing section scores will be available when your official scores are released, usually 10-15 days after your test administration. Institutions that receive your scores will not receive a copy of your responses; they will only receive your cumulative section score.

Scoring Rubric

The Analytical Writing essay reviewers use a holistic approach to scoring essays. Essentially, they assess the essay on its overall cohesiveness and argumentation instead of assigning points based on set criteria. However, there are certain elements raters consider when calculating an overall score. So, what are the characteristics of an essay that receives a score of 6? The following general rubric outlines the typical characteristics that correspond to each possible whole score on the section. In the subsequent chapters, we will explore the scoring rubric specific to each essay task.

Top to Mid-Range Percentile Analytical Writing Scores

6.0 – Outstanding

- Well-structured, logically sound, and demonstrates a clear understanding of the essay task and analysis of the evidence/argument.
- Essay is well-organized, ideas are presented clearly, and transitions are smooth.
- Key components of the argument/issue are addressed and reflects clear insight and understanding.
- Strong support offered for arguments, and evidence used appropriately to support or critique the position advanced by the writer.
- Excellent command of writing, sentence structure, and vocabulary.
- Minimal grammatical and spelling errors.

5.0 – Strong

- Offers a well-developed and organized assessment of the issue/argument and demonstrates strong writing and understanding of the prompt and evidence.
- Ideas are clearly developed and articulated, transitions are smooth and the essay flows logically.
- Evidence is used appropriately to support or critique the present issue/argument.
- Demonstrates strong command of writing though may contain minor grammatical and spelling errors.

4.0 – Satisfactory

- Offers a satisfactory assessment of the issue/argument and demonstrates an understanding of writing and the question task.
- Identifies main issues and addresses most of the key components of the prompt.
- Offers sufficient support for or critique of the argument and presented evidence.
- Writing is structured but contains little complexity and some minor and critical grammatical flaws.

Prep Fact: According to ETS, 90% of all Analytical Writing Essays earn scores in the 2.0-6.0 range.

3.0 – Limited

- Generally organized though offering a flawed critique of the issue/argument; limited understanding of the evidence, and below average command of writing.
- Fails to marshal evidence to form cohesive and well-supported arguments.
- Limited range of complexity in sentence structure and vocabulary.
- Writing contains grammatical, spelling, and syntax errors.

2.0 – Seriously Flawed

- Unsatisfactory essay that demonstrates a clear disconnect from the main components of the issue/argument and is generally disorganized and illogical.
- Evidence not leveraged to support argument and critique is not well-supported.
- Limited analysis of main components and little to no insight and understanding demonstrated.
- Contains critical grammatical, spelling, and syntax errors and exhibits limited vocabulary and sentence structure variation.

1.0 – Fundamentally Deficient

- Essay demonstrates poor understanding of the main components of the argument and fails to provide a logical, organized analysis.
- Limited analysis and insight on the issue/argument and inability to clearly express ideas.
- Writing contains critical grammatical, usage, and mechanical errors, and lacks cohesiveness.

0.0 – Unscorable

- Reserved for essays that are completely off-topic, contain only random keystrokes, or simply copies the essay prompt without providing an answer.
- A score of "0" is rarely assigned and is not to be confused with a score notation of NS-Not Scored which is assigned to essays where the input field is left completely blank.

Characteristics of a Top-Scoring Essay

In order to make your essay stand out and increase your chances of earning a top score, your essay needs to not only be well-written, but also fully address the prompt and align with the essay tasks. If the essay asks you to choose a side and you write a well-developed essay that argues the merits of both sides and how both options are a good idea, then you are not going to score well, even with a well-written essay. The key to scoring well on the Analytical Writing section is more than writing well; you need to follow instructions, use the provided evidence, and adequately support your claims.

Organization & Clarity

Essay reviewers have lots of essays to review and don't have time to re-read your essays in order to grasp your point. As such, it is critical that your essay is well-organized and clearly articulates your argument and analysis of the prompt. Essay reviewers should not have to guess your position or search for your supporting evidence. Your position should be clearly stated and supported by both the provided evidence and relevant evidence you chose to introduce. The flow of the essay should be logical and easy to follow. Make sure you divide your essay into paragraphs, grouping together ideas that are directly related to each other and ensuring your transitions make sense. We will discuss some strategies on how to organize your essay logically and align with the key elements essay reviewers are looking for when deriving your score.

Appropriate Use of Evidence

Creating a well-organized, logically sound, and clear essay largely depends on how you use evidence to support your argument. A well-written essay will marshal not only the provided evidence in support of your position, but will also include relevant evidence introduced by you to further strengthen your argument and support your position. The use of examples, real-world occurrences, and logical assumptions can all be helpful in constructing a well-supported, logical essay.

Vocabulary, Grammar and Sentence Variety

Though content is the most important factor essay reviewers consider when scoring your essay, it is important to ensure your essay is grammatically sound and demonstrates a strong command of written English. With the computerized exam, you will not have access to the typical word processing functions, like grammar and spell check, that you are likely accustomed to using. So, you will need to be diligent and ensure you leave a few minutes at the end of each essay to proofread and correct mistakes.

While minor issues may not count against you, major issues or a lack of variety and complexity in your writing may significantly impact your cumulative score. Reviewers want to see that you understand proper syntax and grammar, and can use a variety of complex sentence structures and vocabulary. However, this isn't an invitation to break out all your championship spelling bee words. Use vocabulary that is appropriate and makes sense in the context. Remember that there are ample opportunities in the Verbal Reasoning section for you to demonstrate your vocabulary prowess.

Critical Analysis and Logical Reasoning

Having an essay that is logically sound and provides a critical analysis of the issues and evidence is an important component if you want to score in the upper percentile for the Analytical Writing section. Your goal is to convince your reader of your point of view by providing a well-supported logically sound case. Having a logically sound argument also means that you have avoided common logical pitfalls and interpreted the issue and evidence without the use of fallacious reasoning.

A Note on Essay Length

You may have noticed that essay length wasn't listed as one of the key characteristics of a high-scoring essay. While there is no prescribed length for your essay, you should ensure that your essay is comprehensive enough to address the prompt. Your essay length is certainly important, but it should be a secondary focus. If you are thinking about how to articulate logical arguments in an organized and cohesive manner by using sufficient evidence to support your position, the length will likely happen organically.

The essay reviewers know that you have a limited amount of time to construct a well-reasoned, complete essay; they understand that you can only do so much in the 30 minutes you are given and that the final product won't be the most polished and extensive analysis of the presented issue or argument. What is expected is that your writing will demonstrate an understanding of the main concepts and sufficiently address the major components of the section according to the prompt. Covering all these bases is rather hard to do in a few sentences.

So, while there is no specific length that is required, an essay that includes a brief introduction, two to three body paragraphs, and a conclusion stands a greater chance of receiving a 5 or 6 than one with just a paragraph or two. Essays should generally be between 400-600 words. But, make sure you are going for quality over quantity and not just adding superfluous information to make your essay seem longer. Doing so can adversely affect your score.

Chapter Overview

In this chapter, we covered the basics of Analytical Writing, scoring, and characteristics of a strong essay. The Analytical Writing section is designed to test your ability to think critically and formulate cohesive, analytical arguments on a given topic. Even if you are a strong writer, it is important to spend an adequate amount of time preparing for the section and understanding the essay tasks.

Analytical Writing Essay Tasks and Scoring

Essay Task	About the Prompt	Scoring
Analyze an Issue	The Analyze the Issue prompt will present you with specific instructions on how to analyze a given topic. The topic lends itself to multiple perspectives, and there is no "correct" answer.	Essays are scored on a scale of 0.0-6.0 in half-point increments. Your scores on both essay tasks are averaged to arrive at your cumulative Analytical Writing score.
Analyze an Argument	The Analyze an Argument prompt will present you with an argument and ask you to evaluate its merits and logical soundness. Unlike the Analyze an Issue prompt, you will not choose a side for this prompt.	

Key Components of a Good Essay

Organization and Clarity: Your essay should be organized and your position clearly articulated and supported.

Vocabulary, Grammar, and Sentence Variety: Use a variety of sentence structures, appropriate vocabulary, and be mindful of grammar and spelling.

Appropriate Use of Evidence: Use the evidence provided to offer support or critique of the issue/argument and introduce relevant evidence of your own when appropriate.

Critical Analysis and Logical Reasoning: Offer a critical analysis of the main components of the prompt and ensure your reasoning flows logically and avoids common logical flaws.

Appropriate Length: Ideally, your essay should be between 400-600 words, though there is not a specified length. Ensure you write enough to fully address the essay tasks and provide a well-supported argument.

Prompts Available on the ETS Website

Remember that all the prompts for both essay tasks are available on the ETS website. Use these prompts to practice writing essays and to gain greater insight into the prompts themselves and the specific instructions for each essay task.

UP NEXT: In the next chapter, we will discuss how to study and prepare for the Analytical Writing section and lay out a strategic approach to outlining and writing your essay on test day.

ARGO
BROTHERS

4 HOW TO PREPARE: ANALYTICAL WRITING

How to Prepare for the Analytical Writing Section

In the previous chapter, we discussed how test-takers are often underprepared for the Analytical Writing section, devoting significantly less time to studying for it compared to the Verbal and Quantitative Reasoning sections. Having reviewed the criteria for scoring and the key characteristics essay reviewers look for when assigning scores, hopefully, you now understand the importance of spending an adequate amount of time building your proficiency in this section.

So, how do you prepare to write organized, logical, and well-supported essays? There are several tools included in this text and offered by ETS that will help you hone your approach to the Analytical Writing section and position you to be able to produce strong, high-scoring essays.

Writing Primer

Before launching into the Analytical Writing chapters on the Analyze an Issue and Analyze an Argument prompts, it is recommended that you work through the Writing Primer in the back of this book. The Writing Primer will:

- Walk you through common writing mistakes
- Discuss key characteristics of good, logically sound writing that essay graders are looking for in your essays
- Provide a review of grammar, mechanics, sentence structure, punctuation, and other critical technical areas of writing
- Provide an overview of logical constructs, common reasoning errors, and examples of solid writing that demonstrate the characteristics of high-scoring GRE Analytical Writing essays

In terms of structuring your study plan for this section of the exam, the Writing Primer should be your first step even if you are a strong writer. It will best situate you to attack the section, avoid costly mistakes, and draft essays that resonate with the essay reviewers, thus increasing your chances of earning a higher score.

Essay Prompts

As we discussed in the last chapter, you have access to all the Analytical Writing prompts used for the GRE. They are the perfect resource for you to get direct exposure to prompts you will encounter on the exam. Try to tap into your network of professors or peers to read your essays and provide you with feedback since errors are not always apparent when reading your own work.

ScoreItNow™

ScoreItNow!™ is an online scoring service offered by ETS that allows you to submit your practice essays to be graded by an e-grader. The scoring service will simulate testing conditions for you, present you with a test prompt, and provide you with an immediate score once you are done with your essays. The system is fee-based depending on the number of essays you wish to have scored.

ScoreItNow!™ is a useful practice tool that allows you to see how your writing measures up to the guidelines that essay reviewers use to score your essay. None of the scores earned in the system are valid to be sent to schools; they are also not recorded or stored in any database. You can use the confidential scoring system and not have to worry about your scores being seen by anyone but you.

> **Prep Tip:** While ScoreItNow!™ is a great tool, it is fee-based and may not be accessible to everyone who could benefit from it. Tapping into your network and asking professors, colleagues, or peers to review your essays using the outlined criteria is also a helpful way to get feedback on your essays.

Developing a Strategy

You only have 30 minutes to write each essay in the Analytical Writing section. With such limited time, your approach is crucial and above all things, it must be strategic. With the time limit, you simply don't have the luxury of digging deep into the material and spending lots of time exploring all the possible angles from which to approach the essay. You have to dive in and attack the essay, and to do that, you must have a strategy that you have gained a level of comfort using.

A strategic approach to the Analytical Writing section merits attention to several key areas:

Time Management
- Understanding how to best use the allotted time to strategically approach the essays

Essay Format
- Structuring your essay so that it is organized, contains a proper introduction and conclusion, and addresses the main components of the prompt

Critical Writing Components
- Clearly articulating your position in an appropriate tone, ensuring that you proofread for errors

Understanding the Differences Between the Prompts
- Understanding the Analyze an Issue and Analyze an Argument prompts are very different in terms of the type of response they require and ensuring your essays aligns with essay task

You should work to implement your strategy while preparing for the exam and continue to refine it as you practice with the sample prompts; test day is not the time to try out new strategies! Let's look at the some of the key strategic areas more closely.

Time Management

Managing your time on the entire exam is critical. However, the Analytical Writing section arguably presents that greatest challenge in this area. Your time limit starts when the prompt is displayed on the screen. You are tasked with writing a cohesive essay that offers critical analysis and insight into a randomly generated topic...all within a 30-minute time limit!

As you begin to work through prompts and write your sample essays, you should first focus on constructing logical arguments without much worry about the time restraints. It is important to spend some time refining your writing and making sure you understand key logical constructs and how to avoid common errors first, and then incorporate the element of time into your study plan. Once you've practiced a few essays focusing on writing, then it's time to start exploring how to put together a high-scoring essay under time restraints.

Your time should be divided among four key tasks:
- Reading
- Brainstorming and Outlining
- Writing your Essay
- Proofreading

Prep Tip: Since the word processing software does not include grammar or spell check, it is a good idea to practice typing your essays with those functions disabled on your computer. Practicing without these tools helps you better simulate actual testing conditions and spot errors on your own while proofreading.

Read: 2 minutes

Make sure you fully read the presented argument or issue and the instructions that follow. You want to walk away from the prompt with a clear understanding of the essay task. Underline key terms and instructions as you read. It may seem like 2 minutes is not enough time, but remember, since you have access to the prompts ahead of time, you have likely seen most of the instructions, even if the argument and issue presented are not familiar to you. Practicing with the provided prompts and familiarizing yourself with the essay tasks will allow you to spend less time reading and trying to understand the prompt.

Brainstorm and Outline: 5 minutes

After you have read the prompt and are clear on the essay task, spend the next couple of minutes brainstorming and outlining your essay. The first step here is to decide your position. Once you know what direction you are going in, you can then brainstorm some counterpoints and supporting evidence before outlining how to lay out your essay. As you work through the Analyze an Issue and Analyze an Argument essay tasks, you will find useful tools to help you refine and systemize your approach to the essays. The more you practice writing sample essays using a strategic approach, the easier it will likely be on the exam.

Write: 18 minutes

Writing the essay is, of course, the most important task. Spend about 18 minutes writing your essay using your outline as a guide. Your essay should include a brief introduction, 2-3 body paragraphs, and a conclusion.

Proofread: 5 mins

You aren't expected to produce a flawless essay in 30 minutes. But you should reserve some time at the end to look over what you've written and correct any grammar, punctuation, spelling, or other critical errors discussed in the Writing Primer.

Essay Format

Organization is a critical aspect of the Analytical Writing essay. If you want to score in the higher percentiles, your essay needs to be well-organized and flow logically. There is no specific format outlined for the test. However, going into the exam, you should have a general idea on how to best structure your essay for each of the essay tasks: Analyze an Issue and Analyze an Argument. While each essay task will require a slightly different approach, there are some key components of the essay format that should be present in both essays.

Introduction

Your introduction should clearly state your position on the issue or argument. It should be succinct and to the point; you should try to avoid long-winded introductions with superfluous information and phrases. You should avoid addressing the reader directly ("What would you do if this happened to you?"), or including an otherwise instructive prompt ("Imagine a world without crime.") Demonstrate you understand the presented issue or argument, state your position, firm up your thesis statement, and move on to the body of the essay.

Body

This is the meat of your essay. You want to craft two to three paragraphs based on your outline that critically analyze the main components of the prompt. You should start a new paragraph for each key point you introduce, making sure to support your viewpoint with the appropriate evidence. Your transitions between paragraphs should be clear and logical so the essay reviewer can easily follow along.

Conclusion

For the conclusion, you want to drive your point home. Re-emphasize your thesis, and close out your argument. Avoid phrases like "As I have shown" or "As you can see." If you have clearly articulated your argument, these types of statements will not be necessary.

Critical Writing Components

Clarity of Position

Your essay should very clearly articulate your position. Be certain to take a firm stance on the issue and make your point. Particularly with the Issue prompt, you want to make sure that you don't straddle the fence and try to address the merits of both sides of the argument. A key consideration for scoring is your ability to clearly defend your position. If you haven't taken a clear stand, it will be hard to meet this expectation. Taking time to outline your essay will help you construct an organized and logical argument. Avoid broad statements and generalizations that cannot be supported by evidence or that add little value to your argument. Relevant examples, coherent analysis, and proper use of evidence will play a major role in helping you draft an essay that clearly states and defends your position.

Logical Flow of Ideas

Having a logically sound argument is also a critical component of a good essay. Essay reviewers want to see that you have solid critical thinking skills and understand the basic principles of a logical argument and logical fallacy. For the Analyze an Argument prompt, you will often need to address logical flaws in the prompt. To do so, you will need to have a clear understanding of those as well as the ability to form a logical rebuttal.

Tone

Essay reviewers expect that your essays may not be as polished as they would be if you had more time. However, you should still treat the essay as a piece of formal writing. You should ensure that your language is appropriate, vocabulary is used correctly, and that you avoid the use of informal speech. While there is no articulated preference for first-person or third-person, third-person is your safest choice to ensure your essay flows well and accurately advances your argument.

Key Differences between the Essay Tasks

The Analytical Writing section has two distinct essay tasks that both require a different approach. One of the most common mistakes test-takers make is devising a single approach and applying it to both essays. While the essays have some similar characteristics and will have some of the basic key elements, their differences do need to be accounted for when you are writing.

The differences between the two essays lend themselves to much discussion. We will take a detailed look at the different expectations and approaches for each of these essays. But, let's first briefly explore the key differences between the Analyze an Issue and Analyze and Argument prompts.

Primary goals for the **Analyze an Issue** prompt:

- Choose one side of the issue. This is the most critical aspect of this essay. It is important to clearly argue for one side of the issue or the other.
- Provide an analysis of a general issue that is often presented without comment or additional information. The issue is usually derived from some aspect of politics, popular culture, the arts, or history.
- Use your own evidence and appropriate examples to support your thesis.

Primary goals for the **Analyze an Argument** prompt:

- Provide critical analysis of the position presented in the prompt. Unlike the Analyze an Issue prompt, you will not be picking a side. Instead, you will analyze the presented argument.
- Assess the logical soundness of the prompt and highlight any logical fallacies.
- Analyze the given evidence and comment on the effectiveness of the evidence in supporting the argument.

Chapter Overview

In this chapter, we covered the key preparation strategies to prepare you for the Analytical Writing section, including available resources to help you prepare, timing strategies, and critical writing components that will help you develop a good essay.

Prep Resources for the Analytical Writing Section

Resource	Benefits
Writing Primer	The Writing Primer should be your first step, even if you are a strong writer. It will best situate you to attack the section, avoid costly mistakes, and draft essays that resonate with the essay reviewers, increasing your chances of earning a higher score.
ETS Prompts	You have access to all the Analytical Writing prompts used for the GRE. They are the perfect resource for you to get direct exposure to prompts you will encounter on the exam. Try to tap into your network of professors or peers to read your essays and provide you with feedback since errors are not always apparent when reading your own work.
ScoreItNow!™	ScoreItNow!™ is a useful practice tool that allows you to see how your writing measures up to the guidelines essay reviewers use to score your essay. The scoring service will simulate testing conditions for you, present you with a test prompt, and provide you with an immediate score once you are done with your essays.

How to Manage Your Time When Writing Your Essay

Task	Objective	Time Allotted
Read	Read the presented issue and the essay task. Underline key pieces of evidence and important information included in the instructions	2 minutes
Brainstorm and Outline	Decide your position, chart your pros and cons, and briefly outline your paragraphs and evidence you plan to use to support your argument	5 minutes
Write	Write your essay using the outline you drafted.	18 minutes
Proofread	Proofread your essay, checking for grammar, spelling, logical flaws, and glaring errors.	5 minutes

UP NEXT: In the next chapter, we will discuss the fundamentals of the Analyze an Issue essay prompt and outline an approach to the prompt.

ARGO
BROTHERS

5 THE ANALYZE AN ISSUE PROMPT

Analyze an Issue Prompt: The Basics

The Analyze an Issue prompt will always appear first in the Analytical Writing section. For the Analyze an Issue essay task, you will write a concise, well-reasoned response to the presented prompt; the prompt expresses a particular viewpoint or viewpoints about a general issue. Your task is to develop your own argument, provide supporting evidence for your position and use the additional instructions to further explain various aspects of your decision. You will have 30 minutes to complete the Analyze an Issue essay. For those taking the computer-adaptive exam, the essay is typed using the word-processing functionality.

Components of the Prompt

The Analyze an Issue prompt is broken into two distinct parts: the issue and the instructions. The issue is typically very brief, including only a sentence or two. The topics are general in nature and require no advanced or specialized knowledge for you to draft a response. The instructions will provide you with specific points to address in your argument outside of simply choosing a side of the issue.

There is no right or wrong answer for the prompt. Since this essay task measures your ability to chose a side of the issue and use appropriate and convincing evidence to support your position, it is absolutely essential for you to choose a clear side: **do not straddle the fence.** Make a decision and explain the merits of your choice!

Essay Task Directions

At the start of the Issue essay task, you will see directions that outline your task and explain how your essay will be evaluated. Let's look at an example of the directions you may see on the exam:

> **Directions:** You will be presented with a brief statement that addresses a particular topic of interest and specific instructions on how to respond. No specific knowledge of the topic is needed to answer the question. Your response will be evaluated based on your ability to:
>
> - Clearly articulate and support your point of view using specific, relevant examples
> - Organize your response so that it flows logically
> - Analyze and address complex nuances of the issue
> - Articulate your point of view using standard English and a demonstrated understanding of proper grammar, usage and mechanics

The directions are straightforward and consistent. Given the time constraints on the exam, it is best to familiarize yourself with the directions prior to the exam so that you do not have to spend valuable time re-reading them on test day.

The Issue and Writing Instructions

A sample prompt includes the presentation of the issue and the specific writing instructions. It may read as follows:

Issue
Homeschooled students often miss out on critical social interactions that lead to the development of important social skills and competencies.

Instructions
Write a response that discusses how much you agree or disagree with the claim and include the most persuasive reasons and/or examples that someone could use to challenge your viewpoint.

On the actual exam, the prompt will be presented without the **Issue** and **Instructions** labels used above. As you can see, the additional instructions move beyond you simply stating your position on the issue. The prompt is designed for you to go a step further and address several other elements of the issue in your argument including:

- Instances when your position might prove to not be true
- Circumstances under which your position may not have the intended outcome
- Possible consequences of acting based on your position
- Possible challenges to your position
- Additional arguments that support your position

Analyze an Issue Writing Instructions

While the presented issues will run the gamut of topics, you will be asked to approach the essay according to one of six sets of instructions. The wording may vary slightly from what you see on the actual exam but the instructions below closely reflect the instructions you will encounter for the Analyze an Issue task.

- Discuss the extent to which you agree or disagree with the statement and explain your position. Also discuss instances when the statement may or may not be true and how these instances impact your viewpoint.
- Discuss the extent to which you agree or disagree with the statement and explain your position. Citing specific examples, explain how the circumstances under which the recommendation could be adopted would or would not be advantageous in developing and supporting your view point. Explain how the specific circumstances affect your point of view.
- Discuss the extent to which you agree or disagree with the claim and cite the most compelling reasons someone could use to dispute your stance.
- Ensuring you address both viewpoints provided, discuss which more closely aligns with your own views. Be sure to use specific evidence to support your position.
- Discuss how much you agree or disagree with the claim and the support offered in defense of the claim.
- Discuss your viewpoint on the proposed plan and the reasons for your perspective. Consider potential consequences of implementing the policy and the extent to which these consequences influence your stance.

Analyze an Issue Scoring Rubric

In the previous chapter, we looked at the general scorings scale for the Analytical Writing essays. That scoring rubric outlined the holistic characteristics that essay reviewers look for when scoring an essay. The rubric below and the rubric found in the next Analyze an Argument chapter outline the essay-specific characteristics reviewers look for when scoring your individual essays.

6.0

- Essay takes a clear stance on the issue and provides a complete response to the issue
- Essay is organized and contains sufficient connections between presented ideas
- Essay uses persuasive evidence to support the position and incorporates specific examples and other appropriate premises
- Every sentence is structured and uses appropriate vocabulary
- Contains only minor grammatical, usage, and spelling errors

5.0

- Essay takes a clear stance on the issue and presents a cogent and focused response
- Essay is clearly organized and proper connections are drawn between presented ideas
- Proper evidence is used to support the selected position and includes appropriate examples, insight, and a persuasive argument
- Exhibits varied sentence structures, proper word choice, and a clearly advanced understanding of writing
- Contains only minor grammatical, usage, and spelling errors

4.0

- Takes a clear stance on the issue and presents a near complete response to the question task
- Essay is logically organized and utilizes appropriate evidence
- Sentences and vocabulary use are clear and appropriate
- Essay generally adheres to grammatical, usage, and spelling conventions, though some errors do exist

3.0

- Essay takes a generally clear stance on the issue and addresses the question task in a manner that maybe unclear or incomplete
- Ideas in the essay are not clearly linked and evidence is inadequate or unrelated
- Essay is loosely organized and does not flow in a manner that is easily understood
- Sentence structure and vocabulary choices sometimes hinder rather than help organization and flow
- Occasional grammatical, usage, and spelling errors that impact flow and clarity of the essay

2.0

- Takes a position that is unclear or poorly articulated and does not sufficiently address the question task
- Evidence used is incomplete, illogical, or unclear; ideas of the passage do not connect with each other
- Organization is lacking and the overall flow of the passage lacks clarity and understanding
- Sentence structure and vocabulary use negatively impact flow of the essay
- Consistent grammatical, usage and spelling errors significantly impact the flow and clarity of the essay

1.0

- Position taken on the issue is uncertain and the question task is unaddressed
- Evidence is poorly marshaled, is illogical and/or irrelevant
- Essay is poorly organized and reflects no clear structure
- Sentence structure and vocabulary significantly impact the flow the essay
- Consistent grammatical, usage, and spelling errors significantly impact the flow and clarity of the essay

0.0

- The response is written in a language other than English
- The response includes nothing but a copy of the question task or the issue
- The response is not legible (paper exam) or contains only non-English characters (computer-adaptive exam)

Developing a Strategy

With only 30 minutes to write your essay, you want to be strategic in your approach. During your preparation for the exam, it is wise to outline some key elements that should be part of your essay regardless of what the prompt may be. This minimizes the time you spend thinking about how to organize your essay and allows you to test out your format since you have the prompts available to you ahead of the exam.

Having a plan going into the essay helps you create a cogent, organized essay that addresses the issue and the instructions. In turn, you increase the chances of your essay being scored higher. Let's look at some of the key concepts you should keep in mind when responding to the Issue prompt.

Clear Statement of Your Position

The most critical element of the Issue essay is the statement of your position. The reviewer should not have to guess what side of the issue you have taken. Remaining neutral is not an option; doing so will significantly impact your score. A clear thesis that directly states your position should be included in the first paragraph. An effective approach to ensure the reader is clear on your position is to clearly articulate your position in the first sentence of your essay and then follow up with content that both supports your stance and addresses the additional instructions provided in the prompt.

Address the Essay Task

Make sure you answer the task. With limited time allocated to finish your response, you might hurry to get all of your ideas down. Remember to go back to the prompt to make sure you are doing what the task asks of you, addressing all points of view, bringing up possible objections, and not just agreeing or disagreeing with the argument.

Get Organized

Having a clear structure for your response will allow the reviewer to easily follow your line of reasoning. Once you have an outline, organize your paragraphs so that they logically flow from one to the next as you build upon your main idea and accompanying evidence. When writing your paragraphs, do not begin them with, "the first reason the argument is flawed is", or, "my second support is". You should also avoid using phrases like, "in conclusion" or "as I have shown". Use transitional words and phrases to wrap up your conclusion. Transitional words and phrases allow paragraphs to flow from one to the next by pinpointing the connections in your writing.

Use Strong Supporting Evidence

Developing adequate support is crucial to your success on this task. Begin with a clear and concise statement of your opinion in your introduction and follow a clear line of reasoning as you develop each additional paragraph.

Connect Your Ideas

The organization of your essay does not need to be based on tradition or on what you learned in college. However, it needs to be logical and concise. Make sure your ideas are linked together logically with supporting evidence. Use transitional words and phrases to help link your ideas together.

Organizing Your Essay

Similar to the characteristics we just reviewed as part of your strategic approach to the prompt, having an idea of how you want to organize your essay regardless of the prompt will help you best utilize your time and optimize your score. The outline below models a layout that addresses the essay task and presents your position in an organized manner.

Opening Paragraph

- Make a clear and concise statement of your position. Do not straddle the fence.

First Body Paragraph

- Explain and support your first reason for taking the side of the issue you have chosen.

Second Body Paragraph

- Explain and support your second reason for taking the side of the issue you have chosen.

Third Body Paragraph

- This paragraph is best reserved to address the additional directions from the essay task. If you have been asked to consider counter-arguments to your position, address specific parts of the prompt in more detail, or consider potential consequences or outcomes, then this is the paragraph to do so.

Concluding Paragraph

- This is your last paragraph to make your point. Try to reserve your strongest point for this paragraph and fully support it using appropriate evidence. Reiterate your position and close your argument.

Do I Have to Use this Format?

While there is no standard organization expected by ETS, it is advantageous to practice using a standard organizational structure to ensure your essay on the exam flows well, communicates your position, and fully addresses the essay task.

Each paragraph should provide support for your point of view. In addition to stating and supporting your position, the body paragraphs should address the specific instructions in the essay tasks. Everything you argue should be explained and supported. Remember to include any possible objections to your argument that you think of with reasons why those objections are not valid.

> **Prep Tip:** Whether you are taking the computer-adaptive exam or the paper exam, you will have access to scratch paper to jot down notes, outline your essay, and organize the points you plan to present in your body paragraphs. Be sure to use this valuable resource to your advantage. While you cannot bring your own scratch paper into the exam, if you run out, you can request more.

Paragraph Structure

If you are aiming for a top score, it is not enough to just organize your paragraphs logically. Each sentence you write in each paragraph must be organized logically and provide support for your position. Paragraphs should follow a traditional structure in the body of your response.

Topic Sentence

Your topic sentence should give the reader an idea of what the rest of your paragraph is about. The sentence should support your point of view, introduce the counterexample, or address the specific directions of the essay task. For example, if you are arguing that zoos should be shut down because of their mistreatment of animals, your topic sentence might suggest that keeping animals locked in cages at zoos is bad for their well-being.

Evidence and Examples

Once you have your topic sentence, there are several ways you can develop the rest of your paragraph. Your goal in this paragraph is to make your topic sentence persuasive by including supporting evidence. In discussing the well-being of animals in zoos, you might talk about the quality of care provided for the animals, and you could emphasize the number of deaths of animals at the zoo. Make sure your examples are both relevant and compelling.

Compelling Conclusion

Your conclusion should be compelling. In your conclusion, you should strive to clearly reiterate your point of view and use your stronger piece of support to solidify your stance on the issue. You don't want to leave the reviewer with a lackluster feeling, so make sure you leave a lasting impression. You can state your main point of view again, summarize your main points, or make the reader aware of a larger issue.

Analyze an Issue Practice Writing Exercise

Now that we have reviewed how to approach the Issue section and the elements that contribute to a high-scoring essay, let's look at an essay prompt. The tasks below will help you solidify your position on the issue, organize your argument, and draft your essay. Practicing with these questions in mind can help you firm up your strategic approach to writing the Analyze an Issue essay. As you work through the ETS prompts, try to answer these questions as you outline your essay.

Issue Prompt

When we know our history, we are less likely to repeat it.

Discuss the extent to which you agree or disagree with the statement and explain your position. Also discuss instances when the statement may or may not be true and how these instances impact your viewpoint.

Brainstorm and Outline Your ideas

Do you agree or disagree with the presented issue?

What are some specific examples that can help support your position?

What are some possible counter-arguments against your position?

Using your strongest points from above, briefly outline the evidence or counter-argument you will address in each paragraph.

Paragraph 1:

Paragraph 2:

Paragraph 3:

Paragraph 4:

Issue Prompt
When we know our history, we are less likely to repeat it.

Discuss the extent to which you agree or disagree with the statement and explain your position. Also discuss instances when the statement may or may not be true and how these instances impact your viewpoint.

Using your outline, write an essay in response to the prompt.

When writing your response for Analyze an Issue & Analyze an Argument, use a computer, and turn off the spell-check feature to simulate real testing conditions. You may use this space for note-taking or brainstorming.

Chapter Overview

The Analyze an Issue task measures your ability to respond to a general issue by taking a clear stance and using appropriate examples to support your decision. The Analyze an Issue essay always appears first in the Analytical Writing section; you will have 30 minutes to complete the essay.

Essay Tasks

In addition to responding to the issue, you will also be presented with specific writing instructions that require you to go a step further than simply stating and defending your position. Pay close attention to these instructions and familiarize yourself with the eight common prompts ahead of the exam.

Scoring

Essays are scored on a scale of 0.0-6.0 and your score is averaged with your score from the Argument essay to derive your cumulative Analytical Writing score. You will not receive a separate score for the Analyze an Issue essay.

Tips for a Solid Analyze an Issue Essay

- Ensure your essay takes a clear stance on the issue, is well-organized, and address all components of the essay task.
- Your overall essay organization is important, but make sure each paragraph is well-organized as well.
- Take a few minutes to proofread your essay and check for missing words, awkward sentence constructions, and grammatical errors.

ARGO
BROTHERS

6 THE ANALYZE AN ARGUMENT PROMPT

The Analyze an Argument Prompt: The Basics

The Analyze an Argument prompt always appears at the end of the Analytical Writing section. For the Analyze an Argument prompt, your task is not to develop your own opinion, but rather to write an essay that analyzes the presented argument and its evidence and to evaluate its persuasiveness and logical soundness. You will have only 30 minutes to complete this essay. For those taking the computer-adaptive exam, the essay is typed using the word-processing functionality.

Components of the Prompt

Like the Analyze an Issue prompt, the Analyze an Argument prompt is broken into two distinct parts: the argument and the instructions.

The **argument** is a brief statement, usually a couple of sentences, with supporting evidence that advances a specific conclusion on a topic drawn from a wide range of subjects. No specific knowledge on the topic is needed to draft a response. The **instructions** will provide you with specific points to address in your argument and prompt you to evaluate the evidence and the overall logical merits of the argument.

The arguments presented for this prompt will **always** be flawed in some way. We will explore common flaws in logical reasoning and argumentation in this chapter. While there is no right or wrong answer to this prompt, it is important to be able to clearly outline the weaknesses in the argument and respond to the specific essay task.

Essay Task Directions

At the start of the Argument essay task, you will see directions that outline your task and explain how your essay will be evaluated. Here's an example of the directions you may see on the exam:

Directions: You will be presented with a brief statement that addresses a particular topic of interest and specific instructions on how to respond. No specific knowledge of the topic is needed to answer the question. Your response will be evaluated based on your ability to:

- Clearly articulate and support your point of view using specific, relevant examples
- Organize your response so that it flows logically
- Analyze and address the evidence used in the passage
- Examine assumptions and assess the logical soundness of the argument
- Articulate your point of view using standard English and a demonstrated understanding of proper grammar, usage and mechanics

The directions are straightforward and consistent. Given the time constraints on the exam, it is best to familiarize yourself with the directions prior to the exam so that you do not have to spend valuable time re-reading them on test day.

The Argument and Writing Instructions

A sample prompt includes presentation of the issue and the specific writing instructions. It may read as follows:

Argument

The results of a four-year study of the common cold examined the possible therapeutic effects of a vegan diet. While many foods are naturally rich in antioxidants, food processing companies also sell isolated antioxidants. The four-year study found a strong correlation between a vegan diet and significant decline in the average number of colds reported by participants. A control group that increased its antioxidant intake using supplements did not have a decrease in the number of colds. Based on these results, some health experts recommend a vegan diet over the use of package antioxidants.

Instructions

Discuss the questions that must be answered in the argument to determine if the advice provided is reasonable. As part of your response, explain how the answers would help in evaluating the validity of the argument.

On the actual exam, the prompt will be presented without the **Argument** and **Instructions** labels used above. As you can see, the additional instructions ask you to analyze the merits of the argument, identify fallacious reasoning, and/or present cogent counter-arguments that challenge the articulated position. While reading the argument, it is important to pay close attention to and examine:

- The evidence used to advance the argument
- Additional evidence that can be used to weaken or strengthen the argument
- Assumptions the author makes and whether the provided evidence supports them
- The logical soundness of the overall argument
- Alternate explanations that could realistically compete with the explanation

You will need to examine the structure of the argument and the way that the author forms the line of reasoning. You will need to identify the flow of logic in the passage and consider whether or not the movement from each step makes sense. In order to do this, look for transition words that reveal that the author is trying to make a logical connection.

For the Analyze an Argument task, it is also important to remember what you are **not** being asked to do:

- You are not being asked to examine if what is stated in the argument is true or false.
- You are not being asked to agree or disagree with the argument.
- You are not being asked to discuss your personal opinion on the matter.

Analyze an Argument Writing Instructions

The second part of the prompt lists the instructions to follow to complete your response to the argument successfully. You must be specific in explaining your evaluation of the argument, while reviewing the evidence and examples provided. As you prepare your response, remember the goal is to identify problems in the argument's reasoning. The set of instructions below is an example of what you can expect on the exam.

- Discuss the evidence needed to fully assess the argument. Include examples and an explanation of how the evidence provided strengthens or weakens the argument.
- Discuss the additional evidence or information needed to establish if the argument it is based on is reasonable.
- Discuss the stated and unstated assumptions in the argument and discuss what the consequences might be if those assumptions are shown to be unwarranted.
- Discuss the questions that must be answered in the argument to determine if the advice provided is reasonable. As part of your response, explain how the answers would help in evaluating the validity of the argument.
- Discuss the questions that need to be asked about the argument to determine if the proposed outcome is likely. In your response, explain how these answers will aid in evaluating the argument.
- After reviewing the author's argument, examine any alternate explanations that could reasonably compete with the proposed explanation. In your response, explain how your analysis challenges the assertions provided in the argument.
- Discuss what, if any, additional information is needed to determine whether or not the proposed recommendation will provide the predicted result.

Analyze an Argument Scoring Rubric

6.0

- Essay provides a logically sound, well-supported response to the question task.
- Evidence is appropriate and persuasive, provides insight, and makes way for in-depth analysis of the argument presented in the prompt.
- Essay reflects a high-level of organization and clearly and concisely draws connections between the main ideas and the evidence used to support those ideas.
- Sentence structure and vocabulary reflects a level of complexity characteristic of strong writing skills.
- Contains only minor grammatical, usage, and spelling errors, if any.

5.0

- Essay provides a logically sound well-supported response to the question task.
- Evidence is appropriate, logical and flows well along side of the main ideas of the essay.
- Essay is well-organized and logically flows.
- Sentence structure and vocabulary are varied and complex.
- Contains only minor grammatical, usage, and spelling errors.

4.0

- Essay provides a response that adequately addresses the question task.
- Evidence is generally sound, though some evidence introduced may not adequately support the main ideas of the essay.
- Essay is generally organized, though the connection between some of the main ideas may not be particularly clear.
- Sentence structure and vocabulary are sufficient but not always used properly.
- Contains grammatical, usage, spelling errors.

3.0

- Essay does not adequately address all components of the question task.
- Evidence used is illogical and/or unrelated to the key points of the essay.
- Essay is loosely organized and does not flow in a manner that is easily understood.
- Sentence structure and vocabulary choices sometimes hinder rather than help clarify the intended meaning.
- Occasional grammatical, usage, and spelling errors that impact flow and clarity of the essay.

2.0

- Essay does not adequately address the question task.
- Lack of evidence to support the main ideas of the essay and/or evidence used is irrelevant, incomplete, or illogical.
- Essay is poorly organized and reflects no logical structure.
- Sentence structure and vocabulary negatively impact flow of the essay.
- Significant grammatical, usage, and spelling errors that impact the flow of the essay.

1.0

- The question task is unaddressed.
- Evidence is poorly marshaled, is illogical and/or irrelevant.
- Essay is poorly organized and reflects no clear structure.
- Sentence structure and vocabulary significantly impact the flow the essay.
- Consistent grammatical, usage, and spelling errors significantly impact the flow and clarity of the essay.

0.0

- The response is written in a language other than English.
- The response includes nothing but a copy of the question task or the issue.
- The response is not legible (paper exam) or contains only non-English characters (computer-adaptive exam).

Developing a Strategy

Having a plan going into the essay helps you create a cogent, organized essay that addresses the argument and the instructions. In turn, you increase the chances of your essay being scored higher. Let's look at some of the key concepts you should keep in mind when responding to the Argument prompt.

Read Actively

A GRE argument analysis should begin with a careful reading of the passage. As you read, write key points on your scratch paper as well as your ideas about their validity. Do not simply evaluate individual statements; consider how all these statements interact with each other. Determine whether the conclusions flow logically from the statements made earlier in the prompt or if the prompt relies on logical fallacies or biased assumptions. The prompt will generally contain significant flaws, and your task is to address these problems in your essay.

Curb Your Opinion and Analyze

For the Analyze an Argument essay, you are analyzing an argument, not creating a new argument of your own. Your opinion on the topic is not relevant. Instead, evaluate the logic and content of the argument given to you. Read the prompt carefully and identify errors in reasoning and the use of evidence.

Structure Your Response

The GRE essay raters have no particular preference for how you organize your essay. However, your essay should flow logically and address all aspects of the essay task. Before you write your essay, create a brief outline to organize your ideas according to this format.

In the Analyze an Argument section of the writing exam, there are a few crucial elements that must be included as you construct your response. Your goal is to create a clear and concise response that analyzes the argument thoroughly and demonstrates the ability to identify the main parts of the argument, missing information and evidence, and assumptions the prompt makes.

- The argument will always be flawed. A passage containing only a few sentences is hardly going to provide solid, logical evidence and go in-depth on the topic. Do not be distracted by the one or two valid points in the argument. Your goal is to analyze, not agree with the argument. Be prepared for the argument to have several flaws for you to dissect.

- Be specific with your argument, examples, and evidence. You do not need to have advanced knowledge or education on the topic. When you bring up an idea or state an objection to the argument, you need to follow that up with specific evidence to support your statement. Evidence can come from the prompt and/or real world sources or personal experiences, as long as they directly relate to the topic. Stick to evidence that directly supports your point. The weaker your evidence, the harder it will be for you to argue your point.

- Remember, the GRE doesn't expect you to have advanced knowledge on a topic to be able to argue it. This task is evaluating your analytical writing capabilities and your rhetorical logic. They want to see critical thinking, not research. Successful responses use 3-5 paragraphs to dissect the argument, review the assumptions and evidence, offer alternate explanations and evidence, and bring up possible objections that arise out of developing the argument.

- Before you begin writing your response, it is important to structure your essay clearly. Having an outline will keep you from going off on a tangent. Let's review how to organize your essay.

Organizing Your Essay

Similar to the characteristics we just reviewed as part of your strategic approach to the prompt, having an idea of how you want to organize your essay regardless of the prompt will help you best utilize your time and optimize your score. The outline below lays out an essay that addresses the essay task and presents your position in an organized manner.

Introduction

- Briefly describe the author's point of view and make a clear statement of your position on whether or not the argument is flawed.

First Body Paragraph

- Discuss your first point of analysis of the argument and assess its validity and what assertions can weaken or strengthen the argument.

Second Body Paragraph

- Discuss your second point of analysis of the argument and assess its validity and what assertions can weaken or strengthen the argument.

Third Body Paragraph

- This paragraph is best reserved to address the additional directions in the essay task that have not been addressed in the previous two paragraphs. If you have been asked to address a question that needs to be answered to assess the validity of the argument, examine alternate explanations, or discuss potential consequences that result from acting according to the presented reasoning, this is the place to do so.

Conclusion

- This is your last paragraph to make your point. Reiterate your position and evaluate the strength of the argument based on the analysis you presented.

Paragraph Structure

If you are aiming for a top score, it is not enough to just organize your paragraphs logically. Each sentence you write in each paragraph must be organized logically and provide both support for your position. Paragraphs should follow a traditional structure in the body of your response.

Topic Sentence

- Your topic sentence should give the reader an idea of what the rest of your paragraph is about. The sentence should critique a particular logical flaw in the prompt, introduce a counterexample, or address the specific directions of the essay task.

Evidence and Analysis

- Once you have your topic sentence, there are several ways you can develop the rest of your paragraph. Your goal is to make your topic sentence persuasive by including supporting evidence or an analysis of the logical reasoning, statistical, or data errors.

Compelling Conclusion

- Your conclusion should be compelling. In your conclusion, you should strive to clearly reiterate your point of view and use your stronger piece of support to solidify your assessment of the argument. You don't want to leave the reviewer with a lackluster feeling, so make sure you leave a lasting impression. You can state your main point of view again, summarize your main points, or make the reader aware of a larger issue.

Using a Standard Format

As mentioned in the previous section, there is not a standard way to organize your essay. However, as with the Analyze an Issue essay, it works to your advantage to develop a standard format for responding to the Argument prompt. The prompts, which are made available to you before the exam, are consistent in their presentation, and the essay tasks do not change. So, you have the opportunity to hone your approach to your essay before the exam and practice with real GRE prompts.

For the Analyze an Argument essay, you want to reflect your understanding of the logical shortcomings of the essay and demonstrate your ability to follow instructions by answering all components of the question tasks. If you go into the exam with a solid foundation in analyzing argument, garnered from practicing with the prompts and refining your essay structure, you can best position yourself to earn a top score.

Logical Flaws and Errors in Reasoning

The arguments you encounter in the prompts for the Analyze an Argument essay will be flawed in some way. Logically, it is important to understand the common flaws in logic so that when you encounter them on the exam, you cannot only recognize them, but also articulate why the reasoning is not sound. This is the crux of the Argument essay. You will also see these logical flaws arise in the Verbal Reasoning section of the exam, especially in Reading Comprehension passages. There are nearly one hundred logical flaws. Don't panic. We could not possibly cover them all here, and most of them will not occur on the exam. A majority of the body of your essay will be spent addressing the flaws in the reasoning that you have identified. So, in order to draft an essay that meets the expectations of the essay reviewers, it is imperative that you provide a clear and accurate analysis of the argument's flaws.

Let's take a look at the most common logical flaws, many of which you will encounter in the Analyze an Argument prompt.

Part of the Whole/Whole of the Part

These types of flaws occur when the author assumes that because something is true of the part it is also true of the whole. Conversely, the author may also erroneously assume that whatever is true of the part. For example, if the author asserts that he read a page in a book and it was good and then concludes that the book must be good, his reasoning is flawed. He has assumed that because a part of something was good (page), that the entire thing must be good (book). Similarly, if the author asserted that because the book was good, then every page in the book must be good, his reasoning is also flawed. You cannot attribute the characteristics of part of something to the whole or characteristics of the whole of something to each of its individual parts without proper evidence to establish the veracity of your claim.

Errors in Conditional Reasoning

Conditional reasoning is the logical relationship characterized by "if-then" statements where "if" is the sufficient and "then" is the necessary. Conditional reasoning is also commonly symbolized as A ⟶ B, which is "If A, then B." Errors in conditional reasoning occur when the author fails to properly understand the sufficient/necessary relationship and makes inappropriate conclusion based on an erroneous understanding. Conditional reasoning has many complex nuances; many of these will not occur on the exam. But, you will need to understand the basics. If you encounter a conditional relationship in the argument prompt, you should always examine it closely to ensure that it conforms to the conditional reasoning conventions. If it does not, then the argument is flawed and you will need to explain the why. Let's look at a conditional reasoning statement and examine both the logical and illogical conclusions that can be made.

> If it rains tomorrow, then the store will be closed.
> The sufficient is "if it rains" while the necessary is "the store will be closed"

The only correct conclusions that you can draw from this statement are outlined below:

- If it rains, the store will be closed. Whenever the sufficient happens, the necessary **always** happens. If the author asserts that it rained but also asserts that the store is closed, the argument is flawed since the necessary must occur whenever the sufficient occurs.
- If it does not rain, the store can be open or closed. The necessary can **always** occur without the sufficient. So, if the author concludes that since the store is closed, it must have rained, the argument is flawed since it fails to consider the the necessary can occur without the sufficient.

Faulty Analogies

Reasoning by analogy functions by comparing two similar things. The false analogy flaw occurs when the author assumes that because similar things or people are alike in some way that they share the same characteristics or outcomes in every instance.

Here's an example of a faulty analogy flaw:

Ted and Jim excel at both football and basketball. Since Ted is also a track star, it is likely that Jim also excels at track.

In this example, numerous similarities between Ted and Jim are used as the basis for the erroneous inference that they share additional traits.

Biased Sample

A biased sample occurs whenever an inadequate sample is used to justify the conclusion drawn. Here's an example of a biased sample flaw:

I have worked with 3 people from New York City and found them to be obnoxious, pushy and rude. It is obvious that people from New York City have a bad attitude.

The data for the inference in this argument are insufficient to support the conclusion.

Source Argument

The source argument flaw, also known as an ad hominem flaw, occurs when an argument is rejected because of irrelevant characteristics of the person presenting the argument. These types of flaws are common and are usually easy to spot. Here's an example:

Governor Bates' new DUI law should be repealed since he was recently himself caught driving under the influence.

While Governor Bates being caught driving under the influence is certainly not a good thing for a number of reasons in this case, the argument provides no reasoning relevant to the actual law that supports its claim that the law should be repealed. The author only offers an assessment of Governor Bates, the person responsible for the law.

Appeal to Authority

Another type of fallacious reasoning is appeal to authority. Sometimes, an author will cite the opinion of an expert or other authority on an issue as the only means of support for the argument. Some appeals to authority are logical, like citing the research of the foremost expert in the treatment of Dissociative Identity Disorder to support an argument about the most effective psychological interventions for the disorder. But, a fallacious appeal to authority either appeals to an irrelevant authority or improperly assumes that citing the position of the authority figures is the only justification needed to support the argument. Here's an example:

Leonardo DiCaprio spoke about climate change in his Oscar speech. Clearly, this should put to the rest the ill-informed arguments of those who contend global warming does not exist.

Leonardo DiCaprio is not an expert on climate change. While he is a celebrity who may have some influence, his speaking on the issue in no way validates or invalidates the global warming argument on either side.

Analyze an Argument Practice Writing Exercise

Now that we have reviewed how to approach the Analyze an Argument section and the elements that contribute to a high-scoring essay, let's look at an essay prompt. The tasks below will help you solidify your position on the issue, organize your argument, and draft your essay. Practicing with these questions in mind can help you firm up your strategic approach to writing the Analyze an Argument essay. As you work through the ETS prompts, try to answer these questions as you outline your essay.

Argument Prompt

The results of a four-year study of the common cold examined the possible therapeutic effects of a vegan diet. While many foods are naturally rich in antioxidants, food processing companies also sell isolated antioxidants. The four-year study found a strong correlation between a vegan diet and significant decline in the average number of colds reported by participants. A control group that increased its antioxidant intake using supplements did not have a decrease in the number of colds. Based on these results, some health experts recommend a vegan diet over the use of package antioxidants.

Instructions

Discuss the questions that must be answered in the argument to determine if the advice provided is reasonable. As part of your response, explain how the answers would help in evaluating the validity of the argument.

Brainstorm and Outline Your Ideas

Identify any logical flaws in the argument?

How does the evidence the author uses weaken or support the argument?

What questions need to be answered for the presented argument to flow logically? What holes are in the author's argument?

Using your strongest points from above, briefly outline the evidence or logical flaw you will address in each paragraph.

Paragraph 1:

Paragraph 2:

Paragraph 3:

Paragraph 4:

Using your outline, write an essay in response to the prompt.

When writing your response for Analyze an Issue & Analyze an Argument, use a computer, and turn off the spell-check feature to simulate real testing conditions. You may use this space for note-taking or brainstorming.

Chapter Overview

The Analyze an Argument task measures your ability to analyze a presented argument and its evidence to evaluate its persuasiveness and logical soundness. The Analyze an Argument essay always appears last in the Analytical Writing section; you will have 30 minutes to complete the essay.

Essay Tasks

In addition to assessing the argument, you will also be presented with specific writing instructions that require you to both understand and explain the errors in logical reasoning and potential weaknesses in the argument. Pay close attention to these instructions and familiarize yourself with the prompts ahead of the exam.

Scoring

Essays are scored on a scale of 0.0-6.0, and your Analyze an Argument essay score is averaged with your score from the Analyze an Issue essay to derive your cumulative Analytical Writing score. You will not receive a separate score for the Analyze an Argument essay.

Tips for a Solid Analyze an Argument Essay

- Evaluate the argument and identify logical flaws, areas of weakness, and/or issues with data.
- Analyze the merits of the argument and leave your opinion out of the equation.
- Your overall essay organization is important, but make sure each paragraph is well-organized as well.
- Take a few minutes to proofread your essay and check for missing words, awkward sentence constructions, and grammatical errors.

Checklist for Argument Essay Prompt

When reading through the prompt and planning your essay, ask yourself these key questions:

- Is the argument logically sound?
- What flawed reasoning has the author used to advance the argument?
- Has the author introduced any statistics and, if so, are they used appropriately?
- What evidence and counter-examples can you use to provide an organized analysis of the argument and address all components of the essay task?

Common Flaws

- Assuming that characteristics of a group apply to each member of that group
- Assuming that a certain condition is necessary for a certain outcome
- Drawing a weak analogy between two things
- Relying on inappropriate or potentially unrepresentative statistics
- Relying on biased or tainted data (methods for collecting data must be unbiased and poll responses must be credible)

Up Next: In the next chapter, we will switch gears and look at the Verbal Reasoning section and explore the questions, some general strategies and resources for helping you prepare for the section.

ARGO
BROTHERS

7 INTRODUCTION TO VERBAL REASONING

Verbal Reasoning: The Basics

The Verbal Reasoning section is designed to test your ability to read, comprehend, and evaluate written material using your logical reasoning and critical thinking skills. This section also measures your understanding of sentence structure, punctuation, and proper use of vocabulary.

The question tasks are presented in various forms from short sentences to multi-paragraph passages. Two scored Verbal Reasoning sections will appear in any order on the exam following the Analytical Writing section. You will have 30 minutes to complete each section. Each section on the computer-adapted exam consists of 20 questions.

Why is this section important?

Graduate programs use your performance on the Verbal Reasoning section to evaluate your critical thinking ability, analytical skills, and aptitude for using context and logical reasoning to infer meaning from written material. These skills are critical to successfully navigating graduate-level work. Graduate programs use your scores along with your application materials to assess whether you're a fit for graduate-level study.

Scoring and Computer-Adaptive Testing

The section is scored on a scale of 130-170, in one-point increments. A 170 is the highest possible score. The score reflects your combined Verbal Reasoning performance; you will not receive a separate score for each verbal section.

When taking the computer exam, you are able to answer questions in each section in any order you wish. You can skip questions or use the built-in system tools to mark a question for review and come back to it later as time permits. As we discussed in the section on computer-adaptive testing, the difficulty of your second scored section of Verbal Reasoning is determined by your performance on your first section. This section of the book will outline strategies to help you manage your time, understand the question tasks, and deploy various strategies to help optimize your Verbal Reasoning score.

Question Types

Your exam will consist of **two** scored Verbal Reasoning sections that consist of three question types. Each question type typically appears at the same frequency across exams. The chart below details the question types and the approximate number of questions you are likely to encounter on each of the two Verbal Reasoning sections.

Question Type	Question Task	Approx. # of Questions
Reading Comprehension	Reading Comprehension questions require you to read the given passages and select the answer choice that best completes the question task. Content of the passages can come from a wide-range of subject matters, and there is often more than one question that corresponds to each passage.	9-10 questions
Text Completion	Text Completion questions require you to identify the appropriate term (or terms) that best completes a given sentence. Text Completion questions can have anywhere from one to three terms that need to be identified. A strong vocabulary and the ability to understand context clues are essential in this section.	5-6 questions
Sentence Equivalence	Sentence Equivalence questions require you to identify two terms for a single blank in a sentence that will create two similar sentences that express the same main idea. Similar to the Text Completion questions, this section requires a strong vocabulary and command of context clues.	4-5 questions

Timewise, answering 20 questions in 30 minutes allots you 1.5 minutes per question. This does not mean you need 1.5 minutes for each question or more than 1.5 minutes on some questions, especially Reading Comprehension. While you are preparing for the exam, you should first focus on strategies and understanding the content and then gradually incorporate timing into your study plan to try to work toward getting to all the questions in the allotted time frame.

Reading Comprehension

Reading Comprehension questions appear in some form on all standardized exams. You may be familiar with them from the SAT or other graduate entrance exams you may have taken. These questions make up a majority of the questions on the Verbal Reasoning section, with about nine to ten questions per section.

Reading Comprehension questions contain passages taken mostly from actual textbooks, articles and books in the humanities, social sciences, arts, and the sciences. Passages are a minimum of one paragraph while some are more robust. While some passages will only have one question that corresponds to it, most passages will have several corresponding questions.

Sample Reading Comprehension Question

A popular publishing house in California estimated that 60,000 to 80,000 people in the United States would be interested in an anthology that includes all of William Shakespeare's works. The publishing house and literary scholars who study Shakespeare's work attribute this interest to the complex psychological nature of Shakespeare's characters, which they assert still intrigue people in the present day.

The paragraph above best supports which one of the following assertions?

A. Shakespeare was an expert in psychology
B. Californians are particularly inclined to enjoy Shakespeare's work
C. Shakespeare's characters are more interesting than characters of more recent works
D. Shakespeare's characters play a major role in people's interest in his work
E. Academic scholars agree on the reason people tend to enjoy Shakespeare's work

Text Completion

Text Completion questions focus heavily on your understanding of advanced vocabulary. Each section of the Verbal Reasoning assessment will contain five to six Text Completion questions that will require you to select one, two, or three answers to fill in the corresponding blanks.

Like the Reading Comprehension questions, the specific content runs the gamut of subjects. You do not need to be an expert on the presented subject matter. Instead, your task is to use the context clues to choose the appropriate word that best completes the sentence.

Sample Text Completion Question

He ____________ the article's ideas with current events to demonstrate how closely they were related.

A. nixed
B. aligned
C. juxtaposed
D. juggled
E. merged

Text Completion questions have one, two, or three blanks. You will have three to six answer choices to select from depending on the number of blanks in the sentence.

Sentence Equivalence

Similar to the Text Completion questions, Sentence Equivalence questions also rely heavily on vocabulary and your ability to use context clues to identify the correct answer. Each section of the Verbal Reasoning assessment will contain four to five Sentence Equivalence questions.

Sentence Equivalence prompts are usually one sentence long and contain one blank. Your task is to identify **two** separate answer choices that can be inserted into the blank and have the sentence retain the same meaning.

Sample Sentence Equivalence Question

You cannot become a certified personal trainer without completing the __________ fitness test and client contact hours.

A. typical
B. requisite
C. optional
D. mandatory
E. physical

For Sentence Equivalence questions, you will always select two answer choices to complete one blank.

How to Prepare for the Verbal Reasoning Section

In the Verbal Reasoning section, you will be asked to read and synthesize information presented in various forms from short sentences to multi-paragraph passages. This assessment area is designed to test your ability to comprehend and evaluate written material. The Verbal Reasoning section also measures your understanding of sentence structure, punctuation, and proper use of vocabulary.

In addition to the strategies we will explore in the subsequent chapters, there are several tools included in this text to help you hone your approach to the Verbal Reasoning assessment.

Vocabulary Lists

Having a strong vocabulary is key as it plays a critical role in the Verbal Reasoning section. The vocabulary lists in the Appendix of this text provide you with commonly used words on the exams as well as an overview of prefixes, suffixes, and root words to help you better understand words you may not know.

Problem Sets and Explanations

After each question type in the Verbal Reasoning section, you will have the opportunity to test out your understanding of the concepts. Use these problem sets to apply the strategies discussed in the sections and review the explanations to help you gain a better understanding of how to arrive at correct answer choices and avoid tricky answer choices meant to distract you.

Chapter Overview

Your performance on the Verbal Reasoning section depends heavily on the breadth of your vocabulary and your ability to critically analyze written text. It is essential to have a solid vocabulary, and a good understanding of root words, suffixes and prefixes. You must also be able to draw inferences and use critical analysis to examine passages.

It is important to note that vocabulary alone, however, will likely not be enough to achieve a high score on this section. You must understand how to use and analyze information in context to identify the correct word or words missing from the Text Completion and Sentence Equivalence questions and to understand the content of the Reading Comprehension passages.

The subsequent chapters in this section and the vocabulary resources included with this text will provide you with the tools to bolster your vocabulary, strengthen your reasoning skills, and develop a strategic approach to optimize your test performance.

FAST FACTS: Section Breakdown

- Two scored Verbal Reasoning sections per exam
- Can occur in any order after the Analytical Writing section
- 30 minutes per section
- 20 questions per section
- Depending on your exam, you may have an additional unscored section of Verbal Reasoning. Remember to approach all sections as if they are scored.

Question Breakdown

Question Breakdown	Question Task	Approx. # of Questions
Reading Comprehension	Reading Comprehension questions require you to read the given passages and select the answer choice that best completes the question task. Content of the passages can come from a wide range of subject matters, and there is often more than one question that corresponds to each passage.	9-10 questions
Text Completion	Text Completion questions require you to identify the appropriate term (or terms) that best completes a given sentence. Text Completion questions can have anywhere from one to three terms that need to be identified. A strong vocabulary and the ability to understand context clues are essential in this section.	5-6 questions
Sentence Equivalence	Sentence Equivalence questions require you to identify two terms for a single blank in a sentence that will create two similar sentences that express the same main idea. Similar to the Text Completion questions, this section requires a strong vocabulary and command of context clues.	4-5 questions

Up Next: In the next chapter, we will discuss Reading Comprehension questions, which comprise a majority of the questions in the Verbal Reasoning section. We will explore the anatomy of a Reading Comprehension passage, common question types, and strategies to help you navigate these oftentimes long and complicated questions.

ARGO
BROTHERS

8 READING COMPREHENSION QUESTIONS

Reading Comprehension: The Basics

Reading Comprehension questions require you to read the given passages and select the answer choice that best completes the question task. Content of the passages can come from a wide range of subject matters, and there is often more than one question that corresponds to each passage. Each section of Verbal Reasoning has three to five Reading Comprehension passages with one to five accompanying questions. With a total of nine to ten questions, Reading Comprehension accounts for about half of the questions on each of the scored verbal section.

The passages are generally one paragraph but can be up to five paragraphs in length. They are drawn from a wide range of sources like journals, academic texts, and literature. You can expect to see passages related to the sciences, humanities, social science, and art, to name a few. The passages are intentionally complex and are often replete with complex vocabulary and complicated sentence constructions. Because of this, Reading Comprehension questions can be some of the most difficult in the Verbal Reasoning section.

This chapter will help you understand the types of passages and questions you will encounter on the exam. It will also outline some useful strategies on how to best approach reading and outlining the passages to position yourself to attack the questions.

Prep Fact: You will have a maximum of two longer passages; the rest will be one paragraph long.

Reading Comprehension and the Computer-Adaptive Exam

Reading passages and trying to answer corresponding questions are daunting tasks on their own. But, having to read the passages and answer the questions on a computer screen can complicate the section even further. The creators of the computer-adaptive exam try to make the section as seamless as possible by utilizing a split-screen model. The passage will always be displayed on the screen alongside the question you are currently working on. As we discussed in the Introduction chapter, ETS offers its free PowerPrep II Software so you can walk through the elements of the section like practice reading, selecting answer choices, and navigating the section. Utilize this resource to not only familiarize yourself with the material, but to also get accustomed to the built-in functions of the exam and with reading long passages using the scroll function on a split-screen. Since you cannot annotate the passage, you want to allow yourself time to practice with various strategies to help you keep up with the information in the passage.

As you work on this chapter, practice keeping up with notes on the passage on your scratch paper instead of growing accustomed to writing on the passages. That way, on exam day, you won't need to get accustomed to doing so.

Components of a Reading Comprehension Question

Reading Comprehension questions are comprised of three key components: the passage, the question stem and the answer choices.

Passage: This is the meat of the Reading Comprehension question. The passage will be one to five paragraphs in length with content drawn from a wide-range of sources like journals, academic texts, and popular literature.

Question Stem: The question stem provides you with a specific task based on the passage. There are several question stems that occur frequently on the exam that test different aspects of your critical reading and analytical reasoning skills. We will explore those in greater detail later in this chapter.

Answer Choices: You will have three to five answer choices for each Reading Comprehension question or be asked to select a specific sentence in the text. Be sure to read them all before selecting your answer as Reading Comprehension questions are notorious for having tricky, nearly true answer choices that occur directly before the correct answer choice.

Let's look at an actual Reading Comprehension question.

Sample Reading Comprehension Question

Directions: Questions 1-2 correspond to the following passage:

Passage

Scientists know very little about the eating habits of our ancestors who lived over 2.5 million years ago. To solve this problem, scientists have started examining chimpanzees' hunting behavior and diet to find clues about our own prehistoric past. It is not difficult to determine why studying chimpanzees might be beneficial. Modern humans and chimpanzees are actually very closely related. Experts believe that chimpanzees share about 98.5 percent of our DNA sequence. If this is true, humans are more closely related to chimpanzees than they are to any other animal species.

Question Stem

1. The main purpose of the passage is to:

Answer Choices

A. explore biological and physiological similarities between humans and chimpanzees
B. examine the hunting behavior and diet of chimpanzees and compare them to human activity
C. discuss the health benefits of eating and hunting meat while simultaneously predicting the effect of this behavior on chimpanzee offspring
D. bring attention to the pioneering research of Dr. Jane Goodall in Tanzania
E. educate the public on the impact that tool use had in early human societies

About the Passages

GRE passages are usually complex excerpts from a wide range of scholarly texts. The passages mirror the complexity of reading materials you will encounter at the graduate level. Regardless of the passage length, Reading Comprehension passages can be overwhelming as they contain intentionally complex language and require you to understand the presented information and in many cases, make inferences based on the information provided. The author of each passage will express a viewpoint and/or state a series of facts that outline an argument. You can expect questions that test your understanding of the logical flow of the passage, the organization, the author's tone, and weaknesses in the argument.

Common Characteristics of Passages

Though GRE passages are organized in a number of ways and vary in content, they all share some common elements that you will need to identify and understand in order to accurately answer the questions. Let's look at some key characteristics you can expect to find in all GRE passages.

Main Point

Each passage will have a main point, or conclusion as it is sometimes referred to, and in many cases, a question that asks you to identify the main point of the passage. The main point is always the author's point of view and answers the question, "Why did the author write this passage?"

It is the most central part of the argument. The main point is not limited to the opening paragraph or closing sentence; this is a common misconception. The main point can be found anywhere in the passage and requires you to consider what it is overall that the author is trying to convey.

Premises

The main point is supported by premises in the passage. Premises are statements that provide evidence for the author's argument and in some cases, evidence against a position that conflicts with the author's assertion. Premises can support the main point independently or work together with other premises to support the author's main point. Premises are often correct answer choices for questions; you should be able to distinguish between the main point and evidence that supports the main point as some questions will ask you to do just that.

Take this passage for example:

> Scientists have hypothesized that disturbing rainforests to gain access to fossil fuels may alleviate the country's impending energy crisis. This is nonsense. While the fossil fuels may temporarily alleviate some of the energy issues, the larger problem it creates will not only exacerbate the energy crisis, but will also create an entirely new set of issues.

What is the main point of this passage?

Why did the author write this passage? What is her stance on the issue being discussed? To identify the main point of this passage, it's important to identify the author's perspective since there are two perspectives expressed: the author's and scientists'. The main point of the passage is that disturbing the rainforests to gain access to fossil fuels is not a viable solution to the impending energy crisis. This is the author's assertion; it is important not to confuse what the scientists are assuming with what the author is arguing.

What are the premises?

The author directly responds to the scientists' claims by saying "this is nonsense." She then goes on to explain why: fossil fuels are a temporary fix and will only create more issues. These premises support her argument and the contention that disturbing the rainforests in order to fix the energy problem is nonsense.

Reading Comprehension Question Tasks

The Reading Comprehension questions are not meant to test your knowledge or opinion about a particular subject. You should answer questions based only on the information presented in the passage, and not on any prior knowledge that you might have of the subject. You might be asked to draw a conclusion or make an inference, but you should do so based only on what the author actually states or implies.

Main Idea

Main Idea questions ask you to identify or infer the main idea of the passage. The question type may also ask you to draw other inferences based on the main point of the passage. Main Idea questions account for a large portion of the questions in this section. It is important to note that the main idea is not geographically defined; you won't always find it in the concluding sentence or the opening paragraph.

Examples of Main Idea Question Stems

- Select the sentence that best represents the author's central argument.
- The primary purpose of the passage is to...
- Given the author's point of view, which one of the following would be an appropriate title for the passage?

> **Prep Tip:** Developing a familiarity with the types of questions you are most likely to see for Reading Comprehension can help you hone both your approach to reading the passage and time management. If you are reading and annotating key points and are familiar with the question tasks, you can use your time effectively and stand a better chance of selecting the correct answer choices.

Supporting Ideas

Supporting Idea questions ask you to identify premises and evidence in the passage that support the main idea. The question type may also ask you to infer supporting ideas not explicitly mentioned in the passage or select an answer choice that explains why a particular supporting idea was included.

Examples of Supporting Ideas Question Stems

- The author mentions the "think-tank" experience in order to...
- The passage lists all of the following consequences of the regulations except...
- Select the sentence that best supports the author's main point.

Author's Attitude

Author's Attitude questions ask you to infer the author's tone about various issues presented in the passage or to use information presented in the passage to infer how the author might feel about similar situations. It is important to be able to separate the author's point of view from other viewpoints presented in the passage.

Examples of Author's Attitude Question Stems

- The author's attitude toward contemporary art can be best described as...
- The author would most likely agree with which of the following policies relating to copyright laws?

Specific Reference

These questions ask you to respond to the question based on information located in a specific location of the passage. The question will often direct you to a particular sentence or term. In this case, it is best to read a few lines before and after to get some context and avoid missing critical connections or transitions that may impact your understanding of the specific line or term in question. These type of questions can encompass a wider scope and ask you to identify points specifically addressed or not addressed in the passage.

Examples of Specific Reference Question Stems

- The author uses the term "precarious" in line 14, most likely to communicate...
- The passage mentions each of the following as reasons for the policy, EXCEPT:

Strengthen/Weaken

These questions ask you to identify answer choices that will either strengthen or weaken the presented argument. An answer choice that strengthens an argument might add to an assumption that the author has made but has not explicitly stated or add additional information that clears up problematic statistics presented in the argument. The correct answer choices will add relevant value to the passage and make the argument stronger, if only by a smidge. An answer choice that weakens an argument will address holes in the reasoning including unjustifiable assumptions, issues with data, and lack of evidence. The answer choice must hurt the argument; it is not necessary for the answer choice to completely invalidate the argument in order for it to be correct.

Examples of Strengthen/Weaken Question Stems

- Which of the following, if true, would most **weaken** the author's argument?
- Which of the following, if true, would most **strengthen** the conclusion drawn in the passage above?

Passage Organization

These questions test your understanding of how the passage is organized and how the organization impacts the author's argument. As you read through the passage, pay close attention to how the paragraphs flow, whether the author uses enumerations (first, second, third) and any chronological information like dates. Understanding the organization of the passage is not only helpful in answering Passage Organization questions, but will also help you better understand the author's point of view, refer back to passage quickly to locate information, and answer other types of questions .

Example of Passage Organization Question Stems

- Which of the following best outlines the organization of the passage?
- Which of the following best describes the organization of the third paragraph?

Parallel

These questions test your understanding of the organization and reasoning in the passage. Because of this, they can be both lengthy and complicated. Oftentimes, answering these questions require you to make inferences not explicitly stated in the passage, or apply the reasoning and/or structure to similar situations that are unrelated to the passage.

Examples of Parallel Question Stems

- Which one of the following is most similar to the process Davis used to compose new pieces in the 1940's?
- Which of the following would best match the reasoning outlined in the passage?

Should I Read the Questions First?

When to read the question is a common point that is discussed among test-takers. Often there are differing opinions and rationale presented to justify one side or the other. When thinking about how to strategically approach the section, taking into account the limited amount of time you have for each question and the information you are usually required to read, we suggest you read the questions after the passage.

There is a reason the Reading Comprehension question is organized the way that it is: the passage, the question stem, and then the answer choices. This is because it makes logical sense to read the passage, understand the question task, then approach the questions. Aside from simply reading the passage as it is presented, there are some other key justifications for reading the questions after you read the passage:

- You have 30 minutes to answer 20 questions. So, every second is valuable. Oftentimes, when people read the question first, they then read it again after reading the passage. That time could be better spent navigating the answer choices or referencing the passage for additional information again if needed.

- A common justification for reading the questions first is that it helps the reader identify what they are looking for in the passage. While this may ring true in some instances, given the complex reasoning included in many of the passages, this typically has the opposite effect. When you read the question first, it primes you to look only for specific information, often at the expense of overlooking other critical premises and supporting evidence that is necessary to consider in order to get to the correct answer.

- Sometimes the question stems introduce new information that is not in the actual passage. If you are looking specifically for that information, you may be confused when going back to the passage and may end up spending more time trying to re-read and understand the question task than if you had simply read the passage first.

Reading Comprehension Answer Choices

You will encounter a number of different answer choice options on the Verbal Reasoning section. For Reading Comprehension passages you can expect to see questions that ask you to select one, two, or three answer choices, and questions that ask you to select specific text within the passage. Let's look more closely at these answer choice types.

Multiple-choice: Choose One Answer Choice

These questions ask you to select the **one** answer choice that best answers the question stem. You will be presented with five answer choices and must select only one. This question type is the most popular type on the exam. In order to select the best answer, you must read all the answer choices. The GRE is commonly littered with attractive answer choices that are not correct. These often occur right before the correct answer. Read all the answer choices to be sure.

Multiple-choice: Choose One or More Answer Choices

These questions ask you to select one, two, or three answer choices to answer the question stem. You will often be presented with three answer choices. As such, it is possible that all three answer choices are correct. There is no partial credit for these questions; you must select all and only the correct answers in order to receive credit for your response. Assess each answer choice on its own to determine if it answers the questions. As with the previous question type, make sure you read all the answer choice options.

Select-in-Passage

These questions ask you to select the sentence in the passage that best addresses the question stem. The part of the passage that the question wants you to focus on will be marked with an arrow, and you are only able to select a sentence from that section.

Incorrect Answer Types

Having an understanding of the common types of incorrect answers you may encounter in the Reading Comprehension section can help you avoid falling for many of the tricky answer choices and psychometrics built into the exam. One of the most important components of Reading Comprehension questions is the understanding that because you are making inferences from the provided passages, most of your answers **must be true based on the passage**. Reading Comprehension questions will ask you about the main point, the author's point of view, and inferences you can draw from the passage. You will always be able to map the correct answers to these questions directly back on the passage. In these instances, do not be enticed by answers that could be true; instead look for the answer choice that, based on the passage, absolutely must be true.

The test writers create intentionally misleading but attractive answer choices and co-mingle them with the correct answer. These answer choices typically fall into several consistent categories. Let's explore some common incorrect answer types.

Out of Scope

These answer choices introduce information that is not included in the passage, though it may be closely related. Since you are typically looking for answers that must be true, it will be difficult to prove that something not mentioned in the passage or able to be inferred must be true. Out of Scope answers occur in a myriad of ways. Some of the trickier instances occur when dates are involved. A passage may address events that happened in the 1900's and an answer choice may make an assertion about what happened in the previous century. While it may be tempting to make common sense assumptions or incorporate your personal knowledge on the matter, remember that your task is to use **only** the information presented in the passage to guide you to the correct answer.

Partially Correct

Your correct answer choice will accurately and completely answer the question. You will sometimes encounter answer choices that are mostly true or only address part of the question. Make sure your answer choice addresses all aspects of the question and is correct in its entirety.

True but Not Correct

Not all answer choices that are true are correct. And, just because you can map it directly back to the passage and confirm its validity does not mean it properly answers the question. Before selecting an answer choice, be sure you are clear about what the question task is asking of you and that your answer both responds to the question task and is drawn from and supported by the passage.

Too Extreme

Be wary of answer choices that use words like always, never, everyone, etc. While use of these terms do not always signify an incorrect answer, they do merit additional attention. When you encounter this type of absolute language in an answer choice in Reading Comprehension (example: all the neighborhoods will be affected by the drought), you want to be sure that you can map it directly back to the passage. If the passage indicates that most of the neighborhoods have experienced some negative consequences as a result of the drought, you cannot logically conclude that all of them have.

Navigating the Answer Choices

In order to select the best answer choice and avoid enticing but incorrect answers, you should make a habit of reading all of the answer choices before making a selection. As you work through the answer choices, some will immediately stand out as incorrect. You can eliminate those and move on the next answer choice.

If you find yourself considering an answer choice for more than a few seconds, mark it as a possible answer and move on to the next answer choice. Using your scratch paper, you can jot down your eliminated and possible answer choices using a t-chart:

Eliminated	Possible
A	B
C	D
E	

In the example above, A, C and E were eliminated in the first pass. Once you have eliminated several answer choices and narrowed your options, carefully consider the remaining options in your second pass.

With only 30 minutes for the entire section, you will need to manage your time effectively. Since you cannot simply mark out the eliminated answer choices on the computer-adaptive exam like you would be able to on the paper exam, keeping track of the answers you already eliminated allows you to focus on the possible answers.

Prep Tip: Reading Comprehension questions are concerned with your ability to critically analyze written information, not your ability to express your personal opinion on the passage. Keep your opinion under wraps and ensure you are only using the information in the passage and logical inferences drawn from it to select answer choices.

Developing a Strategy

Many people fail to prepare adequately for the Reading Comprehension questions because they mistakenly equate their ability to "read" and "comprehend" with their ability to tackle this section. Reading Comprehension questions require more than simply being able to recap what you have read. You must be able to critically assess the reasoning, understand the structure, and pinpoint why particular evidence, vocabulary, and counter-examples are introduced... all within a short time period.

Developing an effective approach to answering these questions is of critical importance. But, part of developing that approach has nothing to do with outlining the steps you should follow when you encounter a Reading Comprehension question on the exam. Instead, developing your approach starts with honing your vocabulary, and most importantly, the pace at which you are able to read, process, and correctly answer Reading Comprehension questions.

Reading Comprehension and Vocabulary

While you will not be explicitly asked to outline definitions of words or fill in missing words like in the other sections, a strong vocabulary is critical for the Reading Comprehension section. The passages require no specific knowledge on the subject matter presented, but they do use complex language that models the level at which a graduate-level student should be able to read and understand.

Study the vocabulary lists in the back of this text along with the root words and prefixes and suffixes to help build your vocabulary and make better educated guesses about the meaning of a word you have not seen before.

Improving Your Reading Pace

The passages are typically replete with complex vocabulary, and sometimes the facts are buried in a dense web of rhetoric. Luckily, some of the passages are quite straightforward. But, dealing with the dense and long passages can greatly impact the amount of time you have for the rest of the section, which of course, affects your overall score. Reading at a good pace and retaining information often present the largest challenges with Reading Comprehension questions. There are, however, ways that you can actively work to improve your reading speed. One of the most effective ways is to incorporate reading complex material into your study plan. For example, many people find science-related passages daunting even though the subject matter of the passage should be a non-issue. Nonetheless, they struggle to process the unfamiliar terms and grow anxious about retaining the information, often re-reading and losing valuable time. Whether this describes you or not, try to increase your reading speed and your ability to clearly understand a passage by regularly reading material that is unfamiliar to you. Great examples include the abstracts of scientific and social science articles; academic journals; and newspapers and editorials from reputable journalism outlets. These all include the types of passages you might see in the Reading Comprehension section.

One of the key misconceptions about reading passages on the Reading Comprehension section is that when you are finished with the passage, you should have an in-depth understanding of what was discussed so that you can answer the questions without referring back to the passage. This is absolutely not the case. You can and should always refer back to the passage to ensure you are selecting the correct answer choice. When reading the passage, prioritize using your scratch paper to annotate the main point of the passage, key transitions, tone, and the general structure of the passage. Understanding these key things will give you the necessary information to navigate the more global questions and refer back to the passage for those questions that require a bit more investigation.

Approaching the Passages

Though the length of short and long passages can vary significantly, your approach to them should be the same. Your main goals are to **Read, Assess, Predict**, and **Answer**.

Read

Read the entire passage and look for the key components discussed above: main point, key transitions, tone, and general organization of the passage before moving on to the question stem and answer choices. You should commit to reading the entire passage so you do not miss critical information that may be integral to answering the questions. Some strategies suggest you should read only the topic and concluding sentences. This is generally not an effective strategy and will oftentimes cause you to have to go back and re-read that passage again. As a result, you spend more time re-reading than actually answering questions, a situation that can significantly impact your score.

Assess

Once you have read the passage, take a quick second to assess and process. What is the main point? What type of attitude does the author have about whatever is being discussed in the prompt? Are there any weaknesses in the argument? If you have a shorter prompt, all these considerations may not be relevant. However, every passage will have a main point; you should pinpoint that before moving on to the questions.

Predict and Answer

After you have read the passage and the question stem, take a second to pause and think about what the answer might be. Remember that your answers should be based on the information stated in or inferred from the passage. Predicting your answer can help you avoid tricky incorrect answer choices and save you time when you are eliminating incorrect answers. Once you have evaluated all the answer choices, select the answer or answers that best address the question stem.

Chapter Overview

Reading Comprehension questions require you to read the given passages and select the answer choice that best completes the question task. Content of the passages can come from a wide range of subject matters, and there is often more than one question that corresponds to each passage. Each Verbal Reasoning section has three or five Reading Comprehension passages with one to five accompanying questions. With a total of nine to ten questions, Reading Comprehension accounts for about half of the questions on each of the scored verbal section.

Components of a Reading Comprehension Question

Passage: The passage will be one to five paragraphs in length with content drawn from a wide range of sources like journals, academic texts, and literature.

Question Stem: The question stem provides you with a specific task based on the passage. There are several question stems that occur frequently on the exam that test different aspects of your critical reading and analytical reasoning skills.

Answer Choices: You will have three to five answer choices for each Reading Comprehension question or be asked to select a specific sentence in the text.

Approaching the Passage

Though the length of short and long passages can vary significantly, your approach to them should be the same. Your main goals are to **Read, Assess, Predict,** and **Answer**.

Multiple-choice: Choose One Answer Choice

These questions ask you to select the one answer choice that best answers the question stem. You will be presented with five answer choices and must select only one. This question type is the most popular type on the exam.

Multiple-choice: Choose One or More Answer Choices

These questions ask you to select one, two or three answer choices to answer the question stem. You often will be presented with three answer choices. As such, it is possible that all three answer choices are correct. There is no partial credit for these questions; you must select all and only the correct answers in order to receive credit for your response.

Select-in-Passage

These questions ask you to select the sentence in the passage that best addresses the question stem. The part of the passage that the question wants you to focus on will be marked with an arrow, and you will only be able to select a sentence from that section.

Incorrect Answer Types

Having an understanding of the common types of incorrect answers you may encounter in the Reading Comprehension section can help you avoid falling for many of the tricky answer choices and psychometrics built into the exam. One the most important components of Reading Comprehension questions is the understanding that because you are making inferences from the provided passages, most of your answers must be true based on the passage. Reading Comprehension questions will ask you about the main point, the author's point of view, and inferences you can draw from the passage.

Up Next: In the next chapter, we will discuss Text Completion and Sentence Equivalence questions. We will explore the different types of questions and strategies to help you select the proper words to complete the sentences.

Reading Comprehension Practice Set

In this chapter we have explored how to read and analyze Reading Comprehension passages, reviewed the types of questions you might encounter, and discussed how to select your answer choice while being careful to avoid common incorrect answer choice types. Now let's put those strategies to the test and get some practice with both short and long Reading Comprehension passages.

Obesity is a serious medical condition that affects millions of people across the globe. The condition is characterized by an excess of body fat and a high body mass index (BMI), which is a proportional measurement of a person's height and weight. People with a BMI that reaches a certain threshold are considered obese and can be prone to a variety of health complications as a result of their excess body weight. People diagnosed as obese often are more at-risk for debilitating diseases likes diabetes, heart disease, and cancer.

While there are many causes of obesity, the combination of poor dietary habits and a sedentary lifestyle are often responsible for the onset and progression of the disease. However, active individuals who normally eat a healthy diet can also be obese as a result of genetics, thyroid or other endocrine disorders, medication, or poor lifestyle habits like lack of sleep or alcohol abuse. There are several pharmacological and surgical interventions to help individuals reduce their body weight to a healthy weight. However, experts contend that regardless of the cause of the onset of obesity, the best way to curb the progression of the disease and thwart some of the negative consequences of carrying excessive body weight, is to get active and to make smart dietary choices.

Obesity can be deadly, and healthcare providers throughout the world continue to try to coach their patients to make smarter choices and live healthier lives. In parts of the world where weight is often conflated with prosperity and wealth, healthcare providers have a harder time convincing patients to make what could be life-saving changes to their diet and exercise regime.

1. What is the main point of the passage?

A. To discuss the parameters and warning levels for BMI
B. To discuss obesity, its causes, and the long-term impact being overweight has on individuals
C. To caution people against surgical interventions for weight-loss

2. The author would most likely agree with which one of the following?

A. Lack of exercise is the primary reason people are obese
B. There are no effective treatments currently available for obesity
C. Even a person who exercises regularly, eats a proper diet, and gets proper sleep may be obese

Out of all the farm animals, farm goats make the best pets because of their co-dependence on and affection for human connection. Even as they grow old, goats display no interest in branching off and being independent.

3. The writer implies that most farm animals:

A. are generally hard to train
B. have an affinity for human interaction
C. become independent as they grow older
D. are communal being only within their own species

Cities across the world are essentially blends of smaller cultural environments that lead people to have vastly different experiences. Each city typically contains a broad spectrum of dining establishments along with various art institutions like museums and theatres. Yet with all these blends of dining, art and night lives, what is the one characteristic that can distinguish a city? History. The undeniably unique history of each city provides rich traditions and a bond between the local people that overshadows any other city's mélange of dining and art institutions.

4. Which of the following would the author likely agree is the most important city attraction or characteristic?

- **A.** An Italian fine dining restaurant in the European district
- **B.** The Museum of Natural History
- **C.** Ruins from the Berlin Wall in the center of a local community
- **D.** Wrigley Field
- **E.** A democratic government

5. Based on its use in the passage, which word most closely defines mélange?

- **A.** history
- **B.** variety
- **C.** tradition
- **D.** unique
- **E.** scarcity

Beyond the great prairies and in the shadow of the Rockies lie the Foothills. For nine hundred miles, the prairies spread themselves out in vast level reaches, and then begin to climb over softly-rounded mounds that ever grow higher and sharper till, here and there, they break into jagged points and at last rest upon the great bases of the mighty mountains. These rounded hills that join the prairies to the mountains form the Foothill Country. They extend for about a hundred miles only, but no other hundred miles of the great West are so full of interest and romance. The natural features of the country combine the beauties of prairie and of mountain scenery. There are valleys so wide that the farther side melts into the horizon, and uplands so vast as to suggest the unbroken prairie.

Nearer the mountains the valleys dip deep and ever deeper till they narrow into canyons through which mountain torrents pour their blue-gray waters from glaciers that lie glistening between the white peaks far away. Here are the great ranges on which feed herds of cattle and horses. Here are the homes of the ranchmen, in whose wild, free, lonely existence there mingles much of the tragedy and comedy, the humor and pathos, that go to make up the romance of life. Among them are to be found the most enterprising, the most daring, of the peoples of the old lands. The broken, the outcast, the disappointed, these too have found their way to the ranches among the Foothills. A country it is whose sunlit hills and shaded valleys reflect themselves in the lives of its people; for nowhere are the contrasts of light and shade more vividly seen than in the homes of the ranchmen of the Albertas.

6. Based on the context, what is the best definition for 'pathos'?

- **A.** shade
- **B.** hunger
- **C.** passage
- **D.** sadness

7. What two types of landscapes comprise the Foothill Country?

- **A.** mountains and coastline
- **B.** prairies and mountains
- **C.** prairies and foothills
- **D.** foothills and mountains

8. Which word best describes the author's feelings about Foothill Country?

- **A.** admiration
- **B.** indifferent
- **C.** incredulous
- **D.** benign

Reading Comprehension Practice Set Answers

1. B.
2. C. Genetics could be the primary contributor.
3. C.
4. C.
5. B.
6. D. Not humorous
7. B.
8. A.

ARGO
BROTHERS

9 TEXT COMPLETION & SENTENCE EQUIVALENCE QUESTIONS

This chapter will help you understand single and multi-blank text completion questions and provide you with strategies on how to use the context provided to navigate the answer choices and identify the correct answer. This chapter will also help you understand how to navigate Sentence Equivalence questions and provide you with strategies to use the context provided to navigate the answer choices and identify the correct answer.

Text Completion: The Basics

Text Completion questions require you to read short passages that have words omitted from them. Your task is to use the context of the passage to correctly identify the missing word or words. For each Text Completion question, there will be one, two, or three blanks and you will have three to six answer choices from which to select each answer. You can expect to see about four to six Text Completion questions per each section of Verbal Reasoning.

A strong vocabulary is essential for the Text Completion questions. But, it is not enough just to study the definition of common words found on the exam; you must understand how to use them in context and how to use context clues to properly identify the correct word that fits with the rest of the sentence.

Regardless of the number of blanks, each Text Completion question is worth one point, like every other question on the exam. For questions with multiple blanks, you must answer all of them correctly to receive credit for your response. There is no partial credit.

Question Formats

Aside from the number of omitted words, there is not much variation in how Text Completion questions are presented. The questions will be shorter than Reading Comprehension questions, containing a couple of sentences at most.

For each blank, you will have a corresponding column of answer choices. The blanks do not need to be answered in any particular order; you should fill in the blanks in the way that best makes sense to you. For example, if the correct answer to the third blank is immediately obvious to you, selecting the answer choice for that blank first can make it easier to identify the remaining blanks. Some blanks are designed to test vocabulary, while others are more concerned with comprehension. Be sure to spend some time studying the vocabulary and root word lists in the back of this text to help strengthen your vocabulary and ability to surmise the meaning of words that you may not be familiar with already.

As mentioned above, Text Completions will have one, two, or three blanks. You must select all of the correct answers for a question in order for your response to be credited. Let's take a closer look at the one, two, and three-blank Text Completion questions.

Prep Tip: When reading Text Completion questions, be sure to look for transition words like "however" or "in contrast" to determine if the sentence is moving in the opposite direction. This may impact your answer choice selection.

One Blank Text Completion Questions

The one blank Text Completion questions will present you with a sentence and five answer choices. You are to select the answer choice that best completes the sentence.

The celebrity designer is known for her outlandish and over-the-top formal wear, but her new line of gowns seems to be more ________________ than her previous works.

A. transparent
B. lackluster
C. fancy
D. succinct
E. extravagant

In this one blank question, there is a transition word, "but", that sends the argument in a different direction. So, instead of looking for an answer choice that describes something similar to over-the-top and outlandish, you are looking for an answer choice that demonstrates the new line of gowns had less of a "wow" factor than the previous work of the designer. The logical answer here is **B**. The line is more lackluster compared to her previous works. Lackluster is a logical contrast to outlandish. When you plug lackluster into the sentence, it nestles in perfectly with the transition and sensibly completes the thought.

Two and Three Blank Text Completion Questions

Text Completion questions with two or three blanks are similar to their one blank companions. However, each blank will have its own corresponding set of three answer choices. You are to select an answer choice for each blank. Remember, there is no partial credit. You must select the correct answer for each blank in order for your response to be credited.

Lacking any sense of (i) ____________, David had no problem (ii) __________ credit for work that was not his own.

Blank (i)	Blank (ii)
A. ethics	**D.** providing
B. urgency	**E.** claiming
C. dishonor	**F.** assigning

Although many new discoveries in quantum physics are often (i) _______ shortly after being accepted as valid, physicists do not shy away from hasty conclusions, (ii) ______ that the (iii) ________nature of what is considered fact has not impeded their desire to innovate nor their confidence in promulgating their findings.

Blank (i)	Blank (ii)	Blank (iii)
A. purged	**D.** forbidding	**G.** hostile
B. disproved	**E.** denying	**H.** illusory
C. heralded	**F.** examining	**I.** predictable

Approaching the Blanks Strategically

Text Completion questions are rather straightforward: find the missing word or words that best complete the sentence. But, instead of just diving into them, you still want to be strategic about your approach. Keep these strategies in mind as you work through the Text Completion questions in the Verbal Reasoning section.

Read and Understand

Read the entire sentence before moving on to the answer choices. Do not confuse yourself by oscillating back and forth between the sentence and the answer choices before you actually have an understanding of what is happening in the sentence. Look for words like "but" or "however" that might change the direction of the sentence or words like "moreover" or "since" that continue the same thought. Even the use of a semicolon can indicate that relationship between the two clauses. Pay close attention to the language of the sentences before considering what the missing word(s) might be.

Predict and Answer

Once you have an understanding of the flow of the sentence, think about what word could feasibly fill the blank and make sense in the sentence. If the questions have more than one blank, consider each blank individually and in an order that makes the most sense to you. If the second blank in a question jumps out as obvious to you early on, you can start there and begin the process of looking for the answer. This may help you complete the other blanks with greater ease. Once you have predicted your answer, scan the answer choices and select the word that best completes the blank. If your question has more than one blank, repeat this process until you have selected an answer for all the blanks.

Re-read

Once you have an answer selected for each blank, re-read the sentence to make sure it makes sense and flows logically.

Sentence Equivalence: The Basics

Sentence Equivalence questions require you to identify two answer choices from a slate of six that best complete the sentence. When inserted into the sentence, both words will form its own sentence but the sentences will both be close in meaning. Like the multi-blank Text Completion questions, there is no partial credit for these questions. You must select two answers, and both answers must be correct in order for you to receive credit. Each question is worth one point, the same as every other question on the exam. You can expect to see about four to five Sentence Equivalence questions per section of Verbal Reasoning.

A strong vocabulary is essential for the Sentence Equivalence questions. But, just like with Text Completion questions, it is not enough just to study the definition of common words found on the exam; you must understand how to use them in context and how to use context clues to properly identify the correct word that fits with the rest of the sentence.

Sample Sentence Equivalence Question

All Sentence Equivalence questions will look the same. You will always have one sentence, with one blank, followed by five answer choices.

As start-ups continue to proliferate limit the available market share, the success of a business is dependent upon two things; the degree to which it can __________ borrowed money, and its ability to endure uncertainty and fluctuations in the market.

A. capitalize
B. repudiate
C. collect
D. leverage
E. expend
F. reallocate

You will need to identify the correct **two** answer choices for the blanks. Both choices, when plugged into the sentence will communicate a similar thought. It is important to note that just because the answer choice yields two similar sentences, it does not mean the words will be synonyms. Likewise, avoid automatically selecting synonyms from the answer choices just because they are alike. You will often see pairs of words that are similar in meaning in the answer choices that are not the correct answer.

Also keep in mind that even though a word may fit into the sentence does not mean that it is correct. You are not looking for two words that make sense; you are looking for two words that both make sense and create a sentence that is similar in reasoning.

Approaching the Blanks Strategically

Sentence Equivalence questions are rather straightforward: find the missing words that best complete the sentence. But, instead of just diving into them, you still want to be strategic about your approach. Keep these strategies in mind as you work through the Sentence Equivalence questions in the Verbal Reasoning section.

Read and Understand

Read the entire sentence before moving on to the answer choices. Do not confuse yourself by oscillating back and forth between the sentence and the answer choices before you actually have an understanding of what is happening in the sentence. Pay close attention to the language of the sentences before considering what the missing words might be.

Predict and Answer

Once you have an understanding of the flow of the sentence, think about what word could feasibly fill the blank and make sense in the sentence. Once you have predicted your answer, scan the answer choices and select the two words that best completes the blank. Remember, just because **two** answer choices are similar does not mean they fit into the sentence. Make sure the words you chose actually make sense and create two similar sentences.

Re-read

Once you have your two answers selected for the blank, re-read the sentence to make sure it makes sense and flows logically.

Chapter Overview

Text Completions

Text Completion questions require you to read short passages that have words omitted from them. Your task is to use the context of the passage to correctly identify the missing word or words. A strong vocabulary is essential for the Text Completion questions. But, it is not enough just to study the definition of common words found on the exam; you must understand how to use them in context and how to use context clues to properly identify the correct word that fits with the rest of the sentence.

Quick Facts About Text Completions

- Text Completions will have one, two, or three blanks.
- You must select all of the correct answers for a question in order for your response to be credited.
- For questions with multiple blanks, you must answer all of them correctly to receive credit for your response. There is no partial credit.

Strategy Overview

Read and Understand

Read the entire sentence before moving on to the answer choices. Do not confuse yourself by oscillating back and forth between the sentence and the answer choices before you actually have an understanding of what is happening in the sentence.

Predict and Answer

Think about what word could feasibly fill the blank and make sense in the sentence. Look for the blank that closely matches your prediction.

Re-read

Once you have selected your answer, plug the word or words back in to sentence to see if it makes sense.

Sentence Equivalence

Sentence Equivalence questions require you to identify two answer choices from a slate of six that best complete the sentence. When inserted into the sentence, both words will form its own sentence but the sentences will both be close in meaning.

Quick Facts About Sentence Equivalence Questions

- Sentence Equivalence questions will always have one blank and two correct answer choices.
- Some answer choices may complete the sentence but still be incorrect. Remember that the sentences created from both words must be similar.
- You must select both correct answers to receive credit for your response. There is no partial credit.

Text Completion and Sentence Equivalence Practice Set

Choose the word that best completes the blank(s).

1. Tony was (i)__________ when he discovered Martin had erased Game of Thrones from the DVR. He (ii) __________ him for almost a week.

Blank (i)	Blank (ii)
A. pungent	**D.** flouted
B. incensed	**E.** eschewed
C. desperate	**F.** upbraided

2. Since losing her prestigious internship after a run-in with the law, Gina avoided family gatherings, afraid that her conservative and religious family would _______ her.

A. begrudge
B. pervade
C. vex
D. deride
E. embrace

3. Chiang Mai has earned the _________ "Digital Nomad Capital of the World" since so many location-independent computer programming professionals tend to flock there.

A. veneration
B. repeal
C. sobriquet
D. syncopation
E. misnomer

4. In 2008, The American Geological Society initiated The Living History of Geology Project to chronicle senior members who have made (i) _____________ contributions during their career to the (ii) ______________ of the discipline and profession of geology. Each esteemed Geologist will be interviewed for (iii) ______________, and the footage will remain on file at the American Geological Society Headquarters.

Blank (i)	Blank (ii)	Blank (iii)
A. remarkable	**D.** progression	**G.** corroboration
B. belabored	**E.** continuation	**H.** posterity
C. ostensible	**F.** thwarting	**I.** practicality

5. Brand loyalty plays a(n) (i) _______ role in a consumer's purchasing habits. Market research supports the notion that consumers are likely to spend more on a product they grew up using rather than try a generic brand that offers the same (ii) ________ at a lower price point. How much more are shoppers willing to spend for (iii) ________?

Blank (i)	Blank (ii)	Blank (iii)
A. marginal	**D.** quality	**G.** familiarity
B. appreciable	**E.** composition	**H.** paranoia
C. speculative	**F.** accolades	**I.** exposure

Select the two answers choices that when inserted into the sentence create two sentences that are similar in meaning.

6. Kristen was ______________ new employee, eager to take initiative and perform up to standard. Unfortunately, her lack of industry knowledge made it impossible for her to move beyond her probationary period.

   A. a prudent
   B. an assiduous
   C. an enthusiastic
   D. a sullen
   E. a punctilious

7. Everyone agreed that the Valedictorian's speech was profound and ___________ in its delivery; it was enjoyed and understood by the audience overall.

   A. pernicious
   B. pellucid
   C. majestic
   D. perspicuous
   E. regal
   F. berated

8. Olivia continuously warned Mellie about the need to run a clean campaign for President since voters tend not to favor candidates who attack the character of other candidates. But, Mellie continued to run campaign ads that ____________ her competitors' personal shortcomings to the media.

   A. expressed
   B. expunged
   C. divulged
   D. propagated
   E. elevated

9. Despite receiving an outstanding performance review for his work and an impressive raise, Sean still felt _______ about his job security in the unstable economy.

   A. confident
   B. solid
   C. anxious
   D. apprehensive
   E. suspicious
   F. perspicacious

10. Valerie looked absolutely _______ when all her children surprised her for her 55th birthday. She had not see them all together in over a year.

   A. ecstatic
   B. pensive
   C. ebullient
   D. lugubrious
   E. morose
   F. eclectic

Text Completion and Sentence Equivalence Practice Set Answers

1. **B, F.** Tony was incensed, which means angry. The second blank is tricky. Flouted and eschewed both mean avoid, which is a very plausible reaction for Tony. However, flouted means to avoid or disregard, usually in terms of a law or convention, and eschewed typically means to refrain or abstain from something and is often used in a religious context. Neither of these fit into the sentence. Upbraided means to reprimand or scold, which works in this context.

2. **D.** To deride is to ridicule which is ostensibly what Gina is trying to avoid.

3. **C.** Digital Nomad capital of the world, as it is established in the sentence is a nickname of sorts for Chiang Mai. Sobriquet means assigned name or title.

4. **A, D, H.** You are looking for a positive word that describes the senior members' contributions and explains why they would be honored; remarkable covers that base. Since the geologists have made remarkable contributions it makes sense that those contributions progressed the field of study and that their interviews should be available for posterity, or for future reference.

5. **B, D, G.** For blank one, appreciable is measureable, like consumer studies. Blank two equates the quality of the products while blank 3 questions how much using something familiar versus something of comparable quality and a lower prices means to consumers.

6. **B, E.** Kristen was eager and took initiative to meet the outlines standards, regardless of her skill level. Both assiduous and punctilious refer to an attention to detail and working to meet standards.

7. **B, D.** The speech was powerful and everyone understood it. Pellucid and perspicuous both fit when plugged in.

8. **C, D.** Mellie disregarded the advice of Olivia to run a clean campaign. So you are looking for words that suggest Mellie may not have acted with good will towards her competitors. Propagated and divulged corroborates that she intentionally made their personal business public.

9. **B, C.** Look for the transitions. While Sean performs well and has received positive reinforcement (bonus), he is still unsure of how stable his job is. Anxious and apprehensive both yield similar sentences when plugged in the blank.

10. **A, C.** You are looking for a positive word to express the joy Valerie felt when she had the chance to see all of children. Ebullient means high-spirited while ecstatic means thrilled or excited.

ARGO
BROTHERS

10 INTRODUCTION TO QUANTITATIVE REASONING

Quantitative Reasoning: The Basics

In this section, you will be asked to solve mathematical problems drawn from the subject areas of arithmetic, geometry, algebra, and data analysis. This section tests your ability to solve quantitative problems, understand real-world applications of mathematical principles, and interpret statistical data from charts and graphs.

The Quantitative Reasoning sections can appear in any order on the exam following the Analytical Writing section. Your exam will consist of **two** scored Quantitative Reasoning sections that include the following question types: Quantitative Comparisons, Problem-Solving, and Data Interpretation. We will discuss the question types in more detail later.

You will have 35 minutes to complete each of the two sections. Each section on the computer-adapted exam consists of 20 questions. The section is scored on a scale of 130-170, in one-point increments. A 170 is the highest possible score. The score reflects your combined Quantitative Reasoning performance; you will not receive a separate score for each quantitative section.

This section of the book will outline strategies to help you refresh your understanding on tested math concepts, manage your time, understand the question tasks, and deploy various strategies to help optimize your Quantitative Reasoning score.

Prep Tip: You can use the on-screen calculator for the Quantitative Section to help you solve expressions. The calculator includes basic functions like addition, subtraction, division, and multiplication. You can also use the calculator to solve square roots.

Why is this section important?

Graduate programs use your performance on the Quantitative Reasoning section to evaluate your ability to solve quantitative problems, interpret data, and apply mathematical principles to a wide range of commonplace situations. Depending on the program to which you are applying, your Quantitative Reasoning scores may be of less concern for an institution, for example, a graduate literature program. Nonetheless, you should try to do your best as your Quantitative Reasoning scores factor into your overall exam score.

In this chapter, we will discuss the format of each question type and provide you with specific strategies for successfully answering the GRE quantitative questions. The Math Primer in the following chapter provides a comprehensive overview of the topics tested in the Quantitative Reasoning section and will help you address gaps in your in mathematics knowledge and refresh topics you may not have visited for some time.

Scoring and Computer-Adaptive Testing

The section is scored on a scale of 130-170, in one-point increments. A 170 is the highest possible score. The score reflects your combined Quantitative Reasoning performance; you will not receive a separate score for each verbal section.

When taking the computer exam, you are able to answer questions in each section in any order you wish. You can skip questions or use the built-in system tools to mark a question for review and come back to it later as time permits. As we discussed in the section on computer-adaptive testing, the difficulty of your second scored section of Quantitative Reasoning is determined by your performance on your first section.

Question Types

Your exam will consist of two scored Quantitative Reasoning sections that consist of three question types. Each question type typically appears at the same frequency across exams. The chart below details the question types and the approximate number of questions you are likely to encounter on each of the two Quantitative Reasoning sections.

Question Type	Question Task	Approx. # of Questions
Quantitative Comparison	Quantitative Comparison questions require you to analyze the relationship between two given quantities and select the answer choice that best describes the relationship. These questions focus more on understanding mathematical relationships and less on actual mathematical calculations.	7-8 questions
Problem-Solving	Problem-Solving questions require you to use various mathematical formulas and processes to solve for the correct answer to the given problems. These are multiple-choice questions that can have either one or multiple correct answers. These questions may also require you to input your own answer without being provided any answer choices to select from.	9-10 questions
Data Interpretation	Data Interpretation questions require you to interpret data from charts and graphs in order to solve for the correct answer. These questions are a sub-set of the Mathematical Problem-Solving questions and occur as part of a set where you will use one chart or graph to answer multiple questions.	2-3 questions

Quantitative Comparison

Quantitative Comparison questions ask you to compare quantities in two columns and determine whether one is greater than or equal to one another, or if there is not enough information to determine a relationship between the two quantities. Some questions include additional information that is centered above the two columns that concerns one or both of the quantities. These questions do not require that you solve for the particular value. You are instead assessing the relationship between the expressions in the two columns. There is only one correct answer for Quantitative Comparison questions.

Sample Quantitative Comparison Question

A. Quantity A is greater
B. Quantity B is greater
C. The two quantities are equal
D. The relationship cannot be determined from the information given

$$\frac{x}{y} = \frac{3}{4}$$

Column A	Column B
$\frac{2x - y}{y}$	$\frac{x}{x + y}$

In this sample problem, you are given additional information $\frac{x}{y} = \frac{3}{4}$ to consider when analyzing the relationship of Column A and B. These instructions should be applied to both quantities before you make a comparison. Remember, you are not looking for a value but rather an understanding of how the two columns relate.

Problem-Solving

Problem-Solving questions are the catch-all questions on the GRE. These questions draw from all the math content areas and are presented as either word problems, finding the angle of a triangle, or pure calculations of algebraic expressions. You will have access to the on-screen calculator to help you with any necessary calculations, though some of the questions will require scratch paper to work out an expression with variables. Problem-Solving questions have a variety of options when it comes to answer choices; there may be more than one response to the question. You will have to select all of the correct answer choices in order to receive credit for the exam. The Math Primer in the following chapter will help you prepare for the Quantitative Reasoning section overall, but it provides an extensive overview of the concepts most likely to appear in relation to the Problem-Solving questions. Unlike the Quantitative Comparison questions, your answer for Problem-Solving questions will be an actual value.

Sample Problem-Solving Question

What is the value of the following expression?

$$(2\sqrt{2})(\sqrt{6}) + 2\sqrt{3}$$

A. 20
B. $6\sqrt{8}$
C. $6\sqrt{3}$
D. $4\sqrt{2} + 2\sqrt{3}$
E. $12\sqrt{3}$

For this problem, you will need to solve the equation and select the corresponding answer choice. This problem has only one correct answer.

Data Interpretation

Data Interpretation questions are more of an extension of Problem-Solving questions than a unique question type. For these questions, you will interpret data from charts, graphs, and other images and use this information to solve for the correct answer. Like Problem-Solving questions, these questions have a variety of answer choice options and can have more than one correct answer. Remember, you need to select all the correct answers in order to receive credit for the question.

Sample Data Interpretation Question

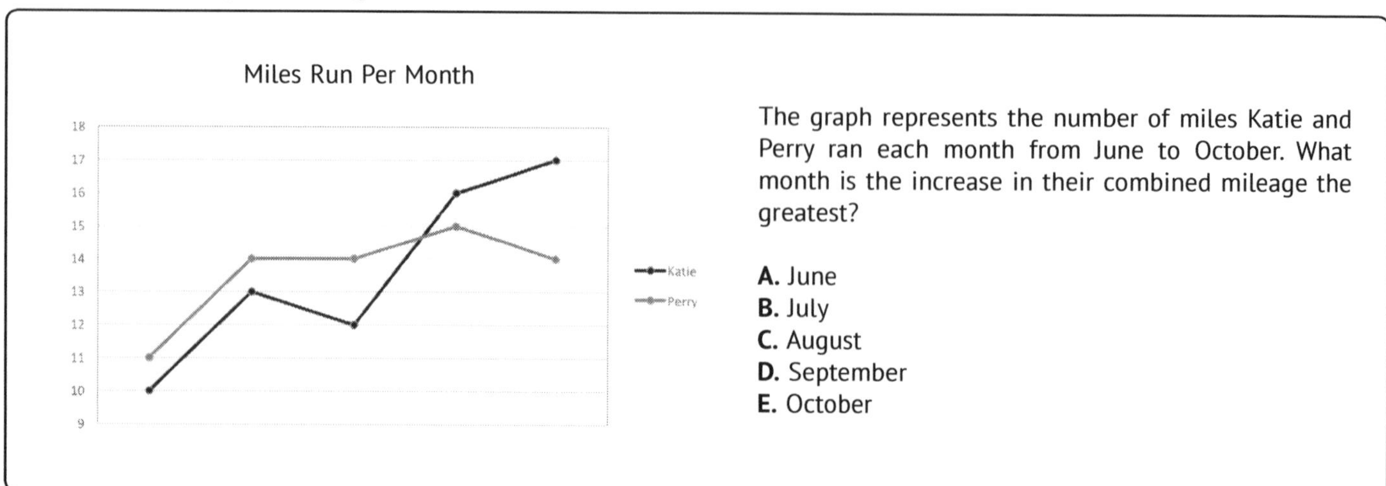

The graph represents the number of miles Katie and Perry ran each month from June to October. What month is the increase in their combined mileage the greatest?

A. June
B. July
C. August
D. September
E. October

Answer Choice Types

You will encounter a number of different answer choice types on the Quantitative Reasoning section. You can expect to see questions that ask you to select one or multiple answer choices, and questions that will not provide any choices but will instead prompt you to fill in your own. Let's look more closely at these answer choice types.

Multiple-choice: Choose One Answer Choice

You will be presented with five answer choices. Only one will be correct. Quantitative Comparison questions will always fall into this category. You can always plug your answer in the check to see if it is correct. However, be careful not to use substitution as your primary strategy as it can cost you a lot of time. Once you have simplified the problem and eliminated incorrect answers, try plugging the remaining answer choices into the problem if you are not sure which answer is correct.

Multiple-choice: Choose One or More Answer Choices

These questions have one or more answer choices that are correct. Select all the answers that you think are correct. There is no partial credit for these questions; you must select all and only the correct answers in order to receive credit for your response. Assess each answer choice on its own to determine if it answers the questions. As with the previous question type, make sure you read all the answer choices.

Numeric Entry Questions

Numeric Entry questions present a unique challenge in that you do not have answer choices to choose from. Instead, you must complete the necessary calculation and key in (or write in) your answer in the designated box. A numeric entry question may look like this:

$$2^2 + 2^8 =$$

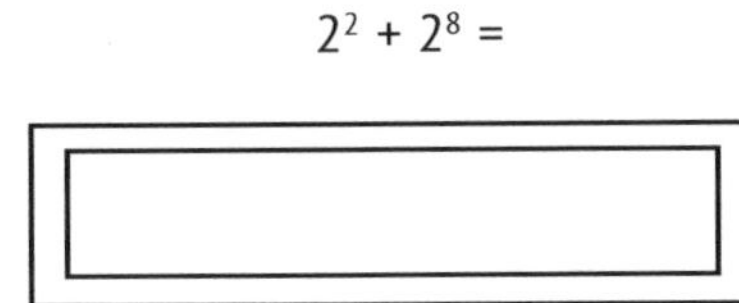

Once you perform the calculation, you will enter your answer into the box. If your answer is an integer or a decimal, you will enter into a single box. If your answer is a fraction, you will enter the numerator into one box and the denominator in a second box. You should enter the entire outcome of the calculation unless instructed not to do so. Let's look at some other considerations related to numeric entry questions:

- Because you do not have answers to choose from, it may not be as easy to realize when you have made a mistake in your calculations. Read the question carefully and ensure you are performing the correct calculation and reporting the answer in the correct units, if applicable.

- Round your number only after you have completed the entire calculation. Oftentimes, decimals can be entered as calculated. However, if the question asks you to round your number, make sure you do so, but not until after you arrive at your final answer.

- You have some flexibility in how you record your answer as all equivalent answers are credited responses. For example, if your answer is $\frac{8}{16}$, you do not need to further reduce your answer to $\frac{1}{2}$. Both are correct, so save some time by not further reducing the fraction and move on to the next question.

Using Testing Resources

Taking a math exam on a computer is less than ideal for a number of reasons. Probably the most notable fact is that you cannot actively annotate the problem and solve it by hand. So, for the Quantitative Reasoning section, you are going to have to make the best use of the resources you have available to you, namely, your scratch paper and the on-screen calculator.

Scratch Paper

You will be provided scratch paper for the exam that you can use on any (or all) of the sections. It is important to note that you are not permitted to bring your own scratch paper, and you must wait until the exam begins before writing anything on the scratch paper. Scratch paper is a critical resource for the Quantitative Reasoning section, though you should not underestimate its value in helping you keep up with information in the other sections. Use the scratch paper to perform calculations, keep up with eliminated answers, and remind yourself of key formulas. Many of the calculations on the exam can be answered and transferred via the calculator function, which we will discuss shortly. But, scratch paper is quite a useful tool and can help you avoid costly mistakes.

On-Screen Calculator

The on-screen calculator will only be displayed during the Quantitative Reasoning section. You may find the calculator useful for performing operations with larger numbers or finding square roots. While the calculator is a helpful tool, its functionality is only as useful as your knowledge of the concepts being tested. Essentially, the on-screen calculator, with its basic functionality, cannot replace core mathematical knowledge. Using the calculator should not always be your first choice when attacking problems. Some problems can be solved more easily without the calculator, and some cannot be solved with a calculator at all. One of the most useful features of the calculator, aside from its ability to quickly solve complex operations for you, is the *Transfer* button for numeric entry questions. Once you have calculated your response, you can simply click the transfer button and your response will be entered into the numeric entry text box.

How to Prepare for the Quantitative Reasoning Section

In the two Quantitative Reasoning sections you will be asked to solve problems, analyze data, and compare quantities to determine their relationship. This assessment area is designed to test your ability to apply mathematical principles to real-world situations and interpret data from visual presentations. In addition to the strategies we will explore in the subsequent chapters, there are several tools included in this text to help you hone your approach to the Quantitative Reasoning section.

Math Primer

Before launching into the Quantitative Reasoning chapters that discuss Quantitative Comparison and Problem-Solving in more detail, you should ensure that you work through the Math Primer in the following chapter. The Math Primer will review key concepts in arithmetic, algebra, geometry, and data interpretation and provide you with an opportunity to practice various concepts with questions similar to those on the exam. In terms of structuring your study plan for this section of the exam, the Math Primer should be your first step, even if you have a strong math background. Many of the concepts tested are high-school level, and most test-takers will not have seen the content for some time. It will best situate you to attack the section, avoid costly mistakes, and adopt critical time-saving strategies.

Problem Sets and Explanations

After each question type in the Quantitative Reasoning section, you will have the opportunity to test out your understanding of the concepts. Use these problem sets to apply the strategies discussed in the section and review the explanations to help you gain a better understanding of how to arrive at the correct answer choices.

Chapter Overview

Your performance on the Quantitative Reasoning section depends heavily on your understanding of the math concepts reviewed in the Math Primer. It is essential to have a solid understanding of the fundamentals of arithmetic, algebra, geometry, and problem-solving when approaching this section. You must also be able to draw inferences and use a critical analysis to examine passages.

Memorizing formulas is not enough. You must know how to apply various mathematical concepts to real-world situations and interpret data, find missing data points, and solve equations of varying complexities.

The subsequent chapters in this section and the Math Primer will provide you with the tools to bolster your math proficiency, strengthen your problem-solving skills, and develop a strategic approach to optimize your test performance.

FAST FACTS: Section Breakdown

- Two **scored** Quantitative Reasoning sections per exam
- Can occur in any order after the Analytical Writing section
- **35 minutes** per section. You can only work on one section at a time.
- **20 questions** per section
- Depending on your exam, you may have an additional unscored section of Quantitative Reasoning. Remember to approach all sections as if they are scored.

Question Breakdown

Question Type	Question Task	Approx. # of Questions
Quantitative Comparison	Quantitative Comparison questions require you to analyze the relationship between two given quantities and select the answer choice that best describes the relationship. These questions focus more on understanding mathematical relationships and less on actual mathematical calculations.	7-8 questions
Problem-Solving	Problem-Solving questions require you to use various mathematical formulas and processes to solve for the correct answer to the given problems. These are multiple-choice questions that can have either one or multiple correct answers. These questions may also require you to input your own answer without being provided any answer choices to select from.	9-10 questions
Data Interpretation	Data Interpretation questions require you to interpret data from charts and graphs in order to solve for the correct answer. These questions are a sub-set of the Mathematical Problem-Solving questions and occur as part of a set where you will use one chart or graph to answer multiple questions.	2-3 questions

Up Next: The Math Primer provides an overview of the key concepts related to arithmetic, algebra, geometry, and data interpretation. Understanding the concepts discussed in the next chapter will play a pivotal role in your performance on the Quantitative Reasoning section.

ARGO
BROTHERS

11 | MATH PRIMER

Math on the GRE

The Quantitative Reasoning section tests your understanding of basic mathematical principles in four subject areas: Arithmetic, Algebra, Geometry, and Data Interpretation. On the exam, you will need to be able to recognize and understand the basic principles associated with these subject areas and demonstrate your ability to reason mathematically to solve problems, identify quantitative relationships, and interpret data from visual displays. Problems are often presented as word problems that discuss math concepts in the context of real-world problems. Other problems require pure math calculations.

The Math Primer is a refresher of concepts you will encounter on the exam. It will cover key definitions, operations, theories, and approaches to problem-solving to help you re-familiarize yourself with concepts you may not have seen since high school. The Math Primer is intended as an overview and is not an extensive exploration of the topics you may see on the exam. Not all topics on the exam are covered in the primer. If you find certain concepts are still a challenge for you after reading through the content and working through the problems, you may benefit from a more in-depth exploration of these concepts using the appropriate texts and resources to help you focus on those particular areas.

Remember that you can use a calculator on the math section. However, the calculator cannot replace your understanding of how to apply mathematical concepts. As you prepare for the Quantitative Reasoning section, pay close attention to the application of the concepts you are studying. How do they apply to world situations? Can you recognize a concept in a word problem? Being able to step beyond the basic understanding of the concepts will help you optimize your Quantitative Reasoning score.

Let's explore the major concepts tested in each of the subject areas. Again, this is not an inclusive list.

Arithmetic

- Real numbers including integers, prime numbers, rational numbers and irrational numbers
- Number sequences
- Factors and multiples
- Fractions and decimals
- Arithmetic operations
- Percentages, ratios, and rates
- Absolute Value

Algebra

- Algebraic expressions
- Coordinate planes, slopes, and intercepts
- Functions and relations
- Linear and quadratic equations inequalities
- Rules of exponents and Roots
- Variables and expressions

Geometry

- Right, Isosceles, and special triangles
- Pythagorean theorem
- Properties and measurements of circles
- Polygons
- Perimeter, area, and volume
- Properties and measurements of three-dimensional figures

Data Interpretation

- Descriptive Statistics
- Understanding data from charts and graphs
- Frequency distributions
- Probability
- Permutations

Mathematical Conventions on the GRE

While math can be straightforward at times, there are many nuances that need to be considered when working with problems to determine how you interpret information. The test-writers have narrowed the focus of the problems in the Quantitative Reasoning section and outlined some standard characteristics true of all the questions on the exam. Here are some of the key conventions:

- All numbers on the exam are real numbers. There will be no questions relating to imaginary numbers.
- Geometric figures are not drawn to scale unless otherwise indicated. While you should not assume lengths based on how the figure looks, you should assume that all lines in a figure are straight lines and that the figure lies on a plane unless otherwise indicated.
- Contrary to geometric figures, *xy*-planes and numbers lines are drawn to scale.
- Graphs on the exam, including histograms, pie charts, and line graphs are drawn to scale and you can make assumptions based on the visual presentation of the data.
- π is assumed to represent the value 3.14.
- For geometry questions, the common assumption that the measure of the interior angles of a triangle equal 180° stands.
- For Data Interpretation questions, consider each question separately. No information except what is given in the display of data should be considered from one question to another.

Arithmetic: The Basics

Arithmetic encompasses the fundamental building blocks of math. It includes basic concepts like the mathematical operations addition, subtraction, multiplication and division. Almost all the questions you encounter on the exam will require you to apply principles of arithmetic in some capacity. You will need to understand order of operations, real numbers, ratios, and fractions. The concepts discussed in this section will help you refresh your understanding of basic arithmetic and prepare you to navigate the more difficult exam concepts such as algebraic expressions and geometry. Let's get started!

Math Building Blocks

Before we dive into the specifics of arithmetic and the other concepts tested on the Quantitative Reasoning section of the exam, let's review the fundamental building blocks of math, especially common symbols and types of numbers. These concepts will appear in some form on the exam and a clear understanding of these fundamentals is key to your success in this section.

> **Prep Tip:** For the full list of Mathematical Conventions for the Quantitative Reasoning section, visit the ETS website at: ets.org/gre.

What's that sign?

Most people taking the GRE have not studied basic math in quite some time. While some of the basics may have stuck with you, it doesn't hurt to do a quick check to test your current ability to identify what key symbols and operations on the exam are asking you to do. Below are some of the most common signs used in mathematics; you will encounter these in some capacity on the exam. Some of these will be addressed in more detail in subsequent sections of the Math Primer.

Math Symbol	Common Name	Description
$<$	Less than	This symbol is used to signify that the quantity to the left of the symbol is less than the quantity to the right.
$>$	Greater than	This symbol is used to signify that the quantity to the left of the symbol is greater than the quantity to the right.
$\leq$	Less than or equal to	This symbol is used to signify that the quantity to the left of the symbol is less than or equal to the quantity to the right.
$\geq$	Greater than or equal to	This symbol is used to signify that the quantity to the left of the symbol is greater than or equal to the quantity to the right.
$\sqrt{\ }$	Square root	An irrational number that produces a specified quantity when multiplied by itself.
$\lvert x \rvert$	Absolute value	Reflects the positive distance of the expressed number from zero on a line.
!	Factorial	The product of the numbers between 1 and a given number.
$\parallel$	Parallel Lines	This symbol signifies that two lines are parallel to each other and do not intersect at any point.
$\perp$	Perpendicular Lines	This symbol signifies that two straight lines separated by this symbol intersect to form a right angle.
π	Pi	Pi is common geometric measure of the ratio of a circle's circumference to its diameter; the abridged measure is 3.14.

Real Numbers

You will encounter only real numbers on the GRE, so you need not concern yourself with studying concepts related to imaginary numbers. Real numbers are numbers found on the number line and are, with the exception of zero, either positive or negative. Several classes of numbers are included in the real numbers category and will appear on the exam. Let's look at the various types of real numbers you can expect to see.

Whole Numbers

Whole numbers are positive counting numbers including zero that contain no decimal or fraction parts.

1, 2, 3, 4, 5...

Integers

Integers are all positive and negative numbers, including zero that are whole numbers. Integers that occur in a sequence like the ones below are called consecutive integers.

-2, -1, 0, 1, 2, 3...

Rational Numbers

Rational numbers are any numbers, positive or negative, that can be expressed as a ratio of two numbers. All integers and fractions are considered rational numbers.

$$\frac{1}{2}, \frac{3}{4}, \frac{1}{4}$$

Irrational Numbers

Irrational numbers are all numbers, positive or negative, that are not rational and cannot be expressed as a ratio.

$$\pi, \sqrt{5}$$

Prime Numbers

A prime number is a number that has only two positive divisors, 1 and itself. For example, 5 is a prime number because it is only divisible by 1 and itself, no other number. Prime numbers are tested often on the exam. It is best to familiarize yourself with the most common prime number, which are those that occur below 100:

2, 3, 5, 7, 11, 13, 17, 19, 23, 29, 31, 37, 41, 43, 47, 53, 59, 61, 67, 71, 73, 79, 83, 89, & 97

There are some other properties of prime numbers you should know:

- Neither 0 nor 1 is a prime number
- Only positive numbers can be prime numbers
- 2 is the only even prime number

Factors

A factor is an integer that divides into another integer evenly and has no remainder. Take the number 24 as an example:

- **1, 2, 3, 4, 6, 8, 12,** and **24** are all factors of 24 since they all divide evenly into the number and have no remainder. On the other hand, the number 5 is not a factor since when you divide 5 into 24, there is a remainder.

Greatest Common Factor

The greatest common factor of two numbers is the largest factor shared by both numbers.
Suppose you wanted to find the greater common factor of 48 and 60. You would first start by identifying the factors for each number:

Factors of 48: 1, 2, 3, 4, 6, 8, **12**, 16, 24, 48
Factors of 60: 1, 2, 3, 4, 5, 6, 10, **12**, 15, 20, 30, 60

The greatest common factor of 48 and 60 is **12**. The least common factor is not likely to be tested on the exam.

Multiples

A multiple is essentially the opposite of a factor. Instead of division, multiples are determined by multiplication. A multiple of a number is the product of the number and any other whole number. For example, 8, 16, 24, 32, 40, 64, and 800 are all multiples of 8 because they are the product of multiplying 8 by another number. This is not an exhaustive list of the multiples of 8. When any whole number is multiplied by 8, the product is a multiple. Zero is a multiple of every number.

Least Common Multiple

The least common multiple of two or more whole numbers greater than zero is the smallest whole number divisible by each of the numbers. If you wanted to find the least common multiple of 5 and 6, for example, you would start by identifying the multiples of each.

Multiples of 5: 10, 15, 20, 25, **30**, 35, 40...
Multiples of 6: 12, 18, 24, **30**, 36, 42...

Since you are looking for the least common multiple, you want to select the smallest number that occurs in both lists. In the case, the least common multiple is **30**. The greatest common multiple is not likely to be tested on the exam.

Numerical Operations

The GRE Quantitative Reasoning section includes problems that will require you to add, subtract, multiply, and divide real numbers, including fractions, decimals, roots, and algebraic expressions with non-numeric variables. There are key operations you should keep in mind when dealing with numbers in order to work more efficiently and minimize mistakes.

Laws of Operations

Commutative Property: Addition and multiplication are commutative operations; the order in which they are performed does not impact the answer.

$$a \bullet b = b \bullet a$$
$$a + b = b + a$$

Associative Property: Addition and multiplication are also associative; when written as an expression, they can be regrouped without impacting the final answer.

$$a + (b + c) = (a + b) + c$$
$$(a \bullet b) \bullet c = a \bullet (b \bullet c)$$

Distributive Property: The distributive property outlines how values in an expression should be distributed to the terms being added or subtracted.

$$a(b + c) = ab + ac$$

The distributive property can also be used in division:

$$\frac{a+b}{2} = \frac{a}{2} + \frac{b}{2}$$

Order of Operations

The commutative, associative, and distributive properties outline some standard approaches to dealing with addition and multiplication. But, when other operations are involved, it is important to understand the proper order in which to solve each component of the problem. Let's look at the order of operations rules.

The acronym **PEMDAS** outlines the correct order for mathematical operations. Performing operations out of order, specifically those dealing with more than addition and multiplication, will often lead you to the incorrect answer.

Parentheses	Complete anything in **parentheses** first
Exponents	Next, calculate any **exponents**
Multiplication **Division**	Then attack **multiplication** and **division** elements from left to right

Addition **Subtraction**	Finally, attack **addition** and **subtraction** elements from left to right

Not all equations will contain all these elements. However, be sure to still follow the order when attacking the elements that are present.

Let's look at an example:

$$100 - 4(7 - 4)^3$$

First, you want to solve for the values in the parentheses. You can easily solve (7 – 4) and replace the value in parentheses with 3. You end up with:

$$100 - 4(3)^3$$

Next, let's solve the exponents:

$$100 - 4 \bullet 3^3 = 100 - 4(27)$$

And multiplication and division:

$$100 - 4 \bullet 27 = 100 - 108$$

Finally, let's solve addition and subtraction elements:

$$100 - 108 = \mathbf{-8}$$

The final answer is **-8**. Remember to work equations in the proper order and that multiplication, division, addition, and subtraction should be solved from left to right.

Absolute Value

Absolute value is the distance of a number from zero. The value is always expressed as a positive number. Absolute value is symbolized by a number being enclosed in two vertical bars. Example:

$$|12|$$

The absolute value of a positive number is always just the number itself. So in the case of the example above:

$$|12| = 12$$

The absolute value of a negative number is derived by dropping the negative sign in front of the number:

$$|-14| = 14$$

You may see absolute value appear in a number of ways on the exam, including as expressions where you must solve for a value. Here's an example:

$$4 - 2 + |5 - 7|$$

First, solve what is in the brackets:

$$|5 - 7| = |-2| = 2$$

Next, plug in the value to the rest of the expression and solve:

$$4 - 2 + 2 = 4$$

Fractions

In the last section, we looked at the properties of whole numbers and the key properties associated with them. Now, let's look at non-whole numbers, namely fractions, decimals, and ratios.

There is no shortage of fractions on the GRE. You will see them appear in word problems, as part of algebraic expressions, and in pure problem-solving questions. The two main components of a fraction are the numerator and the denominator.

$$\frac{a}{b} \quad \begin{matrix} \longrightarrow \text{numerator} \\ \longrightarrow \text{denominator} \end{matrix}$$

You will need to know how to perform various operations with fractions, including addition, subtraction, multiplication, division, simplifying, and converting them to mixed numbers. Let's look at some of the key facts about factions and operations related to them.

Reciprocals

The reciprocal of a fraction is found simply by reversing the numerator and the denominator. For example, the reciprocal of $\frac{2}{3}$ is $\frac{3}{2}$. The product of any fraction and its reciprocal is always 1. All whole numbers have a reciprocal where the reciprocal of a is $\frac{1}{a}$

Equivalent Fractions

Since fractions represent the part of a given whole, increasing the whole and the part by the same amount does not change the relationship. Consider the fraction $\frac{1}{2}$. If you multiplied the numerator and denominator by 3, for example, you would end up with the equivalent fraction $\frac{3}{6}$.

Reducing Fractions

There are a number of instances in which you will need to reduce fractions on the exam; in fact, whenever you are able to do so, you should. When you reduce a fraction, you simply express the fraction in its lowest terms. Let's suppose you have the fraction $\frac{40}{80}$.

To reduce the fraction, identify the greatest common factor shared by the numerator and denominator. In this case, 40 and 80 share several factors:

Factors of 40: 1, 2, 4, 5, 8, 10, 20, **40**
Factors of 80: 1, 2, 4, 5, 8, 10, 20, **40**

The greatest common factor of the numerator and the denominator is **40**. To reduce the fraction, determine how many times the greatest common factor divides into both the numerator and the denominator.

Numerator: $\frac{40}{40}=1$ Denominator: $\frac{80}{40}=2$ Reduced fraction: $\frac{40}{80}=\frac{1}{2}$

Mixed Numbers

A mixed fraction is a fraction that is preceded by an integer. For example: $2\frac{3}{7}$. It is often not possible to work with mixed numbers and perform operations like addition and subtraction. So, you much reduce a mixed fraction into a standard fraction with just a numerator and a denominator. Reducing a fraction is rather straightforward. First, you multiply the denominator and the integer, then add the product to the numerator. The denominator from the mixed fraction will remain the same. Let's look at the example from earlier:

$$2\frac{3}{7}=\frac{7 \bullet 2+3}{7}=\frac{17}{7}$$

Adding and Subtracting Fractions

Adding and subtracting fractions is a straightforward operation when the fractions have the same denominator. In these cases, you simply add or subtract the numerators; the denominator remains the same.

Examples: $\frac{2}{4}-\frac{1}{4}=\frac{1}{4}$

$\frac{8}{13}+\frac{23}{13}=\frac{31}{13}$

Adding and subtracting fractions that do not have the same denominator involves a bit more calculation. The most efficient way to approach adding and subtracting fractions is cross-multiplying.

Example: $\frac{11}{12}+\frac{4}{11}$

First, multiply the denominator of the second fraction by the numerator of the first fraction:

$$\frac{11}{12} \nwarrow \frac{4}{11}$$

So, $11 \bullet 11 = 121$

Then, multiply the denominator of the first fraction by the numerator of the second fraction:

$$\frac{11}{12} \nearrow \frac{4}{11}$$

So, $12 \bullet 4 = 48$

The sum of these two operations, is your new **numerator.** So, your numerator is 48 + 121 = **169**. But, you are not done yet.

To find your new denominator, simply multiply both denominators:

So, the sum of the fractions $\frac{11}{12}+\frac{4}{11}=\frac{\mathbf{169}}{\mathbf{132}}$.

The process is the same for subtracting fractions; instead of adding the products of the cross-multiplication to get the new numerator, you will subtract.

Multiplying Fractions

When multiplying fractions, the process is the same regardless of whether or not the denominators are the same. Let's look at an example:

$$\frac{8}{11}\bullet\frac{7}{13}=\frac{8\bullet 7}{11\bullet 13}=\frac{56}{143}$$

Dividing Fractions

Dividing fractions is similar to the process of multiplying fractions since multiplication and division are inverse operations. To divide fractions, multiply the first fraction by the reciprocal or inverse of the second fraction.

$$\frac{1}{5}\div\frac{3}{7}=\frac{1}{5}\bullet\frac{7}{3}=\frac{7}{15}$$

Decimals

A decimal, like a fraction, expresses a part of a whole. Decimals are tested often on the GRE and it is important to understand the fundamentals of a decimal, including how the specific digits of the decimal are described. Take the decimal 123.456, for example. Each digit has its own mathematical label:

1 2 3 . 4 5 6

1: Hundreds	4: Tenths
2: Tens	5: Hundredths
3: Ones	6: Thousandths

Fractions to Decimals

You may occasionally need to change either the expressions in the problem or your answer from fractions to decimals or decimals to factions. Remember that unless otherwise specified, a decimal or fraction that are equivalent are acceptable for numeric entry questions. To change a fraction to a decimal, simply divide the denominator into the numerator.

$$\frac{6}{20}=6\div 20=0.3$$

Decimals to Fractions

Suppose you have the decimal 54.67. To convert a decimal to a fraction, first remove the decimal point and make the resulting whole number your numerator and, for right now, make 1 your denominator:

$$54.67 = \frac{5467}{1}$$

Then, count the number of digits after the decimal point. In this case, .67 follows the decimal point. So, two digits follow the decimal point. Add a 0 to the denominator for each digit that occurs after the decimal point in order to determine the fractional equivalent to your decimal.

$$54.67 = \frac{5467}{100}$$

As we explored above, to make a fraction a decimal, simply divide the denominator into the numerator. If you did that in this case, you would end up right back at 54.67.

Ratios

Ratios are often written as fractions and compare two quantities. Ratios, like fractions deal with parts of the whole, but also express the relationship between two quantities that may not be part of the same whole.

Ratios can be written as fractions or using the common notation $x : y$. So, if a word problem, for example, tells you that the ratio of girls to boys in the class is four boys for every three girls, you can write that as: $\frac{4}{3}$ or 4 : 3.

If a question asks you what the ratio of girls to boys is, whatever follows the term ***of*** is usually the numerator and whatever follows ***to*** is usually the denominator.

Ratios appear on the exam often in word problems. Be careful and make sure you understand what ratio the question is asking you to examine. Ratios run the gamut of difficulty. Let's look at a more straightforward, simple example:

Nathan has 7 sodas and 4 bottles of water in his cooler. What is the ratio of sodas to bottles of water in the cooler?

Since you are looking for the ratio of sodas to bottles of water, your ratio would look like this:

$$\text{sodas:bottles of water } \textbf{or } \frac{\textit{soda}}{\textit{bottles of water}}$$

Once we know what our ratio looks like, we can simply plug in the numbers that represent the ratio:

$$7 : 4 \text{ or } \frac{7}{4}$$

Ratios are not always expressed with just two variables. Suppose Nathan has 7 sodas, 4 bottles of water, and 2 juice boxes. To express the ratio of the drinks in the cooler you simply add the juice boxes to the original ratio:

$$7 : 4 : 2$$

This is a fixed ratio, meaning that each portion of the ratio directly corresponds to a particular item in the cooler. So, if you reordered the ratio so that it read 4 : 7 : 2, you no longer have the ratio of sodas to bottled waters to juice boxes. Instead, you had the ratio of bottled waters, to sodas, to juice boxes.

Now, Let's look at a more complex ratio question:

Tori's soccer team loses 10 games out of every 30 games that it plays. What is the ratio of Tori's soccer team's wins to losses?

First, you want to make sure you understand what the question is asking you to find. You are looking for the ratio of wins to losses. So, win:losses or $\frac{wins}{losses}$.

Be careful not to assume the ratio of wins to losses is 10 : 30. While that is the order the parts are listed in above, the order does not correspond to the question. Further, the question does not explicitly tell you the number of wins. 30 is the number of games played, so we need to calculate the number of wins before we can determine the ratio. To do so, you need to subtract the number of losses, 10, from the total number of games, 30. So, the total number of wins is 20. Now, let's look back at the ratio we determined from earlier:

$$\frac{wins}{losses} = \frac{20}{10}$$

You can (and should) reduce the ratio to $\frac{2}{1}$. You can also write the ratio as **2 : 1**.

Proportions

Proportions are an extension of ratios. Proportions are equations that set two ratios equal to one another and are helpful to determine ratios when quantities in a specific ratio relationship increase or decrease. So, if Nathan has 7 sodas and 4 bottles of water, if that ratio holds, proportions tell us that if Nathan has 14 sodas, he would have 8 bottles of water. This proportion can be expressed as:

$$\frac{14}{8} = \frac{7}{4}$$

Percentages

Percentages, like fractions and decimals, represent a portion of the whole. Percentages are heavily tested on the exam in a number of ways. Percentages are based on the whole of 100. So, 20% of something is essentially 20 parts of 100. Percentages can be written a number of different ways. Let's take 20 percent as an example. We can write 20 percent as follows:

$$20\% \text{ or } \frac{20}{100} \text{ or } .20$$

All of these are equivalent and represent 20 percent of 100 percent.

On the exam, you may be asked to calculate what percentage an integer is of another integer. For example, a problem-solving question may ask you: 5 *is what percentage of* 20?

If you wrote that out using the information we have, you would have something like this:

$$5 = ?\%(20)$$

Initially, you can set up an equation that sets 5 equal to, right now, the unknown percentages of 20. But, remember, you know that percentages are always based on 100.

Since percentages are always based on 100, you can add more information to the equation to help you solve and substitute an unknown variable for the value we are missing:

$$5 = \frac{x}{100}(20)$$

Now let's solve:

$$5 = \frac{20x}{100}$$

You can reduce the fraction to make it easier to work solve:

$$5 = \frac{x}{5}$$

Then, cross-multiply:

$$25 = x$$

So, 5 is **25**% of 20.

You solved the problem here and got the correct answer, but it took a lot of steps, which translates to a lot of time. There are some common formulas you can use on the exam to help approach percentage problems of various types. Let's look at those in more detail.

Part of the Whole Formulas

Problems involving percentages on the exam will normally, like the previous problem, give you two of the values and ask you to calculate the third. In the previous example, you had 5, the part, and 20, the whole. You were looking for the percentage. You can solve the problem with fewer steps that we did above using this formula:

5 is what percentage of 20?

Formula: $\boldsymbol{percent = \frac{part}{whole}}$

So, using the previous question, 5 is what percentage of 20, plug in the variable to the equation:

$$percent = \frac{5}{20}$$

***percent* = .25 *or* 25%**

Let's look at some other ways percentage problems may be presented and the formulas used to address them:

Example 1:
What is 20% of 42?

Here, you have the percentage, 20% and the whole, 42. So, you are looking for the part.

Formula: ***percent • whole = part***
Solve: **.20 • 42 = 8.4%**

Example 2:
12 is 40% of what number?

Here, you have the percent, 40%, and the part, 12. So, you are looking for the whole.

Formula: $\boldsymbol{\frac{part}{percent} = whole}$

Solve: $\boldsymbol{\frac{12}{.40} = 30}$

Percent Increase and Decrease

The GRE commonly tests the percent of increase and decrease. While word problems are most common, questions are presented in a number of different ways and may ask you to determine, for example, a new price based on a price increase of a certain percentage, or the decreased percentage of revenue for one fiscal year compared to a previous year. Like the previous problems, you will be given some pieces of the information and asked to find the missing element. Let's look at some common formulas to help you calculate percentage increase and decrease.

To calculate the percentage decrease:

$$\textit{percent decrease} = \frac{\textit{amount of decrease}}{\textit{original whole}} \cdot 100$$

Example:
The staff at Salsa Kitchen was reduced from 40 to 29 employees. What is the percent decrease in staff?

Amount always refers to a number, not a percentage. In order to calculate the *amount of decrease*, you must find the difference of the number of current employees and the number of original employees. This should always be a positive number. In this case, Salsa Kitchen started with 40 (*original whole*) employees and now has 29. That is a difference of 11. Now, let's solve our equation:

$$\frac{11}{40} \cdot 100 = \textit{percentage decrease}$$

$$\textit{percentage decrease} = .275 \bullet 100$$

So, the staff at Salsa Kitchen decreased by **27.5**%.

To calculate percentage increase:

$$\textit{percent increase} = \frac{\textit{amount of increase}}{\textit{original whole}}$$

Example:
Ansley works in a bookstore for $12.00 per hour. If her pay is increased to $14.00, then what is her percent increase in pay?

In order to calculate the *amount of increase*, you must find the difference of Ansley's current hourly pay and her previous hourly pay. Again, this should always be a positive number. In this case, Ansley started off earning $12.00 an hour before her pay increased to $14.00 an hour. The amount of increase is $2.00. Now, let's solve our equation:

$$\textit{percentage increase} = \frac{2}{12} \cdot 100$$

$$\frac{1}{6} \cdot 100 = \textit{percentage increase} = 16.66\%$$

So Ansley's hourly pay increased by **16.66%**

Combined Percentages

Sometimes questions on the exam will ask you to calculate more than one percentage. You may also be asked to find the percentage of a percentage. It is important to understand that you cannot compare percentages that are not part of the same whole. This is a common trap on the exam and you can count on an answer choice that matches the outcome of this mistake. Let's look at an example of combined percentages and how to avoid erroneously combining percentages in a word problem.

Example:
During the semi-annual sale, dresses were reduced by 20%.
Then, the price was further reduced by 10%. If a dress was originally $200, what is the final price of the dress?

The dress was first reduced by 20% then by 10%. While it may be tempting to calculate the new final price by reducing the original price of $200 by 30%, that is not correct. However, you can almost always count on an answer whose value will represent the 30% off the $200 total.

To correctly calculate the final price, you will need to calculate the first price reduction of 20%. You can do that by finding 20% of 200:

$$.20 \bullet \$200 = \$40.00$$

If the price of dress was reduced by 20%, there would be a $40.00 price difference from the original price. So, after the first reduction, the price of the dress would be $160.00.

Now, you need to perform the same calculations using the new price of the dress and reduce that by 10%:

$$.10 \bullet \$160 = \$16.00$$

So, the price of the dress would be reduced by an additional $16.00. After the second reduction, the final price of the dress would be $144.00.

If you decreased the original price of $200 by 30%, the total cost of the dress would be $140, which is incorrect.

ARGO
BROTHERS

12 ALGEBRA: THE BASICS

Algebra involves many of the same concepts as arithmetic like absolute value, fractions, and numerical operations. Algebra often uses variables, which are letters used to represent an unknown quantity. Variables are incorporated into expressions and you will often be asked to solve equations to find their value. The concepts discussed in this chapter present themselves in various mathematical capacities on the exam. You will need to understand concepts like factoring, polynomials, algebraic expressions, exponents, roots, and inequalities. Let's get started by reviewing some important vocabulary associated with algebra.

Essential Algebra Vocabulary

Coefficient

A multiplier in front of a variable that indicates how many of the variable there are. For example, for the term $5x$, 5 is the coefficient. Whenever a term occurs without a coefficient in front of it, like x, for example, the coefficient is 1.

Constant

A numerical quantity that does not change.

Equation

Equations are the building blocks of algebra. An equation is two expressions linked together with an equal sign where values of each expression can be solved or simplified. $2x + 1 = x - 10$ is an example of an equation.

Expression

An expression is made up of a single or multiple algebraic terms. Expressions do not have an equal sign to equate one side of the quantities to another. Expressions can only be solved if the value of all terms are known. $5x - 6$, $6xy$, and $x - 1$ are all expressions.

Term

A component of an algebraic equation that either represents the product or quotient of a constant and variable or a specific value separated by arithmetic operations. In the expression $4x + 3b - 2$, $4x$, $3b$, and 2, are all terms.

Variable

A letter used to represent an unknown value. Any letter may be used for variables and you many not always need to or be able to find the specific value associated with the variable. In many cases on the exam, however, you will solve to find the value of the variable.

Now that you've reviewed the essential vocabulary, let's look at some common algebraic operations to help you solve equations more efficiently.

Simplifying Algebraic Expressions

Before you dive into solving more complicated equations, you need to understand a few simplification tools that allow you to change algebraic expressions into simpler but equivalent forms.

Algebraic Laws of Operations

Like with arithmetic, algebra also has three basic properties for dealing with equations: commutative, additive, and distributive.

Commutative Property: Addition and multiplication are commutative operations; the order in which they are performed does not impact the answer. The commutative property does not hold for subtraction. Let's look at an example of addition and multiplication using the commutative property:

$$2a \bullet 3b = 3b \bullet 2a$$
$$2a + 3b = 3b + 2a$$

Associative Property: Addition and multiplication are also associative; when written as an expression, they can be regrouped, and like terms can be combined without impacting the final answer. Let's look at an example of addition and multiplication using the associative property:

$$2a - 3a + 5b + 2b$$
$$= (2a - 3a) + (5b + 2b)$$
$$= -a + 7b$$

Multiplication:

$$(6a \bullet 5b) \bullet 4b$$
$$= 6a(5b \bullet 4b)$$
$$= 6a(20b^2)$$
$$= 120ab^2$$

Distributive Property: The distributive property outlines how values in an expression should be distributed when performing more than one operation (addition, subtraction, multiplication). Let's look at an example on how to simplify equations using the distributive property:

$$3a(4b - 6c) = (3a \bullet 4b) - (3a \bullet 6c)$$
$$= 12ab - 18ac$$

The associative, commutative, and distributive properties apply to many of the problems you will see on the exam; in some expressions and equations, you may need to combine the operations of the properties to arrive at your answer.

Combining Like Terms

Combining like terms is an effective approach to simplifying and solving algebraic expressions. As you work through the expression, using the appropriate law(s) of operation, look for terms that have the same characteristics and combine them into a single term. Any term that shares the same variable in the same form can be combined.

$$x^3 + x^2 + 2x + 3x - 4$$

In this case, $2x$ and $3x$ are like terms and can be combined. Your new expression would be:

$$x^3 + x^2 + 5x - 4$$

Notice that x^3 and x^2 cannot be combined. While they share the same base, x, the exponent is different.

Substitution

Substitution is also another effective way to solve algebraic expressions or to express them in terms of other variables. Oftentimes, the question task will provide you with the information to substitute values if the problem itself does not. Let's look at a sample question:

Evaluate $4x^2 - 8x$ *when* $x = 3$

Here, you would substitute the value 3 for every x in the expression:

$$4(3)^2 - 8(3)$$

Remember the order of operations; solve the parentheses and exponents first:

$$\begin{aligned} 4(9) - 24 &= 36 - 24 \\ &= 12 \end{aligned}$$

Substitution may sometimes require you to replace non-mathematical symbols with values or operations. For example, you may see a question that uses a non-mathematical symbol instead of an operation sign (addition, subtraction, multiplication, division). In this case, the question will always outline what the symbol represents. Let's look at an example:

Suppose $x■ = \frac{8-x}{x^2}$, where $x > 0$. Evaluate 3■.

While it may appear confusing at first, this is simply a substitution question. The original statement tells us that x times ■ is equal to $\frac{8-x}{x^2}$. So, 3■ will be three times the expression. You will need to substitute the value 3 wherever we see an x is the expression:

$$\frac{8-3}{3^2} = \frac{5}{9} = 3■$$

Factoring and Polynomials

Factoring is another approach to simplifying algebraic expressions and is essentially the opposite of distribution, though they are commonly used together. Factoring allows you to evaluate complex expressions by breaking it into simpler expressions taking into consideration monomials, polynomials, binomials, and trinomials.

Monomials

A single term expression. For example, $3x$ or $4y$.

Polynomials

An expression with one than one term. For example, $3x^2 + 2y + 3$.

Binomials

A polynomial expression with exactly two terms. For example, $4x + 6$.

Trinomials

A polynomial expression with exactly three terms. For example, $4y^2 + 3x - 2$.

When there is a monomial factor common to all the terms in the polynomial expression, it can be factored out to create simpler expressions. Suppose you have the following expression:

$$4x + 8xy$$

$4x$ is the common factor and can be used to simplify the expression:

$$4x(1 + 2y)$$

Common Polynomial Equations

There are common polynomials that you may encounter on the exam. Knowing how to recognize and factor these can save you time and help you simplify equations to make them easier to solve.

The difference of squares can be factored out into the product of two simpler expressions:

$$a^2 - b^2 = (a - b)(a + b)$$

Some polynomials can be factored into two matching binomials:

$$a^2 - 2ab + b^2 = (a - b)(a - b)$$

Some polynomials are trinomials that are perfect squares:

$$a^2 + 2b^2 + b^2 = (a + b)^2$$

Since factoring is the opposite of distribution, these equations are all commutative.

Exponents

You may have noticed that polynomials often involve exponents. While this is not always the case, exponents are an important component of algebra and have their own set of rules you should be familiar with going into the exam. An exponent tells you how many times to multiply a number by itself to find a particular value. If we have the exponent 3^2, the number 3 is called the base while the number 2 is referred to as the exponent or power.

To solve an exponent, multiply the base by itself the number of times expressed by the exponent. Take 5^3, for example. If you were to rewrite the expression without exponents and solve, it would look like:

$$5 \bullet 5 \bullet 5 = 125$$

Any base with an exponent of 2 is commonly referred to as being squared and any base with an exponent of 3 is referred to as being cubed. It is helpful to be familiar with some of the common exponents you may see on the exam. The following chart outlines common squares and cubes that may appear mainly in arithmetic and algebra problems.

Common Squares	Common Cubes
$1^2 = 1$	$1^3 = 1$
$2^2 = 4$	$2^3 = 8$
$3^2 = 9$	$3^3 = 27$
$4^2 = 16$	$4^3 = 64$
$5^2 = 25$	$5^3 = 125$

Common Squares	Common Cubes
$6^2 = 36$	$6^3 = 216$
$7^2 = 49$	$7^3 = 343$
$8^2 = 64$	$8^3 = 512$
$9^2 = 81$	$9^3 = 729$
$10^2 = 100$	$10^3 = 1000$

Rules of Exponents

Working with exponents is pretty straight forward when you only have a base and a positive exponent like 3^2. But, you will see exponents on the exam that include negative numbers that involve mathematical operations like multiplication and division. The following chart is a helpful tool to familiarize you with the rules of exponents and how to deal with various presentations of exponents on the exam.

Exponent Rule	Example
$x^0 = 1$	Any nonzero number to the zero power is equal to 1. Note that 0^0 has no defined value. *Example:* $5^0 = 1$
$x^1 = x$	Any nonzero number raised to the power of 1 is equal to the number itself. *Example:* $6^1 = 6$
$(x^a)(x^b) = x^{a+b}$	When you multiply exponents with the same base, add the exponents to calculate the value of the expression. *Example:* $(4^2)(4^3) = 4^{2+3} = 4^5 = 1024$
$\frac{x^a}{x^b} = x^{a-b}$	When you divide exponents with the same base, subtract the exponents to calculate the value of the expression. *Example:* $\frac{4^3}{4^2} = 4^{3-2} = 4^1 = 4$
$xy^a = (x^a)(y^a)$	The product of two bases raised to a power can be simplified and solved by raising each number in the expressions to the same power. *Example:* $(4^2)(2^2) = 8^2 = 64$
$(x / y)^a = \frac{x^a}{y^a}$	The quotient of two bases raised to a power can be simplified and solved raising each number in the expressions to the same power. *Example:* $(3/4)^3 = \frac{3^3}{4^3} = \frac{9}{64}$
$x^{-a} = \frac{1}{x^a}$	Any nonzero number raised to a negative power is equivalent to its reciprocal. *Example:* $3^{-2} = \frac{1}{3^2} = \frac{1}{9}$
$(x^a)^b = x^{ab}$	When a power is raised to another power, multiply to exponents. *Example:* $(3^2)^3 = 3^{2 \cdot 3} = 3^6 = 729$

Exponents in Expression and Equations

The exponent rules cover the basics of dealing with exponents that primarily involve multiplication. It is important to note that it is not possible to add and subtract exponents in an expression if they do not have the same base **and** the same exponent. Consider the following expression:

$$2^9 + 2^7$$

This expression is in its simplest form. You cannot add the terms to get new expression of 2^{16}. Each part of the expression should be solved separately to arrive at your answer. But, won't the answers be the same regardless of which way you do it? Well, let's check?

$2^9 = 512$ and $2^7 = 128$. So, when you add the two together, you get 640. Now let's see what happens when you calculate 2^{16}:

$$2^{16} = 65{,}536$$

That's a vast difference in answers! Exponents in these cases must be computed separately. The same goes for subtraction. However, when working with terms that share the same base and have the same exponents, you can add and subtract to simply the expression.

Suppose you have the algebraic expression $3x^4 + 6x^4$. Here your base and exponent, x and 4, respectively, are the same. So, you can add the two terms together, keeping the base and exponents in tact. Your new expression will look like:

$$9x^4$$

You may or may not have the information needed to fully solve the expression, but you can put it in its simplest terms.

Negative Numbers and Exponents

There is another possible situation involving exponents to keep in mind that we have not yet explored: when a negative number is raised to a positive power.

When you raise a negative number to a positive power, the same rules apply that apply to multiplying negative and positive numbers together. The product of a negative and positive number is a negative number, while the product of two negative numbers is a positive number. How does that relate to exponents? Since an exponent represents the number of times you multiply a number by itself, when you have a negative number raised to an exponent, an odd or even exponent will impact whether or not your final answer is positive or negative. Here's an example:

$$-4^2$$
$$= (-4)(-4)$$

In this case, if you calculated the value of the expression, $(-4)(-4)$, the product is 16, an even number. If you decided you wanted to find out the value of -4^3, you would calculate $(-4)(-4)(-4)$.

$$(-4)(-4)\ (-4) = -64$$

When you raise a negative number to a positive even exponent, the result will be a positive number. When you raise a negative number to a positive odd exponent, the result will be a negative number.

Exponents are closely linked to roots, another mathematical concept that deals with figuring out the number of times a number goes into another number. Like exponents, roots appear on the exam in various forms, and an understanding of the basic principles of roots will help you simply expressions and solve equations.

Roots

Roots are an inverse of exponents. The roots you will encounter on the exam are generally confined to square roots and cube roots. You will need to either solve or simply them. A root is symbolized using the root symbol with a number enclosed:

$$\sqrt{4}$$

The example is the standard notation for a square root. In this case, the expression is translated to the square root of 4. To solve, you are looking for the number that, when multiplied once by itself, equals 4. If you look back at common exponents covered in the previous exponents section, you might remember that $2^2 = 4$. So, the square root 4 is 2.

You may see the root symbol with an exponent in front of it:

$$\sqrt[3]{27}$$

In this case, you must take the cubed root of 27. So, you need to identify the number that when multiplied by itself three times, equals 27. Again, if you refer back to the chart of common squares and cubes, you will see that $3^3 = 27$. So, the cubed root of 27 is 3.

The GRE will only ask you to find the root of positive numbers. With the square root, it does not matter if the number is negative or positive, it will always yield a positive number. But if you are comparing quantities, for example, and have the following equation:

$$\sqrt{x} = 10$$

It's easy to assume that the $x = 100$ since the square root of 100 is 10. But, you must consider that x might also equal −100 since the square root of *both* is 10

Simplifying Roots

You cannot add or subtract roots that appear in equations or expressions. You can, however, multiply or divide them in order to solve or simplify. In some cases, you may be able to solve for the value regardless of the operation being performed. For example:

$$\sqrt{4} + \sqrt{16}$$

Here, you can take the root of each of the terms separately, so 2 and 4, then find the sum, 6. You are not adding the roots; instead, you are adding values of the solved roots. So, given the example above, solving for $\sqrt{20}$ would be incorrect.

You can multiply the same roots in a given expression. So, you can multiply two square roots or two cube roots. You cannot, however, multiply a square root by a cubed root. Consider this example:

$$\sqrt{2} \cdot \sqrt{8} \cdot \sqrt[3]{27}$$

This expression can be simplified to $\sqrt{16} \cdot \sqrt[3]{27}$ since you can combine the two squared roots by finding the product of the two. To solve the expression, simply calculate the values of the roots:

$$\sqrt{16} = 4 \qquad \sqrt[3]{27} = 3$$

So, 4 • 3 = 12

You can also divide roots of the same type:

$$\frac{\sqrt{16}}{\sqrt{4}} = \sqrt{\frac{16}{4}} = \sqrt{4} = 2$$

Here, you can complete the division as you would without the roots to simplify the expression. Then, solve the new simplified root to determine your answer.

Using these general principles, you can also reduce numbers under the root sign to create smaller, but equivalent expressions. For example:

$$\sqrt{81}$$

You can simplify the original root and create a new expression that includes simpler terms and solve:

$$\sqrt{9} \cdot \sqrt{9} = 3 \cdot 3 = 9$$

Fractional Exponents

You may have a number raised to a fractional exponent. To simplify and solve, you can convert the exponent to a root. Let's look at an example:

$$4^{\frac{1}{2}}$$

In these instances, the denominator tells you the type of root squared or cubed for example, while the numerator tells you what power to raise the base number or variable to. Using the example above, your root would look like:

$$\sqrt{4^1}$$

You know that any number raised to the first power is simply the number. So, you end up needing to calculate the square root of 4, which is 2.

Solving Algebraic Equations

Equations are algebraic functions that set two expressions equal to each other. Equations consist of numbers, operations, variables, and in some cases, non-mathematical symbols. Your goal is to isolate the variables and solve or simplify as much as possible if you do not have the information to solve completely.

Since equations set two expressions equal to each other, when you manipulate the equation, you much ensure that you perform any operation to **both** sides of the equation. This is the most fundamental principle of working with algebraic equations.

Equations can have any number of variables. On the exam, you will see equations with one variable up to four or five unique variables. Equations that do not contain any exponents are the most common on the exam and are referred to as linear equations. Let's look a linear equation with one variable and examine how to approach solving similar problems.

$$x + 20 = 45$$

The equation is telling you that the sum of x and 20 is equal to 45. So, you want to isolate x in order to solve for its value. To do so, start by subtracting 20 from each side of the equation. This keeps x positive and isolates it at the same time.

$$x = 45 - 20$$
$$x = 25$$

Equations with one variable on one side tend to be easier to solve than those with multiple variables or variables on both side of the equation. Naturally, the latter requires more manipulation and computation. In a time crunch, seeking out one variable equations may help you get to more question in the time you have remaining.

Now, let's look at an equation with the same variable on both sides:

$$5x - 7 = 3x + 10$$

To solve for x, you still need to isolate the variable. Solve to get all the terms with the variable on one side of the equation. First, subtract $3x$ from both sides.

$$5x - 3x - 7 = 10$$

Next, finish isolating the variables by adding 7 to both sides. When you add 7 to the left side of the equation, it cancels out the −7 already there.

$$5x - 3x = 17$$

Since you have isolated x to one side of the variable, you can solve:

$$5x - 3x = 2x$$
$$2x = 17$$
$$x = 8.5$$

To make sure you have the right answer, you can plug the value you have for x into the original equation.

$$5(8.5) - 7 = 3(8.5) + 10$$
$$42.5 - 7 = 25.5 + 10$$
$$35.5 = 35.5$$

Absolute Value Equations

Solving equations with absolute value expressions involves a little more work than equations that do not. Remember, that when you take the absolute value of a number, you end up with the positive distance from zero to that number on a number line. When you have absolute value expressions in algebraic equations, you will have two answers: one that assumes the expression is positive and one that assumes the expression is negative. Here's an example:

If $|x+3| = 10$, then $x =$

Just like you would in any other equation, you want to isolate the variable. You can worry about the implications of the absolute value later. In fact, write the equation out, without the absolute value notation:

$$x + 3 = 10$$
$$x = 10 - 3$$
$$x = 7$$

You have solved for x, but you are not done yet. Since the expression on the left side asks you to take the absolute value of the expression, and absolute value is always expressed as a positive number, you need to consider that instead of 10, the expression can also yield an answer of −10. To do so, adjust the right side of the equation to −10 and solve.

$$x + 3 = -10$$
$$x = -10 - 3$$
$$x = -13$$

Of course, you can plug your answers back in to the original equations to see if they are correct. Both these answer choices are correct and complete. It is important to consider both possibilities when dealing with absolute value although the question may not specifically prompt you to so.

Variables in the Denominator

When variables are in the denominator, they warrant special attention. You still want to isolate the variable and solve or simplify. Consider this example:

$$\frac{1}{x+3}+5=9$$

Start by subtracting 5 from both sides to try to isolate the variable:

$$\frac{1}{x+3}=4$$

Next, multiply each side for the reciprocal of the expression in the denominator:

$$(x+3)\bullet\frac{1}{(x+3)}=4(x+3)$$

The expression $x + 3$ on the left side cancels out.

$$1 = 4(x + 3)$$

You could distribute the 4, but you are trying to isolate the variable. So, manipulate the 4 instead and divide each side by 4 to further isolate the variable.

$$\frac{1}{4}=x+3$$

Now, subtract 3 from both sides to solve for x:

$$\frac{1}{4}-3=\frac{3}{12}-\frac{36}{12}$$

$$=-\frac{33}{12}=-2\frac{3}{4} \text{ or } -2.75.$$

Equations with More than One Variable

Of course, the test creators couldn't let you slide with solving for just one variable equations. Sometimes, you will see equations with two variables. As with one variable expressions, your goal is to either solve or simplify. And, you can do so using many of the methods previously discussed. Equations with more than one variable, as you might imagine, can be more challenging than their one variable counterparts, and require more steps to arrive at the answer. You are also given two separate equations to help you arrive at the answer. The equations are set equal to each other like expressions in one variable equations. Let's look at an example:

Solve for x and y if $2x + 5y = 7$ and $x + 4y = 2$

First, solve for one of the variables in terms of the other variable. Let's solve for x in terms of y in the second equation:

$$x + 4y = 2$$
$$x = 2 - 4y$$

Now plug in the expression for x into the first equation and solve for y:

$$2(2 - 4y) + 5y = 7$$
$$4 - 8y + 5y = 7$$
$$4 - 3y = 7$$
$$-3y = 3$$
$$y = -1$$

Now that you have the value for y, plug it in and solve for x:

$$x = 2 - 4(-1)$$
$$x = 2 + 4$$
$$x = 6$$

Remember, plug in the values you calculated to check your answers. To determine which variable to try to solve for first, look for the equation where one variable is easier to isolate and start there.

Quadratic Equations

The quadratic equation is a special equation where specific polynomials are set to equal zero.

$$ax^2 + bx + c = 0$$

For the quadratic equation, $a \neq 0$, and a, b, and c are constants representing the coefficients that precede the variable x. Earlier in this section, we reviewed factoring and binomials, which are key components to finding values in a quadratic equation. Consider the example:

$$x^2 - 5x + 6 = 0$$

To solve for x, first factor out the binomial terms:

$$(x - 2)(x - 3)$$

If you are unsure if you have factored properly and identified the correct binomials, check your work using distribution. As you multiply in order, write out the products; if you have factored correctly, your distribution should yield the original equation:

Distribute the first term in the first binomial into both terms in the second binomial:

$$(x)(x) = x^2 \text{ and } (x)(-3) = -3x$$

Next, do the same with the second term in the first binomial:

$$(-2)(x) = -2x \text{ and } (-2)(-3) = 6$$

Now, combine the products to see if it matches your original equation:

$$x^2 - 3x -2x +6 = x^2 - 5x + 6$$

Everything looks good! Now, let's get back to solving the problem.

Our original equation was $x^2 - 5x + 6 = 0$ and we factored it out to $(x - 2)(x - 3)$.

Quadratic equations **always** have two solutions. The two solutions may be the same number though they are solved using a different equation. To solve for the values of x, set each of the binomials to 0.

$$x - 2 = 0 \qquad x - 3 = 0$$
$$x = 2 \qquad x = 3$$

Both 2 and 3, are viable solutions to the equation. Plug in your answers to check if the values are correct.

$$(2)^2 - 5(2) + 6 = 0$$
$$4 - 10 + 6 = -6 + 6 = 0$$

$$(3)^2 - 5(3) + 6 = 0$$
$$9 - 15 + 6 = -6 + 6 = 0$$

The values check out when plugged in. So, the solution for the quadratic equation is $x = 2$ or $x = 3$.

The quadratic equation is derived from the quadratic formula, $x = \frac{-b \pm \sqrt{b^2 - 4ac}}{2a}$. The quadratic formula is not tested on the exam.

Inequalities

Inequalities are a type of equation. But, instead of setting two expression equal or setting them to zero like the quadratic equation, inequalities describe how the two quantities are not equal. You may see an inequality equation that resembles the following:

$$x + 5 > 10x$$

The equation reads: the sum of x and 5 is greater than the product of 10 and x. Inequalities express four quantity comparisons:

x greater than y: $x > y$
x less than y: $x < y$
x greater than or equal to y: $x \geq y$
x less than or equal to y: $x \leq y$

Solving Inequalities

Inequalities are equations; so you approach them like you have approached other equations in this section. Your goal is still to isolate the variables and solve for their value, if possible. As with regular equations, whatever function you perform on one side of the equation, you must perform on the other. Inequalities have one oddity that can impact your answer choice if you are not careful. Whenever you divide or multiply both sides by a negative number, you must flip the inequality sign to ensure the inequality remains valid. Let's look at an inequality equation.

Consider the inequality:

$$3 - \frac{x}{4} \geq 2$$

First, try to isolate the variable:

$$-\frac{x}{4} \geq 2 - 3 = -\frac{x}{4} \geq -1$$

$$(-4)\left(-\frac{x}{4}\right) \leq 4$$

Since we multiplied both sides by a negative number we changed the direction of the inequality sign. The x variables cancel out, so:

$$x \leq 4$$

The expression reads x is less than or equal to 4. While you have solved for x, this is not your answer. The complete answer is all the values equal to or less than 4. Inequalities are sometimes represented on a number line. The above example on a number like would look like:

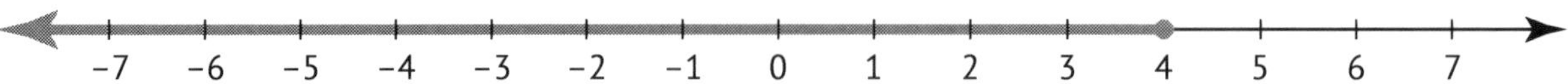

The filled in point on over the 4 indicates that 4 is included in the possible list of values. If the final answer was $x < 4$, the circle would not be filled in. The number line in that case would look like:

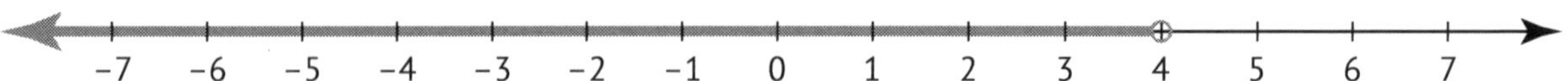

Coordinate Geometry

Coordinate geometry is the transition point from algebra to geometry and involves the use of algebraic expressions to create graphical displays on a coordinate plane. The coordinate plane is composed of a vertical and horizontal axis that run perpendicular to each other. All points on a coordinate plane can be plotted on these axes, which intersect in the center at zero. This meeting point is commonly referred to as the point of origin.

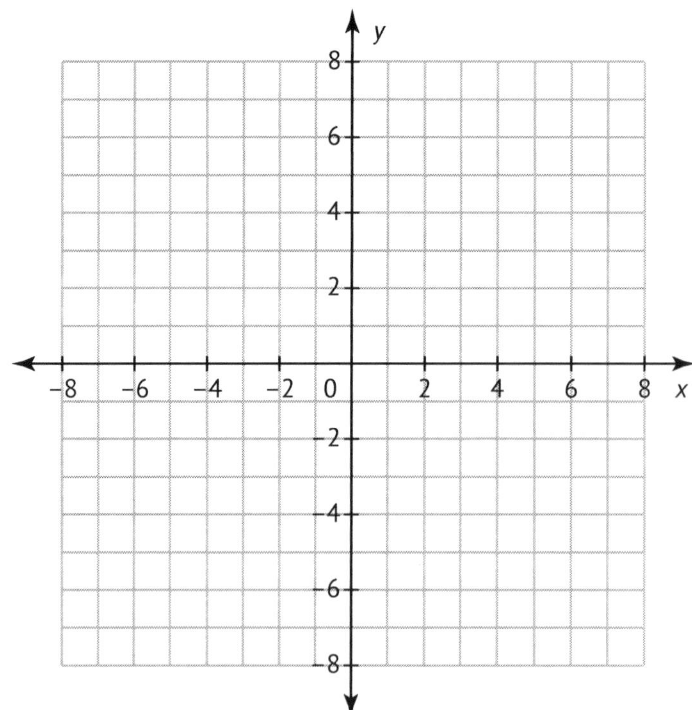

The coordinate plane has four distinct quadrants. Quadrant I is in the upper right corner, quadrant II is in the upper left corner, quadrant III is in the lower left corner, and quadrant IV is in the lower right corner.

Points are plotted on a coordinate plane. Every point has two coordinates, one on the x-axis and one on the y-axis. The center of origin that sits at the intersection of the two axes has points (0, 0). The coordinates of points not at the center are determined by their positive or negative difference from the origin. Coordinates are always written with the with the x coordinate first. So, (x, y). You can determine whether the x and y coordinates are positive or negative based on the quadrant they fall in.

Quadrant	*x*-coordinate	*y*-coordinate
I	positive	positive
II	negative	positive
III	negative	negative
IV	positive	negative

On the exam, it is helpful to know these common locations for coordinates to save time and prevent you from plotting the points on the coordinate plane each time.

Graphing Coordinates

Sometimes you need to either graph coordinates or determine the value of coordinates already on the graph. When given a set of coordinates, simply start at zero and plot the distance across, either left or right, first for the value of the *x*, then plot the distance up or down, for the value of *y*.

Let's look at a set of coordinates and how to graph them on the coordinate plane. Suppose you are asked to identify a graph that has a point with the coordinates (3, 2), your graph would look like this:

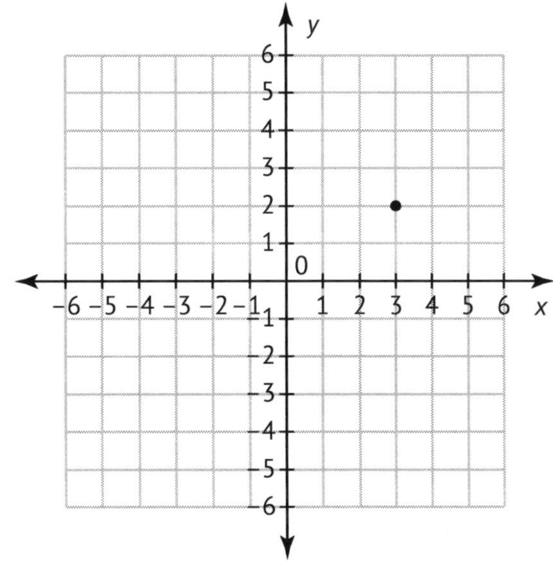

You can see the coordinates start at the point of origin, shifts 3 spaces to the right, then shifts 2 spaces up. If you refer back to the quadrant chart, you can see that it predicted our coordinates, which are both positive, would be in quadrant I.

Calculating Distance on the Coordinate Plane

You may be asked to calculate the distance between two points on a coordinate plane. Or, for an added level of fun, you may be asked to find the midpoint. If the points are in the same vertical or horizontal plane, you can simply count the spaces between the points. The midpoint is the center point of the distance between the two points. Distance is always positive.

You can also use the distance formula to plug in coordinates and calculate the distance between the two points.

$$distance = \sqrt{(x_2 - x_1)^2 + (y_2 - y_1)^2}$$

To find the distance between two coordinates, let's say (5, −2) and (−4, 9), plug in the values in the equation and solve.

$$distance = \sqrt{(-4-5)^2 + (9-(-2)^2}$$

$$= \sqrt{(-9)^2 + 11^2}$$

$$distance = \sqrt{202}$$

Midpoint

The midpoint is also a measure of distance between points on a coordinate plane. Instead of the distance from one point to another, the coordinates of the midpoint are the average of the endpoints. To find the midpoint of two points, take the average of your endpoints using the midpoint formula:

$$midpoint = \frac{x_1 + x_2}{2}, \frac{y_1 + y_2}{2}$$

Suppose you have the points (−1, 2) and (3, −6). Plug in the coordinates to find the midpoint: midpoint $= \frac{-1+3}{2}, \frac{2-6}{2} = (1, -2)$.

Slope

Points on a coordinate plane connect to form lines. The slope is the measure of how steep a line is in relation to the x and y-axis. The equation of a straight line is ***y* = *mx* + *b***, where *m* is equal to the slope and *b* is equal to the y-intercept and *x* and *y* represent possible coordinate values. This equation is commonly referred to as **slope-intercept form**.

The *y*-intercept is just another way of describing the point that falls directly on the *y*-axis. Likewise, the *x*-intercept describes the point that falls directly on the *x*-axis. All lines will have exactly one *x* and *y* intercept.

The slope is the measure of *rise over run* of a line, or the difference between the *y*-coordinate values (rise) and the difference between the *x*-coordinate values (run). You need two coordinate points to find the slope of a line.

Consider the coordinates (4, 3) and (−2, −1). Calculate the change in *x* and *y* to find the slope, *m*.

$$m = \frac{\text{change in } y}{\text{change in } x} = \frac{3-(-1)}{4-(-2)} = \frac{4}{6} = \frac{2}{3}$$

You may sometimes be asked to find the slope of a line from an equation instead of coordinates. Suppose you have the equation $2x + y = 5$. To find the slope, put the equation in slope-intercept form, $y = mx + b$:

$$2x + y = 5$$
$$y = -2x + 5$$

So, the slope of this line is −2.

Properties of Slopes

Knowing some of the common properties of slopes and what they look like graphically can help save you time and calculation on the exam. Let's look at some of these properties.

- The slope of a line can be either positive or negative.
- Slopes do not have to be whole integers, they can be fractions as well.
- Parallel lines on the same coordinate plane will always have the same slope. So, if the slope of line a is 3, **all** lines parallel to that line will also have a slope of 3.
- The slope of a line on the same coordinate plane that is perpendicular to another line is the negative reciprocal. So, if a line has a slope of 2, **all** lines perpendicular to that line will have a slope of $-\frac{1}{2}$.

A **positive** slope rises from left to right.

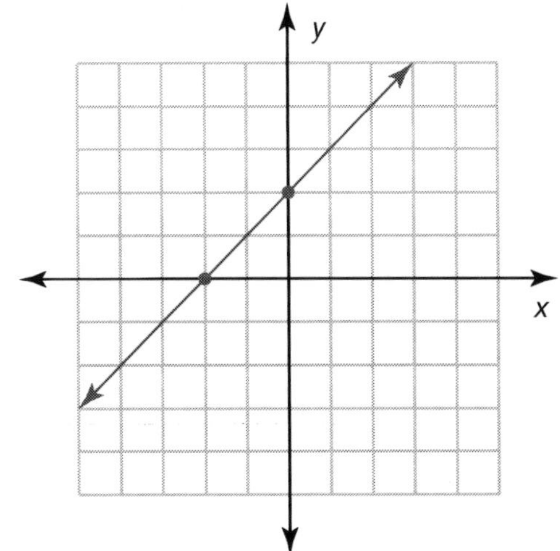

A **negative** slope falls from left to right.

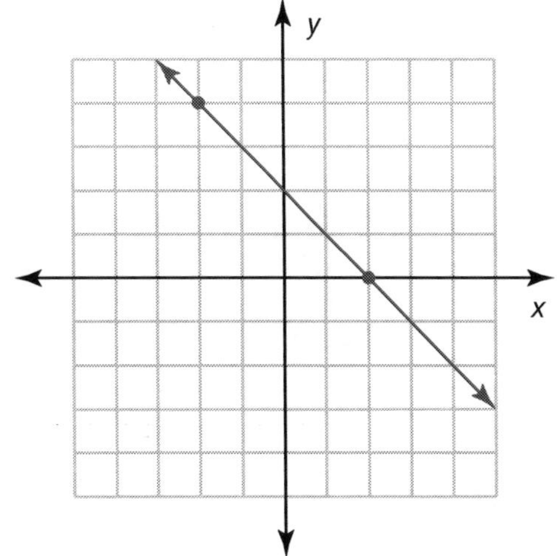

Any straight **horizontal** line has a slope of 0 since there are no points on the y-axis.

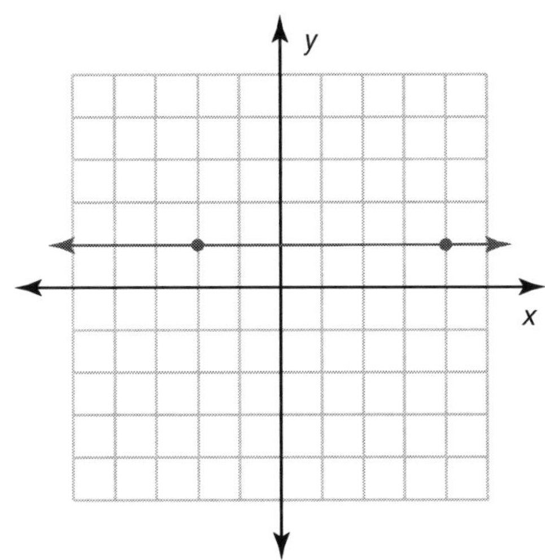

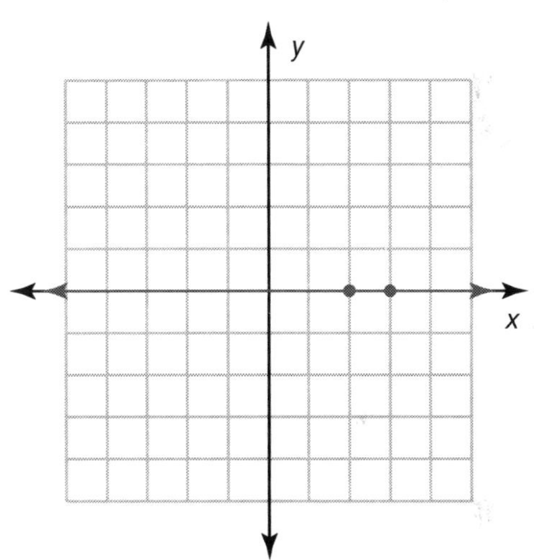

The slope of any straight **vertical** line cannot be defined since all of its points have the same x-coordinate.

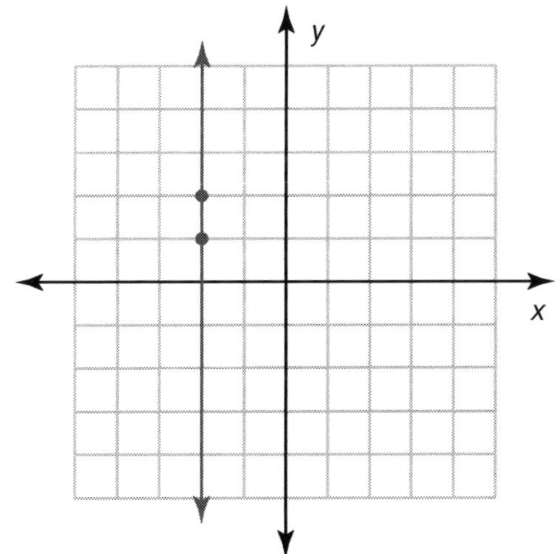

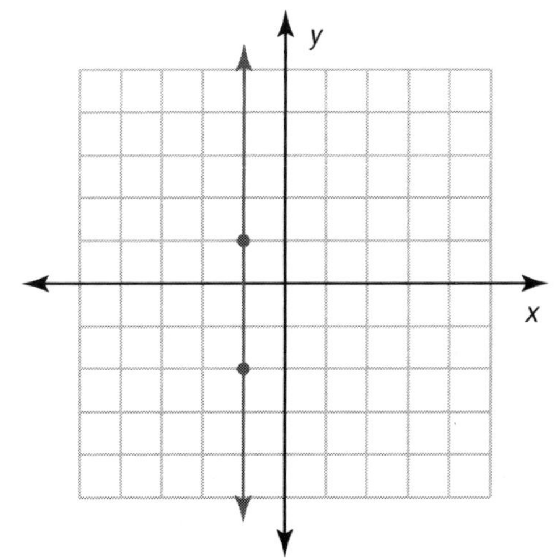

Functions

Algebraic functions can be expressed as a graph or as an equation and describe a relationship between corresponding inputs and outputs. Functions are typically represented by the notation $f(x)$ and dictates what the output is when certain values are substituted for x.

For example, you may see something similar to the following:

$$f(x) = 2x + 4$$

For the function above, f is the name of the function. Any letter can be used in place of f to rename the function.

A question may present you with the above equation and ask you to solve $f(3)$. To solve, replace each x in the equation with the input, 3. So, for $f(3)$:

$$f(3) = 2(3) + 4$$
$$f(3) = 10$$

Functions can also be graphed on a coordinate plane. And, depending on the equation, the graph may not always be a straight line. Instead, functions are often parabolas like in the examples below.

$f(x) = -x^2 - 8x - 15$

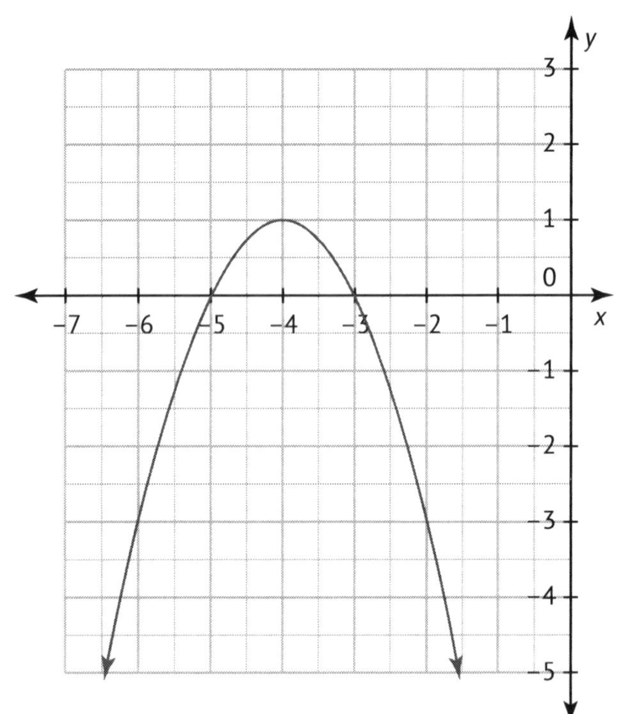

$f(x) = -x^2 + 8x - 19$

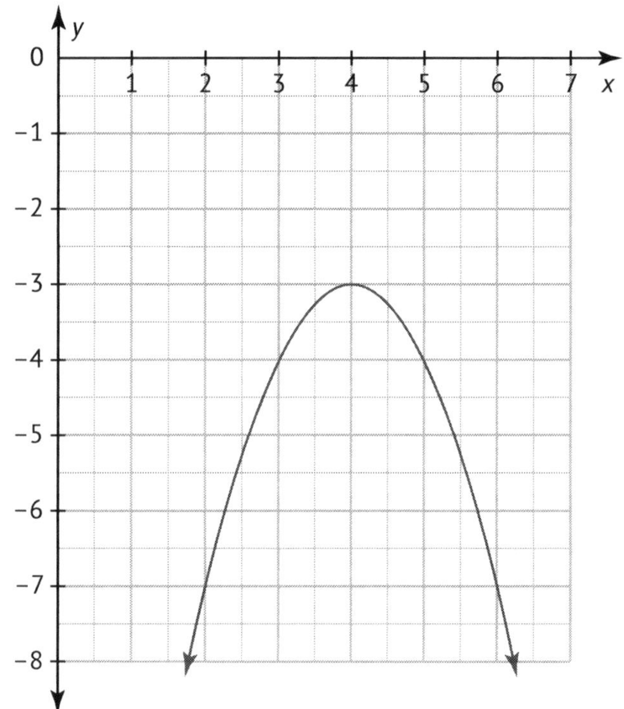

ARGO
BROTHERS

13 GEOMETRY: THE BASICS

Geometry focuses primarily on the measurements of shapes, lines, angles, and planes. Several keys areas of geometry are tested on the GRE. You will see problems that involve triangles, circles, and two-dimensional shapes of various sizes with different numbers of sides. This section will help refresh your memory of all the formulas and concepts you thought you left behind in high school, outline key geometric concepts that occur frequently on the exam, and equip you with problem-solving strategies to improve your accuracy.

Diagrams and Formulas

Most of the geometry questions on the exam will be accompanied by a diagram. In most cases, this works to your advantage. Often the diagrams contain useful information to help you answer the question. For example, if you have a diagram of circle and the diameter is noted as 4 cm you can deduce the radius of the circle, which is half the diameter.

It is important to note that geometry diagrams on the exam are typically not drawn to scale. You should not make assumptions based on how diagrams “look.” Instead, you should use the information presented in the questions and any given measurements to calculate the information you are looking for and find a corresponding answer choice.

We will review key geometric formulas in this section. While the formulas are helpful to know, they are useless if you are unsure of how to use them. Questions on the exam, particularly those dealing with triangles, will require you to think beyond simply plugging in numbers to a formula. Instead, you will have to critically analyze the given components to arrive at the correct answer.

Lines, Angles, Planes, and Shapes (L.A.P.S)

The building blocks of geometry are shapes, lines, angles, and planes. You will encounter one or more of these components in all the geometry questions on the exam. While geometry is a dense subject matter that includes some very complex principles, remember that the GRE is a test of your understanding of high-school level math and is primarily concerned with your basic math skills. As such, complex topics like differential geometry, model theory, and geometric proofs will not appear on the exam.

The exam will focus specifically on coordinate plane geometry. Planes are two-dimensional flat surface areas that extend infinitely in all directions. The surfaces of geometric shapes like polygons, triangles, hexagons, are all planes; lines and points also are essential components of geometric planes. Using points, angles, and other units of measurement, you can calculate other critical information about a shape, plot coordinates on a plane, and draw conclusions about angle measurements. This section will cover the **L.A.P.S** fundamentals, including key definitions, formulas, approaches to various problems, and sample problems for you to test your understanding of each concept.

Let’s get started with some L.A.P.S!

Lines

A line is a one-dimensional figure on a plane. Lines are always straight and drawn with arrows capping each end to indicate their infinite nature. Essentially, lines go on in both directions infinitely.

Lines are uniquely determined by two points. Points are found on all geometric shapes. They are not measurable units, though the distance between two points is a common calculation you will be asked to determine. In the diagram below, **A** and **B** are points on the line. These points are unique and only one line runs through them. And remember, that line goes on infinitely.

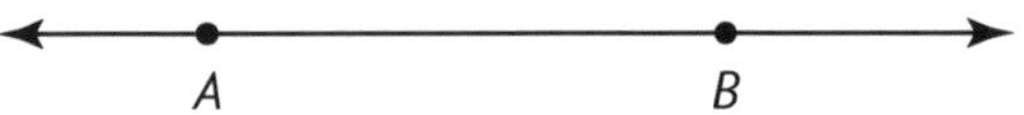

Instead of figures, you may see the common notation $\overleftrightarrow{AB}$ used. The notation indicates that you have a line, with no defined end, that crosses through points **A** and **B**.

Rays

A ray is a straight line that begins at a single point and extends infinitely in one direction. A ray has one end point that marks where it begins. End points mark the beginning or end of a line segment or ray. Line segments have two endpoints with defined lengths. Rays, however, only have one end point, so the length of a ray cannot be measured.

In the diagram below, the ray begins at point **A**, passes through point **B**, and continues infinitely in one direction. Like with a line, you can use a shorthand notation for this figure. The notation $\overrightarrow{AB}$ shows the points on the ray and that it continues infinitely in one direction.

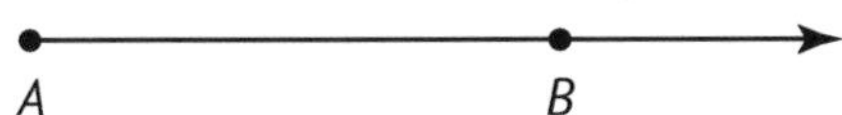

Line Segments

A line segment is a part of a straight line. However, segments have a measurable length. Unlike a line, segments do not continue on infinitely. The annotation for a line segment is written as $\overline{AB}$.

The key characteristics of a line segment are its two end points and its midpoint. The end points mark both finite ends of a segment while the midpoint is positioned at the center of a segment.

In the diagram below, **A** and **B** are the end points of the segment. **M** represents the midpoint or center of the segment.

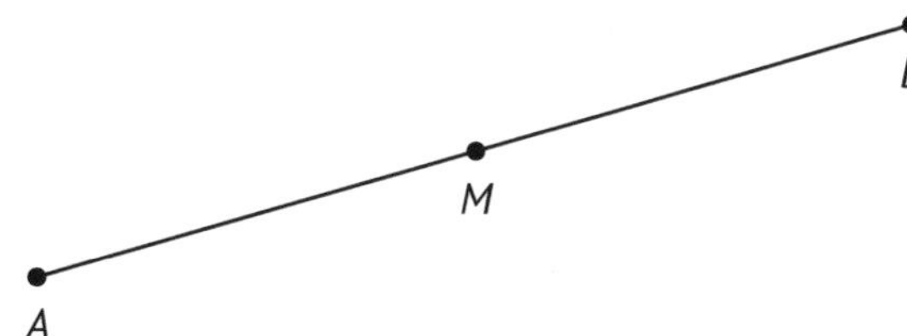

A and **B** are the same distance from the midpoint, **M**. So, $\overline{AM} = \overline{MB}$. If you have an exam question that tells you **M** is the midpoint of segment $\overline{AB}$ and that $\overline{MB} = 3$, you can deduce that $\overline{AM}$ is also 3.

Only segments have midpoints. Because lines and rays go on infinitely in one or both directions, it is not possible to determine the length of the line nor its center.

Parallel Lines

Parallel lines are two straight lines that never intersect each other. You should not assume that because two lines are not touching that they are parallel lines since it is possible they may intersect at some point. For exam questions addressing parallel lines, the question will explicitly state the lines are parallel or will use the common notation for parallel lines.

$\overleftrightarrow{AB}$ and $\overleftrightarrow{CD}$ are parallel lines. Their relationship can be annotated as $\overleftrightarrow{AB} \parallel \overleftrightarrow{CD}$.

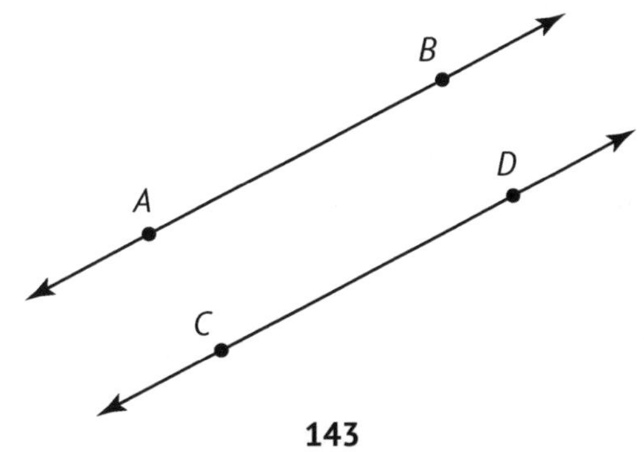

Perpendicular Lines

Perpendicular lines are two straight lines that intersect each other forming a 90° angle. We will discuss angles in more detail later in this chapter. Just like with parallel lines, never assume you are dealing with perpendicular lines unless the instruction specifically tell you are or you can identify the 90° angle. The standard notation for two lines that are perpendicular is $\overleftrightarrow{AB} \perp \overleftrightarrow{CD}$.

Line Intersection

A line intersection, as its name implies refers to the point where two lines, segments, or rays intersects. Perpendicular lines have an intersection point, but not all lines that intersect are perpendicular since they do not all form 90° angles.

Angles

Angles are formed when two lines intersect at a vertex, or point. Angles are measure in degrees and can be either acute, obtuse, right or straight. The measure of the angle determines its classification.

Type of Angle	Degree Measurement	Visual Representation
Acute	Acute angles are angles that measure less than 90°.	
Right	Right angles measure **exactly** 90°.	
Obtuse	Obtuse angles are angles that measure between 91° and 180°.	
Straight	Straight angles are angles that measures exactly 180°, so a straight line.	

Naming Angles

The typical naming convention for angles is to use the markers for the three points labeled on the triangle making sure to place the vertex in the middle. The common symbol to represent an angle is $\angle$.

This angle can be written as $\angle ABC$ or $\angle CBA$. This angle can also be simply named $\angle B$. However, only use this notation when there are no other angles that share B as the vertex.

Other types of Angles

Any time a line intersects another line, at least one angle is formed. Oftentimes questions will ask to you identify the measures of intersecting angles. Knowing a few fundamentals about different type of angles occurring on the same line and how they relate to each other will help you save a lot of time. Let's look at the key angle relationships.

Supplementary and Complementary Angles

Two angles with a sum of 180° are called **supplementary angles**.

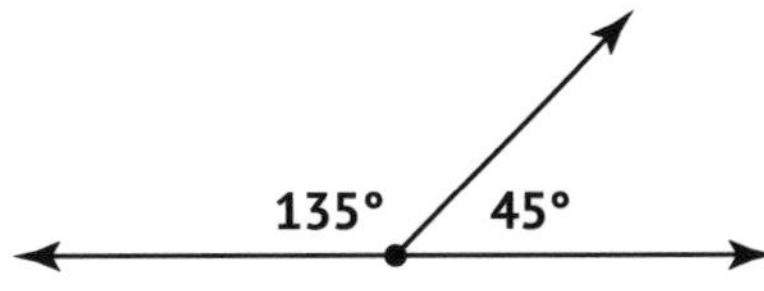

Two angles with a sum of 90° are called **complementary angles**.

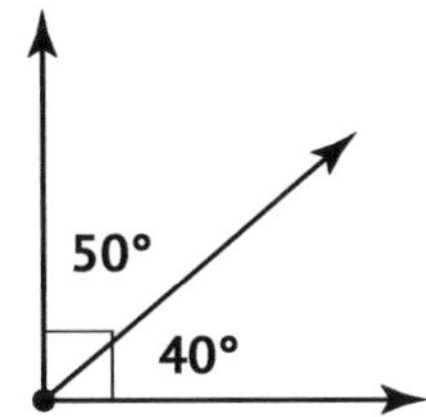

Vertical Angles

Two lines or line segments that intersect form **vertical angles**. Vertical angles, or opposite angles, are congruent and have the same angle measurement.

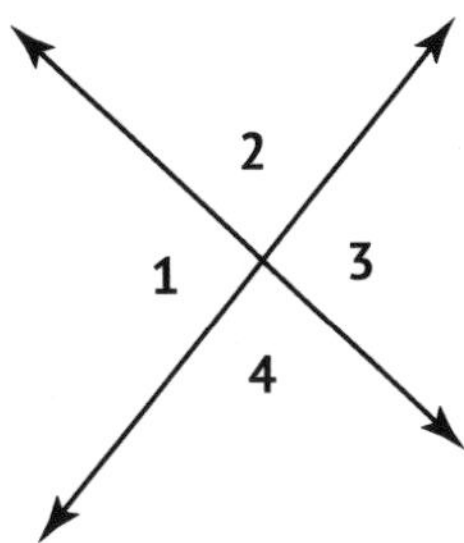

In the figure above, $\angle 2$ and $\angle 4$ are vertical angles. $\angle 1$ and $\angle 3$ are also vertical angles.

For example, if the $m\angle 4 = 50°$, then the $m\angle 2 = 50°$ since they are vertical angles. Moreover, if $m\angle 4 = 50°$, then $m\angle 1 = 130°$ because $\angle 4$ and $\angle 1$ are supplementary.

Adjacent Angles

Angles that share a common vertex are called **adjacent angles**. Take a look at the following example.

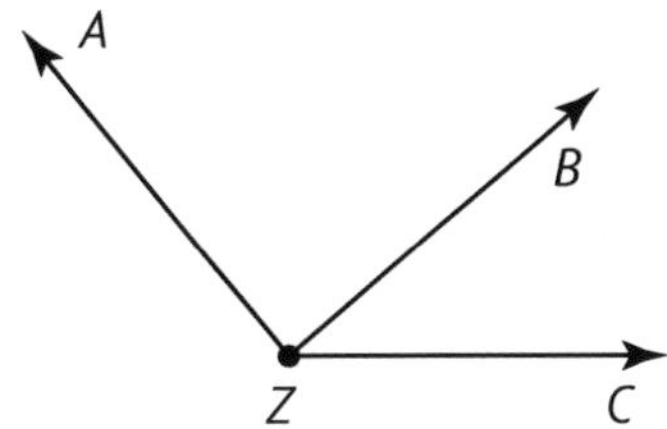

$\angle AZB$ and $\angle BZC$ are adjacent angles because they share a common vertex, Z.

Traversals

A transversal is a line that intersects two or more lines at two or more points.

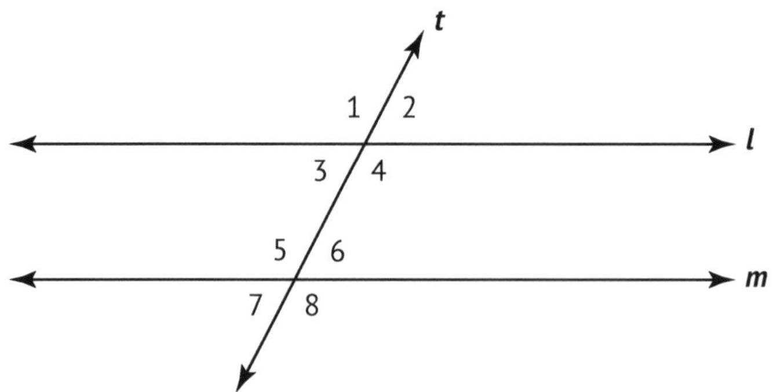

When a transversal intersects a pair of parallel lines, the resulting angles are related in some way:

- Angles 1, 4, 5, and 8 are equal.
- Angles 2, 3, 6, and 7 are equal.
- The sum of any two adjacent angles, like 1 and 2 or 7 and 8, equals 180° since they form a straight angle on a line.
- The sum of any large angle + any small angle = 180°, since the large and small angles in this figure combine into straight lines and all the large angles are equal and all the small angles are equal.

You will see these concepts of angles appear again in the next sections where we will explore properties and measurements of polygons.

Shapes

You will encounter a number of different types of polygons on the exam. A polygon is a two-dimensional enclosed figure with three or more straight sides. Polygons are named based on the number of sides they have.

Polygon Name	Number of Sides
Triangle	3
Quadrilateral	4
Pentagon	5
Hexagon	6
Heptagon	7
Octagon	8
Nonagon	9
Decagon	10
Dodecagon	12

Polygons can be either regular or irregular. Regular polygons have all equal sides and equal angles. Irregular polygons do not. It is important to understand the difference so that you do not make erroneous assumptions about the size of a figure that could lead you to an incorrect answer. The test questions will tell you if you are dealing with a regular or irregular polygon.

While all polygons are different in the number of sides they have, they do share some fundamental characteristics.

- The area of a polygon is the measure of the area of the region inside the polygon while the perimeter is the sum of all the sides
- A polygon with equal sides and equal interior angles is a regular polygon
- The sum of the exterior angles of any polygon is 360°
- The perimeter of a polygon is the sum of the lengths of its sides

Geometry questions will focus primarily on finding various measurements, like volume, area, and circumference, of the polygons. A majority of the polygons on the exams will be triangle and four-sided polygons, also known as quadrilaterals.

This section will look at the basic properties of polygons, and the formulas used to calculate the measurement of the sides and angles. It will also discuss circles and how to approach figures that include more than one polygon or circle. Triangles have many properties, rules, and calculations and merit a deeper review given their complexity and popularity on the exam. First, let's look at some general principles of quadrilaterals.

Quadrilaterals

Quadrilaterals are four-sided polygons. Quadrilaterals can be regular or irregular and the sum of their interior angles is 360°. The most common quadrilaterals tested on the exam are squares and rectangles. But, there are several other quadrilaterals you may encounter. Let's take a look.

Rectangles

A rectangle is a quadrilateral where the opposite sides are parallel and the interior angles are all right angles. The opposite sides of a rectangle are equal. The diagonals of a rectangle also have equal sides.

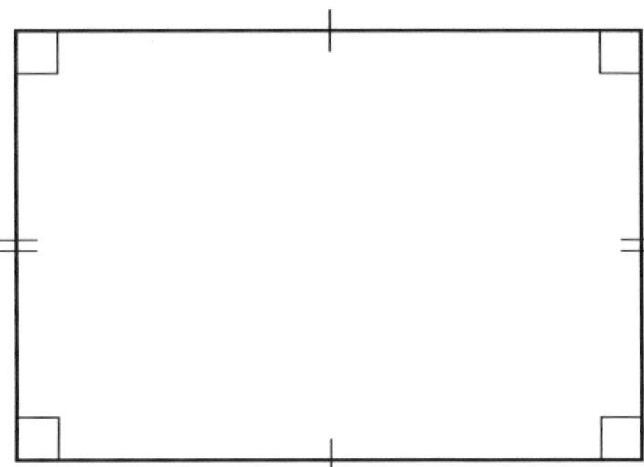

Area of a Rectangle

The formula for the area of a rectangle is:

$$area = base \cdot height$$

To calculate, multiply the length by the width to determine the area of a rectangle.

Diagonals of a Rectangle

The two diagonals of a rectangle are always equal to each other. Both diagonals divide the rectangle into two equal right triangles. Since the diagonals of the rectangle form right triangles that include the diagonal and two sides of the rectangle, if you know two of the values, you can calculate the third with the Pythagorean equation, which we will discuss later.

Square

A square is rectangle with four equal sides. All squares are rectangles but not all rectangles are squares.

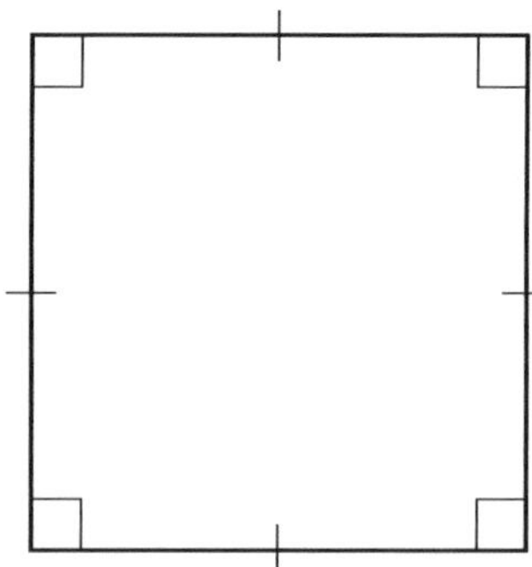

Area of a Square

The formula for the area of a square is:

$$area = s^2$$

In the formula, *s* is the length of a side. Since the sides of a square are all equal, all you need is one side to find the area.

Diagonals of a Square

The diagonals of a square bisect each other at right angles and have equal lengths.

The diagonals also cut the square into two 45-45-90 triangles. So, if you know the length of one side of the square, you can calculate the length of the diagonal.

Parallelogram

A parallelogram is a quadrilateral with two sets of parallel and equal sides. The length and width do not need to be the same in a parallelogram but the opposing sides will always be equal and the adjacent angles will be supplementary.

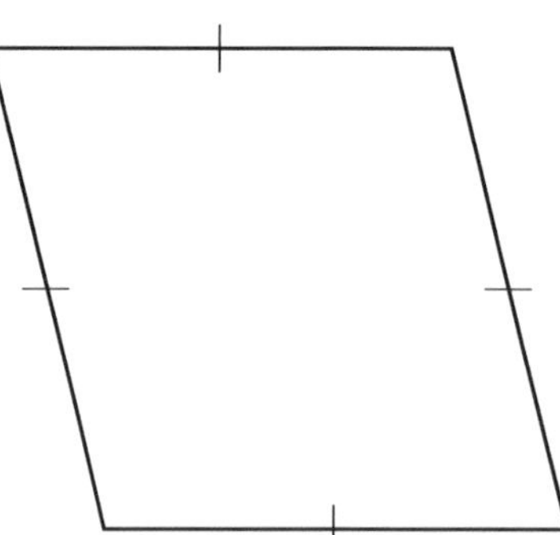

Area of a Parallelogram

The area of a parallelogram is determined by the formula:

$$area = b \cdot h$$

In the formula, *b* is the length of the base and h is the height.

Diagonals of a Parallelogram

The diagonals of a parallelogram divide the figure into two congruent triangles.

Polygon Angles

The sum of the angles inside of a polygon, interior angles, is determined by the number of sides in the figure; this holds for regular and irregular polygons. The figures you will see most often on the exam, triangles and quadrilaterals, both have set measures for their interior angles. Triangles will always total 180 degrees and quadrilaterals will total 360 degrees.

You can always figure out the total measurement of the internal angles of a polygon by using the formula:

$$(n - 2) \cdot 180$$

n equals the number of sides

Triangles

Triangles are three-sided polygons with three straight sides. The sum of the interior angles adds up to 180 degrees. The height of the triangle in the perpendicular distance from the vertex to opposite leg and can be found inside or outside of the triangle.

Area of a Triangle

The formula for the area of a triangle is:

$$area = \frac{1}{2} base \bullet height$$

You must plug in the correct values for the base and height; they are specific parts of the triangle, not just any two sides like some of the other polygons.

Equilateral Triangles

An equilateral triangle has three equal sides and three equal angles:

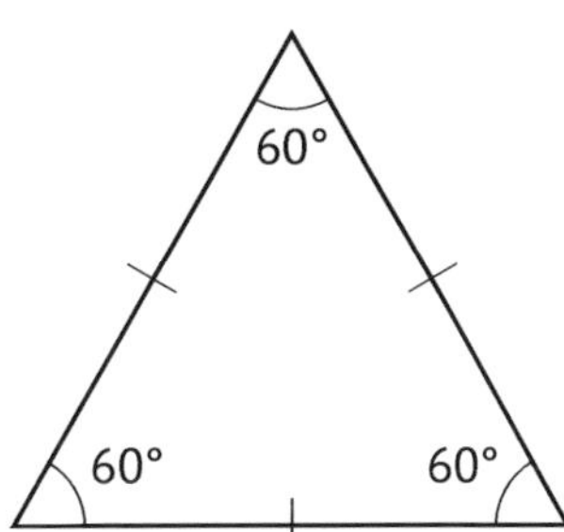

Once you know the length of one side of triangle or you realize you have two 60 degree angles, you can assume you are dealing with an equilateral triangle.

Isosceles Triangles

An isosceles triangle has two equal sides and two equal angles.

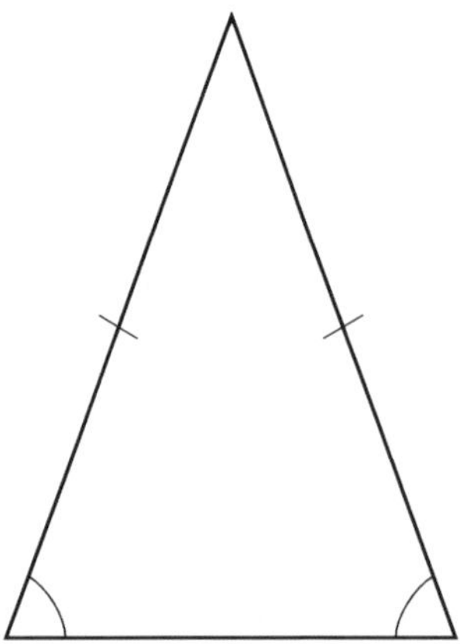

The two equal angles are opposite of the two equal sides. The sides opposite equal angles are always equal, and the angles opposite equal sides are always equal.

Right Triangles

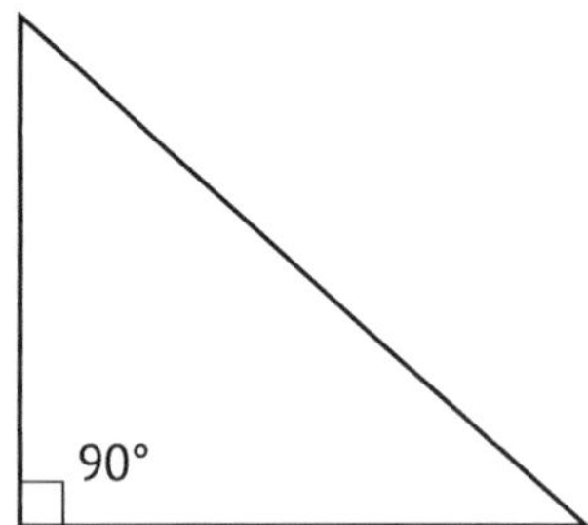

Right triangles are tested more than any type of triangle on the exam. A right triangle is any triangle that contains a right angle. The side opposite the right angle is the hypotenuse. The other two sides are called legs. The remaining two angles add up to 90 degrees.

Right Triangles and the Pythagorean Theorem

The Pythagorean theorem is one of the most tested theories on the exam, which makes sense since its only applies to right triangles and right triangles are tested frequently. The theory establishes the relationship of the legs to the hypotenuse.

$$a^2 + b^2 = c^2$$

In this equation, **a** and **b** are the legs and **c** is the hypotenuse. Plug in the values you know, then solve.

Pythagorean Triples

Since right triangles adhere to the Pythagorean theorem, they rarely yield integers for the lengths of the legs. But, a few integer triplets perfectly conform to the theorem. These are referred to as Pythagorean triples. The ones you will see on the exam include:

- 3, 4, 5
- 5, 12, 13
- 7, 24, 25
- 8, 15, 17

Also note that any multiples of these triples conform. For example, 6, 8, 10 are multiples of the triples 3, 4, 5. Memorizing these will help you identify measurements and answer questions more quickly.

Circles

Circles are not polygons because they do not have straight sides. Circles are tested on the exam and you will mainly be asked, like with the other polygons, to find some part of its measurements. Here are some quick facts about circles:

- All circles contain 360°
- The distance from the center to any point on the circle is called the radius. The radius of a circle is a critical piece of because if you know a circle's radius, you can figure out all its other measurements.
- The diameter of a circle stretches between endpoints on the circle and passes through the center.
- A chord also extends from endpoint to endpoint on the circle, but it does not necessarily pass through the center.
- In the figure below, point C is the center of the circle, *r* is the radius, and AB is a chord.

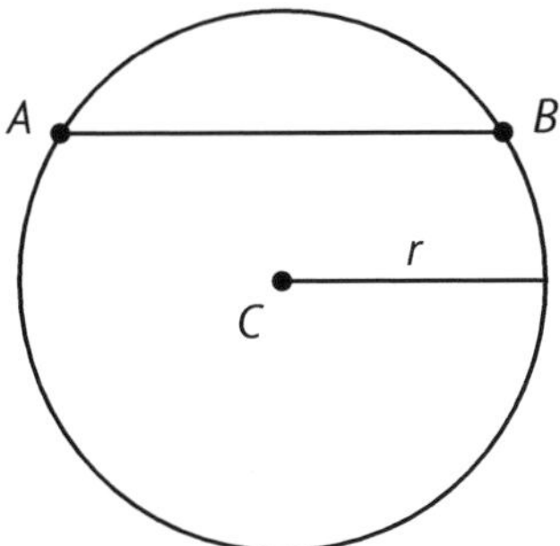

Circumference of a Circle

The circumference is the distance around the circle. The formula for circumference of a circle is:

$$circumference = 2\square r$$

The standard value for pi on the exam is 3.14.

Area of a Circle

The formula for area is:

$$area = \square r^2$$

In this formula, *r* is the radius. So when you need to find the area of a circle, your real goal is to figure out the radius. For an added challenged, sometimes a question may give you the diameter or the circumference and you will need to calculate the radius (half the diameter) to solve for the area.

Rectangular Solids

A rectangular solid is a prism with a rectangular base and edges that are perpendicular to its base.

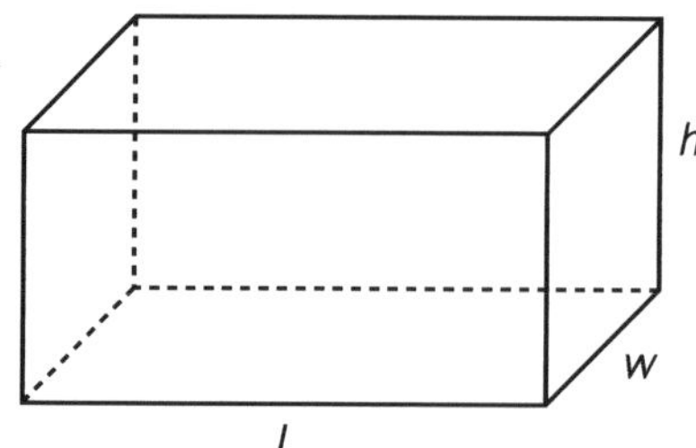

A rectangular solid has three key dimensions, length, width, and height. If you know these three measurements, you can find the solid's volume and surface area using the following formulas:

Surface area: $A = 2wl + 2lh + 2hw$
Volume: volume = lwh

Cubes

A cube is a three-dimensional square with sides that are all equal. Cubes have six faces, each of which is a square, meaning the length, width, and height are equal.

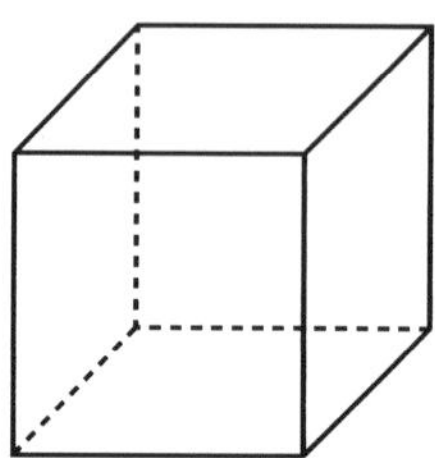

Volume of a Cube

$$volume = s^3$$

Once you know one side of the cube, you can easily calculate the volume. So, if the measure one side is 4, the volume would be 4^3 or 64.

Surface Area of a Cube

$$volume = 6s^2$$

A cube is a rectangular solid with 6 equal sides. To find the surface area, you will need to take the sum of all the faces. Since all the sides are the same, the above formula to simplify the calculation. Using the previous example, if the length of one side is 4, the surface area of the cube would be: $6(4)^2 = 96$.

Right Circular Cylinders

A right circular cylinder is a geometric solid that has two circular bases. A right circular cylinder has a lateral measurement, and its height contains a rectangle.

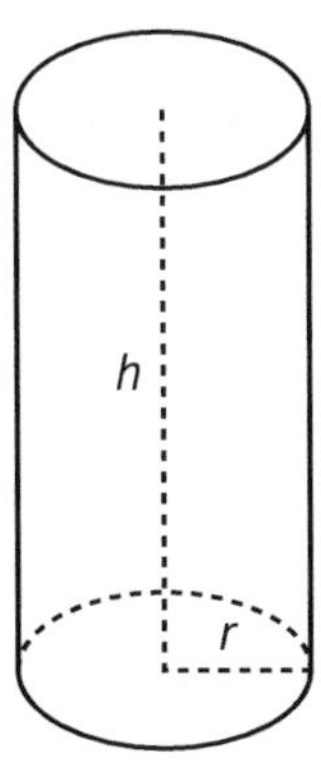

The only measurement you will be asked to calculate for right cylinders is the volume.

$$volume = \square r^2 h$$

Now, let's look at a few of the concepts not covered in the previous sections that are related specifically to data interpretation questions you might see on the exam.

Data Interpretation

Data interpretation questions test your ability to derive information from graphs, charts, and other visual displays. Data interpretation questions are more of an extension of problem-solving questions than a unique question type or concept. For these questions, you will interpret data from charts, graphs, and other images and use this information to solve for the correct answer. A sub-section of Problem-Solving questions, these questions have a variety of answer choice options and can have more than one correct answer. Remember, you need to select all the correct answers in order to receive credit for the question.

This section will provide a brief overview of central tendency, probability, and frequency distributions. Data interpretation is so closely linked to the concepts in the other chapters; so much of the concepts tested for data interpretation fall under the previous sections of this guide. Data interpretation questions simply test your ability to apply those concepts to a variety of situations.

Measures of Central Tendency

Measures of central tendency identify the location of center distributions of values in an attempt to make data more understandable and allow for more accurate interpretation. The three main measures of central tendency: the mean, median, and mode.

Mean

The mean, or the average as it is commonly referred to, is the sum of all terms divided by the number of all terms. To express the mean as an equation, simply set the mean equal to its relationship with the terms in the data set:

$$mean = \frac{sum\ of\ terms}{number\ of\ terms}$$

Suppose on your last four statistics exams, you received the following scores: 84, 92, 93, 87. If you wanted to find the mean of your scores, calculate using the equation for the mean:

$$mean = \frac{84+92+93+87}{4} = \frac{356}{4} = 89$$

Sometimes, instead of all the terms, a test question might provide you with the mean and ask you to identify the other values. Like with other equations you have seen, you can rearrange, simplify, and substitute to arrive at your answer.

Median

The median of a set of data is the middle term when the numbers are written in order. For example, to calculate the median of the group 7, 12, 14, 6, 4, 3, 17, you would first list the numbers in order.

3, 4, 6, 7, 12, 14, 17

Then find the middle number, which is in this case is 7. If two numbers are left in the middle, take the mean of those numbers to determine the median.

Mode

The mode is simply the number that occurs the most. In the group 1, 2, 3, 3, 3, 3, 4, 7
The mode is 3 since it appears the most in the group.

Range

The range of a data set is the difference between the largest term and the smallest term. For example, the range of 12, −24, 13, 2, and 4 is 13 − (−24) = 37.

Probability

Probability is the measure of the number of specific outcomes compared to the number of possible outcomes:

$$p = \frac{\#\ of\ specific\ outcomes}{\#\ of\ possible\ outcomes}$$

If you have 10 cookies in a bag: 3 chocolate chip, 2 oatmeal, 4 lemon, and 1 peanut butter, the probability of you reaching in the bag and selecting a lemon cookie is $\frac{4}{10}$ or $\frac{2}{5}$. Probability can be written as a fractions or a decimal.

You may be asked to determine multiple-event probability. For example, the probability of reaching into the bag of cookies a second time and grabbing a lemon cookie. In these instances, you must find the probability for each event and then multiply them.

Frequency Table/Frequency Distribution

A frequency distribution is a table used to describe a data set. Its also lists intervals or ranges of data values called data classes together with the number of data values from the set that are in each class.

Consider this example: Suppose that the exam scores of 20 psychology students are as follows:

97, 92, 88, 75, 83, 67, 89, 55, 72, 78, 81, 91, 57, 63, 67, 74, 87, 84, 98, 46

You can construct a frequency table with classes 90-99, 80-89, 70-79 etc., by counting the number of grades in each grade range.

Class	Frequency (f)
90-99	4
80-89	6
70-79	4
60-69	3
50-59	2
40-49	1

Note that the sum of the frequency column is equal to 20, the number of test scores.

ARGO
BROTHERS

14 PRACTICE PROBLEM SET

The Math Primer walked you through key concepts in arithmetic, algebra, and geometry in order to prepare you tackle questions that will appear on the Quantitative Reasoning section on the exam. The following problems test your understanding of these concepts. The problems primarily ask you to perform calculations of values like area and volume, and to simplify and solve equations. While some these questions appear as they will on the exam, the primary purpose of this section is reinforce the key concepts discussed in the primer.

Evaluate each expression.

1. $(-1) + (-3)$

2. $(-6) + (-6)$

3. $1 - 2$

4. $(-2) + (-5)$

5. $\left(-\frac{3}{2}\right)+\left(-\frac{3}{2}\right)$

6. $\left(-3\frac{3}{8}\right)-3\frac{7}{8}$

7. $6-\frac{4}{5}$

8. $4\frac{7}{8}-\frac{5}{4}$

9. $2-\frac{10}{-2}$

10. $(-2)\left(\frac{4}{2}\right)$

11. $(-3 + -6 - 3)(-3)$

12. $(2)(6 + -3 - 2)$

13. $3\frac{1}{4}+1\frac{3}{5}$

15. $\frac{1}{2}+\frac{3}{4}$

14. $4\frac{2}{3}+4\frac{5}{6}$

16. $3\frac{1}{3}+\frac{1}{4}$

Find each quotient.

17. $\frac{14}{9}\div\frac{-6}{7}$

18. $\frac{-3}{4}\div 2$

Find each product.

19. $-1\frac{8}{9}\bullet\frac{7}{10}$

20. $1\frac{2}{5}\bullet-\frac{7}{4}$

Simplify. Your answer should contain only positive exponents.

21. $4n^2 \bullet 8n$

23. $7m^2 \bullet 7m^4$

22. $8n \bullet 6n^2 \bullet 3n^2$

24. $4n^2 \bullet 2n^2$

25. $-8k^3 \cdot 4k^2$

26. $6x \cdot -7x^4$

27. $-6 \cdot (-6)^2 \cdot (-6)^3$

28. $-2 \cdot (-2)^3$

Find each square root.

29. $\sqrt{64}$

30. $\sqrt{121}$

31. $\sqrt{49}$

32. $\sqrt{144}$

Solve each equation.

33. $|-9x| = 36$

34. $|-8a| = 48$

35. $\left|\frac{r}{8}\right| = 2$

36. $|2k| = 12$

Solve each inequality and graph its solution.

37. $|9m| \le 63$

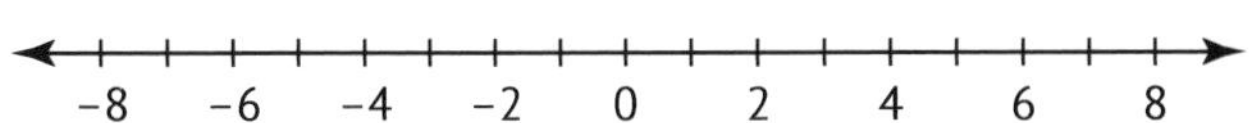

38. $\left|\frac{v}{9}\right| > 2$

−20 −15 −10 −5 0 5 10 15 20

39. $|2 + n| \le 10$

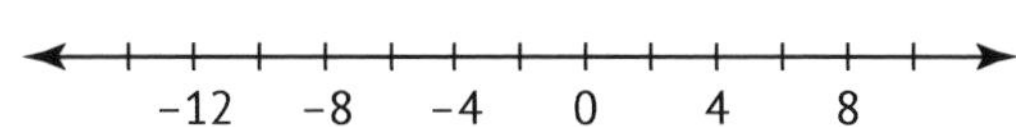

40. $|3x| \le 3$

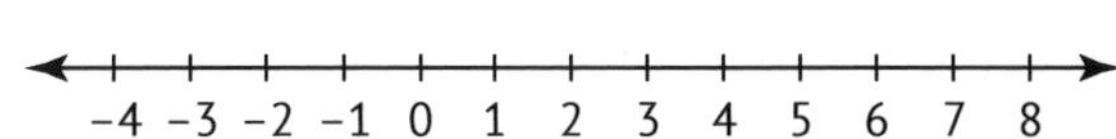

Simplify each expression.

41. $4 - 2(a + 2)$

42. $6x - 2(7 - x)$

43. $5n + 5(1 - 4n)$

44. $-10(1 - 5k) - 8$

Solve.

45. $(36n^6 + 3n^5 + 27n^4) \div 9n$

46. $(36n^3 + 27n^2 + 5n) \div 9n^3$

47. $(2n^3 + 10n^2 + 50n) \div 10n$

48. $(5x^3 + 3x^2 + 6x) \div 6x^3$

Simplify.

49. $\frac{3}{3+2\sqrt{5}}$

50. $\frac{4}{-1+5\sqrt{2}}$

Solve each equation.

51. $-123 = -6 + 3(-8m - 7)$

53. $5(6 - 6x) = -120$

52. $6(7 - 7k) = 336$

54. $266 = 7(3 - 7a)$

Solve each equation by factoring.

55. $x^2 = 6x$

57. $p^2 = 10\,p - 16$

56. $n^2 + 10n = -21$

58. $x^2 + 2x = 8$

Factor each completely.

59. $7x^3 - 14x^2 + x - 2$

60. $15a^3 + 9a^2 + 10a + 6$

Find the slope of each line.

61.

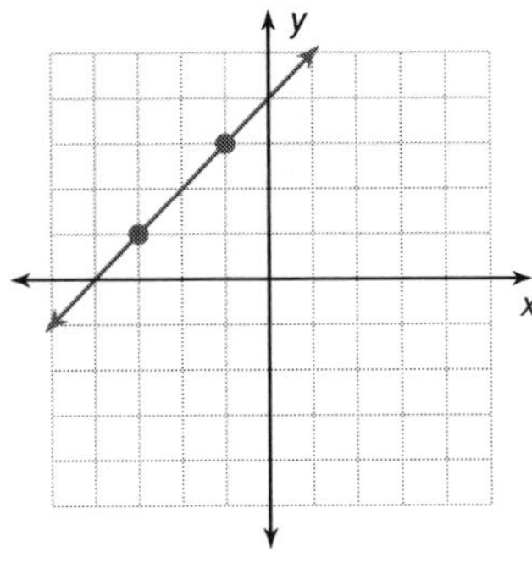

63.

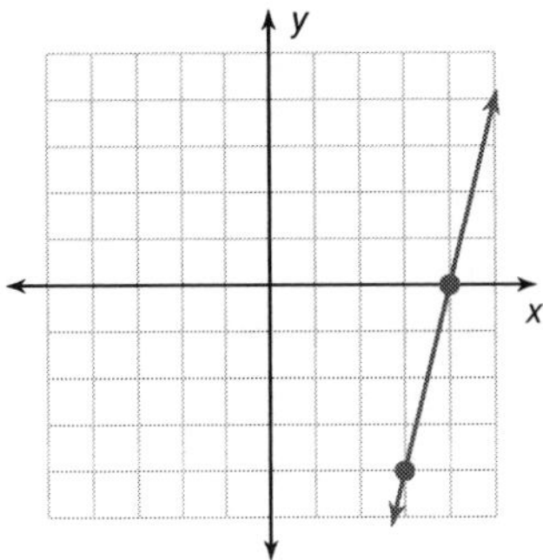

62.

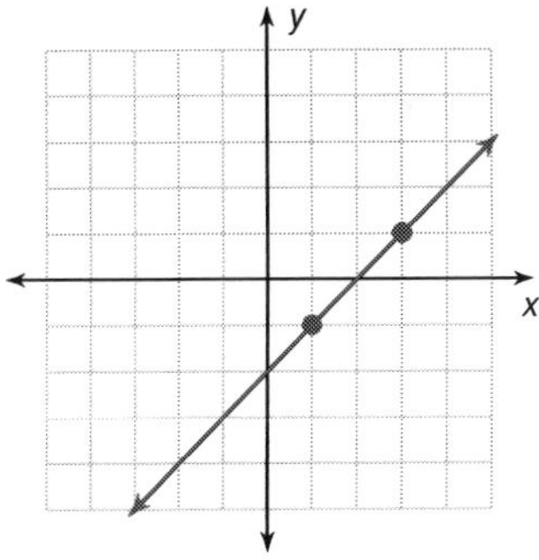

64.

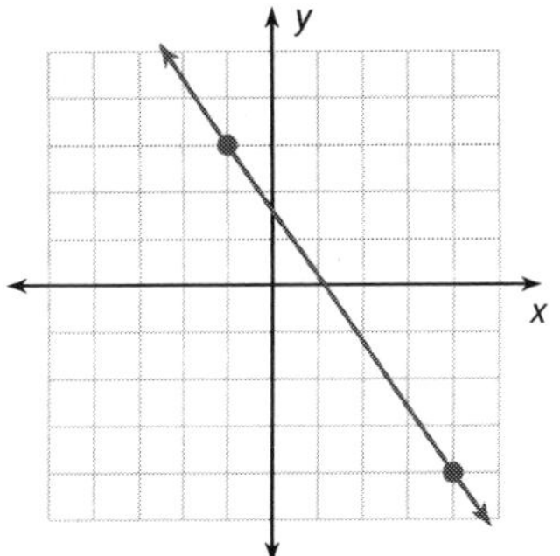

Find the slope of the line through each pair of points.

65. (−17, 13), (−18, 14)

66. (16, 5), (−7, −10)

67. Castel traveled to the ferry office and back. The trip there took five hours and the trip back took six hours. What was Castel' average speed on the trip there if he averaged 30 km/h on the return trip?

68. Lisa left the science museum and drove west. Willie left one hour later driving at 45 mph in an effort to catch up to Lisa. After driving for two hours Willie finally caught up. Find Lisa's average speed.

Solve each question. Round your answer to the nearest hundredth.

69. Ming can pick forty bushels of apples in 10 hours. Imani can pick the same amount in 13 hours. If they worked together how long would it take them to pick 40 bushels?

70. Working alone, Imani can pick forty bushels of apples in 8 hours. Nicole can pick the same amount in 13 hours. Find how long it would take them if they worked together.

Find the measure of angle b.

71.

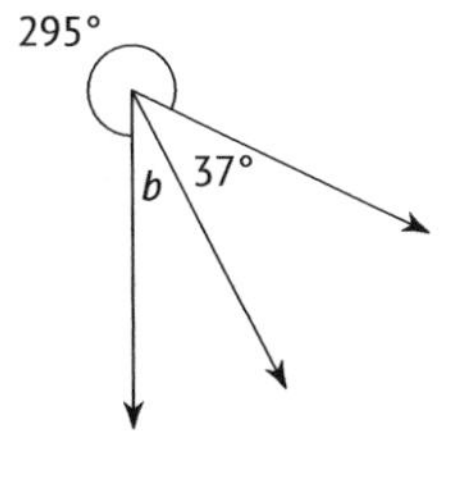

72.

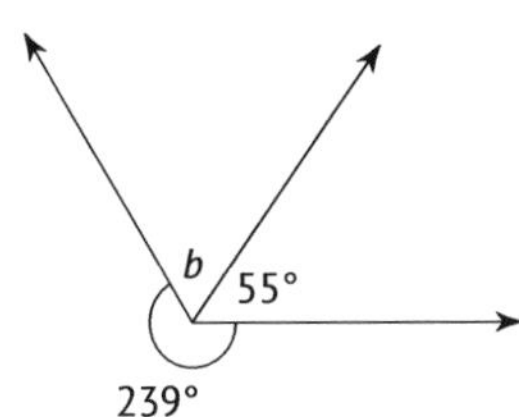

73.

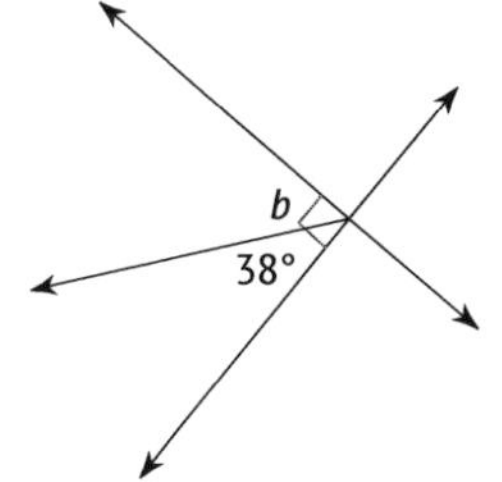

74.

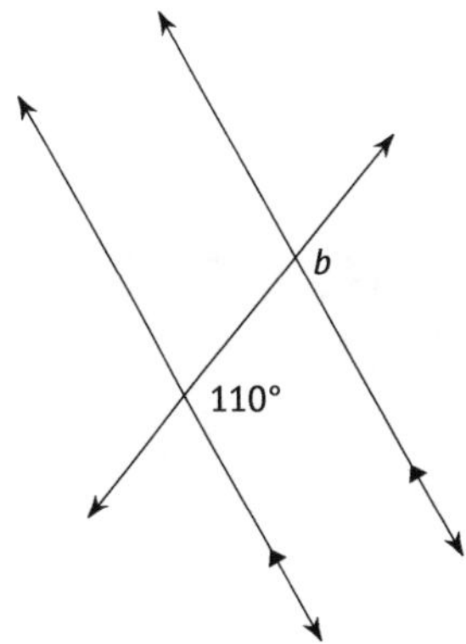

75.

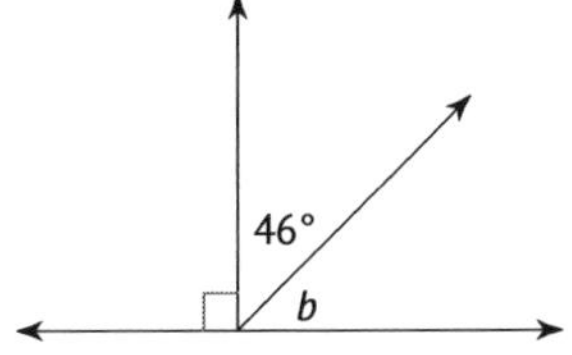

76.

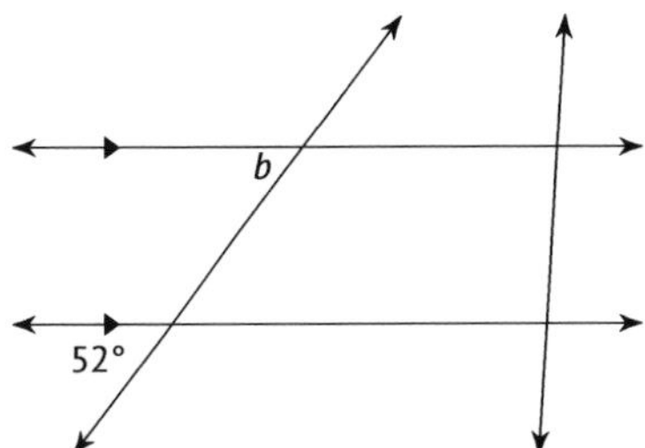

Find the measure of each missing angle.

77.

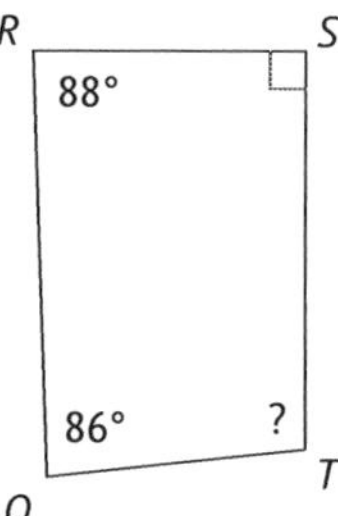

79.

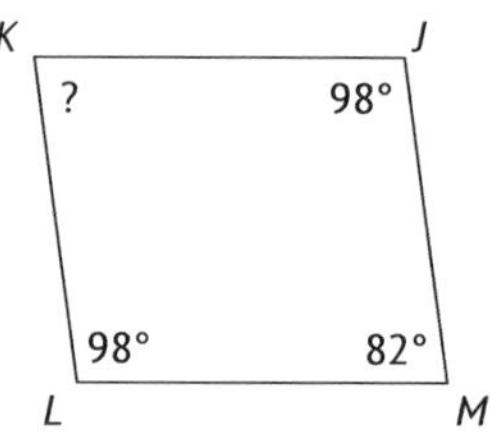

78.

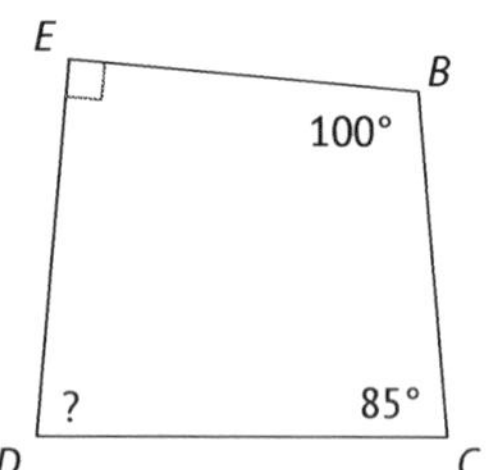

80.

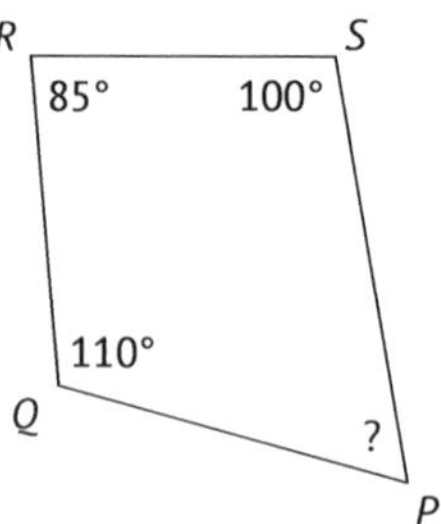

Find the area.

81.

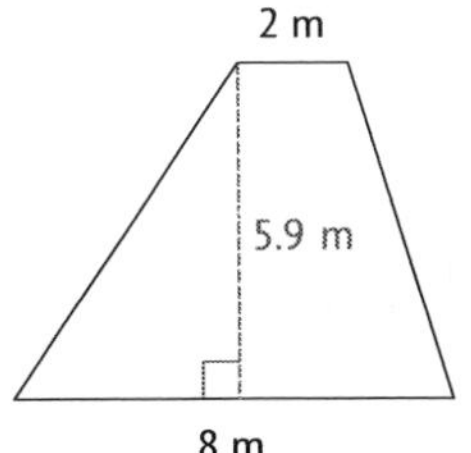

84.

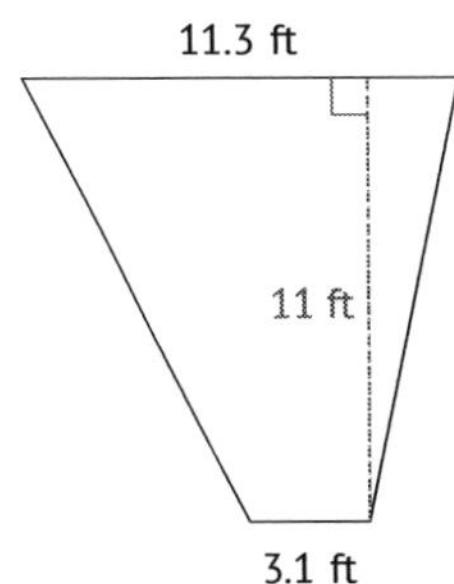

82.

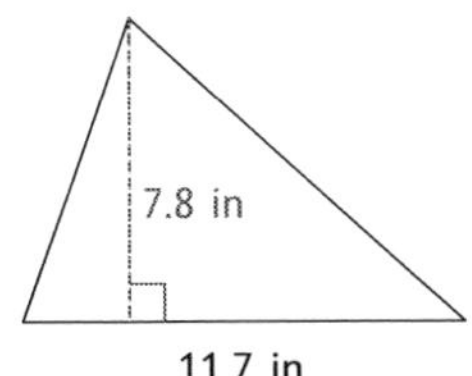

85.

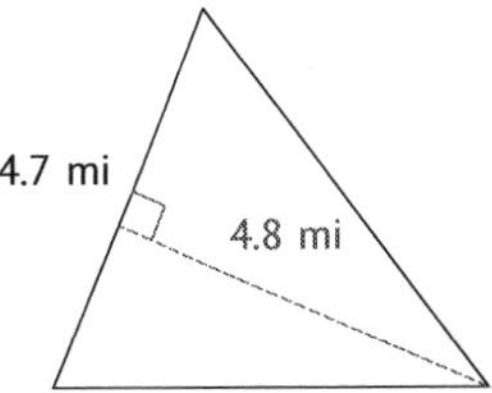

83.

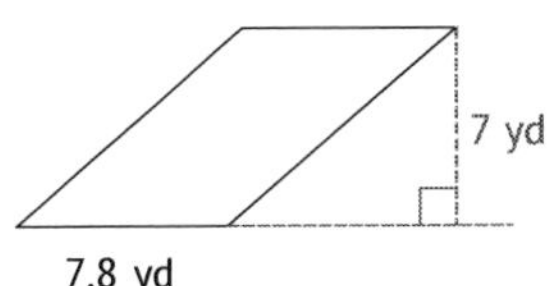

86.

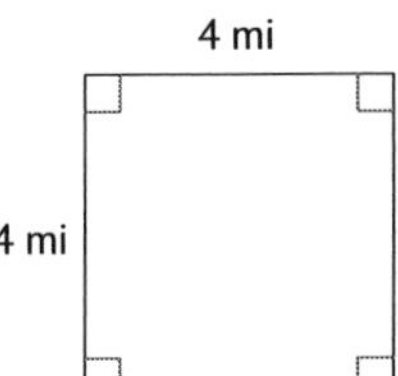

Find the measure of the arc or central angle indicated. Assume that lines which appear to be diameters are actual diameters.

87. $m\overset{\frown}{SU}$

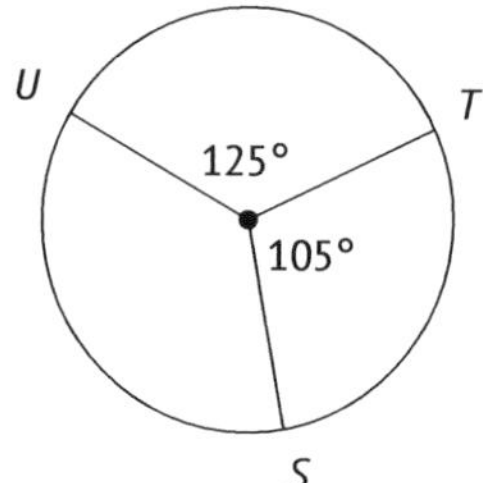

88. $m\angle TRU$

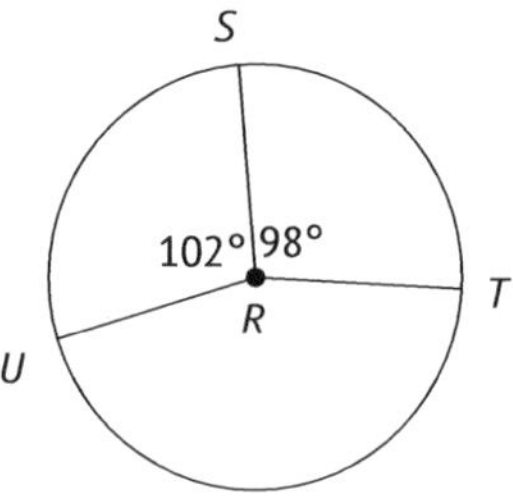

Find the circumference.

89.

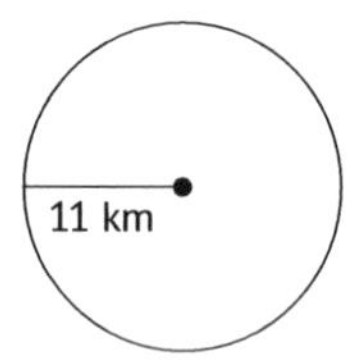

90.

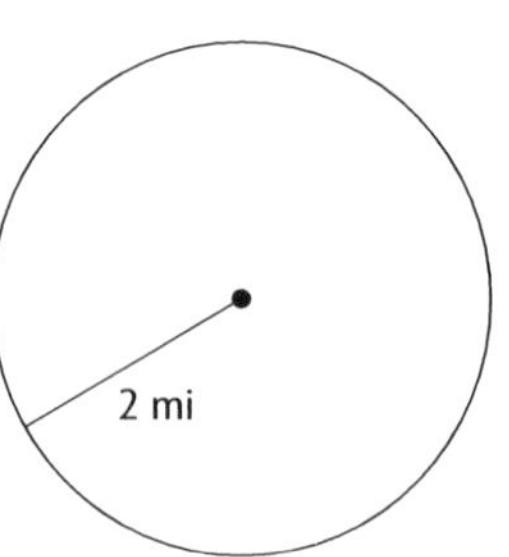

91. area = 49□ ft^2

92. area = 81□ ft^2

Find the radius of each circle.

93. area = 36□ km^2

94. area = 100□ m^2

Find the diameter of each circle.

95. area = 25□ yd^2

96. area = 144□ m^2

Find the probability of each event.

97. A car dealership has nine cars in the lot. Unfortunately, the keys to the cars have been mixed up. The manager randomly grabs a key and tries to start a car. A salesman also randomly picks a different key and tries to start another car. What is the probability that both cars start?

98. Jimmy and Heather each purchase one raffle ticket. If a total of fourteen raffle tickets are sold and two winners will be selected, what is the probability that both Jimmy and Heather win?

99. A basketball player has a 50% chance of making each free throw. What is the probability that the player makes at most four out of six free throws?

A. $\frac{29}{128} \approx 22.656\%$

B. $\frac{247}{256} \approx 96.484\%$

C. $\frac{57}{64} \approx 89.063\%$

D. $\frac{191}{256} \approx 74.609\%$

100. A gardener has thirteen identical-looking tulip bulbs, of which eight will produce yellow tulips and five will become pink. He randomly selects and plants five of them and then gives the rest away. When the flowers start to bloom, what is the probability that exactly three of them are yellow?

A. $\frac{175}{572} \approx 30.594\%$

B. $\frac{560}{1287} \approx 43.512\%$

C. $\frac{10}{21} \approx 47.619\%$

D. $\frac{25}{77} \approx 32.468\%$

Find the volume of each figure.

101.

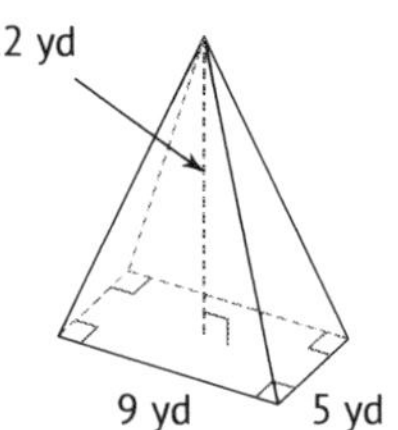

103.

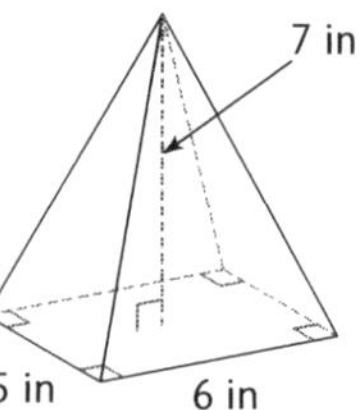

102.

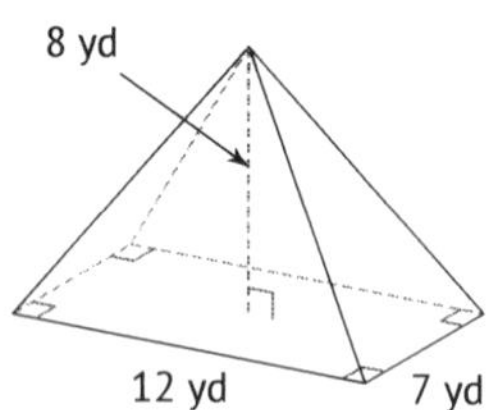

104.

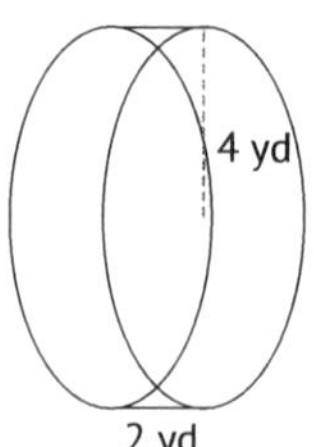

Find the distance between each pair of points.

105. (7, −1), (7, 7)

106. (8, −2), (1, −3)

Find the value of *x*.

107.

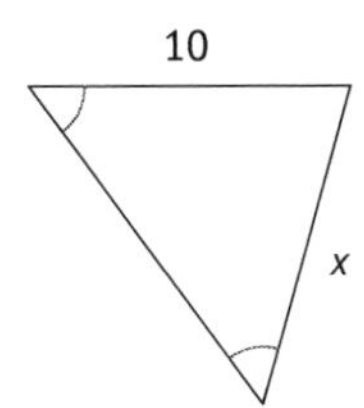

108.

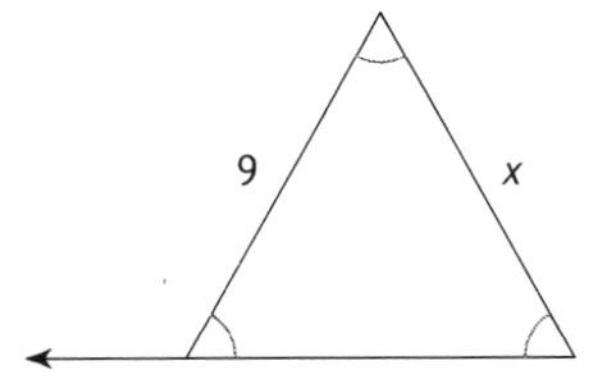

109.

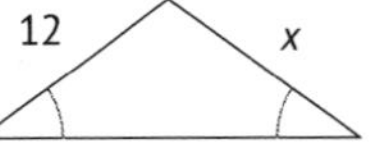

110.

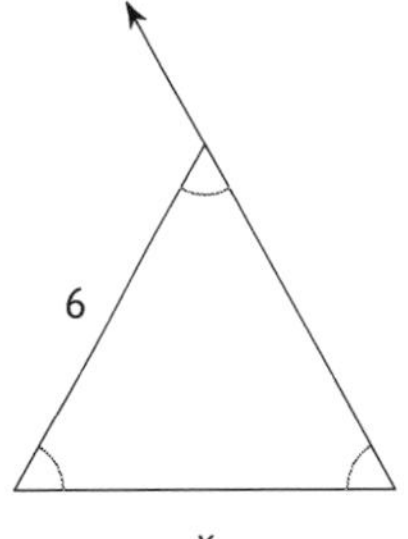

Find the midpoint of each line segment.

111.

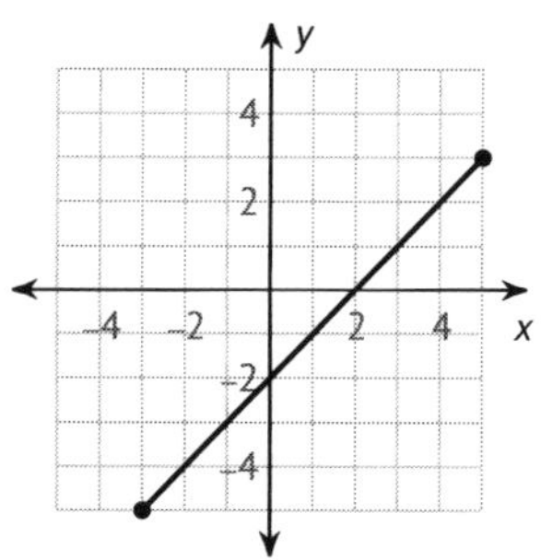

112.

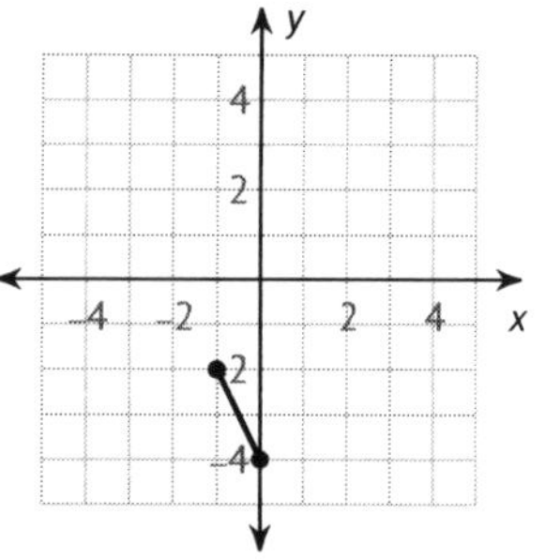

Find the missing side of each triangle.

113.

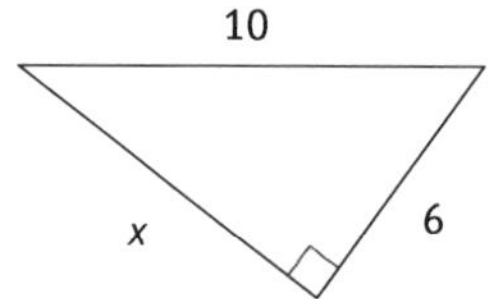

114.

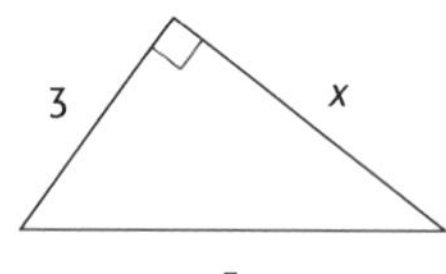

115.

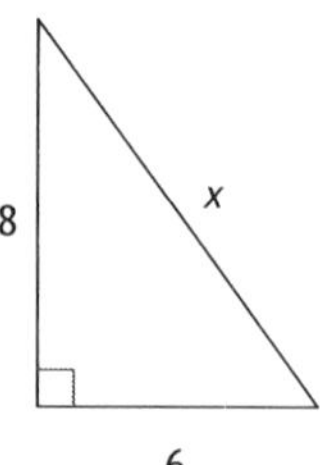

116.

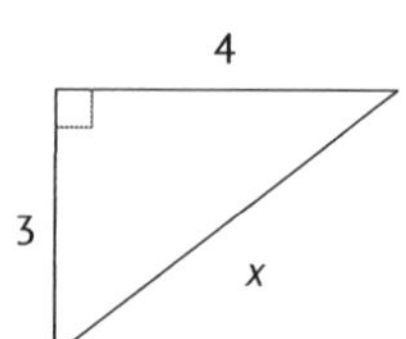

Find the area.

117.

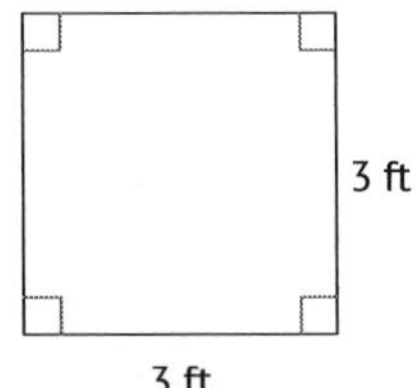

Find the missing side lengths. Leave your answers as radicals in simplest form.

118.

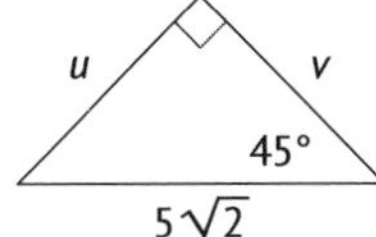

119.

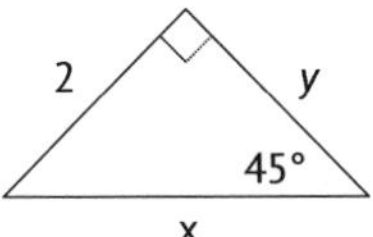

120.

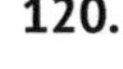

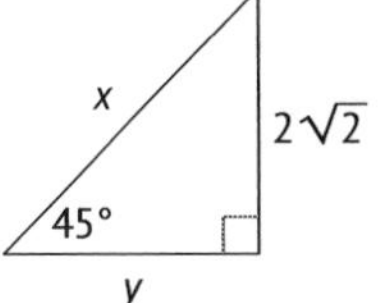

1. -4

2. -12

3. -1

4. -7

5. -3

6. $-7\frac{1}{4}$

7. $5\frac{1}{5}$

8. $3\frac{5}{8}$

9. 7

10. -4

11. 36

12. 2

13. $4\frac{17}{20}$

14. $9\frac{1}{2}$

15. $1\frac{1}{4}$

16. $3\frac{7}{12}$

17. $-1\frac{22}{27}$

18. $-\frac{3}{8}$

19. $-1\frac{29}{90}$

20. $-2\frac{9}{20}$

21. $32n^3$

22. $144n^5$

23. $49m^6$

24. $8n^4$

25. $-32k^5$

26. $-42x^5$

27. $(-6)^6$

28. $(-2)^4$

29. 8

30. 11

31. 7

32. 12

33. $\{-4, 4\}$

34. $\{-6, 6\}$

35. $\{16, -16\}$

36. $\{6, -6\}$

37. $-7 \le m \le 7$:

−8 −6 −4 −2 0 2 4 6 8

38. $v > 18$ or $v < -18$:

−20 −15 −10 −5 0 5 10 15 20

39. $-12 \le n \le 8$:

−12 −8 −4 0 4 8

40. $-1 \le x \le 1$:

−4 −3 −2 −1 0 1 2 3 4 5 6 7 8

41. $-2a$

42. $8x - 14$

43. $-15n + 5$

44. $-18 + 50k$

45. $4n^5 + \frac{n^4}{3} + 3n^3$

46. $4 + \frac{3}{n} + \frac{5}{9n^2}$

47. $\frac{n^2}{5} + n + 5$

48. $\frac{5}{6} + \frac{1}{2x} + \frac{1}{x^2}$

49. $\frac{-9 + 6\sqrt{5}}{11}$

50. $\frac{4 + 20\sqrt{2}}{49}$

51. $\{4\}$

52. $\{-7\}$

53. $\{5\}$

54. $\{-5\}$

55. $\{6, 0\}$

56. $\{-3, -7\}$

57. $\{8, 2\}$

58. $\{2, -4\}$

59. $(7x^2+1)(x - 2)$

60. $(3a^2 + 2)(5a + 3)$

61. 1

62. 1

63. 4

64. $-\frac{7}{5}$

65. -1

66. $\frac{15}{23}$

67. 36 km/h

68. 30 mph

69. 5.65 hours

70. 4.95 hours

71. 28°

72. 66°

73. 52°

74. 110°

75. 44°

76. 52°

77. 96°

78. 85°

79. 82°

80. 65°

81. 29.5 m^2

82. 45.63 in^2

83. 54.6 yd^2

84. 79.2 ft^2

85. 11.28 mi^2

86. 16 mi^2

87. 130°

88. 160°

89. 22□ km

90. 4□ mi

91. 14□ ft

92. 18□ ft

93. 6 km

94. 10 m

95. 10 yd

96. 24 m

97. $\frac{1}{72} \approx 1.389\%$

98. $\frac{1}{91} \approx 1.099\%$

99. C

100. B

101. 180 yd^3

102. 224 yd^3

103. 70 in^3

104. 100.53 yd^3

105. 8

106. $5\sqrt{2}$

107. 10

108. 9

109. 12

110. 6

111. (1, −1)

112. (−0.5, −3)

113. 8

114. 4

115. 10

116. 5

117. 9 ft^2

118. $u = 5$, $v = 5$

119. $x = 2\sqrt{2}$, $y = 2$

120. $x = 4$, $y = 2\sqrt{2}$

ARGO
BROTHERS

15 | QUANTITATIVE COMPARISON

Quantitative Comparison: The Basics

Quantitative Reasoning questions require you to compare two quantities and assess their relationship to each other if there is enough information to do so. Each section of Quantitative Reasoning has seven or eight Quantitative Comparison questions that typically occur near the beginning of the section.

The presentation of Quantitative Comparison questions and their answer choices will always be the same. You will be given two columns, each with the given quantity, and you will choose from the same four standard answer choices. Some questions will provide you with additional information to consider; this information should be applied to the quantities in both columns before you select an answer choice. Oftentimes, the questions have variables but do not include sufficient information to solve for those variables. This is not a problem in this section since you are not solving for a value in Quantitative Comparison question. Instead, you are looking to determine how the quantities in the two columns relate.

This chapter will help you understand Quantitative Comparisons and discuss strategies to attack the question quickly and accurately.

> **Prep Tip:** Quantitative Reasoning questions are the only questions on the exam that present you with the same four answer choices each time. Memorize these to save time!

Sample Quantitative Comparison Problem

$$\frac{x}{y} = \frac{3}{4}$$

Column A	Column B
$\frac{2x-y}{y}$	$\frac{x}{x+y}$

A. Quantity A is greater
B. Quantity B is greater
C. The two quantities are equal
D. The relationship cannot be determined from the information given

As you can see, Quantity A and Quantity B are listed in separate columns. You are given additional information: $\frac{x}{y} = \frac{3}{4}$ to consider when analyzing the relationship of Quantity A and Quantity B. These instructions should be applied to both quantities before you make a comparison. Remember, you are not looking for a value but rather an understanding of how the two columns relate. All Quantitative Comparison questions will mirror this sample, though some of them may not have the additional information listed at the top.

Answer Choices

Quantitative Comparison Answer Choices

A. Quantity A is greater
B. Quantity B is greater
C. The two quantities are equal
D. The relationship cannot be determined from the information given

The answer choices for Quantitative Comparison questions will **always** be the same and will appear in the same order. Let's examine them a bit more closely.

Since these answer choices will not change, it is best to try to memorize them so you can navigate Quantitative Comparison questions more quickly. However, do not hesitate to refer back to the listing if you need to.

Quantity A is greater: (A) is the correct answer when the quantities are compared and any additional information is applied to both columns and the quantity of column A is greater.

Quantity B is greater: (B) is the correct answer when the quantities are compared and any additional information is applied to both columns and the quantity of column B is greater.

Quantities are Equal: (C) is the correct answer when the quantities are compared and any additional information is applied to both columns and the quantities of both columns are equal.

Not enough information: (D) is the correct answer when it is not possible to determine how the two quantities relate to each other. (D) is never the answer when both quantities are values. For example, if Quantity A = 10 and Quantity B = 2^5, (D) will not be the answer since we can solve it in its entirety and determine that 10 is less than 32 (2^5 solved). So, the answer would be (B).

Quantitative Comparison Strategies

We already discussed how knowing the answer choices ahead of time can help you quickly navigate through the questions. Don't forget that (D) should not be selected when both columns are determined values. Now, let's look at some other time-saving strategies to help you navigate the questions.

Substitute

If one or both of the quantities are algebraic expressions, substitute a variety of numbers in place of the variables and then compare the quantities. To confirm the comparison, be sure that the substitute numbers will create different outcomes like negative numbers, positive numbers, large numbers, and small numbers. Remember, zero is also a number and warrants consideration when comparing quantities. Consider all kinds of appropriate numbers before you give an answer: e.g., zero, positive and negative numbers, small and large numbers, fractions and decimals.

Size Up the Figures

You can expect to see geometric figures appear in Quantitative Comparison questions as well. One thing to keep in mind is that the shapes are not typically drawn to scale, and you should assume it is this way unless the instructions tell you so. When working with geometric figures, do not make presumptions based on how a figure "looks." Instead, be sure to use the given information and/or measurements to make your comparison.

> **Prep Tip:** When plugging in a variety of numbers (negatives, positives, large, small, etc.), if you discover that Quantity A is greater than Quantity B in one instance and Quantity B is greater than Quantity A in another case, it is not possible to determine the relationship between the quantities. Choose answer choice D and move on.

Simplify

Many of the Quantitative Comparison questions will have expressions that can be simplified. You generally will not have to perform all of the calculations necessary to reach a definitive answer. Simplify or estimate one or both of the quantities only as much as is necessary to compare them. Once you establish one is always greater or that the quantities must always be equal, you can stop and make your answer choice selection. Again, the goal is not to solve but to understand how the quantities compare.

Simplify by Elimination

Sometimes, quantities share similar terms that can help you simplify the equation in order to assess the comparison of the quantities. For example, if both columns featured $2x$, you could simply subtract it from the equations and evaluate the remainder of the expression.

Understand the Centered Information

Remember that sometimes a question will provide you with additional information to consider when comparing the quantities. This information will always be centered and positioned atop the two columns. You must consider this information and apply it to **both** quantities.

Let's revisit the sample program we saw earlier to better understand how to work with this information.

$$\frac{x}{y}=\frac{3}{4}$$

Column A	Column B
$\frac{2x-y}{y}$	$\frac{x}{x+y}$

A. Quantity A is greater
B. Quantity B is greater
C. The two quantities are equal
D. The relationship cannot be determined from the information given

In this example, you are given additional information: $\frac{x}{y}=\frac{3}{4}$ to consider when analyzing the relationship of Quantity A and Quantity B. These instructions should be applied to both quantities before you make a comparison. Here, we can take the centered information and substitute it into the expressions in both columns. Since we know $\frac{x}{y}=\frac{3}{4}$, we can go ahead and plug in the values for x and y and solve:

Column A: $\frac{2(3)-4}{4}=\frac{6-4}{4}=\frac{2}{4}$ Column B: $\frac{3}{3+4}=\frac{3}{7}$

Here Column A has a value of $\frac{2}{4}$ or $\frac{1}{2}$. This quantity is greater than the quantity of Column B which is $\frac{3}{7}$. So, in this instance, Quantity A is the greatest. But, remember that we need to test more than just one type of number in order to accurately compare the quantities. So, let's try a negative number.

$$\frac{x}{y} = \frac{3}{4}$$

Column A	Column B
$\frac{2x-y}{y}$	$\frac{x}{x+y}$

A. Quantity A is greater
B. Quantity B is greater
C. The two quantities are equal
D. The relationship cannot be determined from the information given

Since we know that $\frac{x}{y} = \frac{3}{4}$, the variables we plug in x and y must equal $\frac{3}{4}$. If we think back to the Math Primer and our review of fractions, we know that when we have a negative denominator and negative numerator, for example, $\frac{-3}{-4}$, it simplifies to a positive numerator and denominator, $\frac{3}{4}$. So, we could plug in a negative numerator and a negative denominator that we would simplify to $\frac{3}{4}$. Let's try -6 and -8.

Column A: $\frac{2(-6)-(-8)}{-8} = \frac{-4}{-8} = \frac{1}{2}$ Column B: $\frac{-6}{-6+(-8)} = \frac{-6}{-14} = \frac{3}{7}$

After plugging in a negative number, the quantity of Column A is still and will always be greater. So, the correct answer is (A).

Understanding the Fundamentals

Quantitative Comparison questions rely heavily on your knowledge of the fundamental principles covered in the Math Primer. Think back to the last question. That one question alone required you to demonstrate your understanding of fraction rules, order of operations, and simple algebraic expressions. Not all questions will include so many different concepts. But, some questions may include more. As you work through the Quantitative Comparison problem set, refer back to the Math Primer to refresh your understanding of concepts that may still be confusing for you.

The following problem set will present you with Quantitative Comparison questions that incorporate skills from arithmetic, algebra, and geometry. Remember that figures in this section are not drawn to scale and that you must consider the outcome of a variety of numbers, including negative number and zero where appropriate to compare the column quantities.

Chapter Overview & Practice Set

Quantitative Comparison questions ask you to compare quantities in two columns and determine whether one is greater than or equal to one another, or if there is not enough information to determine a relationship between the two quantities.

Quantitative Comparison questions are all uniform in both presentation and answers choices. Occasionally, you will be given additional information on the columns; be sure to apply the information to both columns before making a comparison.

$$\frac{a}{b}=\frac{1}{2}$$

Column A	Column B
a	b

A. Quantity A is greater
B. Quantity B is greater
C. The two quantities are equal
D. The relationship cannot be determined from the information given

The answer questions will always look the same. Become familiar with the answer choices to help you to save time when on the exam.

Quantitative Comparison Answer Choices

A. Quantity A is greater
B. Quantity B is greater
C. The two quantities are equal
D. The relationship cannot be determined from the information given

- Because Quantitative Comparison questions ask only for a comparison, don't get hung up on trying to find exact values for every question. Simplify until you have the information you need to determine how the quantities compare.

- You can often plug in numbers to determine how columns compare. Be sure to use a variety of numbers including positive and negative numbers, and zero when appropriate.

- Use substitution and simplification to make the two columns look as similar as possible. Find the connection between the columns and use that in addition to any center information as the building block for your approach.

Quantitative Comparison Practice Set

1.

$$3a - 10 = b$$
$$3b - 10 = a$$

Column A	Column B
a	b

A. Quantity A is greater
B. Quantity B is greater
C. The two quantities are equal
D. The relationship cannot be determined from the information given

2.

$$a < 0 < b$$

Column A	Column B
$-2(a + b)$	$-ab$

A. Quantity A is greater
B. Quantity B is greater
C. The two quantities are equal
D. The relationship cannot be determined from the information given

3. DEF is a triangle such that the measure of angle D is 45°. The measure of angle F is twice the measure of angle E.

Column A	Column B
Measure of Angle D	Measure of Angle E

A. Quantity A is greater
B. Quantity B is greater
C. The two quantities are equal
D. The relationship cannot be determined from the information given

4.

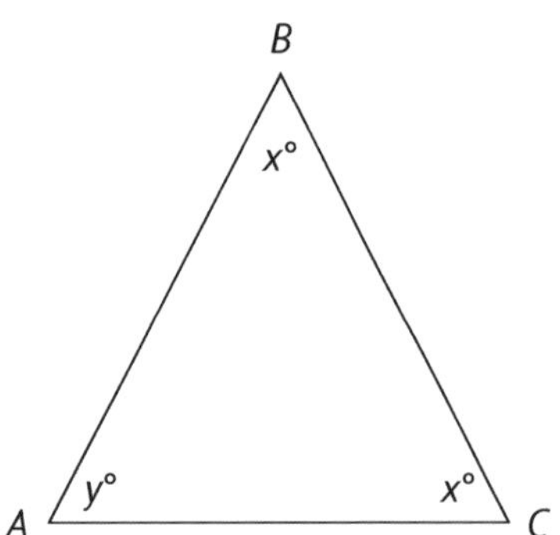

Use the figure above to answer the question.

Column A	**Column B**
AB	BC

A. Quantity A is greater
B. Quantity B is greater
C. The two quantities are equal
D. The relationship cannot be determined from the information given

5. A bag contains green, blue and yellow glass marbles. The ratio of green to blue glass marbles is 2 : 7. The ratio of green to yellow glass marbles is 3 : 5.

Column A	**Column B**
Number of blue glass marbles	Number of yellow glass marbles

A. Quantity A is greater
B. Quantity B is greater
C. The two quantities are equal
D. The relationship cannot be determined from the information given

6.

$$\sqrt{a^2 + 39} = 8$$

Column A	**Column B**
a	4

A. Quantity A is greater
B. Quantity B is greater
C. The two quantities are equal
D. The relationship cannot be determined from the information given

7.

$$■x = -x + \frac{1}{x}$$

Column A	Column B
Value of $■x$ if $x = 4$	Value of $■x$ if $x = 3$

A. Quantity A is greater
B. Quantity B is greater
C. The two quantities are equal
D. The relationship cannot be determined from the information given

8. Line q on a coordinate plane is defined by the equation $-2x + 3y = 6$.

Column A	Column B
Should be a line perpendicular to line q	The slope of a line parallel to line q

A. Quantity A is greater
B. Quantity B is greater
C. The two quantities are equal
D. The relationship cannot be determined from the information given

9.

Column A	Column B
3^3	2^7

A. Quantity A is greater
B. Quantity B is greater
C. The two quantities are equal
D. The relationship cannot be determined from the information given

10. A set has exactly five consecutive positive integers.

Column A	Column B
The percentage decrease in the average of the numbers when one of the numbers is dropped from the set	20%

A. Quantity A is greater
B. Quantity B is greater
C. The two quantities are equal
D. The relationship cannot be determined from the information given

Quantitative Comparison Practice Set Answers

1. **(C).** Substitute $3b - 10$ for a in the first equation and solve for b. Then, plug your resulting value into the equation to find a. Your calculations will yield a value of 5 for both a and b, so C is correct.

2. **(D).** The center information tells you that a is negative and b is positive since a is less than 0 and b is greater than 0. Since b is always positive and a is always negative, their product will be a negative number. The expression in column b, then, will always be positive since the result will always be a negative product with a negative sign in front of it ($-ab$). Plug in values to try to determine how the quantities relate. If you plug in -1 for a and 2 for b and solve, column b is greater. But, if you plug in a large enough negative number, say -49, column a will be greater. Because of these different outcomes, we cannot determine the relationship.

3. **(C).** You are given the quantity of column a. Using your understanding of triangles, calculate the value of column b.

$$A + B + C = 180$$
$$45 + B + 2B = 180$$
$$45 + 3B = 180$$
$$3B = 135$$
$$B = 45$$

4. **(D).** In a triangle, equal angles have equal opposite sides. So, AB = AC. You have not information about angle y, so you cannot determine any information about side BC.

5. **(A).** First consider the ratios of green marbles to blue marbles and green marbles to yellow marbles: $\frac{2}{7}$ and $\frac{3}{5}$, respectively. The ratio of blue marbles to green marbles is $\frac{7}{2}$. Then, multiply the ratios of green to yellow and blue to green of together: $\frac{g}{y} \bullet \frac{b}{g} = \frac{3}{5} \bullet \frac{7}{2} = \frac{21}{10}$. Since the equation $\frac{g}{y} \bullet \frac{b}{g}$ simplifies to $\frac{b}{y}$ then $\frac{b}{y} = \frac{21}{10}$. So $b = 21$ and $y = 10$.

6. **(D).** Square both sides of the equation to get rid of the square root. Solve for a. Be careful not to pull the plug too early on this one. You end up with 5 as the value for a, but you solved a that by taking the square root a number, the value could also be -5. When you plug in both possible answers, the results favor column a in one instance and column a in the other. The quantities cannot be compared.

7. **(B).** Plug in 3 from column a and 4 from column b for x into the equation $\blacksquare x = -x + \frac{1}{x}$; solve, then simplify the mixed fraction. The quantity of B is greater.

8. **(B).** Determine the slope of both a parallel and perpendicular line. Solve using $y = mx + b$.

$$-2x + 3y = 6$$
$$y = \frac{2}{3}x + 2$$

You have the slope intercept. Remember that perpendicular lines are negative reciprocals of each other and parallel lines have identical slopes. So, column $a = -\frac{3}{2}$ and column $b = \frac{2}{3}$.

9. **(B).** Solve the exponents.

10. **(B).** The average of the five consecutive positive integers can be represented as:

$$\frac{x + (x+1) + (x+2) + (x+3) + (x+4)}{5}$$

$$= \frac{5x+10}{5} = x+2$$

Calculate the new average by dropping the largest term:

$$\frac{x+(x+1)+(x+2)+(x+3)}{4}$$

$$\frac{4x+6}{4} = x + \frac{3}{2}$$

Calculate the percentage decrease using the formula:

$$\frac{\textit{previous average} - \textit{new average}}{\textit{previous average}} = \frac{(x+2)-(x+\frac{3}{2})}{x+2} \bullet 100 = \frac{\frac{1}{2}}{x+2} \bullet 100$$

To find the maximum percentage, set x at its minimum. The center information tells you x is a positive integer, so its lowest possible value is 1. Plug in 1 for x and solve.

$$\frac{\frac{1}{2}}{1+2} \bullet 100 = \frac{\frac{1}{2}}{3} \bullet 100$$

$$= \frac{100}{6} = 16.666\%$$

This is the value for column a. So, column b is greater.

Up Next: Next we will look at Problem-Solving questions and their subset Data Interpretation questions. Together, these make up a majority of the Quantitative Reasoning questions and test the full range of concepts found in the Math Primer.

ARGO
BROTHERS

16 PROBLEM-SOLVING & DATA INTERPRETATION

When it comes to describing Problem-Solving in the Quantitative Reasoning section, it is pretty straight-forward. Quite simply, the questions ask you to solve the problem you are presented with and select the correct answer choice. Problem-Solving questions are the catch-all questions on the GRE. They draw from all the math content areas and are presented as either word problems, geometric figures, or algebraic expressions. Some Problem-Solving questions might ask you to interpret data from a graph or chart; these are a sub-set of questions we call Data Interpretation questions. We will look more at these later.

All of the necessary calculations for these questions can be done using scratch paper or the on-screen calculator. Some will require no calculations at all, but rather an understanding of fundamental mathematics concepts. You will encounter nine to ten Problem-Solving questions per section of Quantitative Reasoning.

This chapter will outline the common types of Problem-Solving and Data Interpretation questions and provide you with strategies and how the address them efficiently and how to appropriately apply the mathematical concepts need to answer the questions.

Sample Problem-Solving Question

If Erica can complete a project in four hours and Corey can complete the same project in six hours, how many hours will it take Erica and Corey to complete the project if they work on the project at the same time?

A. 3

B. $2\frac{2}{5}$

C. 2

D. $2\frac{3}{4}$

E. $5\frac{1}{2}$

Word problems are a common occurrence in the Quantitative Reasoning section. This is a classic rate of work problem where you need to determine how long it would take to complete a project with two people working together at a different rate. To calculate the rate of work, find the product of the time it takes both Corey and Erica to compete the project individually, then divide by the sum of the time it takes them: $\frac{(4)(6)}{(4+6)} = \frac{24}{10} = 2\frac{2}{5}$. Since your answer choices are written as fractions, you do not need to reduce further. This question is a word problem that has only one correct answer. Before we dig deeper in more problems, let's review what we know about answer choices in the Quantitative Reasoning section.

Prep Tip: Questions that have more than one response are usually preceded by a square instead of an oval. This is true for all sections on the exam.

Answer Choice Types

Problem-Solving questions have a variety of options when it comes to answer choices; there may be more than one response to the question or you may have to input your answer into a text box.

Multiple-choice: Choose One Answer Choice

You will be presented with five answer choices. Only one will be correct. Once you select an answer, you can plug your answer in the check to see if it is correct. Remember, substitution is not a primary strategy. Once you have simplified the problem and eliminated incorrect answers, try plugging the remaining answer choices into the problem if you are not sure which answer is correct.

Multiple-choice: Choose One or More Answer Choices

These questions have one or more answer choices that are correct. Select all the answers you think are correct. There is no partial credit for these questions; you must select all and only the correct answers in order to receive credit for your response. Assess each answer choice on its own to determine if it answers the questions. As with the previous question type, make sure you read all the answer choices.

Numeric Entry Questions

Numeric Entry questions present a unique challenge in that you do not have answer choices to choose from. Instead, you must complete the necessary calculations and key in (or write in) your answer in the designated box. A numeric entry question may look like this:

$2^3 + 2^8 =$

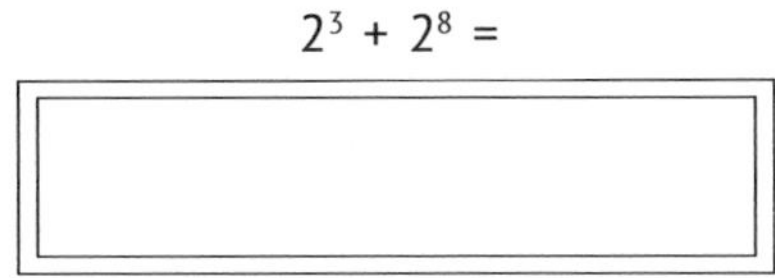

Once you perform the calculation, so 8 + 256 = 264, you will enter just your answer into the box. If your answer is an integer or a decimal, you will enter into a single box. If your answer is a fraction, you will enter the numerator into one box and the denominator in a second box. You should enter the entire outcome of the calculation unless instructed not to do so. Let's look at some other considerations related to numeric entry questions:

- Because you do not have answers to choose from, it may not be as easy to realize when you have made a mistake in your calculations. Read the question carefully and ensure you are performing the correct calculation and reporting the answer in the correct units, if applicable.

- Round your number only after you have completed the entire calculation. Oftentimes, decimals can be entered as calculated. However, if the question asks you to round your number, make sure you do so, but not until after you arrive at your final answer.

- You have some flexibility in how you record your answer as all equivalent answers are credited responses. For example, if your answer is $\frac{8}{16}$, you do not need to further reduce your answer to $\frac{1}{2}$. Both are correct, so save some time by not further reducing the fraction and move on to the next question.

Characteristics of the Problems

The problems you will be asked to solve run the gamut in terms of difficulty. Sometimes you will be able to answer quickly with little to no calculations while others may take a little longer and require more computation. The difficulty of the questions often increases when multiple concepts are tested. The less difficult questions often require the application of just a single concept.

As we discussed, all the mathematical concepts in the Math Primer are fair game when it comes to problem-solving. Make sure you are familiar with these not only in theory, but also in application. This way, you can be equipped to approach the questions regardless of the number of concepts test.

Developing a Strategy

All the Problem-Solving questions can be approached with the same general strategy. The critical pieces to the approach are to identify the question task, determine your plan of attack, then select and check your answer. Let's explore these steps in more detail.

Understand the Problem

The first step is figuring out what your question task is. What math concepts are being tested in this question? Does the problem have more than one calculation that needs to be made? Make sure you are clear on the final value you are trying to find.

Scan the Answer Choices & Determine your Approach

With some questions you are asked explicitly which of the choices has a particular property. In this case, scan the answers and eliminate those that don't meet the requirement. Then determine your approach to the problem. Depending on the question, you might decide to substitute the answer choice into the expression. In other questions, it may be helpful to work backward from the choices. You may also need to apply various theories and principles, with triangles for example, to solve the problem.

Use the Calculator Smartly

Using the calculator should not always be your first choice when attacking problems. Some problems can be solved more easily without the calculator, and some cannot be solved with a calculator at all. One of the most useful features of the calculator, aside from its ability to quickly solve complex operations for you, is the *Transfer* button for numeric entry questions. Once you have calculated your response, you can simply click the transfer button and your response will be entered into the numeric entry text box.

Data Interpretation Problems

Data Interpretation questions are more of an extension of Problem-Solving questions than a unique question type. For these questions, you will interpret data from charts, graphs, and other images and use this information to solve for the correct answer. Like Problem-Solving questions, these questions have a variety of answer choice options and can have more than one correct answer. You may also have more than one question that corresponds to the graph or chart. Remember, you need to select all the correct answers in order to receive credit for the question.

Like the rest of the questions in the Quantitative Reasoning section, you do not need an advance level of knowledge to approach these questions. You will, however, need to understand the basics of reading graphs and charts and deriving meaning from the data. You can expect to see 2-3 of these questions on the exam.

Data Representations

For Data Interpretation questions, you will see data represented in a number of different ways including:

- Bar graphs, including stacked bar graphs
- Pie Charts
- Line Graphs, often with multiple variables charted on the axes.

Prep Tip: On the computer-adaptive exam, working with graphs can be a challenge. If necessary, use your scratch paper to sketch out a general replica of the draft so that it provides you with the essential information and so that you can jot down notes and explore relationships in the data.

Developing a Strategy

Data Interpretation questions are an extension of Problem-Solving questions. The major difference is of course the chart or graph. They can be approached with the same general strategy, though there are some particular things you should be on the lookout for when you encounter these question types.

Understand the Graph

What data is being represented? What are the variables? Before moving on to the questions, make sure you have a clear understanding of what the graph or chart is representing. Read all the information on the graph or chart and try to determine how they relate to each other.

Be Careful with the Data

Some of the charts and graphs can be confusing since they can have many variables. When you have pinpointed what the question is asking you to analyze, double-check the graph to make sure you are analyzing the proper data.

Number and Percentages

Perhaps one of the most common mistakes in the conflation of numbers and percentages. It is important to note that the two are quite different and will yield different results in your analysis. In some case, you may have both in the graph. So double-check your calculations and the question to make sure you are using and analyzing the correct terms.

Chapter Overview and Problem Set

Problem-Solving questions are the catch-all questions on the GRE. They draw from all the math content areas and are presented as either word problems, geometric figures, or algebraic expressions. Some Problem-Solving questions might ask you to interpret data from a graph or chart; these are sub-set of questions we call Data Interpretation questions.

Problem-Solving questions have a variety of options when it comes to answer choices; there may be more than one response to the question or you may have to input your answer into a text box.

Approaching the Problems

Understand the Problem

The first step is figuring out what your question task is. What math concepts are being tested in this question? Does the problem have more than one calculation that needs to be made? Make sure you are clear on the final value you are trying to find.

Scan the Answer Choices & Determine your Approach

Some questions you are asked explicitly which of the choices has a particular property. In this case, scan the answers and eliminate those that don't meet the requirement. Then determine your approach to the problem.

Use the Calculator Smartly

Using the calculator should not always be your first choice when attacking problems. Some problems can be solved more easily without the calculator, and some cannot be solved with a calculator at all.

Data Interpretation

Data Interpretation questions are more of an extension of Problem-Solving questions than a unique question type. For these questions, you will interpret data from charts, graphs, and other images and use this information to solve for the correct answer. These problems will be accompanied a number of visual representations including:

- Bar graphs, including stacked bar graphs
- Pie Charts
- Line Graphs, often with multiple variable charted on the axes

Approaching the Problems

These questions follow the same general principles as Problem-Solving questions but have some unique considerations you should keep in mind.

Understand the Graph

- What data is being represented?
- What are the variables?
- Read all the information on the graph or chart and try to determine how they relate to each other

Be Careful with the Data

- Some of the charts and graphs can be confusing since they can have many variables
- Double-check the graph to make sure you are analyzing the proper data

Number and Percentages

- Confusing numbers and percentages is one of the most common mistakes in this section
- Understand that the two are different and yield different results in your analysis
- Double-check calculations and the question to make sure you are using and analyzing the correct terms

Problem-Solving and Data Interpretation Practice Set

1. The average of all consecutive integers from x to y inclusive is 39. Which of the following could be x and y? Be sure to select all the possible answers.

   A. 33 and 45

   B. 21 and 35

   C. 25 and 53

   D. 29 and 61

   E. 33 and 45

2. Circle K has a total area of 9□. Circle M has a total area of 49□. Suppose the circles intersect at exactly one point. Which of the following could be the distance from the center for Circle K to the center of Circle M?

   A. 8

   B. 21

   C. 10

   D. 29

   E. 58

3. For her upcoming vacation, Jade packed three shirts, two pair of shoes, and four skirts. How many different outfits consisting of one skirt, one pair of shoes, and one shirt can Jade make with the clothes she packs? Enter you answer in the box below.

4. Which of the following is less than the sum of all the prime factors of 330? Select all the apply.

   A. 17

   B. 15

   C. 19

   D. 21

   E. 23

5. What is the area of a triangle that has two sides that are 10 units in length and has a perimeter equal to that of a square that has an area of 81?

   A. 36

   B. 28

   C. 48

   D. 60

   E. 24

6. Suppose $f(x) = (x - 4)^2$ and $g(x) = x^2 - 5$, what is the value of $f(2) - g(2)$?

A. 5

B. 9

C. −1

D. 0

E. 3

7. Find the value of b in the figure below. Write you answer in the text box.

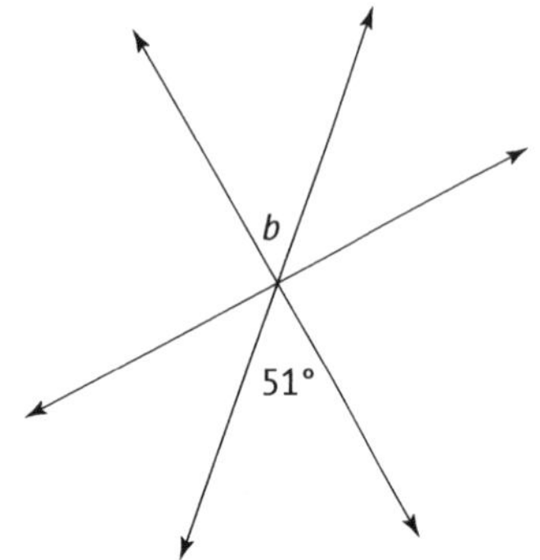

8. The chart details the age at which several U.S. Presidents were took office. What is the median age of inauguration for the Presidents listed?

Age At Inauguration

President	Age
Richard Nixon	56
James Buchanan	65
Franklin Pierce	48
Thomas Jefferson	57

President	Age
Grover Cleveland	47
George W Bush	54
James A Garfield	49
Franklin D Roosevelt	51

President	Age
Ulysses S Grant	46
William McKinley	54
Milllard Fillmore	50
James K Polk	49

President	Age
George Washington	57
William H Harrison	68
Barack Obama	47
Chester A Arthur	51

A. 51

B. 47

C. 53

D. 56

E. 50

9. Find the area of the figure below.

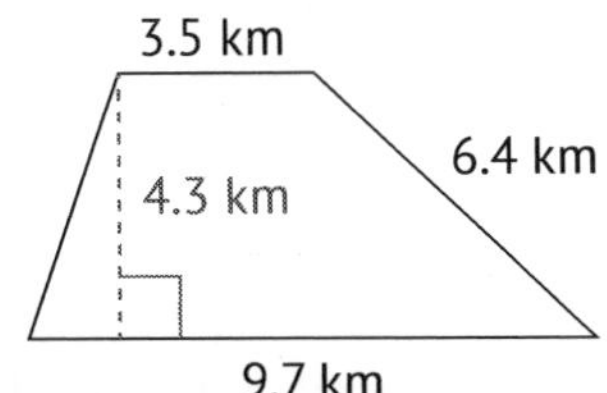

A. 28.38

B. 33.78

C. 31.25

D. 56.76

E. 50.25

10. Find the slope of the line on the coordinate plane below.

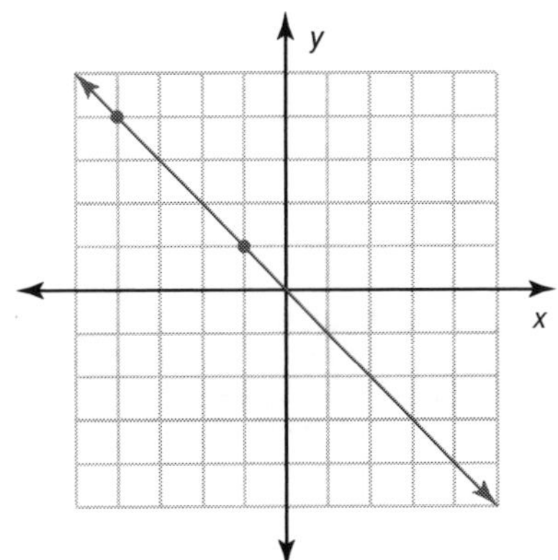

A. 1

B. −1

C. Undefined

D. 0

E. 2

Problem-Solving and Data Interpretation Practice Set Answers

1. **C, E.** To find the average of a set of consecutive integers, take the average of the largest and smallest integers. Since you know the average you are looking for is 39, and answer choices with an average of 39 is correct.

2. **C.** You have two circles and you know the area for each circle. Since the circles only intersect at one point, find the radius of each circle so you can measure the distance from the center of one circle to the center of the other. If the area of Circle K is 9□ and the equation for the area of a circle is A = □r^2, for Circle K, r = 3. If the area for Circle M is 49□, for Circle M, r = 7. So, if the circles are next to each other, which they will need to be in order to share one point, the total distance from the the center of Circle K to the center of Circle M, simply add the distance of each radius, for a distance of 10.

3. **24.** Jade can create 3 · 2 · 4 outfits based on her packing 3 shirts, 2 pair of shoes, and 4 skirts. She can create 24 different outfits.

4. **A, B, C.** The prime factors of 33 at 2, 3, 5, and 11. The sum of the factors is 21. So, 17, 15, and 19 are all less than 21.

5. **C.** This question is about triangles, but requires knowledge of squares as well. The perimeter of a square that has an area of 81 is 36 is the value of one side, squared. Take the square root of 81 to determine that each side of the square is 4. So, the perimeter of the triangle will also be 36. Since you already know the two equal sides at both 10, the base of the triangle is 16, so that the sides add up to 36. Now, solve for h so that you can calculate the area. $h=\sqrt{a^2-\frac{b^2}{4}}=\sqrt{10^2-\frac{16^2}{4}}=\sqrt{100-64}=6$.

   Now, solve the area equation by plugging in 6 for h.

6. **A.** Plug in values for x is each function, then solve.

7. **51.** The angles are vertical and have the same measurements.

8. **A.** The median is the center number or sum of the two center numbers when all the terms are listed in order.

9. **A.** $\boldsymbol{A}=\frac{\boldsymbol{a}+\boldsymbol{b}}{2}(\boldsymbol{h})=\frac{3.5+9.7}{2}(4.3)$

10. **B.** Line trends downward from left to right.

ARGO
BROTHERS

17 | WRITING ON THE GRE

Writing on the GRE

The Analytical Writing section tests your ability to create cogent and well-supported arguments. The section is of particular importance to graduate and business schools, and was introduced specifically to ascertain the writing skills of candidates and their ability to meet the often writing-intensive curriculum characteristic of a majority of graduate school programs.

Though content is the most important factor essay reviewers consider when scoring your essay, it is important to ensure your essay is grammatically sound and demonstrates a strong command of written English. For the computerized exam, you will not have access to the typical word processing functions like grammar and spell check that you are likely accustomed to using. So, you will need to be diligent and ensure you leave a few minutes at the end each essay to proofread and correct mistakes. While minor issues my not count against you, major issues or a lack of variety and complexity in your writing may significantly impact your cumulative score.

Reviewers want to see that you understand proper syntax and grammar, and can use a variety of complex sentence structures and vocabulary words. Use vocabulary that is appropriate and makes sense in context. Remember that there are ample opportunities in the Verbal Reasoning section for you to demonstrate your vocabulary prowess. Let's look at the characteristics of a top-scoring essay.

Characteristics of a Top-Scoring Essay

In order to make your essay stand out and increase your chances of earning a top score, your essay needs to not only be well-written, but also fully address the prompt and align with the essay task. If the essay task asks you to choose a side and you write a well-developed essay that argues the merits of both sides and how both options are a good idea, then you are not going to score well, even with a well-written essay. The key to scoring well on the Analytical Writing section is more than writing well; you need to follow instructions, use the provided evidence, and adequately support your claims.

Organization & Clarity

Essay reviewers have lots of essays to review and don't have time to re-read your essays in order to grasp your point. As such, it is critical that your essay is well-organized and that it clearly articulates your argument and analysis of the prompt. Essay reviewers should not have to guess your position or search for your supporting evidence. Your position should be clearly stated and supported by both the provided evidence and relevant evidence you chose to introduce. The flow of the essay should be logical and easy to follow. Make sure you divide your essay into paragraphs, grouping together ideas that are directly related to each other and ensuring your transitions make sense. We will discuss some strategies to organize your essay logically and align with the key elements essay reviewers are looking for when deriving your score.

Appropriate Use of Evidence

Creating a well-organized, logically sound, and clear essay largely depends on how you use evidence to support your argument. A well-written essay will marshal not only the provided evidence in support of your position, but will also include relevant evidence introduced by you to further strengthen your argument and support your position. The use of examples, real-world occurrences, and logical assumptions can all be helpful in constructing a well-supported, logical essay.

Critical Analysis and Logical Reasoning

Having an essay that is logically sound and provides a critical analysis of the issues and evidence is an important component if you want to score in the upper percentile the Analytical Writing section. Your goal is to convince your reader of your point of view by providing a well-supported logically sound case. Having a logically sound argument also means that you have avoided common logical pitfalls and interpreted the issue and evidence without the use of fallacious reasoning.

About the Writing Primer

The Analytical Writing chapters of this book address essay organization, use of evidence, and critical analysis and logical reasoning. This Writing Primer will walk you through common writing mistakes, discuss key characteristics of good, logically sound writing that essay graders are looking for in your essays, and provide a review of grammar, mechanics, and punctuation. This guide provides a high-level review of grammar, mechanics, and usage. Further study may be necessary to provide the understanding needed to master areas that may still present a challenge for you.

Grammar Review

Grammar plays a key role in your developing strong essays for the Analytical Writing section. Your writing must be clear, and your ideas must flow in a logical sense that does not confuse the essay reviewers. Essay reviewers are looking for how well you respond to the prompt using concise, but varied sentences that exhibit a clear understanding of grammar and an ability to clearly communicate your ideas. ETS asserts that essays receiving high scores "will demonstrate facility with the conventions (i.e., grammar, usage and mechanics) of standard written English." Let's look at some key grammatical conventions that can help you draft a high-scoring essay.

Subject-Verb Agreement

Basic Premise: The subject and verb of a sentence must agree in person and number. Singular subjects must be paired with singular verbs and plural subjects must be paired with plural verbs.

Person refers to whether the subject is the author (first person), the reader (second person), or someone/something else (third person).

First Person:	<u>I</u> will bake the cake for you. *The author is the subject who is causing the action.*
Second Person:	<u>Tom</u> should tell me what type of icing he wants before I begin. Tom *refers the subject who is causing the action.*
Third Person:	<u>My mom</u> will pick up the ingredients for the icing from the grocery store. *Here, the author's mom is the subject causing the action.*

Number refers to whether the subject is about one person, place, or thing (singular), or multiple persons, places, or things (plural).

Singular:	<u>James Bailey</u> was honored as one of the top philanthropists in Atlanta. *The subject is one person: James Bailey, so the verb was* is *singular.*
Plural:	The new playgrounds have seesaws and swing sets to accommodates lots of kids. The subject includes multiple playgrounds, so the verb *have* is plural.

Some words and word groups are governed by special rules to ensure proper subject-verb agreement.

Subject-Verb Agreement Rules	Example	Example
Two or more subjects joined by "and" require a plural verb	The players and the coach are going to celebrate their win.	Jenny and Peter are going to the basketball game together later tonight
Collective nouns require a singular verb	The group was unable to come to a consensus.	The committee is unsure of how to move forward.
Two or more subjects joined by "or" or "nor," require that the verb agree with the subject closest to it	Neither the manager nor the the employees agree with new policy change.	Neither the employees nor the manager agrees with the new policy change.
Some indefinite pronouns are singular (e.g., anything, everyone, either, no one, each, etc.) and others are plural (e.g., few, many, several, etc.)	Everyone was excited about the upcoming reunion since they had not seen each other in years.	Many of the new recruits were nervous about playing in their first game.
Indefinite pronouns can be plural or singular in some cases depending on the context in which they are used.	Jim turned in the project and indicated that some was completed by him and the rest by his lab partner.	Jim turned in the lab reports and indicated that some were completed by him and some by his lab partner.
The subject is not always a noun or pronoun. When a verb or gerund is used as a subject, it requires a singular verb	Shopping is a good way to de-stress after a long week.	Shopping online minimizes the time you spend waiting in line and searching the store for a particular item.
The subject and verb must agree regardless of their proximity to each other	Each of the articles suggests that stress is a precursor to cardiovascular disease.	The goal of the campaign was to raise awareness about heart disease.
In statements that begin with "there is" or "there are," the noun or pronoun that follows is the subject that must match the verb	There are many options for font colors.	There is only one appro-priate option that meets the required criteria.

Subject-Pronoun Agreement

Basic Premise: Pronouns must match the nouns they replace in person, number, and gender. Sentences that contain pronouns without a clear antecedent are not grammatically correct.

Person indicates whether the noun is the author (first person), the reader (second person), or someone/something else (third person).

First Person:	I will bake the cake for you. The pronoun "I" references the author of the statement
Second Person:	<u>You</u> should be able to pick them up soon. The pronoun "You" references the reader of the statement
Third Person:	<u>They</u> will be packed securely so you can transport them. The pronoun "They" references, something other than the author/reader. In this case, the cakes.

Number indicates whether the noun is about one person, place, or thing (singular), or multiple persons, places, or things (plural).

Singular:	I will bake the cakes. The pronoun "I" references one person.
Plural:	I will bake the cakes. They will be ready for pickup tomorrow. The pronoun "They" references multiple cakes.

Gender indicates whether the noun is masculine, feminine, or an object.

Masculine:	Send an email to Peter. He will confirm your attendance at the conference. The pronoun *He* references the masculine noun *Peter*.
Feminine:	Send an email Cynae. She will confirm your attendance at the conference. The pronoun *She* references the feminine noun *Cynae*.
Object:	Send an email to Peter. He will confirm that he received it. The pronoun *it* references the object *request*.

Some words and word groupings have specific rules that apply to them to ensure agreement.

The pronoun *who* always refers to a person or people. The pronoun *that* always refers to objects.

Incorrect:	I will never understand people that travel so much.
Correct:	I will never understand people who travel so much.
Incorrect:	Countries who limit free speech suppress the free flow of ideas.
Correct:	Countries that limit free speech suppress the free flow of ideas.

When a pronoun references a singular noun and a plural noun joined by *or* or *nor*, it should agree with the noun closest to it.

Incorrect:	Either the students or the teacher will represent their class at the carnival.
Correct:	Either the students or the teacher will represent her class at the carnival.

Although the correction makes the pronouns in the sentence agree, the sentence is still awkward. To be more precise, you could rewrite the sentence:

Either the students will represent their class at the carnival or the teacher will represent the class.

Parallelism

In order to have proper parallel constructions, the items or phrases in any list must be in the same form, either noun, verb or preposition form. Parallelism errors are often for readers awkward because they do not follow the anticipated pattern the reader expects.

Incorrect:	I need to hire an assistant who is able to answer calls, to book travel, and record-keeping.
Correct:	I need to hire an assistant who is able to answer calls, to book book travel, and to keep records.

In this example, the parallelism error is fixed by converting record-keeping to an infinitive form to match how the other job requirements are listed.

Modifiers

Misplaced or dangling modifiers can cause confusion for your reader. It is important to make sure that your sentences are structured properly and that phrases are modifying the proper subjects or objects of your sentence.

Incorrect:	The public received some important information to protect their homes this summer from the fire chief.
Correct:	The public received some important information from the fire chief to protect their homes this summer.

The first sentence is ambiguous in that it appears that the public received information on how to protect their home from the fire chief, as if she was the threat. The correction however, makes it more clear that the fire chief disseminated the information to the public.

Similar to misplaced modifiers, dangling modifiers modify part of a statement, but there is key information missing that is needed to allow the reader to fully connect all the pieces make sense of the sentence. Essentially, a dangling modifier is a word or phrase that modifies a word or words not explicitly articulated in the sentence. Most dangling modifiers are the result of an author omitting a subject of the sentence.

Incorrect:	With a great deal of disappointment, the deal fell through.
Correct:	With a deal of disappointment, Jack announced that the deal fell through.

Since the deal cannot be disappointed, the sentence needs more information in order to make sense. By adding a subject to the sentence capable of experiencing the disappointment, the sentence more clearly expresses the point.

Punctuation and Capitalization

Proper capitalization and punctuation are critical aspects of writing and communicating clearly and concisely with your reader. Improper punctuation can change the intended meaning of your writing and confuse readers. Let's look at a brief overview of proper punctuation and capitalization.

Punctuation	Proper Usage	Examples
Period (.)	To end a complete thought	This long day is finally over.
Question Mark (?)	To signify a question or statement of doubt	How many years did he have to wait before he could re-apply?
Exclamation Point (!)	To show extreme excitement or surprise. Your use of exclamation points should be limited on the GRE.	I can't believe you just did that!
Comma (,)	To separate items in a series	There are bagels, coffee, and donuts in the lounge.
	To separate a string of adjectives	The paper was clear, concise, and well-researched.
	To separate two independent clauses joined by a coordinating conjunction	I was going to go to the beach, but I decided to go to the mountains instead.
	To signify the end of an introductory or prepositional phrase	In order for the team to be successful, they needed to complete the requisite training program.
	To introduce a quotation	He said, "no, please don't do that."
	Between day of the month and year in dates	July 13, 1982
	Between a city and state	Somerville, Massachusetts
	After conjunctive adverbs	She failed her theses defense; therefore, she will not graduate.
Semicolon (;)	To separate two closely-related independent clauses	She was devastated after the loss; we all expected she would be.
	To separate clauses joined by a conjunctive adverb	She took more than a year to complete the project; however, she was still able to graduate with her class.
	To separate a series of equal elements that include commas	The world tour will include Budapest; Sofia; and Tbilisi.
Apostrophe (')	To indicate possessives	It is hard to determines the mothers' motives since they all refuse to talk to the press.
	To make contractions. Your use of contractions on the exam should be minimal since the essays are considered a formal writing tasks.	The dog couldn't figure out how to use the automatic food dispenser.
Quotations (" ")	To signify information quoted directly from an outside source	She said that the professor told her that her argument was "loosely constructed."

Capitalization

Requires Capitalization	Example
First person singular pronoun "I"	I will serve as the marshal for this year's parade.
Proper Nouns	Greg Whitmore is the new director of Housing Operations at the University of Chicago located in Cook county Illinois.
Days of the week and months	Our office is open Monday through Friday.
Proper names of historical periods/events and formally organized groups	The **S**upreme **C**ourt is the highest court in the United States Justice system.
Proper names of races, ethnicities, nationalities, and languages	The school now offers Spanish and Thai.
Names of businesses, trademarks, and brand names	Nike and Adidas are fierce competitors in the sports apparel market.

While grammar plays a critical role in creating cogent essays, writing style also influences how clearly and logically your ideas a communicated in your writing. Writing style has less to do with comma placement and modifiers and more to do with your word choice, arrangement of your ideas, and voice.

Using Active Voice

Most writing is either in active voice or passive voice. Voice simply describes the structure of the action in your sentence; the structure is determined based on who or what receives the action. When using active voice, the subject of the sentence performs the action. When using passive voice, the subject of the sentence is the recipient of the action. Let's look at some examples.

Active Voice: The young musician composed his first original score this year.

Passive Voice: The first original score was written by the young musician this year.

Passive voice is not grammatically incorrect. However, passive voice is often not concise and can cause confusion for your readers. Active voice is much more clear and direct and often eliminates confusion about who is performing or receiving an action. You should endeavor to complete your essays in active voice to ensure you are clearly addressing the prompts and providing a clear road map of your logic for the essay reviewer to follow.

Vocabulary

One of the best ways to clearly articulate your point is to strategic about your vocabulary use. Be consistent in how you describe things and avoid using "big" words for the sake of using big words. Use words that are appropriate for the context; ensure you use words correctly and avoid up terms that are commonly confused. The remainder of this guide is a refresher of commonly misspelled words and commonly confused and misused words.

Commonly Misspelled Words

a lot
acceptable
accidentally
accommodate
acquaintance
acquitted
advice
affect
attendance
beginning
believe
benefit
business
calendar
cemetery
challenge
changeable
commission
committee
conscience
conscientious
conscious
criticize
deceive
definite
definitely
describe
desperate
despise
develop
disappearance
disappoint
discipline
dissatisfied
duel
ecstasy
effect
embarrassment
environment
existence
familiar
fascinate
February
fiery
formerly
gauge
government
grammar
grateful
guarantee
harass
humorous
hypocrisy
immediately
incidentally
independent
irresistible
jewelry
judgment
knowledge
laboratory
latter
led
liaison
loneliness
lose
marriage
medieval
millennium
miniature
mischief
misspell
murmur
necessary
noticeable
occasionally
occurred
paid
parallel
pastime
permissible
perseverance
precedence
preceding
prejudice
principal
privilege
pursue
questionnaire
receive
recommend
reference
relevant
repetition
rhyme
rhythm
ridiculous
sacrilegious
shepherd
siege
seize
separate
sergeant
similar
simile
sophomore
succeed
supersede
tragedy
tries
undoubtedly

Commonly Confused and Misused Words

a/an
a is used ahead of consonants and an is used ahead of vowels.

accept/except
Accept means to receive or take something or someone.
Except means to leave something out.

advice/advise
Advice is a noun that means suggestions or guidance.
Advise is a verb that means to direct or give advice.

affect/effect
Affect means to impact or influence something or someone. Effect is a consequence or outcome of something.

among/between
Between references a relationship consisting of two things.
Among references a relationship of two or more things.

assure/ensure/insure
Assure means to provide comfort to someone.
Ensure means to guarantee that something be happen or be completed.
Insure means to protect against lost or damages from unexpected occurrences.

beside/besides
Beside means close to or next to.
Besides means in addition to.

compliment/complement
Compliment means to offer praise or expresses admiration.
Complement means two more things or people that work well together.

choose/chose
Choose is used to expressing making a choice in the present tense or future tense.
Chose is used to express a choice already made and is in the past tense.

compare/contrast
Compare means to highlight similarities.
Contrast means to highlight differences.

continual/continuous
Continual means repeated intermittingly.
Continuous means occurring without interruptions all of the time.

Disinterested/Uninterested:
Disinterested means to be impartial or unbiased.
Uninterested means having no interested in at all.

e.g./i.e.
The e.g. abbreviation means "for example." It is used to list examples after a general statement. The list is usually considered incomplete.
The i.e. abbreviation means "that is" or "in other words." It is used to clarify something previously stated. When the clarification is a list of items, using i.e. indicates that the list is complete.

equal/equitable
Equal means the same.
Equitable means fair.

farther/further
Farther is used in reference to distance.
Further means refers to additional or can be used to mean to a greater degree or extent.

fewer/less
Fewer is used to refer to things that can be counted.
Less is used to refer to quantities that cannot be counted, usually percentages, volume, etc.

imply/infer
Imply refers to something that expressed indirectly.
Infer refers to an assumption that is made based on given facts.

irregardless/regardless/irrespective
Irregardless is not a word despite it being frequently used colloquially.
Regardless and irrespective mean despite or without consideration.

of/have
Of is often misused as a preposition when have should be used as in would of instead of would have.

their/there/they're
Their is a pronoun and shows possession of something by several people or things.
There refers to a location.
They're is the contraction of *they are.*

who/whom
Who always refers to the person performing whatever action in the sentence.
Whom always refers to the person receiving the action in a sentence.

your/you're
Your refers to something that you possess.
You're is the contraction of *you are.*

ARGO
BROTHERS

18 ANALYZE AN ISSUE: MODEL ESSAY

Prompt

If a goal is worthy, it is justifiable to take a by any means necessary approach to achieving it.

Discuss the extent to which you agree or disagree with the statement and explain your position. Also discuss instances when the statement may or may not be true and how these instances impact your viewpoint.

Essay

Goals are the foundation of personal growth and often are harbingers for many of our achievements and contributions to society. People often go to extraordinary lengths to reach their goals. But, while a stanch commitment to achieve one's goals is typically admirable, it is a mistake to assert that a "by any means necessary" approach is justifiable in all circumstances.

Goals provide a roadmap for an individual's life and endow them with a sense of purpose, a feeling that they are working towards something meaningful. While often mostly beneficial to the individual, personal goals can also contribute to the betterment of society. For example, when individuals set goals to obtain education, to pursue medical careers, or to earn a leadership role in the military, their efforts and achievements impact more than just themselves; the results positively impact their communities and add value to society. If those individuals make extreme personal sacrifices for those goals, then the means are most likely justified assuming they do not irreparably harm others or stand opposed to what is morally acceptable.

Not all goals belong to an individual, however. Nations, businesses, and communities, like individuals, have goals that often prioritize their own interests. But, regardless of the contribution made to society or the interests being protected, if the means by which the goal is achieved deviates from what is morally right or unjustifiably brings harm upon others, the goal loses its value and the novelty of achieving that goal is diminished.

That is not to say that extreme, morally questionable measures are not sometimes justifiable. There have been many instances in history that demonstrate this. During the Third Reich, Nazi Germany had as a goal the extermination of Jews and the proliferation of the Aryan race. Their extreme measures to achieve their goal were met by the extreme measures of the Allied Powers to prevent them from doing so. Some may argue that war is an unjustifiable means to an end. In this instance, the means by which the Allied Powers opted to achieve their goal was justified because, while it may have been morally questionable and caused harm to others, the alternative of not intervening would have had far greater consequences.

Goals are important for the growth of individuals and society as a whole. We should encourage the steadfast pursuit of goals with the understanding that in order for a goal to maintain its worth, the means by which that goal is achieved must be carefully considered. An achievement tainted by moral ineptitude or the unjustifiable sacrifice of others is in essence not an achievement at all.

Analysis

The essay takes a clear stance on the issue in the first paragraph, asserting that it is a mistake to assume that a "by any means necessary" approach is justifiable in all circumstances. The essay provides relevant examples on when "by any means necessary" is acceptable but cogently asserts that if the means by which the goal is achieved deviates from what is morally right or unjustifiably brings harm upon others, the goal loses its value and the novelty of achieving that goal is diminished.

The body paragraphs provide an analysis of individual goals and the goals of larger entities like nations, businesses and communities, and reasserts that means to achieving goals that deviate from what is morally right or cause harm to others are not justifiable. The essay sufficiently addresses the question task by providing examples of when the taken position may not be true. The fourth paragraph addresses the Allied Powers' goal to stop the extermination of Jews by the Third Reich. While the means by which the Allied Powers achieved their goal was morally questionable (war) and caused harm to others, the essay asserts the actions were justified because not intervening would have had far worse consequences.

The examples used are appropriate, persuasive, and align with the position the essay takes. There are minimal spelling and grammar errors, and the essay demonstrates a solid understanding of written English and critical reasoning. The essay receives a score of 6.

ARGO
BROTHERS

19 ANALYZE AN ARGUMENT: MODEL ESSAY

Prompt

The following is an excerpt from a letter drafted by the Nimman Homeowners Association and sent to the current homeowners in Nimman:

"Eight years ago, the nearby neighborhood, Old City, experienced a significant increase in property values after implementing rigid standards that standardized the exterior home colors and landscaping requirements for all homes in the neighborhood. Given their success, Nimman is implementing similar standards for landscaping and exterior paint colors in order to raise the property value of homes in the neighborhood.

Discuss the evidence needed to fully assess the argument. Include examples and an explanation of how the evidence provided strengthens or weakens the argument.

Essay

The letter to homeowners sets forth recommendations to increase property values for Nimman based on the outcomes of similar changes implemented in Old City several years prior. While the logic may initially seem to follow, closer inspection of the evidence challenges the assumptions made by the Homeowners Association. The argument is flawed in a number of ways.

First, the only evidence offered for the author's claim is that a nearby neighborhood implemented similar guidelines eight years ago and experienced an increase in property values. A lot can change in eight years that might impact the likelihood of a similar outcome. For example, people may have different priorities now than they did eight years ago or the area could have changed considerably in that time. Without more information about the full circumstances that lead to the increase in property value, and by using an example so far in the past, the author is at best making a huge logical leap.

Second, the Homeowners Association contends that simply tightening the restrictions on landscaping and standardizing exterior paint colors of the homes will produce the same results in Nimman as they did in Old City. Even when setting aside the time that has lapsed since Old City experienced an increase in property value, this assumption also fails to consider other factors that may have accounted for the increase in property value Old City experienced; it attributes the increase solely to the policy changes. Any number of confounding factors could have contributed to the increase, like an influx of businesses or greenspace that made the neighborhood more attractive and sought after, thereby driving up the property value.

The Homeowner Association's assertion is further questionable in its failing to establish that Old City and Nimman are comparable enough in all other aspects that making similar aesthetic changes would yield the same increase in property value. While the areas may be nearby each other, the communities could vary substantially enough that, even if the changes were the sole factor that accounted for Old City's property value, more would need to be done in Nimman in addition to those changes to make the areas equally desirable. The premises the Homeowners Association uses to support its conclusion are limited in scope and do not follow logically.

The Homeowners Association would have a more compelling argument had they gather evidence directly from homeowners in Old City that ascertained the factors that influenced their willingness to purchase a home in the area and the reasons they believe the property value experienced such an increase eight years ago. In addition to that, the Homeowners Association could have conducted surveys of residents near and in Nimman and Old City to gain an understanding of what qualities homeowners and potential homeowners value in a home and location presently. These two points of inquiry would have equipped the Homeowners Association with an understanding of past trends and present-day values, and provided them with more relevant and complete data to make more appropriate and recommendations more likely to yield expected results than those offered in the letter to residents.

Analysis

The essay examines the provided evidence and its assumptions and clearly articulates the weakness of the argument. The essay explores several considerations that the Homeowners Association has seemingly neglected when drawing its conclusion including other factors that may have prompted Old City's rise in property, and the fact that 8 years had lapsed.

Paragraphs 2 ,3 and 4, deconstruct the faulty logic of the argument, demonstrating why the argument as a whole is weak. The analysis of the evidence sufficiently satisfies the question task to include and discuss the strength or weakness of the evidence presented.

The last paragraph offers clear and appropriate examples of information that could be used to formulate better, data-driven recommendations that perhaps stand a better chance of increasing property value than recommendations that worked eight years ago in a different neighborhood.

The essay contains some minor errors that do not detract from the ideas being communicated. There is appropriate sentence variation and a strong grasp of grammar and vocabulary. The response overall is cogent, properly addresses the question task, and demonstrates a clear mastery of written English and critical reasoning. The essay receives a score of 6.

ARGO
BROTHERS

GRE®

PRACTICE TESTS

ARGO
BROTHERS

PRACTICE TEST 1

GRE®

Graduate Record Examinations

- This exam is 3 hours and 45 minutes long. Try to take this full exam in one sitting to simulate real test conditions.
- While taking this exam, refrain from listening to music or watching TV.
- When writing your response for Analyze an Issue & Analyze an Argument prompt, use a computer, and turn off the spell-check feature to simulate real testing conditions.
- Use a basic calculator, do not use a graphic or scientific calculator. On the real exam, you will have an on-screen calculator with only basic operation functions and a square root key.
- Concentrate and GOOD LUCK!

To calculate your score visit our web site and download excel calculator:

www.einstein-academy.com/GRE

ANALYTICAL WRITING | ESSAY 1

ANALYZE AN ISSUE | 30 MINUTES

The government has a responsibility to closely regulate herbal supplements that are made available for sale to ensure their safety and validate their claims about health outcomes.

Discuss how much you agree or disagree with the claim and the support offered in defense of the claim.

GO TO THE NEXT PAGE

ANALYTICAL WRITING | ESSAY 2
ANALYZE AN ARGUMENT | 30 MINUTES

The following memo was issued by the sales manager of Wappy Waffle restaurants.

"We recently made the decision to replace all our syrups with a sugar-free substitute. We have been soliciting customer feedback and determined that the change, however, has had little impact on our customers. To date, only about 4 percent of customers have complained, indicating that an average of 96 people out of 100 have happily greeted the change. Additionally, many servers have reported that a number of customers who ask for syrup do not complain when they are given the sugar-free variety instead. Clearly, these customers cannot distinguish between the two.

After reviewing the author's argument, examine any alternate explanations that could reasonably compete with the proposed explanation. In your response, discuss how your alternate explanations challenges the assertions provided in the argument.

VERBAL REASONING | 20 QUESTIONS
SECTION 3 | 30 MINUTES

DIRECTIONS: Answer each question according to the directions given.

For questions 1 to 8, you are to choose one answer for each blank from the corresponding column of choices.

1. Ash worked hard to accomplish his goal of bench-pressing twice his body weight. When he finally achieved the feat, he was ______________ .

Ⓐ rapturous
Ⓑ deflated
Ⓒ stoic
Ⓓ exasperated
Ⓔ smitten

2. Alana blamed her emotional distress on those around her instead of accepting personal responsibility for her actions. As a result, she ______________ herself from friends, causing them to believe she no longer wanted to be bothered.

Ⓐ bolstered
Ⓑ sequestered
Ⓒ illuminated
Ⓓ diminished
Ⓔ excused

3. Realizing his final grade in the course was not high enough to graduate, Josh ______________ his teacher to allow him to complete extra credit to raise his grade.

Ⓐ instructed
Ⓑ permitted
Ⓒ beseeched
Ⓓ commanded
Ⓔ expected

4. Considering how (i) ______________ the available evidence is against the defendant, the prosecution is unlikely to be able to build a (ii) ______________ case to present to the jury.

Blank i	Blank ii
Ⓐ insubstantial	Ⓓ persuasive
Ⓑ aggressive	Ⓔ circumstantial
Ⓒ erudite	Ⓕ sufficient

5. Joe tried to (i) ______________ the effects of the medicine by drinking coffee to reduce his drowsiness. His plan was unsuccessful and he only (ii) ______________ the effects.

Blank i	Blank ii
Ⓐ accelerate	Ⓓ exacerbated
Ⓑ mitigate	Ⓔ inflamed
Ⓒ aggravate	Ⓕ imputed

6. The (i) ______________ auditor combed through hundreds of records to piece together the carefully executed embezzlement scheme that (ii) ______________ hundreds of thousands of dollars to ghost companies.

Blank i	Blank ii
Ⓐ punctilious	Ⓓ averted
Ⓑ boorish	Ⓔ allotted
Ⓒ steadfast	Ⓕ diverted

7. The (i) _____________ of available financial resources made it difficult for the charter school to satisfy its (ii) _____________ responsibilities. Not only did the bills fall behind, but teachers also lacked the necessary supplies to provide innovative and engaging classroom activities. If the school is going to continue to thrive, it is (iii) _____________ for it to analyze its financial situation and make a plan to ameliorate the dearth of resources.

Blank i
Ⓐ concomitant
Ⓑ preponderance
Ⓒ paucity

Blank ii
Ⓓ managerial
Ⓔ pecuniary
Ⓕ mercurial

Blank iii
Ⓖ imperative
Ⓗ advisable
Ⓘ insincere

8. From the early 1880s onward, author Oscar Wilde found it hard to escape the (i) _____________ belief that he happily (ii) _____________ other people's ideas. By far the most controversial conflict in Wilde's career arose from criticisms that the socially competitive painter James McNeill Whistler made about Wilde's unacknowledged (iii) _____________ of his witticisms.

Blank i
Ⓐ entrenched
Ⓑ transient
Ⓒ unfounded

Blank ii
Ⓓ expunged
Ⓔ espoused
Ⓕ filched

Blank iii
Ⓖ acknowledgement
Ⓗ approbation
Ⓘ appropriation

VERBAL REASONING

Questions 9 to 11 are based on the following passage. Select one answer unless otherwise indicated.

The following is an excerpt from The Pursuit of Happiness by Charles Dudley Warner.

Perhaps the most curious and interesting phrase ever put into a public document is "the pursuit of happiness." It is declared to be an inalienable right. It cannot be sold. It cannot be given away. It is doubtful if it can be left by will. The right of every man to be six feet high and of every woman to be five feet four was regarded as self-evident, until women asserted their undoubted right to be six feet high also, when some confusion was introduced into the interpretation of this rhetorical fragment of the eighteenth century.

The pursuit of happiness! It is not strange that men call it an illusion. But I am satisfied that it is not the thing itself, but the pursuit, that is an illusion. Instead of thinking of the pursuit, why not fix our thoughts upon the moments, the hours, perhaps the days, of this divine peace, this merriment of body and mind, that can be repeated, and perhaps indefinitely extended by the simplest of all means, namely, the disposition to make the best of whatever comes to us? Perhaps the Latin poet was right in saying that no man can count himself happy while in this life, that is, in a continuous state of happiness; but as there is for the soul no time save the conscious moment called "now," it is quite possible to make that "now" a happy state of existence. The point I make is that we should not habitually postpone that season of happiness to the future.

Sometimes wandering in a primeval forest, in all the witchery of the woods, besought by the kindliest solicitations of nature, wild flowers in the trail, the call of the squirrel, the flutter of the bird, the great world music of the wind in the pine-tops, the flecks of sunlight on the brown carpet and on the rough bark of the immemorial trees, I find myself unconsciously postponing my enjoyment until I shall reach a hoped-for open place of full sun and boundless prospect. The analogy cannot be pushed, for it is the common experience that these open spots in life, where leisure and space and contentment await us, are usually grown up with thickets, fuller of obstacles, to say nothing of the labors and duties and difficulties, than any part of the weary path we have trod.

The pitiful part of this inalienable right to the pursuit of happiness is, however, that most men interpret it to mean the pursuit of wealth, and strive for that always, postponing being happy until they get a fortune, and if they are lucky in that, find in the end that the happiness has somehow eluded them, that, in short, they have not cultivated that in themselves which alone can bring happiness. More than that, they have lost the power of the enjoyment of the essential pleasures of life. I think that the woman in the Scriptures who out of her poverty put her mite into the contribution-box got more happiness out of that driblet of generosity and self-sacrifice than some men in our day have experienced in founding a university.

9. In line 52, the author uses the phrase "driblet of generosity" most likely to suggest that the subject:

- (A) Shared what she had without reservations
- (B) Was reluctant to share the little that she had
- (C) Did not give enough to make a difference
- (D) Felt guilty because her contribution was so small
- (E) Cried when she gave all she had

10. The author suggests that the pursuit of happiness is most often closely linked to:

- (A) the pursuit of power
- (B) the pursuit of wealth
- (C) a commitment to a healthy lifestyle
- (D) a spirit of carpe diem
- (E) helping others pursue happiness

11. Which word from the passage is most likely derived from a Latin root that means "age"?

- (A) inalienable
- (B) irreverent
- (C) primeval
- (D) essential
- (E) immemorial

GO TO THE NEXT PAGE

Questions 12 and 13 are based on the following passage. Select one answer unless otherwise indicated.

The stability that marked the Iroquois Confederacy's pro-British position was diminished with the overthrow of James II in 1688, the colonial uprisings that followed in Massachusetts, New York, and Maryland, and the commencement of King William's War against Louis XIV of France. The increasing French threat to English hegemony in the interior of North America was signalized by French-led or French-inspired attacks on the Iroquois and on outlying colonial settlements in New York and New England. The high point of the Iroquois response was the spectacular raid of August 5, 1689, in which the Iroquois virtually wiped out the French Village of Lachine, just outside Montreal. A counterraid by the French on the English village of Schenectady in March, 1690, instilled an appropriate measure of fear among the English and their Iroquois allies.

The Iroquois position at the end of the war, which was formalized by treaties made during the summer of 1701 with the British and the French, and which was maintained throughout most of the eighteenth century, was one of "aggressive neutrality" between the two competing European powers. Under the new system the Iroquois initiated a peace policy toward the "far Indians," tightened their control over the nearby tribes, and induced both English and French to support their neutrality toward the European powers by appropriate gifts and concessions.

By holding the balance of power in the sparsely settled borderlands between English and French settlements, and by their willingness to use their power against one or the other nation if not appropriately treated, the Iroquois played the game of European power politics with effectiveness. The system broke down, however, after the French became convinced that the Iroquois were compromising the system in favor of the English and launched a full-scale attempt to establish French physical and juridical presence in the Ohio Valley, the heart of the borderlands long claimed by the Iroquois. As a consequence of the ensuing Great War for Empire, in which Iroquois neutrality was dissolve and European influence moved closer, the play-off system lost its efficacy and a system of direct bargaining supplanted it.

12. The primary purpose in the passage is to:

Ⓐ disavow the imperialistic policies advanced by the French
Ⓑ highlight the impact the war had on the Iroquois population
Ⓒ examine possible alternate outcomes of the French occupation
Ⓓ describe and assess the effect of European military power had on the Iroquois
Ⓔ provide commentary on the Iroquois' unwillingness to engage in diplomacy

13. With which of the following statements would the author be LEAST likely to agree?

Ⓐ The Iroquois were effective in managing France's aggressive encroachment
Ⓑ The Iroquois were shrewd strategists and often played one side against the other
Ⓒ James II being deposed agitated tension within the colonies
Ⓓ The French resented the British for their success in gaining favor among the Iroquois
Ⓔ The Iroquois ceased to hold the balance of power early in the eighteenth century

VERBAL REASONING

For questions 14-20, select two answers that best complete the blank and produces two sentences that are alike in meaning.

14. Because it is far off the beaten path and imposes stringent restrictions on the number of tourists allowed to visit at any given time, Bhutan has managed to preserve its culture and the natural beauty of its lush mountain villages. Many view the country as a ______________ of sorts and dream about visiting and experiencing the serene surroundings and hospitable people.

Ⓐ utopia
Ⓑ purgatory
Ⓒ haven
Ⓓ paradise
Ⓔ omen

15. To the untrained eye that may only see random and chaotic paint strokes, impressionist works of art may seem ______________.

Ⓐ whimsical
Ⓑ intentional
Ⓒ arbitrary
Ⓓ careful
Ⓔ superfluous
Ⓕ manic

16. When the students learned of the new policies that tightened school uniform regulations, they reacted ______________. Since the new principal had taken over, they had grown accustomed to the implementation of tedious and senseless policies.

Ⓐ impassively
Ⓑ angrily
Ⓒ stoically
Ⓓ offensively
Ⓔ blithely
Ⓕ callously

17. People often blame meteorologists for misreporting the weather when in actuality it is not their fault. Weather is ______________; even when studied closely, it can change in an instant.

Ⓐ fickle
Ⓑ capricious
Ⓒ laconic
Ⓓ unswerving
Ⓔ liable
Ⓕ steadfast

18. Pilar had serious ______________ about joining the team since Amy, her supervisor, was known for taking over projects that she wasn't assigned to and generally being a poor team-player.

Ⓐ misgivings
Ⓑ exceptions
Ⓒ grief
Ⓓ qualms
Ⓔ aberrations
Ⓕ provisions

19. Having travelled to many countries to study their culinary culture, Jenn was a shoe-in to win the cooking competition since a majority of the score was based on the chef's ability to integrate a ______________ of cuisines, techniques, and flavors into their dishes.

Ⓐ mélange
Ⓑ dearth
Ⓒ cacophony
Ⓓ fusion
Ⓔ template
Ⓕ scarcity

GO TO THE NEXT PAGE

20. The doctor told Victor that he needed to better manage his hypertension and lose weight or he could be at serious risk of a heart attack. So, Victor decided to give up eating meat and overall made more ________________ choices when planning his meals.

- (A) austere
- (B) cavalier
- (C) abstemious
- (D) garrulous
- (E) voracious
- (F) conventional

STOP

QUANTITATIVE REASONING | 20 QUESTIONS
SECTION 4 | 35 MINUTES

DIRECTIONS: For questions 1-8, use any provided centered information to help you compare Column A and Column B. Select the answer that describes the relationship between the two quantities, noting that the same answer choices are presented for each Quantitative Comparison question:

- A **Quantity A is greater.**
- B **Quantity B is greater.**
- C **The two quantities are equal.**
- D **The relationship cannot be determined from the information given.**

1.

$$x + y = 16$$
$$y + 4 = 10$$

Column A	Column B
x	y

Ⓐ Ⓑ Ⓒ Ⓓ

2.

$$a < b < 0$$

Column A	Column B
$\lvert b \rvert$	$\lvert a \rvert$

Ⓐ Ⓑ Ⓒ Ⓓ

3.

$$x^2 = 16$$

Column A	Column B
x	-4

Ⓐ Ⓑ Ⓒ Ⓓ

4.

10 cm

Column A	Column B
The area of the circle	2^8

Ⓐ Ⓑ Ⓒ Ⓓ

5.

Column A	Column B
The sum of two acute angles	90°

Ⓐ Ⓑ Ⓒ Ⓓ

GO TO THE NEXT PAGE

QUANTITATIVE REASONING

6.

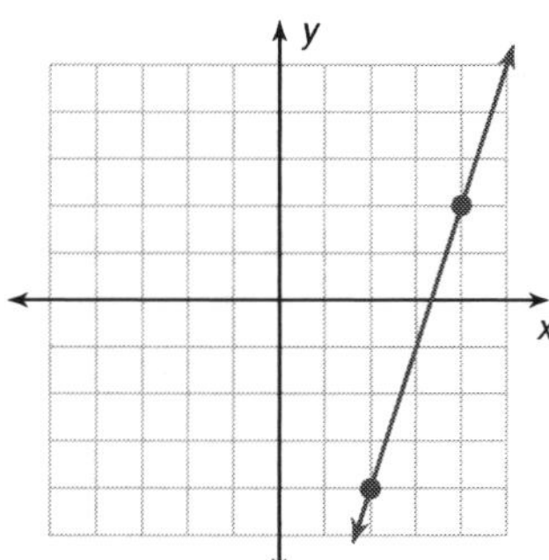

Column A	Column B
$\frac{3}{4}$	The slope of the line in the graph above

Ⓐ Ⓑ Ⓒ Ⓓ

7. There are 8 blue glass marbles and 6 red glass marbles in a box. Two are chosen at random without replacement.

Column A	Column B
The probability of choosing two red glass marbles	The probability of choosing a blue glass marble then a red glass marble

Ⓐ Ⓑ Ⓒ Ⓓ

8. Gabe is 5 years older than Paul. Gabe was twice as old as Paul three years ago.

Column A	Column B
5	Paul's current age

Ⓐ Ⓑ Ⓒ Ⓓ

9. If $y \neq 0$, select all the terms that must be positive:

Ⓐ $|y|$
Ⓑ y^{-2}
Ⓒ $y^2 \bullet y^{-4}$
Ⓓ y^0
Ⓔ $\frac{1}{y^{-5}}$
Ⓕ $(y^2)^3$

10. Sean rode his bike 60 miles between 10:30AM and 1:45PM on Monday. What was his approximate average mileage per hour?

Ⓐ 20.0
Ⓑ 21.5
Ⓒ 18.5
Ⓓ 17.25
Ⓔ 17.75

11. Which one of the following is equivalent to the expression $\frac{(xy)^3(z^0)}{x^3y^4}$ when $abc \neq 0$?

Ⓐ xyz
Ⓑ xz
Ⓒ $\frac{1}{y}$
Ⓓ 1
Ⓔ $\frac{z}{xy}$

QUANTITATIVE REASONING

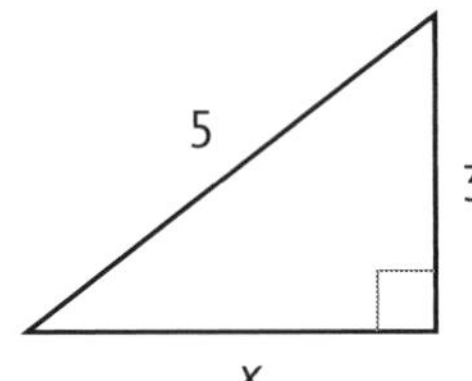

12. For the figure above, find the value of x.

Ⓐ 4
Ⓑ 3.5
Ⓒ 6
Ⓓ 5
Ⓔ 5.5

---

13. Which one of the following could be an integer?

Ⓐ The average of two consecutive integers
Ⓑ The average of 8 consecutive integers
Ⓒ The average of 8 and 11
Ⓓ The average of three consecutive integers
Ⓔ The average of 11 and 22

---

14. If $4(x - 1) = x + 8$, then $x =$

Ⓐ 4
Ⓑ -4
Ⓒ $\frac{1}{2}$
Ⓓ $\frac{1}{3}$
Ⓔ $\frac{1}{6}$

---

15. After a 20% discount at the book store, a recipe book sells for $10. What was the original price of the book? Enter your response in the text box.

---

16. The average of a and b is 16 and the average of a, b, and c is 22. Find the value of c.

Ⓐ 67
Ⓑ 16
Ⓒ 34
Ⓓ 40
Ⓔ 28

---

17. Which of the following is the slope of a line perpendicular to the line $3x + 5y = 10$?

Ⓐ 3
Ⓑ $\frac{5}{3}$
Ⓒ $-\frac{5}{3}$
Ⓓ $\frac{3}{5}$
Ⓔ $-\frac{3}{5}$

QUANTITATIVE REASONING

Use the diagram below to answer question 18 and 19.

A survey was conducted to determine the age at which the members of the Youth Advisory Committee started their first job.

Age at First Job

Age	Frequency
14	1
15	3
16	3
17	4
18	1
19	2
21	1
23	1

18. What was the median age reported by the Youth Advisory Committee?

Ⓐ 15.5
Ⓑ 16
Ⓒ 17.5
Ⓓ 17
Ⓔ 18

19. What is the average age at which the members of the Youth Advisory Committee secured their first job?

Ⓐ 17.19
Ⓑ 20
Ⓒ 17
Ⓓ 16.25
Ⓔ 14.25

20. Suppose $2(a - 3) + 9 = 4a - 7$. What is the value of a?

STOP

QUANTITATIVE REASONING | 20 QUESTIONS
SECTION 5 | 35 MINUTES

DIRECTIONS: For questions 1-8, use any provided centered information to help you compare Column A and Column B. Select the answer that describes the relationship between the two quantities, noting that the same answer choices are presented for each Quantitative Comparison question:

- A **Quantity A is greater.**
- B **Quantity B is greater.**
- C **The two quantities are equal.**
- D **The relationship cannot be determined from the information given.**

1.

Column A	Column B
$x + 9$	$x + 11$

Ⓐ Ⓑ Ⓒ Ⓓ

2.

$a^2 = 9$
$b^3 = 27$

Column A	Column B
a	b

Ⓐ Ⓑ Ⓒ Ⓓ

3.

$x^2 + 9 = 18$
$x > 0$

Column A	Column B
x	-5

Ⓐ Ⓑ Ⓒ Ⓓ

4.

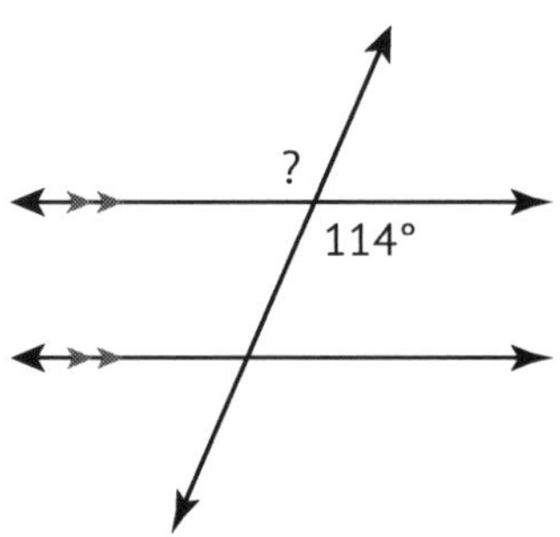

Column A	Column B
The measurement of the missing angle	66°

Ⓐ Ⓑ Ⓒ Ⓓ

5.

Column A	Column B
$(-5)^5$	$(-3)^8$

Ⓐ Ⓑ Ⓒ Ⓓ

6.

Column A	Column B
The sum of integers from 21 to 51 inclusive	The sum of integers from 24 to 49 inclusive

Ⓐ Ⓑ Ⓒ Ⓓ

QUANTITATIVE REASONING

7. A task is completed by x workers in 36 hours. The same task is completed by $(x + 2)$ workers in y hours.

Column A	Column B
36	y

Ⓐ Ⓑ Ⓒ Ⓓ

8.

Column A	Column B
Time to travel 95 miles at 50mph	Time to travel 125 miles at 60mph

Ⓐ Ⓑ Ⓒ Ⓓ

9. For the following equation, find the value for x: $-3(x-6)+2x(x+8)$:

Ⓐ $-29x+9$
Ⓑ $-37x+12$
Ⓒ $-26x+2x^2+34$
Ⓓ $13x+18+2x^2$

10. Find the distance between the two points $(-4,6)$ and $(-8,2)$:

Ⓐ $3\sqrt{29}$
Ⓑ $2\sqrt{2}$
Ⓒ $\sqrt{205}$
Ⓓ $4\sqrt{2}$
Ⓔ $2\sqrt{2}$

11. Working alone, it takes Randy 11 hours to inventory the instrument shop. Liz can complete the same inventory in 10 hours. If they worked together, how long would it take them to complete the inventory of the instrument shop?

Ⓐ 5.24 hours
Ⓑ 5.59 hours
Ⓒ 5.77 hours
Ⓓ 5.6 hours
Ⓔ 5 hours

12. Simplify the expression: $-3\sqrt{6}+2\sqrt{6}$

Ⓐ $-2\sqrt{6}$
Ⓑ $\sqrt{6}$
Ⓒ $-\sqrt{6}$
Ⓓ 1
Ⓔ $-6\sqrt{6}$

13. Consider the equation $\frac{2+n}{-5}=-2$. Solve for n. Write your answer in the text box.

QUANTITATIVE REASONING

14. Find the area of the figure below.

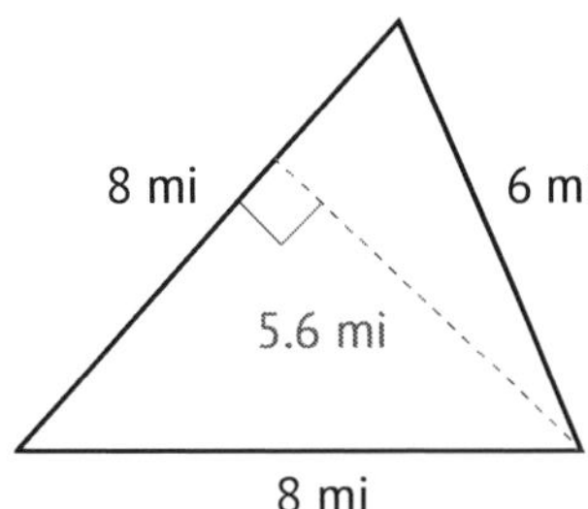

Ⓐ 19.7
Ⓑ 22.4
Ⓒ 11.2
Ⓓ 44.8
Ⓔ 44.2

---

15. A candy shop sells chocolate bars and strawberry rock candy in a ratio of 5:2. The ratio of strawberry rock candy to coconut haystacks is 5:3. What is the ratio of chocolate bars to coconut haystacks?

Ⓐ 3:2
Ⓑ 2:3
Ⓒ 3:5
Ⓓ 25:6
Ⓔ 9:5

---

16. Find the slope of the line perpendicular to the line with the equation $y-2x+3=0$.

Ⓐ - 2
Ⓑ $-\frac{1}{2}$
Ⓒ 2
Ⓓ $\frac{1}{2}$
Ⓔ - 1

---

17. The new video games console was priced at $400 when it was released last year. This year, the price decreased by 15% during the holiday sale period. The game manufacturer recently announced that the same console will be re-released with new updates and expanded functionality. The retail price will be 25% greater than the previous sale price. When the game console is re-released, what will be the retail price?

Ⓐ $360
Ⓑ $425
Ⓒ $380
Ⓓ $415
Ⓔ $395

---

18. Solve the proportion: $\frac{n+4}{10}=\frac{n-8}{2}$

Ⓐ 7.3
Ⓑ - 11
Ⓒ 11
Ⓓ 6.2
Ⓔ - 10

---

19. If A, B, C, D, and E are points on a plane such that line CD bisects $\angle ACB$ and line CB bisects right angle $\angle ACE$, then $\angle DCE$ =

Ⓐ 22.5°
Ⓑ 45°
Ⓒ 57.5°
Ⓓ 67.5°
Ⓔ 72.5°

---

20. Find x.

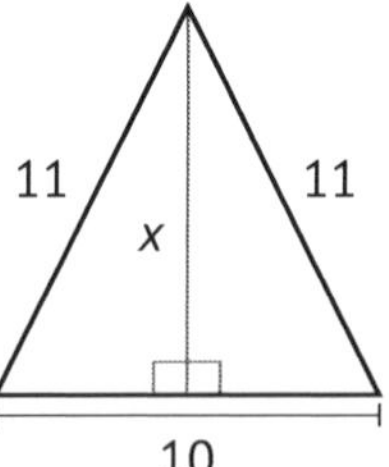

Ⓐ 16
Ⓑ 6
Ⓒ $\sqrt{8}$
Ⓓ $4\sqrt{6}$
Ⓔ $3\sqrt{2}$

STOP

VERBAL REASONING | 20 QUESTIONS
SECTION 6 | 30 MINUTES

DIRECTIONS: Answer each question according to the directions given.

For questions 1 to 8, you are to choose one answer for each blank from the corresponding column of choices.

1. No one was surprised that Gavin decided to join a law firm as a trial lawyer, given his ______________ nature.

Ⓐ potent
Ⓑ litigious
Ⓒ unobtrusive
Ⓓ introverted
Ⓔ exuberant

2. Raye was a ______________ child. By the time she was five, she already played two instruments proficiently and had nearly mastered a language other than her native language.

Ⓐ troublesome
Ⓑ malleable
Ⓒ cantankerous
Ⓓ thwarted
Ⓔ precocious

3. To hide the insecurities she had yet to deal with, Jennifer often acted like a ______________, making people laugh out of fear that if she didn't, people would see her true self and judge her.

Ⓐ buffoon
Ⓑ recluse
Ⓒ diplomat
Ⓓ prude
Ⓔ forerunner

4. Toby's writing style did not match the style desired by the satire magazine. His writings were often (i) ______________ and lacked any sort of sensationalism or (ii) ______________.

Blank i	Blank ii
Ⓐ humdrum	Ⓓ waggishness
Ⓑ academic	Ⓔ depth
Ⓒ scintillating	Ⓕ insight

5. Bobby stood in the winding (i) ______________ for what seemed like hours. But, he was determined to (ii) ______________ tickets to the newly announced Garth concert since it had long been his dream to see the band perform live.

Blank i	Blank ii
Ⓐ cue	Ⓓ procure
Ⓑ stanchion	Ⓔ mislay
Ⓒ queue	Ⓕ scalp

6. Although the start-up had the potential to become a (i) ______________ and thriving business, it failed to capture the attention of venture capitalists, largely because its pitch deck was (ii) ______________; it focused too heavily on insignificant statistics and background and failed to clearly articulate the overall purpose of the company.

Blank i	Blank ii
Ⓐ viable	Ⓓ conflated
Ⓑ venerable	Ⓔ convoluted
Ⓒ vexed	Ⓕ disparate

GO TO THE NEXT PAGE

VERBAL REASONING

7. The careful examination of the stability of banks in the U.S is supposed to reassure (i) ______ investors by affirming that the banks they trust with their money are the most secure. The thorough process is meant to identify both the most stable and the most (ii) ______ institutions and report back to investors. Since the banks are reviewed by an independent firm by individuals with no vested interest in the banks or the investors, their recommendations are viewed as (iii) ______ and are highly regarded.

Blank i
Ⓐ timorous
Ⓑ parsimonious
Ⓒ irate

Blank ii
Ⓓ tenuous
Ⓔ steady
Ⓕ duplicitous

Blank iii
Ⓖ unprejudiced
Ⓗ vacillating
Ⓘ veritable

8. The (i) ______ state of the community college requires immediate attention, but it's important that the action plan be carefully laid out and executed so as not to exacerbate the situation. Faculty need extensive training in classroom management and curriculum development, while administrators need to develop better mechanisms to (ii) ______ progress, using consistent standards and measurements to ascertain compliance. Overall, the community college needs to work to develop a more efficacious approach to teaching and programming if it hopes to increase its student (iii) ______ and maintain an appropriate student body size.

Blank i
Ⓐ execrable
Ⓑ tendentious
Ⓒ chaotic

Blank ii
Ⓓ assess
Ⓔ possess
Ⓕ allocate

Blank iii
Ⓖ resentment
Ⓗ retention
Ⓘ engagement

Questions 9 to 11 are based on the following passage. Select one answer unless otherwise indicated.

The Egyptians taught us many things. They were excellent farmers. They knew all about irrigation. They built temples which were afterwards copied by the Greeks and which served as the earliest models for the churches in which we worship nowadays. They invented a calendar that proved such a useful instrument for the purpose of measuring time that it has survived with a few changes until today. But most important of all, the Egyptians learned how to preserve speech for the benefit of future generations. They had invented the art of writing.

We are so accustomed to newspapers and books and magazines that we take for granted that the world has always been able to read and write. Without written documents we would be like cats and dogs, who can only teach their kittens and their puppies a few simple things and who, because they cannot write, possess no way in which they can make use of the experience of those generations of cats and dogs that have gone before them.

In the first century when the Romans came to Egypt, they found the valley full of strange little pictures which seemed to have something to do with the history of the country. But the Romans were not interested in foreign riddles and did not inquire into the origin of the peculiar figures that covered the walls of the temples and the walls of the palaces and endless reams of flat sheets made out of the papyrus reed. The last of the Egyptian priests who understood the holy art of making such pictures died several years before the Romans arrived. Egypt, deprived of its independence, had become a store-house filled with important historical documents that no one could decipher.

Seventeen centuries went by and Egypt remained a land of mystery. But, in 1798, a French general by the name of Bonaparte happened to visit eastern Africa to prepare for an attack on the British Indian Colonies. He did not get beyond the Nile, and his campaign was a failure. But, quite accidentally, the famous French expedition solved the problem of the ancient Egyptian picture-language, now known as hieroglyphics.

One day a young French officer, much bored by the dreary life of his little fortress on the Rosetta river (a mouth of the Nile) decided to spend a few idle hours rummaging among the ruins of the Nile Delta. He found a stone that initially greatly puzzled him. Like everything else in Egypt, it was covered with little figures. But this particular slab of black basalt was different from anything that had ever been discovered. It carried three inscriptions. One of these was in Greek. The Greek language was widely known. "All that is necessary," so he reasoned, "is to compare the Greek text with the Egyptian figures, and they will at once tell their secrets."

The plan sounded simple enough but it took more than twenty years to solve the riddle. In 1802, French professor Champollion began to compare the Greek and the Egyptian texts of the now famous Rosetta stone. In 1823, he announced that he had discovered the meaning of fourteen hieroglyphic figures. Today the story of the valley of the Nile is better known to us than the story of the Mississippi River. We possess a written record that covers four thousand years of chronicled history.

9. What is the primary purpose of the passage?

- Ⓐ To discuss the origins of the English language
- Ⓑ To recount the discovery and deciphering of the earliest known written language
- Ⓒ To highlight the critical role Egyptians played in deciphering the Rosetta stone
- Ⓓ To demonstrate the close relationship between Greek and hieroglyphics
- Ⓔ To establish the importance of learning about the story of both the Mississippi River and the Nile Valley

---

10. The passage most supports which one of the following inferences?

- Ⓐ Had the Rosetta stone never been found, it would have been impossible to decipher Egyptian hieroglyphics.
- Ⓑ Early Egyptian discoveries and practices persist in some form even in the modern world.
- Ⓒ The Romans were convinced their language was superior and thus had no desire to decipher the hieroglyphics that proliferated throughout Egypt.
- Ⓓ Had Bonaparte's planned attack on the British Indian colonies been successful, the Rosetta stone would have never been found.
- Ⓔ All languages derived from ancient Egypt.

11. What can be inferred by the author's assertion in line 60 that we now know the story of the Nile better than the story of the Mississippi?

Ⓐ Egyptians shared the story of Egypt's rise to power with the French general when he arrived and the story was passed down in perpetuity.
Ⓑ The Rosetta stone helped scholars decipher the hieroglyphics throughout Egypt which chronicled Egypt's long and prosperous history of building an empire along the Nile.
Ⓒ The history of the Mississippi River is similar to that of the Nile River.
Ⓓ The Mississippi River and its history of development is not as important as the story of the Nile.

GO TO THE NEXT PAGE

Questions 12 and 13 are based on this passage. Select one answer unless otherwise indicated.

The World Cup is one of the premier sporting events in the world, drawing large and boisterous crowds whenever it is held. FIFA, the organization that oversees professional soccer, votes to decide where the World Cup is held; it takes bids from interested countries and ultimately makes a decision on which country would best support the event. When FIFA announced that the 2022 World Cup would be held in Qatar, the decision was met with disdain and consternation from soccer fans, humanitarian organizations, and even prominent celebrities. Many felt that the decision was ill-informed given Qatar's extreme climate. Aside from the potentially inhospitable climate conditions players and fans alike would be subjected to, Qatar is also a dry country, so alcohol sales and consumption are not permitted. Many justifiably contend that the unavailability of alcohol would completely change the vibe of the event. Additionally, Qatar would have to build all new facilities to accommodate the large crowds and a stadium since it does not currently have one. Human rights groups have spoken out about the horrid work conditions some of immigrant workers who are building the stadium are subjected to as they work to meet rigorous construction deadlines. FIFA has offered little response to the criticism and has only issued one statement standing by their choice of Qatar as a host country and expressing confidence in their ability to host a spectacular World Cup.

12. Which one of the following statements is the author most likely to agree with based on the passage? Select all that apply.

- [A] FIFA should rescind its decision to host the World Cup in Qatar.
- [B] The availability of alcohol is an important consideration when planning the World Cup.
- [C] FIFA made a controversial decision to select Qatar as the host of the 2022 World Cup.
- [D] Soccer fans will likely not travel to Qatar out of protest of FIFA's decision.
- [E] Qatar will likely make improvements in its labor policies and treat its immigrant workers more fairly.

13. The passage mentions each of the following objections to Qatar hosting the 2022 World Cup, EXCEPT:

- (A) The lack of established infrastructure
- (B) Inability to sell or consume alcohol
- (C) Unfair labor practices
- (D) Conflict of the World Cup with religious holidays
- (E) Inhospitable climate

GO TO THE NEXT PAGE

VERBAL REASONING

Question 14-15 is based on the following passage. Select one answer unless otherwise indicated.

Deadlines often stifle creativity with regards to writing. When forced to write within the confines of a given time frame, writers often have to make difficult decisions to omit content that requires more time than is available to develop. Additionally, since writing is a creative process, deadlines often do not allow enough time for the writer to step away from the material and assess what is missing and what can be refined. As a result, writers often end up frustrated with their final product, feeling like they have not put out their best work. Publishers, whose primary concern is with the distribution of the material, tend to be unaware of writers' need for the space and time to create, as evidenced by the tight deadlines that writers are often under.

14. Which of the following, if true, most challenges the author's argument?

Ⓐ Writers need time to write and rewrite material to make it as polished as possible.
Ⓑ Many writers produce their best work under the pressure of a deadline.
Ⓒ Visual artists also find deadlines stressful and would rather work fluidly until the piece is complete.
Ⓓ Optimal conditions for creativity vary from person to person.
Ⓔ Frustration often leads writers to turn out a better finished product than they originally anticipated.

---

15. Which of the following can be logically inferred from the passage? Select all that apply.

Ⓐ Writers are deadline averse and prefer to never have a time limit placed on their creativity.
Ⓑ If a publisher gave a writer a deadline that reasonably matched the amount of time required to produce a particular written work, the writer would likely have the necessary time to fully assess the work and make needed additions and improvements.
Ⓒ Writers produce their best work when they have the appropriate time to do so.

VERBAL REASONING

For questions 16-20, select two answers that best complete the blank and produces two sentences that are alike in meaning.

16. Sonjia underestimated the ______________ conditions the group would encounter on their group trip to Bolivia; the altitude was much higher than everyone was used to and many of the trip participants experienced unpleasant symptoms.

Ⓐ soporific
Ⓑ vertiginous
Ⓒ placid
Ⓓ dizzying
Ⓔ hazardous
Ⓕ tedious

---

17. Diagnosed with early onset dementia, Donna worked fervently with her daughter to chronicle her life story before her memory began to ______________.

Ⓐ atrophy
Ⓑ digress
Ⓒ wane
Ⓓ wax
Ⓔ dilute
Ⓕ enervate

---

18. Advances in research have helped ______________ the mortality rate of infants born with severe genetic defects.

Ⓐ exacerbate
Ⓑ curtail
Ⓒ restrain
Ⓓ accelerate
Ⓔ numb
Ⓕ upturn

---

19. The exhibition was ______________ as a collegial gathering to discuss that latest innovations in 3D technology. But, it digressed into a series of quarrels amongst the participants.

Ⓐ touted
Ⓑ conceived
Ⓒ touted
Ⓓ heralded
Ⓔ promised
Ⓕ required

---

20. Gina was ______________ in her commitment to practicing Taekwondo and eventually earned her black belt and won a national championship.

Ⓐ steadfast
Ⓑ whimsical
Ⓒ resolute
Ⓓ persnickety
Ⓔ admirable
Ⓕ lenient

STOP

VERBAL REASONING
ANSWER KEY : SECTION 3

1. **A.**
Rapturous means overjoyed or ecstatic.

2. **B.**
The context clues indicate Alana closed herself off from her friends, which matches the meaning of sequestered.

3. **C.**
To beseech is to beg or implore. D is too strong and does not match the context clues.

4. **A, D.**
Though circumstantial is a legal term, it does not fit in the sentence. The prosecution would be unable to build a persuasive case with insubstantial evidence.

5. **B, D.**
Joe tried to slow down, or mitigate the effects, but only made them worse, or exacerbated them.

6. **A, F.**
Punctilious is meticulous. Steadfast typically refers to devotion or commitment rather than a keen attention to detail.

7. **C, E, G.**
Paucity means shortage; context clues lead you to believe there is shortage of funds. Pecuniary relates to finances or budgets. Imperative matches the urgency of the situation in the passage and is a more appropriate fit than advisable.

8. **A, F, I.**
The sentence paints Wilde as a pilfer of others' work. Unfounded does not work in the first blank based on the notion that it appears the claims were valid. Be careful not to confuse approbation (approval) with appropriation (taking).

9. **A.**
The woman, in spite of being impoverished, gave what she had, and derived great joy from it.

10. **D.**
A spirit of carpe diem is a sense of seizing the day. At the end of the first paragraph, the author writes "but as there is for the soul no time save the conscious moment called "now," it is quite possible to make that "now" a happy state of existence. The point I make is that we should not habitually postpone that season of happiness to the future."

11. **C.**
Primeval means ancient or aged.

12. **D.**
While many of the answers choices are discussed in the passage, they do not reflect the main point.

13. **E.**
The question asks which the author is LEAST likely to agree with. The passage discusses the solidarity of the Iroquois and how they managed European powers. Answer choice E is at odds with the facts of the passage.

14. **A, D.**
Utopia and paradise both mean a place of bliss or an ideal environment.

15. **A, C.**
Whimsical and arbitrary match the language in the sentence (random and chaotic). The sentence is about paintings, not painters, so manic, which usually describes an emotion, is incorrect.

16. **A, C.**
The students were unaffected by the announcement.

17. **A, B.**
Fickle and capricious both mean unreliable.

18. **A, D.**
Misgivings and qualms both are used to express feelings of doubt.

19. **A, D.**
You are looking for words that mean mixture. Fusion is often used to describe a mixture of food among other things, as is mélange.

20. **A, C.**
Both austere and abstemious reflect a sense of seriousness and responsibility.

QUANTITATIVE REASONING
ANSWER KEY : SECTION 4

1. **A.**
You are given two equations. In the second equation, $y + 4 = 10$, you can solve for *y*.

$$y + 4 = 10$$
$$y = 10 - 4$$
$$y = 6$$

Plug the value of y into the first equation to solve for *x*.

$$x + 6 = 16$$
$$x = 16 - 6$$
$$x = 10$$

2. **B.**
The inequality tells you that *a* is less than *b* and *b* is less than zero. So, both *a* and *b* are always going to be negative numbers. As negative numbers, *b* will always be greater than *a*. But, since you are taking the absolute value of both terms, *a* will always be greater than *b*.

3. **D.**
When you square a positive or a negative number, the result is always a positive number. You can find the value of *x* by taking the square root of 16 or by recalling common squares. Both 4^2 and -4^2 equal 16. Since *x* could be 4 or– 4, you cannot determine the relationship.

4. **A.**
The area of a circle is calculated using the equation $A = □r^2$. In this case, you have the radius, 10, so you can plug in and solve. Without solving for □, you end up with 100□. The standard value for □ is 3.14. So, when you solve for □ your answers is ≈314. The exponent 2^8 solved is equal to 256. The area of the circle is greater.

5. **D.**
Acute angles measure less than 90°. Since no additional information is given about the angles other than that they are acute, we cannot determine if the sum of their measurement is less than 90°.

6. **B.**
In the diagram, you have two points on the coordinate plane, (4, 2) and (2, – 4). Plug those points into the slope formula to find the slope:

$$\frac{y_1 - y_2}{x_1 - x_2} = \frac{2-(-4)}{4-2} = \frac{6}{2} = 3$$

The slope of the line is 3, which is greater than $\frac{3}{4}$.

7. **B.**
The total number of glass marbles you have is 14. If you choose two marbles at random without replacement, you need to calculate each instance separately and calculate each column individually. For column a, on the first pull, your chances of pulling a red glass marble is $\frac{6}{14}$. Assuming you pulled a red glass marble on the first pull, for the second pull, you only have 13 glass marbles overall, and only 5 of those are red. So, for the second pull, the probability of the marble being a red glass marble is $\frac{5}{13}$. To find the probability of both events occurring, multiply the probability of each event:

$$\frac{6}{14} \bullet \frac{5}{13} = \frac{30}{182} = \frac{15}{91}$$

For column B, for the first pull, the probability of the marble being a blue glass marble is $\frac{8}{14}$. For the second pull, the probability of the marble being a red glass marble is $\frac{6}{13}$. To find the probability of both of these event happening, multiply the probability of each event:

$$\frac{8}{14} \bullet \frac{6}{13} = \frac{48}{182} = \frac{24}{91}$$

The probability of pulling a blue glass marble, then a red glass marble is greater than the probability of pulling two red glass marbles.

8. **B.**
Gabe is 5 years older than Paul. Gabe was twice as old as Paul three years ago.

The centered information tells you that three years ago, Gabe was twice as old as Paul.

To compare the quantities in the columns, create an equation to solve for Paul's current age based on how hold he was three years ago. Let *x* represent Paul's current age.

QUANTITATIVE REASONING
ANSWER KEY : SECTION 4

Three years ago, Paul was $x - 3$. If Gabe is five years older than Paul, three years ago, Gabe was $x + 5 - 3$, so $x + 2$. But, Gabe was twice as old as Paul three years ago. If Paul was $x - 3$ and Gabe was $x + 2$, and Gabe's age was twice that of Paul's, you can create an equation and solve for x:

$$x+2=2(x-3)$$
$$x+2=2x-6$$
$$2=x-6$$
$$8=x$$

So, three years ago, Paul age was x-3, or 8-3. So, Paul was five. Gabe's age was x+2, or 8+2. So, Gabe was 10. To find Paul's current age, simply add three since you already know how old he was three years ago. Paul's current age is 8. So, Column B is greater.

9. A, B, C, D, F.
This question relies heavily on your understanding of the rules of exponents. Answer choice A must be positive since the absolute value of any number is positive. For answer choice B,

$y^{-2}=\frac{1}{y^2}$. Any number squared will yield a positive number. So, if you solved the fraction, it would be positive. For answer choice C, since you are multiplying exponents that share the same base, you add the exponents. When you add the exponents, you end up with the same expression you had in answer choice B, $y^2 \bullet y^{-4}=y^{-2}$. So, as was the case in answer choice B, the outcome will be positive. For answer choice D, any number raised to the zero power is 1. When you have an exponent in the denominator like in answer choice E, $\frac{1}{y^{-5}}$ is equivalent to y^5. The outcome will be positive if y is positive, and negative is y is negative, since the exponent is odd. So, E must not be positive. For answer choice F, multiply the exponents. Any number raised to an even power will yield a positive number.

10. C.
First, you must determine the amount of time Sean spent cycling, which is 3.25 hours. Divide the distance traveled by the time traveled to determine the approximate miles per hour:

$$\frac{60}{3.25}=18.46$$

Sean cycled at a rate of approximately 18.5 miles per hour.

11. C.
Distribute out the numerator:

$$\frac{(xy)^3(z^0)}{x^3y^4}=\frac{x^3y^3}{x^3y^4}$$

$z^0 = 1$, so it can be removed from the numerator since it is being multiplied by the remaining expression. Once you factor out the numerator, you can cancel out x^3 in both the numerator and denominator and y^3 in both the numerator and denominator. You are left with $\frac{1}{y}$.

12. A.
The triangle sides are Pythagorean 3:4:5 triples.

13. D.
This problem tests your understanding of basic number theory. Remember that an integer is a whole number. When you add two consecutive integers, the sum will be odd, and therefore the average cannot be an integer. The sum of three consecutive integers is always even, and the average is an integer. In all the other answer choices, the outcome cannot be a whole number.

14. A.
Distribute the terms:

$$4(x-1)=x+8$$
$$4x-4=x+8$$
$$4x=x+8+4$$
$$3x=12$$
$$x=4$$

15. \$12.50
To find the original price, use the equation $(100\%-20\%)\bullet(\textit{original price})=\$10.00$ and solve:

$$.80x=\$10.00$$
$$x=12.5$$

16. C.
The average of a and b is 16. So, $\frac{a+b}{2}=16$. You can solve to find that $a + b = 32$. You do not need to know the individual values of a and b. The problem is asking for the value of c and you know that the

average of a, b, and c is 22. So: $\frac{a+b+c}{3}=22$ and $a+b+c=66$

You already know that $a+b=32$, so solve for c.

$$\begin{aligned}32+c&=66\\c&=34\end{aligned}$$

17. B.
Be careful not to assume that 3 is the slope. The equation is not in slope-intercept form. Put the equation in slope-intercept form to find the slope of the original line:

$$\begin{aligned}3x+5y&=10\\5y&=-3x+10\\y&=-\frac{3}{5}+2\end{aligned}$$

So, the slope is $-\frac{3}{5}$. To find the slope of a line perpendicular to this line, take the negative reciprocal of slope of the original line. So, the slope is $\frac{5}{3}$.

18. D.
Organize the data in numerical order and find the middle term. Your data set is:

$\{14,15,15,15,16,16,16,17,17,17,17,18,19,19,21,23\}$

19. A.

20. The value of $x = 5$.

$$\begin{aligned}2(x-3)+9&=4x-7\\2x-6+9&=4x-7\\2x+3&=4x-7\\10&=2x\\x&=5\end{aligned}$$

You can substitute to check your answer.

QUANTITATIVE REASONING
ANSWER KEY : SECTION 5

1. **B.**
Column B will always be greater regardless of what number you plug in for x since you are adding a larger number, 11, to the expression.

2. **D.**
You can solve for a. In both cases, the variable is equal to 3. Be careful not to assume too quickly that the quantities are equal. Remember, when you square an integer, the result will be positive whether the integer is negative or positive. In this case, a^2 can be 3 or – 3.

3. **A.**
Solve for x. $x^2+9=18$. So, $x^2=9$. That means x = 3 or x = – 3. But, the centered instructions tell you that $x > 0$, so you can eliminate x = – 3 as a possibility. So x is 3, which is greater than -5.

4. **A.**
The angle is a vertical angle to the angle that measures 114°. Thus, the angle measurement will have the same measurement. A is the greater value.

5. **B.**
Any negative number raised to an odd power is negative. Any negative number raised to an even power is positive. So, the quantity in column A is negative and the quantity in column B is positive. B is greater.

6. **A.**
There is no need to add all the integers up in each set to see which sum is larger. Column A contains more terms and includes higher integers in the same range as column B. The quantity of column A is greater.

7. **A.**
The addition of two workers will decrease the number of hours it takes to complete the task. So, column A is greater.

8. **B.**
There is no need to calculate the actual times to travel each distance. You can estimate. Traveling 95 miles at 50 miles an hour will be less than two hours since you are traveling less than 100 miles; 100 miles at 50mph would take you exactly two hours. Traveling 125 miles at 60mph would take more than two hours since it would take you exactly two hours to travel 120 miles at 60mph. Column B has a greater value.

9. **D.**
Distribute to solve:
$-3(x-6)+2x(x+8)=-3x+18+2x^2+16x$.

Combine like terms: $13x+18+2x^2$

10. **D.**
Solve using the distance formula:

$$d=\sqrt{(x_2-x_1)^2+(y_2-y_1)^2}$$

$$d=\sqrt{(-8-(-4))^2+(2-6)^2}\text{, so, } d=\sqrt{32}=4\sqrt{2}$$

11. **A.**
This is a classic work/rate problem. It takes Randy 11 hours to do one inventory, so his rate of work is $\frac{1}{11}$. It takes Liz ten hours, so her rate of work is $\frac{1}{10}$. Find the least common multiple so you can find their combined rate of work. The least common multiple is 110. So, you end up with $\frac{11}{110}+\frac{10}{110}$. Since there is only one inventory, the combined rate to finish one inventory can be expressed as $\frac{1}{\frac{21}{110}}$. Multiply the reciprocal of the denominator to get $\frac{110}{21}=5.24$.

12. **C.**
The roots are the same, so you can subtract the values in front of the roots to arrive at the answer.

13. **8**

$$\frac{2+n}{-5}=-2$$
$$2+n=10$$
$$n=8$$

QUANTITATIVE REASONING
ANSWER KEY : SECTION 5

14. B.

The formula for the area of a triangle is $\frac{1}{2}bh$. So, plug in the values 8 and 5.6 for the base and height, respectively and solve.

15. D.

This question deals with combined ratios. Since the strawberry rock candy is involved in both ratios, you need to ensure that the strawberry rock candy is the same in each ratio in order to compare. Find the least common multiple of 2 and 5, which represent the number of pieces of strawberry rock candy in each ratio. The least common multiple is 10. The ratio of chocolate bars to strawberry rock candy is thus 25:10 and the ratio of strawberry rock candy to coconut haystacks is 10:6. So, the ratio of chocolate bars to coconut haystacks is 25:6.

16. B.

Perpendicular lines have a negative reciprocal slope.

17. B.

When the price is decreased by 15%, the console is $340. After the upgrade, the price increases from $340 to $425 representing a 25% increase.

18. C.

Cross-multiply.

19. D.

You are given that CB bisects the right-angle $\angle ACE$. So, $\angle ACB = \angle BCE = \frac{\angle ACE}{2} = \frac{90^\circ}{2} = 45^\circ$.

Since CD bisects $\angle ACB$,

$\angle ACD = \angle DCB = \frac{\angle ACB}{2} = \frac{45^\circ}{2} = 22.5^\circ$.

So, $\angle DCE = \angle DCB + \angle BCE = 22.5^\circ + 45^\circ = 67.5^\circ$.

20. D.

Divide the triangle into 2 right triangles. Substitute values in the Pythagorean Theorem and solve.

$$a^2 + 5^2 = 11^2$$
$$a^2 = 121 + 25$$
$$a = \sqrt{96} = 4\sqrt{6}$$

VERBAL REASONING
ANSWER KEY : SECTION 6

1. **B.**
Litigious means argumentative.

2. **E.**
Raye was developed well beyond what was expected for her age. Precocious means talented or gifted above what is expected.

3. **A.**
A buffoon is a fool or a jester.

4. **A, D.**
Context clues steer you in the opposite direction of satirical and witty.

5. **C, D.**
Be careful not to confuse cue (signal) with queue (line).

6. **A, E.**
Venerable means admirable and honorable and does not particularly fit the sentence as well as viable, which means workable or feasible. The pitch deck included too much irrelevant info so it was convoluted.

7. **A, D, G.**
The investors needing to be reassured indicates that they may be nervous or timorous. The second blank calls for the opposite of stable; tenuous is the most appropriate choice. Answer choice I is a distractor answer. Just because the independent firm has no vested interest in the banks or the investors, it does not mean their finding will be true. They will however, be unbiased.

8. **C, D, H.**
The urgency expressed in the topic sentence alludes to an atmosphere that needs immediate attention. Chaotic fits the bill. Administrators need to better understand if progress is being made, so they need better mechanisms to assess, or evaluate the situation. The closing indicates that the student body size not being appropriate is a consequence of not fixing the current issues. You can assume the school is trying to increase student retention, or the rate of students returning.

9. **B.**
The passage mentions hieroglyphics as the first written language and traces the history of the language being deciphered.

10. **B.**
Answer choice A is too absolute of an answer and is not supported by the passage. The passage mentions architecture and things like the calendar as remnants of ancient Egypt that still exist today in some form.

11. **B.**
The author closes saying that the deciphered written record chronicled 4000 years of history.

12. **B, C.**
Choice A is too absolute and is not supported by the passage. B and C are mentioned explicitly in the passage while D and E are assumptions that cannot be properly supported.

13. **D.**
Religious holidays are not mentioned in the passage.

14. **B.**
If many writers produce their best work under a tight deadline, the argument of the author is nullified.

15. **B.**
Answer choices A and C require assumptions that are not supported by the passage.

16. **B, D.**
The second sentence mentions high altitude, giving you clues to fill in the first blank. Vertiginous and dizzying are synonyms for symptoms that can result from altitude changes.

17. **A, C.**
Donna wanted to write her life story down before her memory started to decline. Wane and atrophy are both words for decline.

18. **B, C.**
An advance in technology would likely have positive outcomes. So, you can assume the advances made the situation better by reducing the mortality rate. Curtail and restrain both mean to reduce or cut short.

VERBAL REASONING
ANSWER KEY : SECTION 6

19. A, D.
The exhibition, based on the context clues, was not as expected. It was quarrelsome and seemed to not address the main topic. Touted and heralded mean publicized or promoted. In the sentence it is used in the context that the event was promoted at one things and ended up not being that. Promised does not work grammatically in the sentence.

20. A, C.
Gina worked hard, so she was steadfast and resolute, both of which mean determined.

Raw Score	Scaled Score	Raw Score	Scaled Score
40	170	20	150
39	169	19	149
38	168	18	148
37	167	17	147
36	166	16	146
35	165	15	145
34	164	14	144
33	163	13	143
32	162	12	142
31	161	11	141
30	160	10	140
29	159	9	139
28	158	8	138
27	157	7	137
26	156	6	136
25	155	5	135
24	154	4	134
23	153	3	133
22	152	2	132
21	151	1	131

These practice tests are designed to simulate actual testing conditions as closely as possible. While the questions are similar to those you will encounter on the GRE, the sections are not adaptive for Verbal and Quantitative Reasoning like they will be if you sit for the computer-adaptive exam. The scale above gives you an **idea** of your projected score and can help you monitor your progress as you become more familiar with the material. The scale above is a rough guide to predict your score. **As a reminder**, the PowerPrep II software distributed by ETS offers two free computer-adaptive exams to supplement your study plan. Be sure to include those exams in your study plan in addition to the exams in this section; this will help you get an idea of the areas you need to study more closely in order to reach your scoring goals.

ARGO
BROTHERS

PRACTICE TEST 2

GRE®

Graduate Record Examinations

- This exam is 3 hours and 45 minutes long. Try to take this full exam in one sitting to simulate real test conditions.
- While taking this exam, refrain from listening to music or watching TV.
- When writing your response for Analyze an Issue & Analyze an Argument prompt, use a computer, and turn off the spell-check feature to simulate real testing conditions.
- Use a basic calculator, do not use a graphic or scientific calculator. On the real exam, you will have an on-screen calculator with only basic operation functions and a square root key.
- Concentrate and GOOD LUCK!

To calculate your score visit our web site and download excel calculator:

www.einstein-academy.com/GRE

ANALYTICAL WRITING | ESSAY 1
ANALYZE AN ISSUE | 30 MINUTES

Teachers' salaries should be largely dependent on how well their students perform on standardized tests.

Discuss the extent to which you agree or disagree with the statement and explain your position. Citing specific examples, explain how the circumstances under which the recommendation could be adopted would or would not be advantageous in developing and supporting your view point. Explain how the specific circumstances affect your point of view..

GO TO THE NEXT PAGE

ANALYTICAL WRITING | ESSAY 2
ANALYZE AN ARGUMENT | 30 MINUTES

The following is from a memo released by a prominent pesticide company in Lincoln, Nebraska.

Wheat fields throughout the state are being ravaged by the wheat weevil, a crop pest that can eat through a pound of wheat a day! The wheat weevil is highly mobile and has a short gestation period so an infestation can manifest in no time. To prevent your valuable crops from being destroyed, you must act now. Because the wheat weevil has already infected crops in Lincoln, you can be sure that they will inevitably make it to your land. Call us today so we can help you protect your livelihood. Just two easy treatments guarantee the safety and longevity of your crops.

Discuss the stated and unstated assumptions in the argument and discuss what the consequences might be if those assumptions are shown to be unwarranted.

GO TO THE NEXT PAGE

VERBAL REASONING *SECTION 3* | 20 QUESTIONS 30 MINUTES

DIRECTIONS: Answer each question according to the directions given.

For questions 1 to 8, you are to choose one answer for each blank from the corresponding column of choices.

1. Reddington's ______________ clues made it nearly impossible for Keene to figure out the truth about her past.

Ⓐ cogent
Ⓑ nebulous
Ⓒ nefarious
Ⓓ peculiar
Ⓔ demure

2. One of the most important requirements for being a peer counselor is confidentiality. Those seeking counseling must not have any ______________ that their conversation will remain private.

Ⓐ aspiration
Ⓑ breech
Ⓒ prevision
Ⓓ inkling
Ⓔ misgivings

3. The neighborhood wellness program was charged with not only maintaining the safety of the neighborhood, but also creating a(n) ______________ environment where everyone felt welcomed and connected to each other.

Ⓐ isolated
Ⓑ earnest
Ⓒ affable
Ⓓ tolerable
Ⓔ extant

4. The camp was full of counselors with (i) ______________ dispositions, bursting at the seams with energy and positivity. The hope was that the campers, who often experienced little joy in their lives, would be motivated and invigorated by the positive energy and given the tools to better (ii) ______________ happiness in their lives when they return back home.

Blank i	Blank ii
Ⓐ abstract	Ⓓ obscure
Ⓑ sagacious	Ⓔ manifest
Ⓒ sanguine	Ⓕ compose

5. Climate change often evokes heated debates, especially in the political arena. But, few can deny that areas that were once lush and (i) ______________ are now starting to become (ii) ______________, unable to be inhabited or used for farming or other critical resources.

Blank i	Blank ii
Ⓐ fecund	Ⓓ diaphanous
Ⓑ puerile	Ⓔ barren
Ⓒ aggrade	Ⓕ bombastic

6. Unfortunately, Tom's reputation preceded him. He was known as one of the biggest (i)______________ in the company. Even though he openly flirted and made advances towards other employees often and indiscriminately, he acted (ii)______________ when he was confronted by the manager of Human Resources.

Blank i	Blank ii
Ⓐ imposters	Ⓓ unnerved
Ⓑ coquettes	Ⓔ flummoxed
Ⓒ forerunners	Ⓕ rapt

7. The long-tail boat cruised down the Mekong as the passengers aboard enjoyed the (i) ______________ scenery. It was just what they needed after the (ii) ______________________________ week they all had cleaning up after the massive floods that swept through the area. The boat ride was the first (iii) _______________ any of them had and they were all relishing in the opportunity to simply relax.

Blank i
Ⓐ picturesque
Ⓑ precluded
Ⓒ ornate

Blank ii
Ⓓ melancholy
Ⓔ tumultuous
Ⓕ austere

Blank iii
Ⓖ reprieve
Ⓗ respite
Ⓘ cacophony

8. The only safe basis of psychotherapy is a thorough psychological knowledge of the human personality. Yet such a claim has no value until it is (i) _______________ clear what is meant by psychological knowledge. We can know man in many ways. Not every study of man's inner life is psychology and the (ii) ______________ mixing of different ways of dealing with man's inner life is largely responsible for the vagueness that characterizes the popular literature of psychotherapy. It is not enough to say that a statement is true or not true. It may be true in one aspect and entirely (iii) _______________under another.

Blank i
Ⓐ ineptly
Ⓑ wholly
Ⓒ relatively

Blank ii
Ⓓ slipshod
Ⓔ meticulous
Ⓕ lugubrious

Blank iii
Ⓖ asinine
Ⓗ exacting
Ⓘ conspicuous

VERBAL REASONING

Questions 9 to 12 are based on the following passage. Select one answer unless otherwise indicated.

The following is an excerpt from Eleanor Roosevelt's speech to the Members of the American Civil Liberties Union in Chicago in 1940.

Now I listened to the broadcast this afternoon with a great deal of interest. I almost forgot what a fight had been made to assure the rights of the working man. I know there was a time when hours were longer and wages lower, but I had forgotten just how long that fight for freedom, to bargain collectively, and to have freedom of assembly, had taken.

Sometimes, until some particular thing comes to your notice, you think something has been won for every working man, and then you come across, as I did the other day, a case where someone had taken the law into his own hands and beaten up a labor organizer. I didn't think we did those things any more in this country, but it appears that we do. Therefore, someone must be always on the lookout to see that someone is ready to take up the cudgels to defend those who can't defend themselves. That is the only way we are going to keep this country a law-abiding country, where law is looked upon with respect and where it is not considered necessary for anybody to take the law into his own hands. The minute you allow that, then you have acknowledged that you are no longer able to trust in your courts and in your law-enforcing machinery, and civil liberties are not very well off when anything like that happens. So, I think that after listening to the broadcast today, I would like to remind you that behind all those who fight for the Constitution as it was written, for the rights of the weak and for the preservation of civil liberties, we have a long line of courageous people, which is something to be proud of and something to hold on to. Its only value lies, however, in the fact that we profit by example and continue the tradition in the future.

We must not let those people in back of us down; we must have courage; we must not succumb to fears of any kind; and we must live up to the things that we believe in and see that justice is done to the people under the Constitution, whether they belong to minority groups or not. This country is a united country in which all people have the same rights as citizens. We are grateful that we can trust in the youth of the nation that they are going on to uphold the real principles of democracy and put them into action in this country. They are going to make us an even more truly democratic nation.

9. Based on the passage, what can most likely be inferred about the content of the broadcast Roosevelt references in the first sentence?

- Ⓐ It derided the fair wage movement and its constituents.
- Ⓑ It sparked a sense of nostalgia in Roosevelt perhaps through references to times that preceded fair rights for workers.
- Ⓒ It criticized the amount of time it took for the labor movement to make measurable progress.
- Ⓓ The broadcast contained inaccuracies about the history of the fight for worker's rights.
- Ⓔ The broadcast included a call to action prompting citizens to reflect on the times when freedom of assembly and collective bargaining were not commonplace.

---

10. Select the sentence in the text that expresses Roosevelt's thoughts on the consequences of citizens disregarding the confines of the law and handling issues as they see fit.

---

11. Roosevelt used the word "fight" repetitively in the passage most likely to emphasize her support of protecting:

- Ⓐ Civil liberties
- Ⓑ Lawless citizens
- Ⓒ Labor organizers
- Ⓓ Youth
- Ⓔ Law enforcement officials

---

12. According to Roosevelt, the youth of the country: Select all that apply.

- [A] Can be trusted to continue to fight for civil liberties
- [B] Will influence the furthering of democracy in the country
- [C] Will be subjected to similar struggles encountered by those who came before them.

GO TO THE NEXT PAGE

Questions 13 and 14 are based on the following passage. Select one answer unless otherwise indicated.

The range of the American bison extended over about one-third of the entire continent of North America. Starting almost at tide-water on the Atlantic coast, it extended westward through a vast tract of dense forest, across the Alleghany Mountain system to the prairies along the Mississippi, and southward to the Delta of the great stream. Although the great plains country of the West was the natural home of the species, where it flourished most abundantly, it also wandered south across Texas to the burning plains of northeastern Mexico, westward across the Rocky Mountains into New Mexico, Utah, and Idaho, and northward across a vast treeless waste to the bleak and inhospitable shores of the Great Slave Lake itself. It is more than probable that had the bison remained unmolested and uninfluenced by man, it would eventually have crossed the Sierra Nevadas and the Coast Range and taken up its abode in the fertile valleys of the Pacific slope.

Had the bison remained for a few more centuries in undisturbed possession of its range, and with liberty to roam at will over the North American continent, it is almost certain that several distinctly recognizable varieties would have been produced. The buffalo of the hot regions in the extreme south would have become a short-haired animal like the gaur of India and the African buffalo. The individuals inhabiting the extreme north would have developed still longer hair, and taken on more of the dense hairiness of the musk ox. In the "wood" or "mountain buffalo" we already have a distinct foreshadowing of the changes which would have taken place in the individuals which made their permanent residence upon rugged mountains.

13. Which of the following best describes the author's attitude about the main contributing factor that affected the America bison's migratory course?

Ⓐ ambivalent
Ⓑ critical
Ⓒ neutral
Ⓓ passionate
Ⓔ indifferent

14. If American bison continued to roam freely without interference from man, according the author's assertions, what would be a key characteristic of bison found in the arid and hot areas of Texas?

Ⓐ Thick, long hair
Ⓑ Overly hairy
Ⓒ Short hair
Ⓓ Darker, tougher skin
Ⓔ Thick, short hair

VERBAL REASONING

For questions 15-20, select two answers that best complete the blank and produces two sentences that are alike in meaning.

15. The Republican candidate for President _______________ clamorously on political issues, immigration, and his ideas of patriotism at every-opportunity he received. But, no one was fooled by his lack of viable qualifications to serve as the leader of the free world.

Ⓐ pontificated
Ⓑ castigated
Ⓒ inveighed
Ⓓ maligned
Ⓔ demurred
Ⓕ acceded

16. The fire at the homeless shelter left several hundred _______________ residents without a home and critical necessities since all the shelter's supplies had also been lost in the fire and had yet to be replaced.

Ⓐ indigent
Ⓑ copious
Ⓒ nascent
Ⓓ impecunious
Ⓔ roving
Ⓕ staid

17. Cat owners typically fail to realize how _______________ their obsession is with their pet until an outsider observes their interactions and brings it to their attention.

Ⓐ apposite
Ⓑ bizarre
Ⓒ ominous
Ⓓ eccentric
Ⓔ gauche
Ⓕ morose

18. The conservative teacher stopped allowing students to suggest movies for the weekly movie break after the last one chosen proved to be more _______________ than its PG rating suggested it might be.

Ⓐ utilitarian
Ⓑ lascivious
Ⓒ bawdy
Ⓓ esoteric
Ⓔ mirthful
Ⓕ penetrating

19. Instead of fixing the many logical gaps in his presentation, Al spent hours developing _______________ to possible objections that the audience might have raised.

Ⓐ juxtapositions
Ⓑ frameworks
Ⓒ retorts
Ⓓ pretexts
Ⓔ ripostes
Ⓕ solecisms

20. Erica's exceptional grasp of Public Relations and Marketing has positioned her as a(n) _______________ in the field and, as a result, many have sought her services to help them grow their business.

Ⓐ liaison
Ⓑ authority
Ⓒ proxy
Ⓓ doyen
Ⓔ pioneer
Ⓕ honorary

STOP

QUANTITATIVE REASONING | 20 QUESTIONS
SECTION 4 | 35 MINUTES

DIRECTIONS: For questions 1-8, use any provided centered information to help you compare Column A and Column B. Select the answer that describes the relationship between the two quantities, noting that the same answer choices are presented for each Quantitative Comparison question:

- A **Quantity A is greater.**
- B **Quantity B is greater.**
- C **The two quantities are equal.**
- D **The relationship cannot be determined from the information given.**

1. $1000 > z > 500$

Column A	Column B
$1000 - z$	$z - 500$

Ⓐ Ⓑ Ⓒ Ⓓ

2. $a + b = 12$
$b + 4 = 8$

Column A	Column B
a	b

Ⓐ Ⓑ Ⓒ Ⓓ

3. a, b, and c are positive integers

Column A	Column B
The product of a, b, and c	The sum of a, b, and c

Ⓐ Ⓑ Ⓒ Ⓓ

4.

Column A	Column B
The greatest prime factor of 17	The greatest prime factor of 16

Ⓐ Ⓑ Ⓒ Ⓓ

5.

Column A	Column B
The percentage of increase from 10 to 15	The percentage of increase from 54 to 58

Ⓐ Ⓑ Ⓒ Ⓓ

6. There are 150 people in an auditorium. 75 are women, 60 are men, and the rest are children.

Column A	Column B
10%	The percentage of children in the auditorium

Ⓐ Ⓑ Ⓒ Ⓓ

QUANTITATIVE REASONING

7. x and y are greater than 1

Column A	Column B
$4xy$	$(4x)(4y)$

Ⓐ Ⓑ Ⓒ Ⓓ

8.

Column A	Column B
The number of days in 15 weeks	The number of minutes in 3 hours

Ⓐ Ⓑ Ⓒ Ⓓ

9. A truck traveled 130 miles with 4 gallons of diesel fuel. What distance would the same truck cover, driving the same route, with 6.7 gallons of diesel fuel?

Ⓐ 124 miles
Ⓑ 260.25 miles
Ⓒ 240.50 miles
Ⓓ 217.75 miles
Ⓔ 185 miles

10. $||-10 - 18| - 20| =$

Ⓐ 8
Ⓑ −8
Ⓒ −48
Ⓓ 28
Ⓔ 11

11. The square of the sum of two numbers is 289. The product of the two numbers is 66. What is the sum of the squares of the two numbers?

12.

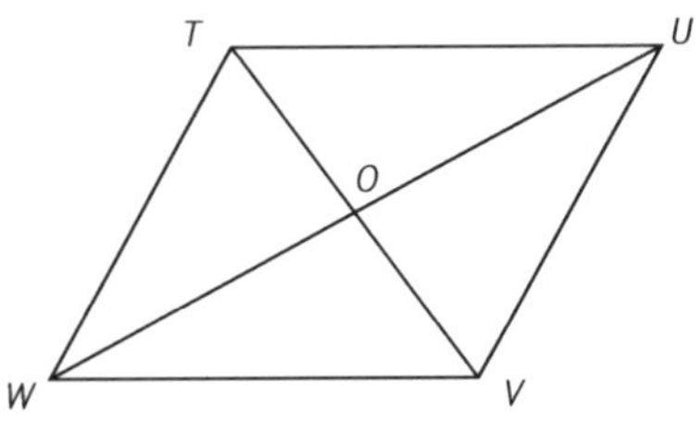

In rhombus $TUVW$, if $\angle TUW = 34°$, find $\angle UVT$

Ⓐ 56°
Ⓑ 68°
Ⓒ 34°
Ⓓ 112°
Ⓔ 72°

13.

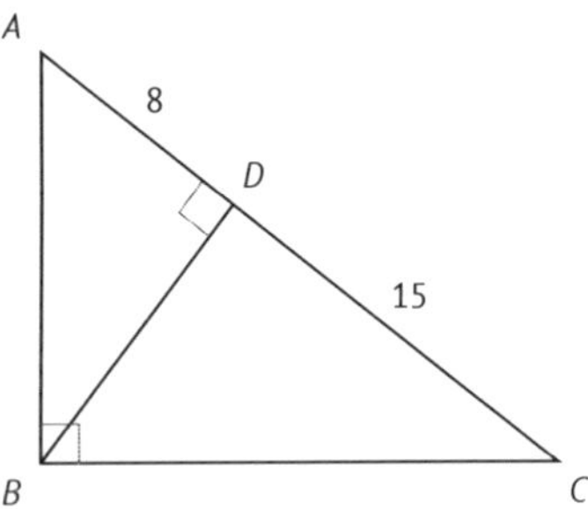

Find the measure of $\overline{BD}$.

Ⓐ 11.3
Ⓑ $2\sqrt{30}$
Ⓒ $\sqrt{23}$
Ⓓ 120
Ⓔ $2\sqrt{26}$

14. Solve the equation $d = vt + \frac{1}{2}at^2$ for a.

Ⓐ $a = \frac{2d}{vt^3}$

Ⓑ $a = \frac{d - vt}{t^2}$

Ⓒ $a = \frac{2(d - vt)}{t^2}$

Ⓓ $a = \frac{2dt^2}{t}$

Ⓔ $a = \frac{2d - vt}{t^2}$

15. Find the missing value indicated on the diagram below.

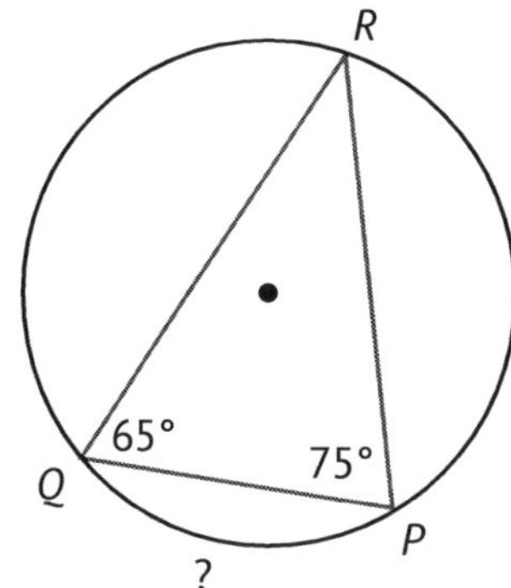

Ⓐ 40°
Ⓑ 50°
Ⓒ 80°
Ⓓ 74°
Ⓔ 92°

Use the graph below to answer Questions 16-17.

At this year's carnival, each child's ticket included the choice of one snack.

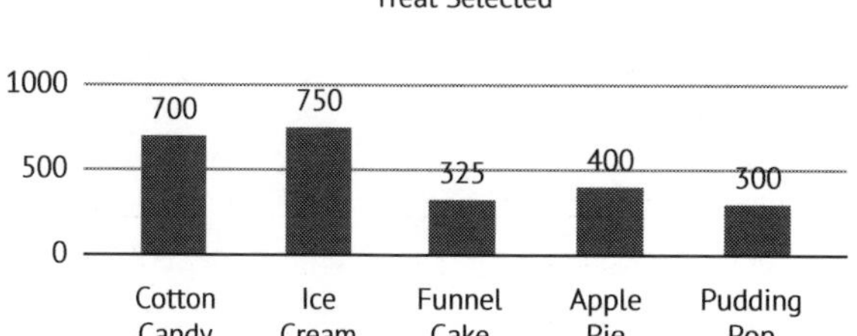

The graph represents the snack each child chose.

16. What is the percentage difference between the kids who selected ice cream and the kids who selected a pudding pop as their treat?

Ⓐ 58%
Ⓑ 62%
Ⓒ 60%
Ⓓ 45%
Ⓔ 45.5%

17. If each of the treats was ordered from most selected to least selected, which treat would represent the median?

Ⓐ Pudding pop
Ⓑ Funnel Cake
Ⓒ Ice Cream
Ⓓ Apple Pie
Ⓔ Cotton Candy

18. Find the distance between the points (−4,5)(8,4).

Ⓐ $3\sqrt{10}$
Ⓑ $\sqrt{145}$
Ⓒ $\sqrt{13}$
Ⓓ $2\sqrt{10}$
Ⓔ $\sqrt{10}$

QUANTITATIVE REASONING

19. What is the perimeter of a rectangular garden that is 16 units wide and has the same area as a rectangular garden that is 10 units wide and 32 units long?

Ⓐ 320
Ⓑ 160
Ⓒ 72
Ⓓ 52
Ⓔ 96

---

20. A circle with a radius of 10 has a circumference of:

Ⓐ 100□
Ⓑ 20□
Ⓒ 25□
Ⓓ 10□
Ⓔ 100

STOP

VERBAL REASONING | 20 QUESTIONS
SECTION 5 | 30 MINUTES

DIRECTIONS: Answer each question according to the directions given.

For questions 1 to 8, you are to choose one answer for each blank from the corresponding column of choices.

1. The rampant product placement in the recent charity advertisement was a(n) _______________ display of commercialism.

Ⓐ errant
Ⓑ allocable
Ⓒ ardent
Ⓓ applicable
Ⓔ gratuitous

2. Though the small surrounding villages worked arduously to maintain their independence, they were eventually _______________ by the larger province.

Ⓐ amalgamated
Ⓑ usurped
Ⓒ emancipated
Ⓓ exculpated
Ⓔ absolved

3. Once the pirates made it to land, they _______________ the nearby villages in hopes of increasing their already large stash of stolen goods.

Ⓐ squandered
Ⓑ eclipsed
Ⓒ marauded
Ⓓ obscured
Ⓔ abetted

4. Toby Stanch was one of the most (i) _______________ performers of all time; concert goers could not get enough of his energy on stage. So, it seemed quite (ii) _______________ that he died alone in his modest home, where he had spent the past 10 years isolated from others.

Blank i	Blank ii
Ⓐ haphazard	Ⓓ enigmatic
Ⓑ reticent	Ⓔ supercilious
Ⓒ fulsome	Ⓕ calculable

5. The scientist was the subject of widespread scorn in his local community after publishing a report (i) _______________ the detrimental effects of high-fructose corn syrup on the brain development of young children. High-fructose corn syrup was a major source of income for the region and many felt the report would (ii) _______________ affect their profits.

Blank i	Blank ii
Ⓐ promulgating	Ⓓ marginally
Ⓑ shrouding	Ⓔ indefinitely
Ⓒ speculating on	Ⓕ adversely

6. The team's conduct after their loss was (i) _______________. They walked off the court without shaking hands with the opposing team and destroyed the locker room before they left. The school was embarrassed and (ii) _______________ apologized for their behavior and made sure that each member of the team was disciplined accordingly.

Blank i	Blank ii
Ⓐ diffident	Ⓓ inertly
Ⓑ deplorable	Ⓔ precariously
Ⓒ defensible	Ⓕ profusely

GO TO THE NEXT PAGE

VERBAL REASONING

7. The mission of the organization was (i) ______________ at best; not even the founder could articulate it when asked. Nonetheless, the organization (ii) ______________ its fundraising goals for three years in a row. Many speculated that the founder was either a(n) (iii) ______________ fundraiser or that there was some type of impropriety involved.

Blank i
Ⓐ despotic
Ⓑ flummoxing
Ⓒ sedulous

Blank ii
Ⓓ flexed
Ⓔ effaced
Ⓕ surpassed

Blank iii
Ⓖ munificent
Ⓗ middling
Ⓘ adroit

8. The notion that all religions of the world can unite under one force seems to be a far-fetched idea; yet it is worth entertaining the possible impact the widespread adoption of certain (i) ______________ may have on ameliorating religious intolerance and conflict. For example, the ideas of non-violence expressed in the Buddhist tradition could not only be (ii) ______________ to all religions, but could, with its adoption across faiths, serve as a means of (iii) ______________ religious tensions and creating a more perfect world.

Blank i
Ⓐ ideologies
Ⓑ exegesis
Ⓒ platitudes

Blank ii
Ⓓ inane
Ⓔ germane
Ⓕ irrelevant

Blank iii
Ⓖ assuaging
Ⓗ inflaming
Ⓘ osculating

GO TO THE NEXT PAGE

Questions 9 to 11 are based on the following passage. Select one answer unless otherwise indicated.

Garret Hardin's *Tragedy of the Commons* broadly and scientifically broached the issue of population growth and its impact on earth's finite resources. Hardin advanced the notion that no technological intervention would be sufficient to address humans outpacing earth's resources and that a growth rate of zero was a viable option to mitigate resource depletion. Additionally, central to his argument was the premise that unallocated common assets, when freely available to everyone, are subject to be indiscriminately consumed without regard for the longevity of the resource itself. This unchecked consumption, Hardin portended, served as a harbinger for destruction of those resources and inevitably the communities that would eventually find themselves in a wealth for none situation.

Hardin used cattle herders to demonstrate his concerns and to highlight his cynical perception of human behavior. According to his example, if cattle grazed on commonly held property and each herder laid claim to personal incentives that correlated to the size of his herd while being only marginally affected by overgrazing, herders would naturally be concerned with increasing the size of their own herd instead of the long-term effects such actions might render. With no regulation, overuse and eventual depletion were inevitable outcomes at the hands of self-serving interests. Along with reducing breeding behavior, it is also cited as self-serving, he argued that privatization and regulation could be feasible solutions for thwarting common resource exhaustion and promoting sustainable use and preservation.

Forgoing the lack of empirical support to back Hardin's assertions, the Tragedy of Commons still yields some clear parallels to many present-day environmental issues especially over-fishing. Fish live in bodies of water that often do not have singular ownership and are accessible to large segments of the population. Naturally, regulation is challenging and with unchecked access, the finite population faces threats. As major employers and food sources, fisheries are critical to many communities, particularly in developing nations. So, over-fishing could have potentially dire consequences. But, with the onslaught of tracking technology and more efficient and industrial fishing practices, fishermen are now able to bring in larger hauls to meet the demand for seafood and likely do so motivated by financial gain instead of concern for conservation. This line of action is exactly what Hardin warned about. If the resource, in this case fish, is readily accessible and not governed by regulation and privatization, it is prone to being exhausted likely more quickly with little collective benefit for the community and more benefit for the individual.

Using Hardin's rhetoric to rethink fishing could help alleviate over-fishing and threats to populations that are fished so aggressively that they do not have adequate time to repopulate. Regulation could lead to restrictions on catching certain types of fish during known breeding times or when populations are experiencing significant declines. These types of measures, however, would take some ownership and buy-in from fishermen who are simultaneously the primary perpetrators and benefactors of the fishing industry. While regulatory measures would inevitably impact the livelihood of fishermen, failing to act and regulate over-fishing would eventually also impact their livelihoods more consequentially if fish species continue to die off.

9. Select the sentence that contains the author's chief objection to Hardin's *Tragedy of the Commons.*

---

10. According to the passage, which of the following are inevitable contributors to over-consumption of resources on commonly-held property? Select all that apply.

- Ⓐ self-serving interests
- Ⓑ over-population
- Ⓒ inequitable resource allocation
- Ⓓ increased demand for resources

---

11. Which of the following is most likely to have a similar affect as the fish-tracking technology mentioned in the passage?

- Ⓐ a sensor that pinpoints the location of the largest diamonds in a mine
- Ⓑ a new technology that milks cows twice as fast designed to increase output

GO TO THE NEXT PAGE

VERBAL REASONING

Ⓒ a tracking device that tracks the trajectory of salmon during its migration season
Ⓓ technological advances that allow duck hunters to easily locate the landing location of their kill
Ⓔ a robot that collects eggs quickly after hens lay them

Questions 12 and 13 are based on this passage. Select one answer unless otherwise indicated.

James Baldwin's *Giovanni's Room* highlights the negative impact of navigating social and moral norms contradictory to one's inherent desires and identity. Baldwin's protagonist, David, faced with the confines of what is arbitrarily deemed to be moral and accepted, struggles to understand and carve out his sexual identity amidst a myriad of sexual encounters and reflections. In search of himself and better clarity on his desires free from the restraints and impositions of America, David travels to Paris. There begins his eventual downward spiral. As he journeys to find himself and experience the freedom of being who he really is, he finds himself unable to shed the same societal and moral norms he sought so earnestly to flee.

David's journey demonstrates the damage societal norms and the pressure to conform to them inflict upon the freedom to be ourselves and be true to our inherent desires; this ultimate suppression of individual freedom arguably makes us all slaves to the confines of societal stipulations and drones of conformity.

12. The author mentions which of the following as themes of *Giovanni's Room*? Select all that apply.

Ⓐ Racial identity issues
Ⓑ The far-reaching impacts of conformity
Ⓒ Suppression of our desires

---

13. The primary purpose of the passage is to:

Ⓐ highlight the themes in James Baldwin's *Giovanni's Room*
Ⓑ dissuade readers interested in purchasing *Giovanni's Room* from doing so
Ⓒ offer an analysis of the weakness in the writing of *Giovanni's Room*
Ⓓ explain the challenges associated with moving to a foreign country
Ⓔ to explore the various aspects of the protagonist's identity discussed in the book and the impact societal norms had on his identity

---

Question 14 is based on the following passage. Select one answer unless otherwise indicated.

Erosion from wind and water has threatened American farmland since the first agricultural settlements cropped up in the early 19th century. By the 1930s, more than 200 million acres of farmland were damaged by erosion. Though conservation efforts tried to curb the decline of fertile lands, erosion has continued alongside new more deleterious issues like increased demands for crops that have led to overuse of the land. If erosion on over-tilling of domestic land continues, food scarcity in America is a real possibility.

14. Which of the following, if true, most weakens the author's assertion that food scarcity is imminent if over-tilling and erosion cannot be thwarted? Select all that apply.

Ⓐ Very little of America's food comes from domestic farms.
Ⓑ Genetically modified food contains nutritional value.
Ⓒ Over-tilled farmlands can be used for other purposes that may be beneficial to Americans.

For questions 15-20, select two answers that best complete the blank and produces two sentences that are alike in meaning.

15. After completing the Wilderness First Aid course, Spence became more ______________ when he greeted the long distance hikers on the trails. He looked for signs of distress that others may have missed or dismissed as simply fatigue.

Ⓐ alert
Ⓑ cavalier
Ⓒ unhinged
Ⓓ fixated
Ⓔ discerning
Ⓕ odiferous

16. Evita's supervisor was taken aback by the ______________ letter of resignation she wrote, since he saw her as reserved and timorous.

Ⓐ peremptory
Ⓑ indolent
Ⓒ chary
Ⓓ guileless
Ⓔ irreverent
Ⓕ farcical

17. While it may be tempting to attribute the criminal's violent behavior to his ______________ upbringing, it is important to note that many people grow up in troubled homes as children and do not turn out to be violent criminals.

Ⓐ obstinate
Ⓑ tempestuous
Ⓒ tenacious
Ⓓ acerbic
Ⓔ pompous
Ⓕ volatile

18. Bikram yoga has long been thought to detox the body through perspiration as a result of the high temperatures of the room during a session. Because of this, practitioners of Bikram often leave a session with a sense of ______________.

Ⓐ stagnation
Ⓑ purgation
Ⓒ exhaustion
Ⓓ exuberance
Ⓔ ablution
Ⓕ dissonance

19. Bill was quite the ______________; he did nothing in moderation and always threw lavish fetes and invited all his friends.

Ⓐ epicurean
Ⓑ prude
Ⓒ philanthropist
Ⓓ sybarite
Ⓔ pragmatist
Ⓕ curator

20. Amy was the epitome of ______________. She would go to extraordinary lengths to gain the favor of her superiors even if that came at the expense of her colleagues and the team dynamic.

Ⓐ collegial
Ⓑ sycophantic
Ⓒ obsequious
Ⓓ staunch
Ⓔ esurient
Ⓕ peevish

STOP

QUANTITATIVE REASONING | 20 QUESTIONS
SECTION 6 | 35 MINUTES

DIRECTIONS: For questions 1-8, use any provided centered information to help you compare Column A and Column B. Select the answer that describes the relationship between the two quantities, noting that the same answer choices are presented for each Quantitative Comparison question:

A **Quantity A is greater.**
B **Quantity B is greater.**
C **The two quantities are equal.**
D **The relationship cannot be determined from the information given.**

1.

$$f(x) = 4x$$
$$g(x) = \frac{1}{2}x$$

Column A	Column B
$f(g(3))$	$g(f(3))$

Ⓐ Ⓑ Ⓒ Ⓓ

2. The sale price for a set of new bike wheels is $65.00, which is 30% of the original price.

Column A	Column B
The original price of the set of bike wheels	$91.00

Ⓐ Ⓑ Ⓒ Ⓓ

3. The ratio of stingrays to blow fish is 2:3. There are a total of 225 stingrays and blow fish.

Column A	Column B
The number of blowfish	100

Ⓐ Ⓑ Ⓒ Ⓓ

4. The sum of two consecutive integers is 83.

Column A	Column B
The difference of three times the smallest integer and 23	The sum of two times the largest integer and 16

Ⓐ Ⓑ Ⓒ Ⓓ

5.

Column A	Column B
(84 + 12)(15 + 91)	(74 + 22)(20 + 86)

Ⓐ Ⓑ Ⓒ Ⓓ

6.

Column A	Column B
75% of 30	30% of 75

Ⓐ Ⓑ Ⓒ Ⓓ

7.

$$0 < a < b$$

Column A	Column B
(a + b)(a + b)	(b – a)(b – a)

Ⓐ Ⓑ Ⓒ Ⓓ

GO TO THE NEXT PAGE

8.

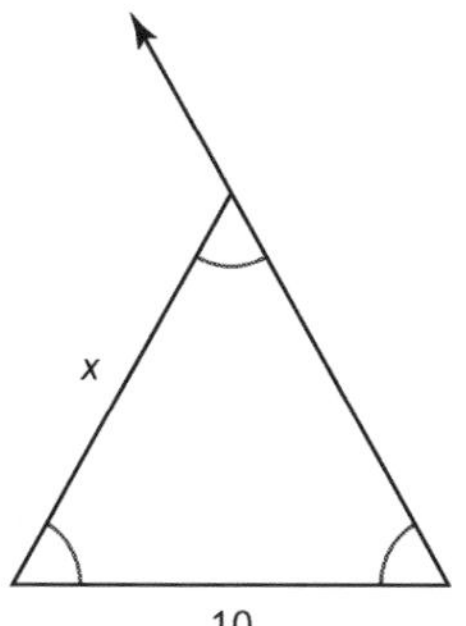

Column A	Column B
The length of x	12

Ⓐ Ⓑ Ⓒ Ⓓ

9. Solve the equation $-3(x-4)+8=4(2x-1)-9$ for x.

Ⓐ $x=\frac{11}{9}$
Ⓑ $x=3$
Ⓒ $x=-\frac{11}{9}$
Ⓓ $x=-3$
Ⓔ $x=1$

10. What is the slope of a line that is perpendicular to the line with the equation $6y - 3x = -18$

Ⓐ -2
Ⓑ -3
Ⓒ $-\frac{1}{3}$
Ⓓ $\frac{1}{3}$
Ⓔ 2

11. Lea's school is selling tickets for the upcoming choral performance. On the first day of ticket sales, the school sold 10 adult tickets and 10 child tickets for a total of $200. On the second day, the school sold 13 adult tickets and 2 child tickets for a total of $172 dollars. How much did each child ticket cost?

Ⓐ $6
Ⓑ $8
Ⓒ $12
Ⓓ $7.50
Ⓔ $5

12. Find the missing angle b in the figure below.

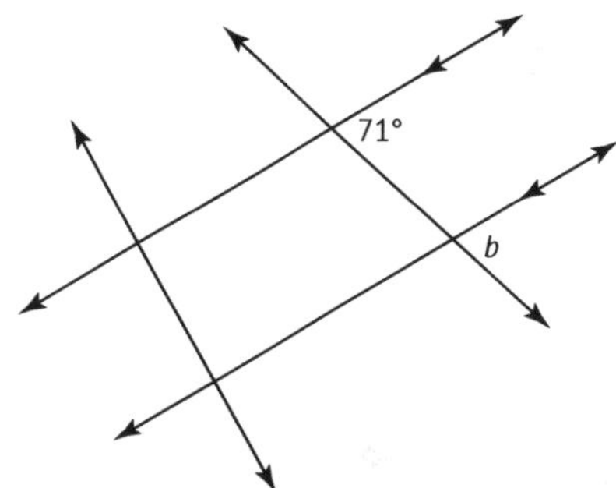

Ⓐ 109°
Ⓑ 89°
Ⓒ 71°
Ⓓ 64°
Ⓔ 180°

13. A newly cleared tract of land has been designated for reforestation. The commission responsible for the project decided to plant 30 trees. 12 of the trees will be oak trees, one-fifth of the trees will be pine trees, 3 are weeping willows, and the rest of the trees will be fruit-bearing trees of a various types. What is the ratio of weeping willows to fruit-bearing trees?

Ⓐ 1:3
Ⓑ 1:2
Ⓒ 3:1
Ⓓ 3:12
Ⓔ 30:3

GO TO THE NEXT PAGE

QUANTITATIVE REASONING

14. If Katie scored a 80, and 83, and an 88 on her first three tests, what must she score on her fourth test if she wants an average of 85? Enter your answer in text box below.

The chart below reflects the total record sales (in thousands) for six major labels: Petra, Jams, AudioPro, Keynote, GSharp, and Lumia.

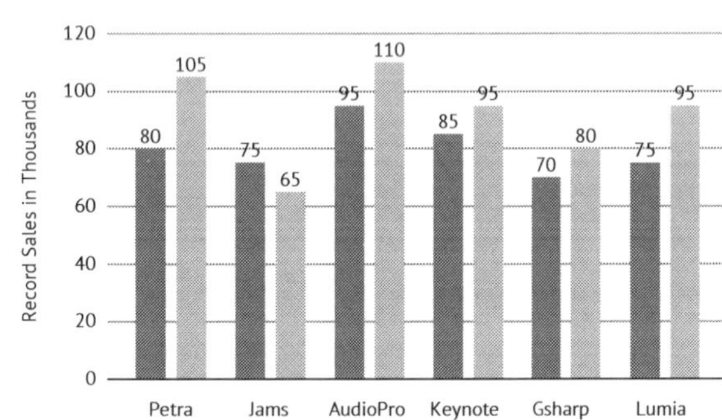

15. What is the mean of the sales from all the record companies in 2016?

Ⓐ 91.6
Ⓑ 101
Ⓒ 80
Ⓓ 85.3
Ⓔ 101.5

16. Lumia's sales in 2015 represents what percentage of the overall sales for that year?

Ⓐ 17.5
Ⓑ 15.6
Ⓒ 19.8
Ⓓ 20
Ⓔ 12.75
Ⓕ 80

17. Which company experienced the greatest percentage increase in sales from 2015 to 2016?

Ⓐ Petra
Ⓑ Audiopro
Ⓒ Keynote
Ⓓ GSharp
Ⓔ Lumia

18. For the equation $-1-4(4m-5)=-13-8m$, solve for m. Enter your response in the text box, rounded to the nearest whole number.

19. What is the slope of a line with coordinates $(-12,-9)$ and $(20,-1)$?

Ⓐ -4
Ⓑ 4
Ⓒ $-\frac{1}{2}$
Ⓓ $\frac{1}{4}$
Ⓔ 2

20. Solve for x to find the missing value.

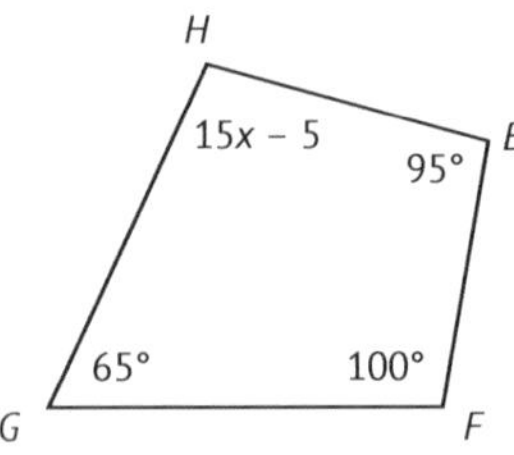

Ⓐ 5
Ⓑ 4.5
Ⓒ 8
Ⓓ 6
Ⓔ 7

STOP

VERBAL REASONING
ANSWER KEY : SECTION 3

1. **B.**
The clues did not aid Keene's ability to decipher her past. The clues were unclear or unhelpful. So, they were nebulous.

2. **E.**
Those seeking counseling want to ensure that their conversations will be held in confidence. A misgiving is a feeling of doubt.

3. **C.**
Affable suggests a pleasant and engaged community whereas tolerable simply indicates a willingness to put up with each other.

4. **C, E.**
The overall tone of the passage is positive, so you are looking for words that resonate with that. The counselors were jovial. Sanguine is another word for jovial or upbeat. They hoped their energy would spread to the campers so that they could create, or manifest, happiness in their own lives.

5. **A, E.**
Phonetically, puerile might remind you of 'pure' but it means infantile or immature. Fecund on the other hand is a synonym for lush and fertile. There is a transition in the sentence that suggests the lands are moving in the opposite direction of what they once were. Barren is the opposite of lush; the sentence leads you to believe this is the fate of the land.

6. **B, E.**
The use of "unfortunately" indicates Tom's behavior may not be innocent. A coquette is a flirt or a charmer. The use of "even though" in the sentence signals a transition and indicates that the second blank will be the opposite of Tom's normal behavior. To be flummoxed is to be confused or flabbergasted, which is how Tom appeared when confronted by HR.

7. **A, E, G.**
The picturesque, or striking scenery provided an escape from a rough week. Tumultuous means turbulent and is the more appropriate word here given that the subjects of the sentence seemed to be actively dealing with cleaning up after flood rather than simply experiencing great sadness, or melancholy about the situation. The last blank has a distractor answer, reprieve. Reprieve is commonly misused and believed to mean the same as respite, which means a break. Reprieve means pardon or to be given a pass.

8. **B, D, G.**
Wholly, or completely, matches "clear" in the second sentence and follows the shift in the sentence to clarify the requirement of the safe basis of psychotherapy. For the second blank, the word that completes it has something to do with creating confusion. If the mixing of different ways of dealing with man's inner life was slipshod, or careless, it would certainly cause or contribute to vagueness. For the third blank, you are looking for something that is opposite of true or relevant. In this case, asinine, which means unintelligent or foolish is the correct word.

9. **B.**
"I almost forgot what a fight had been made..." speaks to the nostalgia Roosevelt experienced thinking about the fight for fair wages for workers.

10. "The minute you allow that, then you have to acknowledge that you no longer able to trust in your courts and in your law-enforcing machinery, and civil liberties are not very well off when anything like that happens."

11. **A.**
The passage largely focuses on civil liberties and the fight to win and retain them.

12. **A, B.**
C is an assumption that is not supported by the facts of the passage and is thus incorrect. Both A and B are explicitly mentioned in the passage.

13. **B.**
The author is critical of the role humans played on altering the migration patterns of bison.

14. **C.**
Bison in arid, hot air areas would have adapted short hair according to the passage.

15. **A, C.**
"At every opportunity he received" gives you a context clue that the candidate never missed an opportunity to clamorously, or loudly and vocally go on about various issues. Pontificate means to expound upon or preach.

VERBAL REASONING
ANSWER KEY : SECTION 3

16. A, D.
Indigent means poor or needy. Impecunious means without financial means.

17. B, D.
If something needs to be brought to someone's attention, it is likely out of the ordinary. The use of the word obsession further affirms this. Bizarre and eccentric both mean odd or strange.

18. B,C.
The context clues, mainly the fact that the conservative teacher was not thrilled with the movie selection, lets you know that the movie sat opposite of conservative. The fact that it seemed to warrant more than the PG rating assigned to it affirms this. Lascivious means lewd or indecent.

19. C, E.
Al chose not to tighten up his presentation and instead prepared responses to objections. Retorts and ripostes both mean comebacks or replies.

20. B, D.
Erica is a notable contributor to the field and others come to her for advice. She would qualify as an expert or a leader. Authority and doyen fit best in the blank. The sentence does not mention her making new novel discoveries or contributions to the field, so pioneer would not be a good fit.

QUANTITATIVE REASONING
ANSWER KEY : SECTION 4

1. **D.**
z is less than 1000 but greater than 500. Plug in 999 and 501 for z. In one instance (999) column B is greater while in the other instance (501) column A is greater. The relationship cannot be determined.

2. **A.**
Solve the second equation for b. $b = 4$. Plug the value into the first equation to solve for a, which is 8.

3. **D.**
If you plug in 1, 2, and 3 to test, the columns would be equal with the product and sum equal to 6. But, if you plug in 4, 5, 6, for example, the product would be greater than the sum. The relationship cannot be determined.

4. **A.**
The greatest prime factor of 17 is itself since it is a prime number. The greatest prime factor of 16 is 2.

5. **A.**
The percentage increase from 10 to 15 is the difference of the current amount and the new amount divided by the original amount. So: $\frac{15-10}{10}=\frac{5}{10}=.5=50\%$. Do the same with Column B to find the percentage change: $\frac{58-54}{58}=\frac{4}{58}=.068=\sim 6.9\%$.

6. **C.**
There are a total of 135 men and women. So, there are 15 children in the auditorium. So, $\frac{15}{150}=10\%$. The quantities are the same.

7. **B.**
While the expressions look similar, they are quite different. Plug in any value greater than 1 for x and y. B will always be greater.

8. **B.**
There are 105 days in 15 weeks and 180 minutes in 3 hours.

9. **D.**
The truck can travel 32.5 $\left(\frac{130}{4}=32.5\right)$ miles per gallon of diesel. With 6.7 gallons, the truck can drive 217.75 miles $(32.5 \bullet 6.7 = 217.75)$

10. **A.**
Solve the inner-most absolute value expression first, then solve the outmost absolute value expression. $|-10-18|=|-28|-20=8$.

11. **157.**
Use x and y to symbolize the two unknown numbers. $(x + y)^2 = 289$. Then, factor.

$$(x+y)^2$$
$$(x+y)(x+y)$$
$$x^2+2xy+y^2=289$$

The question tells you that the product of the two numbers is 66, so plug in and simplify.

$$x^2+2(66)+y^2=289$$
$$x^2+132+y^2=289$$
$$x^2+y^2=289-132$$
$$x^2+2xy+y^2=289$$
$$x^2+y^2=157$$

157 is the sum of the squares.

12. **A.**
The diagonals bisect the angle at 90°. So, $\angle UOV$ = 90°. Since you already know $\angle TUW$ = 34° to find $\angle UVT$ subtract 34° and 90° from 180° to get 56°.

13. **A.**
The diagram consists of two connected 45:45:90 right triangles. The measurements of the legs and hypotenuse in these triangles is x, x, and $x\sqrt{2}$. So, $\widehat{BD}=8\sqrt{2}$. The answer choice solves the radial and expresses it as its decimal equivalent, 11.3.

14. **C.**

$$d=vt+\frac{1}{2}at^2$$
$$d-vt=\frac{1}{2}at^2$$

Next, multiply each side by 2:

$$2(d-vt)=at^2$$

QUANTITATIVE REASONING
ANSWER KEY : SECTION 4

To isolate a, divide each side by t^2.

$$\frac{2(d-vt)}{t^2}=a$$

15. C.
The triangle is inscribed in the circle. First, find the third angle of the triangle by subtracting 65° and 75° from 180°. The missing angle is 40°. The corresponding arc, $\widehat{QP}$ is twice the inscribed angle, so 80°.

16. C.
Calculate percentage difference between 750 and 300: $\frac{750-300}{750}=\frac{450}{750}=.6=60\%$.

17. D.
Organize the treats in order by the number of kids who selected them. 750, 700, 400, 325, 300. 400 is the median and represents apple pie.

18. B.

$$d=\sqrt{8-(-4)^2+(4-5)}$$

$$d=\sqrt{8-(-4)^2+(4-5)^2}$$

$$d=\sqrt{144+1}=\sqrt{145}$$

19. C.
The area of the rectangle with sides 10 and 32 is 320. So, in order to find the missing side of the other rectangle, divide 320 by 16. The missing side is 20 units long. So, the perimeter is 20 + 20 + 16 + 16 = 72.

20. B.
C = 2□r so (10)(2)□ = 20□.

VERBAL REASONING
ANSWER KEY : SECTION 5

1. **E.**
Gratuitous means over the top or uncalled for.

2. **B.**
While amalgamated does mean to unite, it is important to consider the context clues here. The small villages fought hard and were eventually usurped, or taken, by the larger province.

3. **C.**
Marauded means pillaged or robbed.

4. **C, D.**
Fulsome means lavish and exiting which is the opposite of how the end of Toby's life was characterized. His reclusive and modest final years were at odds with his earlier life, a fact that puzzled many. Enigmatic means puzzling.

5. **A, F.**
To promulgate is to make known or share publicly. Indefinitely is a stretch beyond the facts given in the sentence.

6. **B, F.**
You are looking for words that are negative based on the composition of the sentence. Deplorable means disgraceful or shocking. Profusely means abundantly which matches that tone of the sentences based on the level of inappropriateness of the team's behavior.

7. **B, F, I.**
The message was so unclear that even the founder could not articulate it. Flummoxing means confusing or perplexing. Even with an unclear mission, the company seems to be doing well. It surpassed, or exceeded its fundraising goals. Adroit means skilled or astute. The founder was either skilled at fundraising or there were dishonest practices happening.

8. **A, E, G.**
Ideologies are ideas or notions which the sentence alludes should be adopted by religions. The second sentence presents a specific ideology that condemns violence. Germane means appropriate or suitable; in this case these universal ideas would be appropriate tenets for religions to adopt. The sentence contends certain ideas could help ease, or assuage, tensions.

9. Forgoing the lack of empirical support to back Hardin's assertions, The Tragedy of the Commons still yields some clear parallels to many present-day environmental issues especially over-fishing. (Paragraph 3, Sentence 1)

10. **A, D.**
Over-population and demand for resources are addressed in the passage but not in reference to over-consumption of common resources.

11. **B.**
This is a difficult parallel question. First, you must understand the outcome of the fish-tracking technology: the ability to get the maximum about of fish at once. For answer choice (A), the sensor leads you only to large diamonds with no certain quantity. (C) gives no indication of the outcome and whether or not the technology would help maximize the haul like the milking technology enhancement explained in answer choice (B).

12. **B, C.**
Be careful not to let any outside knowledge of this book influence your answer choice. Use only the information provided in the passage, which does not address racial identity though it is a central theme in the book.

13. **A.**
While the passage offers some commentary it's primary purpose is to discuss the themes and encounters of the main character.

14. **A.**
If very little of America's food comes from domestic farms, then the destruction of those farms may not have the purported impact on the food supply, so A is correct. B is incorrect because it is not a strong attack on the argument. Genetically modified food might have nutritional value but that has no bearing on the availability of food. The land being used for other purposes is outside of the scope of the question and the passage.

15. **A, E.**
Spence was not only diligent, he was also able to recognize symptoms that may have not been noticed by someone who was untrained. Discerning and alert both mean to pay close attention to or recognize and fit cleanly into the blank.

VERBAL REASONING
ANSWER KEY : SECTION 5

16. A, D.
You are looking for a pair of words that are opposite of reserved and timorous. Guileless means candid and peremptory similarly means commanding.

17. B, F.
You are look for a word that describes an upbringing that might lead a person towards violent behavior. Tempestuous and volatile both can mean unstable or explosive.

18. B, E.
Yogis feel detoxed after Bikram; so purgation and ablution means to purge or cast out.

19. A, D.
The second part of the first sentence defines the missing term clearly. Bill did nothing in moderation and enjoyed partying. Epicurean and sybarite can both be defined as lavish or indulgent.

20. B, C.
Amy tried to gain favor at any cost. Sycophantic and obsequious are synonyms that means seeking favor or ingratiating.

QUANTITATIVE REASONING
ANSWER KEY : SECTION 6

1. **C.**

Plug in the values of each function and solve.

$$f(g(3)) = \frac{1}{2}(3) = \frac{3}{2}$$

Now, plug in the answer above for x to find f(x).

$$f\left(\frac{3}{2}\right) = 4\left(\frac{3}{2}\right) = 6$$

Now, do the same for column B.

$$f(x) = 4(3) = 12$$

Plug in the answer above to solve for g(f(3)).

$$g(12) = \frac{1}{2}(12) = 6$$

The quantities are the same.

2. **B.**

$65 is 70% of the original price. So, (.70)(*x*) = $65. *x* = $85.71. $91 is greater.

3. **A.**

If the ratio is 2:3 and there are a total of 225 stingrays and blowfish, use the ratio to create an equation.

$$2x + 3x = 225$$
$$5x = 225$$
$$x = 45$$

Solve for the number of stingrays: 3(45) = 135. A is greater.

4. **C.**

The sum of the two consecutive integers is 83. Let *n* represent the integer and create an equation to solve:

$$n + (n+1) = 83$$
$$2n = 82$$
$$n = 41$$

So, the two integers are 41 and 42. Both values work out to be 100. So, the quantities are equal.

5. **C.**
Solve the parentheses first then multiply each term. The value for both columns is 10,176. The quantities are equal.

6. **C.**
To find column A use (.75)(30)=22.5. To find column B use (.30)(75)=22.5 The quantities are equal.

7. **D.**
Both values will be positive so there and infinite number of possibilities. Without more information, it is not possible to determine the values.

8. **B.**

The triangle is equilateral, so all the sides and angles are the same. So x=10.

9. **B.**

$$-3(x-4) + 8 = 4(2x-1) - 9$$
$$-3x + 12 + 8 = 8x - 4 - 9$$
$$-3x + 20 = 8x - 13$$
$$33 = 11x, \text{ so } x = 3$$

10. **A.**
When you isolate y to put the equation in slope-intercept form, you get the equation $y = \frac{1}{2}x - 3$. The slope of a perpendicular line is the negative reciprocal, so -2.

11. **B.**
The school made $200 the first day by selling 10 adult tickets and 10 child tickets. Create an equation to solve.

$$10a + 10c = 200$$
$$10c = 200 - 10a$$
$$c = 20 - a$$

Now, you can plug in the value for *c* in terms of *a*.

$$13a + 2(20 - a) = 172$$
$$13a + 40 - 2a = 172$$
$$11a = 132$$

QUANTITATIVE REASONING
ANSWER KEY : SECTION 6

The adult ticket is \$12. So, the child ticket is \$8.

12. C.
The angles are complementary and share the same measurement.

13. A.
You must first solve to find the number of pine and fruit-bearing trees. 1/5 of the trees is 6, so there are 6 pine and 9 fruit-bearing trees. The ratio of weeping willows to fruit-bearing trees is 3:9 or 1:3.

14. 89.

$$\frac{x+80+83+88}{4}=85$$
$$x+80+83+88=340$$

Solve for *x*.

15. A.
To find the mean, add 105, 65, 110, 95, 80, 94 and divide by 6 to get 91.6.

16. B.
The total sales for 2015 is 480. To find the percentage solve: $\frac{75}{480}=15.6\%$.

17. A.

18. 4

$$-1-4(4m-5)=-13-8$$
$$-1-16m+20=-13-8m$$
$$-16m+19=-13-8m$$
$$32=8m\ ,\ m=4$$

19. D.
Plug the coordinates into the slope formula and solve for the equation of the line.

20. E.
The interior angles of a four-sided polygon add up to 360. With the given sides, 15*x* - 5 = 100. Solve for *x*.

Raw Score	Scaled Score	Raw Score	Scaled Score
40	170	20	150
39	169	19	149
38	168	18	148
37	167	17	147
36	166	16	146
35	165	15	145
34	164	14	144
33	163	13	143
32	162	12	142
31	161	11	141
30	160	10	140
29	159	9	139
28	158	8	138
27	157	7	137
26	156	6	136
25	155	5	135
24	154	4	134
23	153	3	133
22	152	2	132
21	151	1	131

These practice tests are designed to simulate actual testing conditions as closely as possible. While the questions are similar to those you will encounter on the GRE, the sections are not adaptive for Verbal and Quantitative Reasoning like they will be if you sit for the computer-adaptive exam. The scale above gives you an **idea** of your projected score and can help you monitor your progress as you become more familiar with the material. The scale above is a rough guide to predict your score. **As a reminder**, the PowerPrep II software distributed by ETS offers two free computer-adaptive exams to supplement your study plan. Be sure to include those exams in your study plan in addition to the exams in this section; this will help you get an idea of the areas you need to study more closely in order to reach your scoring goals.

ARGO
BROTHERS

PRACTICE TEST 3

GRE®

Graduate Record Examinations

- This exam is 3 hours and 45 minutes long. Try to take this full exam in one sitting to simulate real test conditions.
- While taking this exam, refrain from listening to music or watching TV.
- When writing your response for Analyze an Issue & Analyze an Argument prompt, use a computer, and turn off the spell-check feature to simulate real testing conditions.
- Use a basic calculator, do not use a graphic or scientific calculator. On the real exam, you will have an on-screen calculator with only basic operation functions and a square root key.
- Concentrate and GOOD LUCK!

To calculate your score visit our web site and download excel calculator:

www.einstein-academy.com/GRE

ANALYTICAL WRITING | ESSAY 1
ANALYZE AN ISSUE | 30 MINUTES

Since library books are free to check out, library fines for overdue books should be abolished.

Discuss your viewpoint on the proposed plan and the reasons for your perspective. Consider potential consequences of implementing the policy and the extent to which these consequences influence your stance.

GO TO THE NEXT PAGE

ANALYTICAL WRITING | ESSAY 2
ANALYZE AN ARGUMENT | 30 MINUTES

The following is from a memo released by the Birmingham Country chapter of Uncles Against Texting and Driving:

The number of accidents as a result of texting and driving has continued to rise. In just our small county alone, we have over 15 accidents a day where one or both drivers were on their phone at the time of the collision. Teen drivers are especially at risk since they are more likely to talk or text while driving. This inclination coupled with their overall lack of driving experience leads us to believe that increasing the legal driving age to 21 would best solve the problem by reducing the number of accidents and keeping our teens safe.

Discuss the evidence needed to fully assess the argument. Include examples and an explanation of how the evidence provided strengthens or weakens the argument.

QUANTITATIVE REASONING *SECTION 3* | 20 QUESTIONS 35 MINUTES

DIRECTIONS: For questions 1-8, use any provided centered information to help you compare Column A and Column B. Select the answer that describes the relationship between the two quantities, noting that the same answer choices are presented for each Quantitative Comparison question:

A **Quantity A is greater.**
B **Quantity B is greater.**
C **The two quantities are equal.**
D **The relationship cannot be determined from the information given.**

1.

Column A	Column B
The measure of the interior angles of a regular polygon	The measure of the interior angles of a triangle

Ⓐ Ⓑ Ⓒ Ⓓ

---

2. $f(x) = 5x + 7$

Column A	Column B
Slope of $f(x)$	intercept of $f(x)$

Ⓐ Ⓑ Ⓒ Ⓓ

---

3. A bag has 30 colored pegs. The pegs are either red or blue.

Column A	Column B
The probability of drawing a blue peg on your first pull	The probability of drawing a red peg on your first pull

Ⓐ Ⓑ Ⓒ Ⓓ

---

4. Data Set {60, 20, 30, 15, 10, 14, 80}

Column A	Column B
The mean of the data set	The median of the data set

Ⓐ Ⓑ Ⓒ Ⓓ

---

5. 70% of the students enrolled in a statistics class passed the final exam.

Column A	Column B
The ratio of students who passed the exam to those who failed	$\frac{3}{7}$

Ⓐ Ⓑ Ⓒ Ⓓ

---

6. A line is represented by the equation $6x + 3y = 12$

Column A	Column B
The x-intercept of the line	The y-intercept of the line

Ⓐ Ⓑ Ⓒ Ⓓ

7. a and b are prime numbers and $a + b = 12$.

Column A	Column B
ab	45

Ⓐ Ⓑ Ⓒ Ⓓ

8. $-(x - y) = x - y$

Column A	Column B
x	y

Ⓐ Ⓑ Ⓒ Ⓓ

Kelly recently began raising funds to support the development of her new social enterprise that will help build clean water wells in rural South Dakota. The graph below details the source of the funds, including matched donations from her employer's giving program, that helped Kelly exceed her original goal of $20,000 by exactly 20%.

Source of Funds

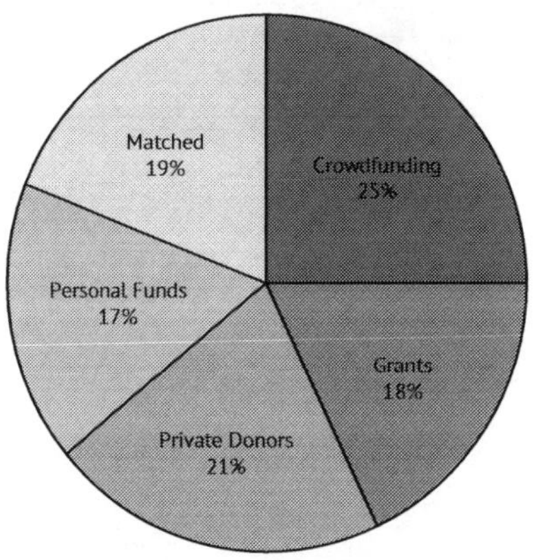

9. How much did Kelly raise via Crowdfunding? Round to the nearest dollar. Write your answer in the text box below.

10. If Kelly's employer had not provided a match from the giving program, how much would she have been short of her initial fundraising goal?

Ⓐ $4560
Ⓑ $560
Ⓒ $800
Ⓓ $4650
Ⓔ $750

11. Line R is perpendicular to the line with the equation $y = -\frac{1}{5}x$ and the point (3,–10) is on line x. Find the equation of line R.

Ⓐ $y = \frac{1}{5}x - \frac{3}{10}$
Ⓑ $y = -\frac{1}{5}x - 25$
Ⓒ $y = 5x - 10$
Ⓓ $y = 5x + 10$
Ⓔ $y = 5x - 25$

12. If a coin is flipped three times, what is the probability that the coin will land on heads exactly twice?

Ⓐ $\frac{1}{2}$
Ⓑ $\frac{1}{12}$
Ⓒ $\frac{3}{8}$
Ⓓ $\frac{2}{7}$
Ⓔ $\frac{1}{3}$

GO TO THE NEXT PAGE

QUANTITATIVE REASONING

13. Find the distance between the two points on the graph below.

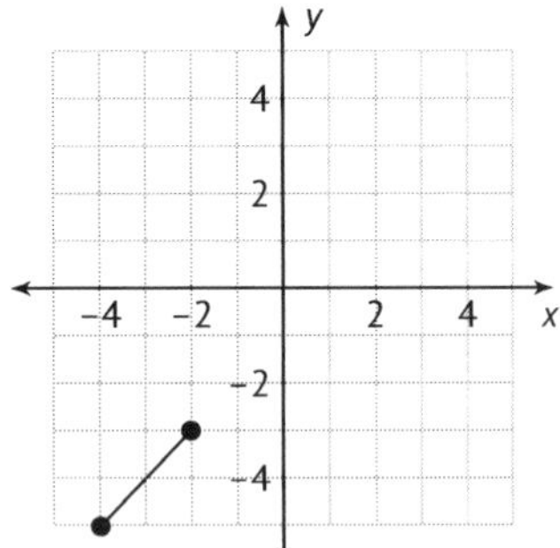

Ⓐ 10
Ⓑ 2
Ⓒ −2
Ⓓ $\sqrt{2}$
Ⓔ $2\sqrt{2}$

14. Solve $-7(3n+5)=-6n+25$ for n.

Ⓐ 6
Ⓑ −20
Ⓒ $\frac{3}{2}$
Ⓓ −4
Ⓔ No solution

15. Based on the diagram below, find the value of a and b.

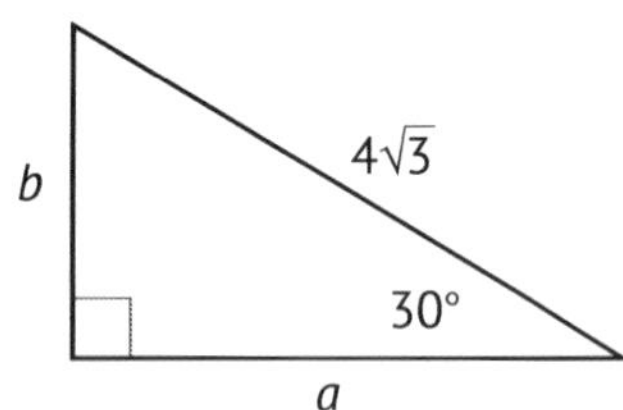

Ⓐ $a=6\sqrt{3}, b=2$
Ⓑ $a=6, b=2$
Ⓒ $a=2, b=6\sqrt{3}$
Ⓓ $a=6, b=2\sqrt{3}$
Ⓔ $a=6\sqrt{3}, b=2\sqrt{6}$

16. Suppose $g \boxtimes k=\frac{g}{2k}$. Solve the expression $7 \boxtimes 28$.

Write your answer in the text box below.

17. The sales rep makes \$100 for each client visit. Because she is a top seller on her team, she also receives 2.5% of all the sales she makes on a visit. If she earned \$900 total from a single client, what was the total amount of sales she made?

Ⓐ \$36,000
Ⓑ \$38,000
Ⓒ \$38,500
Ⓓ \$32,000
Ⓔ \$34,000

18. If $(a + 2)(a - 3)(a + 4) = 0$ and $a > 0$, then $a =$

Ⓐ −3
Ⓑ 3
Ⓒ 2
Ⓓ 0
Ⓔ 7

19. Simply $5a(3a+7)+3(-4+2a)$.

Ⓐ $49a-16a^2+12$
Ⓑ $50a-16a^2+12$
Ⓒ $19a-16a^2+12$
Ⓓ $15a^2+41a-12$
Ⓔ $15a-28a^2+12$

20. Evaluate the following: $\frac{10!}{8!}$.

Ⓐ 20
Ⓑ 90
Ⓒ 75
Ⓓ 60
Ⓔ 95

STOP

VERBAL REASONING
SECTION 4

20 QUESTIONS
35 MINUTES

For questions 1 to 8, you are to choose one answer for each blank from the corresponding column of choices.

1. Nellie argued that selecting everyone who applied for membership challenged the supposed _______________ of the group.

Ⓐ presumption
Ⓑ dynamic
Ⓒ inclusiveness
Ⓓ exclusivity
Ⓔ aura

2. Despite how much he tried to change his mindset, Brody found himself in an inescapable state of _______________ when it came to reading Conrad's work.

Ⓐ ecstasy
Ⓑ respite
Ⓒ ennui
Ⓓ tepidness
Ⓔ augur

3. The massage therapist's _______________ technique quickly eased the tension in Sunny's neck.

Ⓐ amateurish
Ⓑ deft
Ⓒ terse
Ⓓ abrupt
Ⓔ obvert

4. Jodie knew that she did not have the (i) _______________ for the position. But, because of her stubborn personality, she (ii) _______________ refused to entertain the possibility of withdrawing from the candidate pool.

Blank i	Blank ii
Ⓐ requisite	Ⓓ mulishly
Ⓑ recommended	Ⓔ sheepishly
Ⓒ temporal	Ⓕ reluctantly

5. As soon as the jury read the verdict that (i) _______________ the defendant, the courtroom (ii) _______________ into a shocked uproar as they were all sure he was guilty.

Blank i	Blank ii
Ⓐ convicted	Ⓓ effervesced
Ⓑ vindicated	Ⓔ simmered
Ⓒ expunged	Ⓕ erupted

6. Despite the urgency of the matter, the city council decidedly delayed the vote on the pending proposal to decrease after-school program funding until they had time to fully (i) _______________ the impact the decrease would have on learning outcomes. In the interim, the city council voted on a (ii)_______________ plan that explored alternatives to decreased funding.

Blank i	Blank ii
Ⓐ probate	Ⓓ provisional
Ⓑ vet	Ⓔ provincial
Ⓒ appraise	Ⓕ prospective

GO TO THE NEXT PAGE

VERBAL REASONING

7. The researchers could hardly believe their (i) ____________ luck. After months of searching for a specific mushroom variety in the deep woods of France, they not only found the mushroom but also stumbled upon a once (ii) ____________ city that was so well-hidden historians had started to believe it was just a myth. The researchers were able to complete their research project, but they all chose to retire with their sudden (iii) ____________of wealth as a result of award money they received for their find.

Blank i	Blank ii	Blank iii
Ⓐ gravitas	Ⓓ clandestine	Ⓖ serendipitous
Ⓑ calamitous	Ⓔ mythical	Ⓗ boon
Ⓒ auspicious	Ⓕ medieval	Ⓘ demerit

8. The hiring process was largely a (i) ____________ since everyone knew that (ii) ____________ was quite prevalent throughout the organization and the family of the owners were most likely to be hired whether or not they were (iii) ____________ for the job.

Blank i	Blank ii	Blank iii
Ⓐ formality	Ⓓ despotism	Ⓖ qualified
Ⓑ repulsion	Ⓔ nepotism	Ⓗ considered
Ⓒ charade	Ⓕ duality	Ⓘ groomed

Questions 9 to 11 are based on the following passage. Select one answer unless otherwise indicated.

Perceived physical attractiveness has been linked to self-esteem which has been linked to multiple components of mental health. The characteristics that constitute physical attractiveness often vary between and among cultures, but the weight, relative value, and impact that physical characteristics have on one's social context remains consistent.

Historically, as cultures became less isolated and more interactive, populations were exposed, both voluntarily and involuntarily to alternative definitions of physical attractiveness, differing perceptions of the importance of these features, and varying types of social capital distributed to those possessing such traits. Additionally, messages reinforcing the value and meaning of these traits were communicated through various means including, but not limited to, media and social stigmas and rewards.

In recent decades, due, in part, to globalization and the increased availability of various forms of media, idealized Western standards of physical attractiveness regarding skin tones, bone structure, body shape, weight, hair length, facial features (i.e., lips, nose, eye shape, proportion etc.) were exported throughout the globe. Consequently, persons living thousands of miles away from Western countries became exposed to various messages about Western standards of beauty prior to their direct contact with Western cultures. Upon emigrating from their homelands to more Western-oriented countries, many ethnic minorities are presented with the dilemma of either adopting idyllic characteristics of physical attractiveness in the hopes of gaining social acceptance or rejecting these characteristics in favor of their own genetically/culturally distinct traits. Such decisions may create or intensify acculturative stress and negatively impact the self-esteem.

Despite the widespread proliferation and mass-promotion of cultural ideals of physical attractiveness in recent decades, the amount of scientific inquiry and academic discussion into the comparative impact of these ideals on the overall psyche and self-esteem of ethnic minorities worldwide remains lacking. Consequently, additional research is necessary to explore and understand this phenomenon and its relationship to the process of acculturation. Such inquiry could result in the creation and implementation of culturally relevant preventative and ameliorative interventions for populations for whom this psychological and cultural issue is particularly relevant.

9. The passage lists which of the following as features that are idealized by western standards? Select all that apply.

- Ⓐ hair length
- Ⓑ eye color
- Ⓒ skin tone
- Ⓓ body shape
- Ⓔ bone density

---

10. The author would most likely disagree with which one of the following statements?

- Ⓐ Western beauty standards impact the self-esteem of some individuals not born in western cultures.
- Ⓑ Sufficient research exists to examine the impact western beauty standards have on acculturation.
- Ⓒ Technology has aided the proliferation of arbitrary standards of beauty throughout the U.S.
- Ⓓ Perception of physical attractiveness plays a key role in development of self-esteem.
- Ⓔ Western standards of beauty are very dissimilar from those in the Eastern hemisphere.

---

11. What is the primary purpose of the passage?

- Ⓐ To highlight the disparity in attention paid to non-western standards of beauty versus western standards of beauty.
- Ⓑ To discuss the possible reasons for the decline in self-esteem issues among immigrant teens.
- Ⓒ To illuminate the need for more research on the impact western beauty standards have on self-esteem of those who find themselves physically at odds with the standards.
- Ⓓ To criticize western beauty standards for being too stringent and exclusive.
- Ⓔ To express concern over the impact social media has on the proliferation of unhealthy images of women.

VERBAL REASONING

Questions 12 and 13 are based on the following passage. Select one answer unless otherwise indicated.

Couples are often quick to turn to litigation when it comes to a contested divorce and rarely consider the benefits of mediation. Mediation offers an alternative approach and can be quite efficient and successful. Mediation often leads to a quicker resolution, is less expensive, and can lead to creative solutions not always possible in a court of law. Additionally, mediation focuses on mutually acceptable solutions, rather than winning or losing.

12. Which one of the following is most supported by the passage?

- Ⓐ Couples who choose mediation over litigation are happier in the end.
- Ⓑ Some of the agreements reached in mediation are outside of the confines of what would be permitted in a legal proceeding.
- Ⓒ After mediation, couples often choose to get back together and cancel further divorce proceedings.
- Ⓓ Mediation should always be the first choice for settling a contested divorce.
- Ⓔ Mediation is not necessary for uncontested divorces.

---

13. The author's attitude towards the value of mediation can be described as:

- Ⓐ reasonably optimistic
- Ⓑ incredulous
- Ⓒ unabated
- Ⓓ fervent
- Ⓔ ambivalent

Questions 14 and 15 are based on the following passage. Select one answer unless otherwise indicated.

Many of the citizens of Namouth have speciously tried to blame the governor for the ever-increasing wage gap between workers with a college degree and those with just a high school diploma. Over the past two decades, more companies have integrated advanced technology and social media into their business models, a change that has increased their need for more educated and technically proficient employees who are in turn are paid significantly more than those with less education. The wage gap then, is precipitated by the growth of technology in businesses, not by policies enacted by the governor.

14. Which of the following, if true, most weakens the assertion that technology growth and the need for tech savvy workers is responsible for the wage gap between college graduates and high school graduates?

Ⓐ The governor has three college-educated children who are gainfully employed.
Ⓑ The governor recently released a slate of new policies to be voted on by the state senate.
Ⓒ A decade ago, schools in Namouth instituted several technology courses that provided training on the latest technology as a requirement for high school graduation.
Ⓓ The governor has been ridiculed for the impact his policies have had in other areas.
Ⓔ The governor has not made a public statement to refute the claims levied against him.

15. The passage makes which one of the following unwarranted assumptions?

Ⓐ The level of technical proficiency college graduates possess warrants a significant difference in pay from those who do not possess such knowledge.
Ⓑ High school graduates do not possess the skills necessary to be industry leaders.
Ⓒ High school graduates do not possess the skills necessary to meet the needs of the city of Namouth.
Ⓓ Only college graduates possess the necessary education to fill the open jobs.
Ⓔ High school graduates should not be paid as much as college graduates.

For questions 16-20, select two answers that best complete the blank and produces two sentences that are alike in meaning.

16. The board felt that the Director's ______________ of the intern was unwarranted given how minor her mistake was; they surmised it was possibly brought on by the fact that she had previously rejected his advances. As a result, the Director's otherwise stellar career was tarnished and he was asked to step down.

Ⓐ admonishment
Ⓑ depredation
Ⓒ catechization
Ⓓ censure
Ⓔ placating
Ⓕ heurism

17. Freud and his theories continue to be looked upon with skepticism and disdain in the psychological community even though during his lifetime, Freud was often ______________ by scholars and laymen alike.

Ⓐ lauded
Ⓑ precluded
Ⓒ extolled
Ⓓ lambasted
Ⓔ underappreciated
Ⓕ misguided

18. After her surgery, Hannah was reluctant to spend time ______________ but knew that it was necessary in order to heal properly and be ready for the upcoming competition season.

Ⓐ recuperating
Ⓑ prevaricating
Ⓒ convalescing
Ⓓ philandering
Ⓔ exculpating
Ⓕ absolving

GO TO THE NEXT PAGE

VERBAL REASONING

19. After an explosive argument with the other founding members, John vengefully released the company's prized trade secret. He was promptly _______________ by the rest of the founding members; all personal contact was cut off and his access to company records was terminated.

Ⓐ heralded
Ⓑ bemused
Ⓒ spurned
Ⓓ attenuated
Ⓔ ostracized
Ⓕ bludgeoned

---

20. Paul went into the room to break the news about the plane crash to his team. As he approached the conference room, he saw them enjoying each other's company and celebrating the upcoming return of their colleagues unaware of what had happened. He stood there a moment taking in their _______________ dispositions before he went into the room.

Ⓐ mirthful
Ⓑ melancholy
Ⓒ tenuous
Ⓓ jovial
Ⓔ laconic
Ⓕ dubious

STOP

QUANTITATIVE REASONING | 20 QUESTIONS
SECTION 5 | 35 MINUTES

DIRECTIONS: For questions 1-8, use any provided centered information to help you compare Column A and Column B. Select the answer that describes the relationship between the two quantities, noting that the same answer choices are presented for each Quantitative Comparison question:

- A **Quantity A is greater.**
- B **Quantity B is greater.**
- C **The two quantities are equal.**
- D **The relationship cannot be determined from the information given.**

---

1. $x > 0$

Column A	Column B
$x^3 \quad 2$	$x^2 + 2$

Ⓐ Ⓑ Ⓒ Ⓓ

2.

Column A	Column B
$\sqrt{49}$	$\sqrt{64}$

Ⓐ Ⓑ Ⓒ Ⓓ

3.

Column A	Column B
Area of a circle with a diameter of 12	Surface area of a sphere with a diameter of 12

Ⓐ Ⓑ Ⓒ Ⓓ

---

4. The arithmetic mean of four numbers is 36

Column A	Column B
Sum of the four numbers	150

Ⓐ Ⓑ Ⓒ Ⓓ

5.

Column A	Column B
The numbers of faces on a cube that share and edge with any one face	Total number of sides on a square

Ⓐ Ⓑ Ⓒ Ⓓ

6.

Column A	Column B
75% of 90	30% of 80

Ⓐ Ⓑ Ⓒ Ⓓ

GO TO THE NEXT PAGE

QUANTITATIVE REASONING

7. A coin is tossed 3 times

Column A	Column B
The chances of getting tails three times	The chance of the coin never landing on heads

Ⓐ Ⓑ Ⓒ Ⓓ

8.

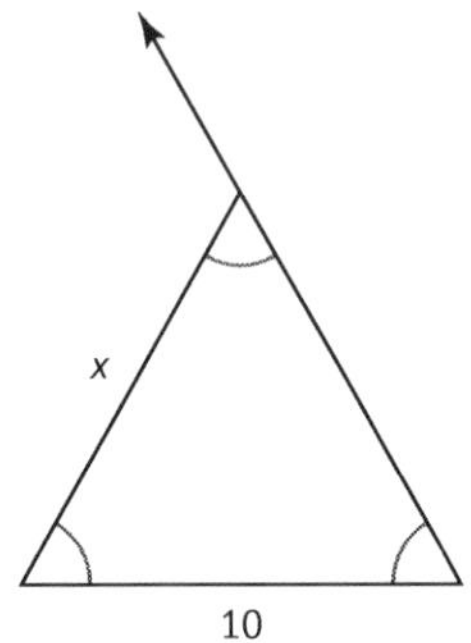

Column A	Column B
The length of x	12

Ⓐ Ⓑ Ⓒ Ⓓ

9. Bob is making mini fondant cakes for the next bake sale. Each cake costs Bob \$1.80 to make. If he sells the cakes for \$3.00 each, how many will he have to sell to make a profit of exactly \$36.00?

Ⓐ 12
Ⓑ 31
Ⓒ 36
Ⓓ 60
Ⓔ 30

10. Solve the proportion $\frac{8}{a} = \frac{9}{6}$.

Ⓐ 72
Ⓑ $\frac{16}{3}$
Ⓒ $\frac{3}{16}$
Ⓓ $\frac{1}{3}$
Ⓔ 2

11. If $x = -1$ and $y = 2$, what is the value of the expression $2x^3 - 3xy$?

Ⓐ -9
Ⓑ 14
Ⓒ 14
Ⓓ 4
Ⓔ -1

12. What is the equation of the line that contains the points (−3, 7) and (5, −1)

Ⓐ $y = x + 10$
Ⓑ $y = x - 10$
Ⓒ $y = 3x - 2$
Ⓓ $y = -x + 4$
Ⓔ $y = x + 4$

QUANTITATIVE REASONING

13. For trapezoid *JKLM, A* and *B* are midpoints of the legs. Find *ML*.

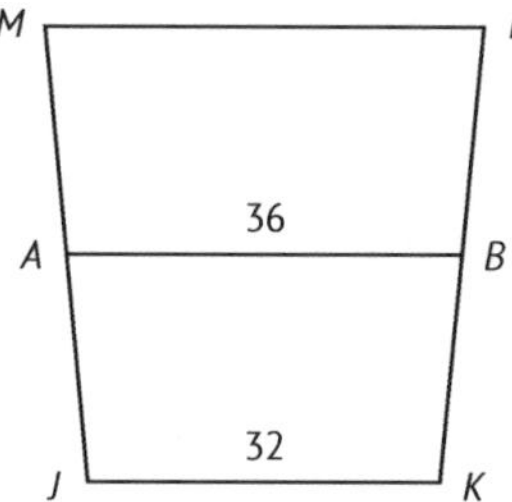

Ⓐ 32
Ⓑ 4
Ⓒ 34
Ⓓ 68
Ⓔ 40

14. Find the value of y in the figure below.

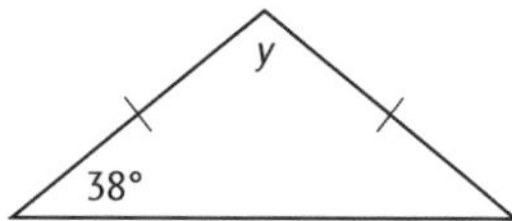

Ⓐ 76°
Ⓑ 180°
Ⓒ 90°
Ⓓ 38°
Ⓔ 104°

15. If Jim scored a 76, and 42, and a 55 on his first three tests, what must his score on his fourth test be if he wants an average of 60? Enter your answer in the text box below.

Use the graph below to answer questions 16-18. Select one answer unless otherwise indicated.

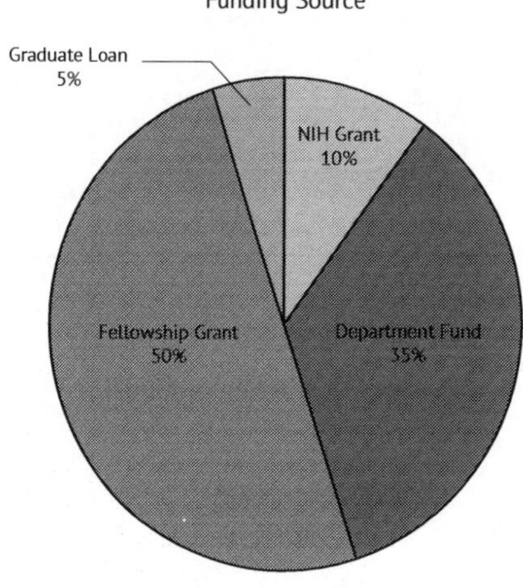

16. The graph represents the funding sources Freda used for her graduate education. If the total amount of her education was $84,000, what was the amount of her graduate loan?

Ⓐ $5000
Ⓑ $5500
Ⓒ $5750
Ⓓ $4200
Ⓔ $5200

17. Freda covered what percentage of her tuition through grants?

Ⓐ 60%
Ⓑ 95%
Ⓒ 10%
Ⓓ 50%
Ⓔ 70%

QUANTITATIVE REASONING

18. Freda started her graduate program during the first year of the 12% tuition increase. If Freda had enrolled the previous year before the increase, how much would her graduate loan have been assuming she received the same percentage of funding from her other funding sources?

Ⓐ $4000
Ⓑ $3500
Ⓒ $3750
Ⓓ $4200
Ⓔ $2200

---

19. $(4^3)^2 =$

Ⓐ 32
Ⓑ 64
Ⓒ 4096
Ⓓ 526
Ⓔ 472

---

20. Solve $\sqrt{144} \bullet \sqrt{64} \bullet \sqrt{49} \bullet \sqrt{169}$. Enter your answer in the text box.

STOP

VERBAL REASONING | 20 QUESTIONS
SECTION 6 | 30 MINUTES

DIRECTIONS: Answer each question according to the directions given.

For questions 1 to 8, you are to choose one answer for each blank from the corresponding column of choices.

1. Multi-level marketing schemes often try to ______________ potential contractors with promises of large payouts and exclusive benefits.

Ⓐ beguile
Ⓑ dilute
Ⓒ derringer
Ⓓ force
Ⓔ deceive

2. After several unfortunate scandals, students were happy to have Mr. Barton, the new Head of School, to ______________ the school's reputation and boost the morale of the student body.

Ⓐ recant
Ⓑ restore
Ⓒ rebrand
Ⓓ supersede
Ⓔ expand

3. Mr. Trent's carefree and ______________ nature was at odds with the serious nature of the other teachers at the school.

Ⓐ decorous
Ⓑ quiet
Ⓒ rollicking
Ⓓ voluble
Ⓔ morose

4. Deb often (i)______________ the use of (ii) ______________ to explain challenging things like death to children as irresponsible. She believed in the importance of being blunt and truthful and that telling children deceased loved ones had gone to visit the rainbow did more harm than good.

Blank i	Blank ii
Ⓐ repudiated	Ⓓ enigmas
Ⓑ decried	Ⓔ eulogiums
Ⓒ espoused	Ⓕ euphemisms

5. Few musicians are able to ever fully master the (i) ______________ of playing the French horn without years of (ii) ______________ training alongside the few experts in the field.

Blank i	Blank ii
Ⓐ intricacies	Ⓓ devoted
Ⓑ chords	Ⓔ specialized
Ⓒ escapades	Ⓕ intentional

6. The growth of technology and the proliferation of widely available digital content has made print material nearly (i) ______________. In spite of that, major publications have still maintained a (ii) ______________ readership that still enjoys print material.

Blank i	Blank ii
Ⓐ bombastic	Ⓓ loyal
Ⓑ innovative	Ⓔ transitory
Ⓒ obsolescent	Ⓕ scholastic

VERBAL REASONING

7. Robert was so upset about his team's loss that he (i) ______________ for days before his wife finally issued him an (ii) ______________ to either get it together or sleep on the couch. Realizing how much his wife was affected, he quickly apologized and (iii) ______________ his sour mood.

Blank i

Ⓐ murmured
Ⓑ sulked
Ⓒ grooved

Blank ii

Ⓓ proviso
Ⓔ provocation
Ⓕ ultimatum

Blank iii

Ⓖ revamped
Ⓗ enervated
Ⓘ portended

---

8. The team of treasure hunters, eager to be the first to get to the location outlined on the map, pushed forward with their march and (i) ______________ warnings to steer clear of the mountain. When the storm started to rage, they realized the (ii) ______________ of the situation and attempted to turn back. But, the descent proved more (iii) ______________ than any of them could imagine; they eventually had to search for cover until the storm passed.

Blank i

Ⓐ flouted
Ⓑ surmised
Ⓒ rescinded

Blank ii

Ⓓ feebleness
Ⓔ gravity
Ⓕ perspicacity

Blank iii

Ⓖ baleful
Ⓗ long-suffering
Ⓘ resigned

GO TO THE NEXT PAGE

Questions 9 to 11 are based on the following passage. Select one answer unless otherwise indicated.

Prior to the arrival of the first foreign explorers on Hawaii, the sovereign nation had a rich tradition of culture and self-governance. Its population was made up of mostly natives who ascribed to the established culture and structure. Soon after the arrival of British explorer, James Cook, the islands transitioned from independent Chiefdoms and instituted a monarchy.

The U.S. first established its foothold on the Hawaiian Islands in the 1820's when missionaries arrived to spread Christianity. Ravaged by disease brought on by contact with Cook and his crews, the population on the once isolated and sheltered islands dwindled drastically. Missionaries took advantage of the natives' misfortune to advance their ideology, and suggested that the natives' sins had provoked god to punish them. The missionaries promised deliverance and eternal life if the natives accepted Christianity. The religious conversion, however, led to generational manipulation carried on by the offspring of the missionaries; they eventually established self-serving governments that allowed them to assert power and drive policies throughout the islands that later served as a harbinger for annexation by the U.S.

Because of its prime location in the Pacific, Hawaii was eyed by competing world powers as a potential asset to their expanding empires. The United States eventually began the process of trying to annex the islands to extend the reach of its pervasive ideology of Manifest Destiny. The U.S. had a vested interest in the Islands for a myriad of reasons, reasons that led to the overthrow of the monarchy, and the acquisition of Hawaii as a territory and eventual U.S state. Of particular note was the opportunity for the U.S. to expand its military presence, gain greater control of the Pacific maritime routes, increase its economic power through access to Hawaii's natural resources, and curb expansion of other global powers who stood to benefit from acquiring the islands.

9. The passage lists which of the following reasons why the U.S was interested in Hawaii. Select all that apply.

- [A] The U.S recognized the value of Hawaii's position in the Pacific and did not want other powers to acquire it.
- [B] Hawaii was known for its natural resources and the U.S wanted to tap into its agricultural potential.
- [C] James Cook was interested in claiming the island as his own and the U.S intervened to prevent him from disturbing the rich culture Hawaii had established.

10. What is the main point of the passage?

- (A) Hawaii was better off being acquired by the U.S since the British only brought with them disease and a hunger for power.
- (B) Hawaii's culture and structure would have persisted as it was without the interference of outside forces.
- (C) Hawaii was a major interest to many world powers because of its position in the Pacific.
- (D) James Cook was an integral part of Hawaii's history and played a major role in it becoming a state.
- (E) The U.S was not interested in Hawaii until it realized other world powers were interested.

11. Select the sentence that best describes Hawaii's population before foreign settlers arrived.

VERBAL REASONING

Questions 12 and 13 are based on the following passage. Select one answer unless otherwise indicated.

Rhesus monkeys use facial expressions to communicate with each other and enforce social order within their habitat. One of their most noticeable expressions is the fear grimace, which is usually expressed when a monkey who is lower on the social hierarchy feels intimidated by a higher-ranking monkey.

12. The fear grimace is most likely to be expressed by:

Ⓐ the leaders in the monkey group.
Ⓑ the females in the group since they lack social rank.
Ⓒ newer monkeys to the group.
Ⓓ a monkey who possess little authority within the group.
Ⓔ a higher ranking monkey in the presence of humans.

---

13. Which one of the following can be inferred from the passage?

Ⓐ Rhesus monkeys often live in chaotic and unchecked groups where power changes constantly.
Ⓑ Female monkeys tend to take on the dominant roles in the groups.
Ⓒ Power dynamics are generally understood and adhered to in groups of Rhesus monkeys.
Ⓓ Dominant Rhesus monkeys often intimidate subordinate monkeys.
Ⓔ The only way a subordinate monkey can reach the top of the Rhesus hierarchy is to kill the most dominant monkey.

Questions 14 and 15 are based on the following passage. Select one answer unless otherwise indicated.

Yogis believe the body to be a means of evolving through this life on earth before transcending into the realm of the Absolute. For them, chanting *om* makes the body acquiescent to the healing and uplifting energies of yoga. Chanting *om* creates vibrations for yogis syncing them with the universe and opening the door for the meeting and adjoining with Braham. The incantation allows the aimless wander of the mind to become focused and intent on an existence outside of anything mundane and material, leaving the devotee open for the blessings that come along with communion with the true and pure self. Chanting *om* serves the purpose of creating an environment of perfect peace for yogis. The silence falling between each chant becomes sort of a metronome and the devotee alternatives between it and vibration, creating a trance-like state.

14. The passage aims to:

Ⓐ Explain the benefits yogis derive from chanting *om*
Ⓑ Assess how effective chanting is in creating a trance-like state
Ⓒ Examine an isolated and rarely practiced component of yoga
Ⓓ Encourage the reader to take up yoga and meditation
Ⓔ Support the separation of the spirit from the material world

---

15. The author uses the word "metronome" most likely to:

Ⓐ Highlight the musical nature of yoga
Ⓑ Allude to how monotonous yoga and chanting can be
Ⓒ Create a visual for the reader to imagine how the yogi alternates methodically between two different states
Ⓓ Attempt to dissuade the reader from chanting in a silent space
Ⓔ Equate chanting to playing music

For questions 16-20, select two answers that best complete the blank and produces two sentences that are alike in meaning.

16. People with a(n) ______________ silence meditation typically find that the world is too busy and noisy for them; this could explain why many of them choose to spend at least some of their time in isolation.

Ⓐ aloofness of
Ⓑ antipathy towards
Ⓒ penchant for
Ⓓ predilection for
Ⓔ aversion to
Ⓕ curiosity about

17. The two marathoners were neck and neck until the final stretch when the reigning champion took a huge lead and finally ______________ the new-comers chances of winning.

Ⓐ amplified
Ⓑ stymied
Ⓒ galvanized
Ⓓ expounded
Ⓔ thwarted
Ⓕ implored

18. Even after burning the Thanksgiving turkey and dropping the cake she had spent hours making, Martha was still in a ______________ mood and thrilled to finally have all of her family together again.

Ⓐ histrionic
Ⓑ genial
Ⓒ retracted
Ⓓ jocund
Ⓔ cantankerous
Ⓕ magnanimous

19. The fraternity house had a distinct ______________ aroma; the likely culprit was the pile of gym socks and pizza boxes that littered the hallway.

Ⓐ honeyed
Ⓑ pungent
Ⓒ tussled
Ⓓ soporific
Ⓔ putrid
Ⓕ inimical

20. The young politician rose quickly in political rank to become the youngest Governor ever elected. But, while his understanding of policy was superlative, his interpersonal and organizational skills were still quite ______________.

Ⓐ pusillanimous
Ⓑ on par
Ⓒ tedious
Ⓓ copasetic
Ⓔ immature
Ⓕ unfledged

STOP

QUANTITATIVE REASONING
ANSWER KEY : SECTION 3

1. **D.**
Because you do not know the number of sides of the polygon, you cannot determine the relationship. A triangle is a regular polygon and the angle measures could be equal. But, if the polygon was a quadrilateral, column A would be greater.

2. **B.**
The function equation is already in slope-intercept form $y = mx + b$. So, the slope is 5 and the y-intercept is 7. The y-intercept is greater.

3. **D.**
The centered information does not tell you how many of each color you have. The relationship cannot be determined.

4. **A.**
The mean of the data set is 32.7 and the median is 20. The mean is greater.

5. **A.**
If 70% of the students passed the exam then 30% failed. The ratio of students who passed to students who failed is 7:3 or $\frac{7}{3}$ which is greater than $\frac{3}{7}$.

6. **B.**
The x and y-intercept indicate where the line hits each axis at the point of origin. Solve the equation for each variable by plugging in 0 for the other variable.

$$6(0)+3y=12$$
$$y=4$$
$$6x+3(0)=12$$
$$x=2$$

7. **B.**
If the sum of prime numbers a and b is 12, then a and b are 7 and 5. Their product is 35, so quantity B is greater.

8. **C.**
Distribute the negative sign for column A.

$$-(x-y)=x-y$$
$$-x+y=x-y$$
$$y-x=x-y$$

Since the expressions are the inverse of each other, x and y must be equal.

9. **6,000**
First, determine the overall amount Kelly raised. Her goal was \$20,000 and she raised 20% more. So, she raised \$24,000 in total. Crowdfunding accounted for 25% of that, so \$6000.

10. **B.**
Kelly raised \$24,000. 19% of that was from matched donations, so \$4560. Notice this is an answer choice, but it is incorrect. The question asks how much she would have fallen short of her *original* goal of \$20000. So, subtract, \$4560 from \$24,000. Without employer matched donations, Kelly would have been \$560 away from her \$20000 goal.

11. **E.**
The slope of a perpendicular line is the negative reciprocal. So, the slope is 5. Next, solve for the y-intercept, using the given points.

$$-10=5(3)+b$$
$$y=-25$$

12. **C.**
Tossing a coin three times leads to 8 possible outcomes, three of which include exactly two heads. So, the probability is 3/8.

13. **E.**
Use the distance equation and plug in points (−2, −3) and (−4, −5).

$$d=\sqrt{(x_2-x_1)^2+(y_2-y_1)^2}$$
$$d=\sqrt{-4-(-2))^2+(-5-(-3))^2}$$
$$\sqrt{4+4}$$
$$\sqrt{8}=\sqrt{4}\bullet\sqrt{2}=2\sqrt{2}$$

14. **D.**

$$-7(3n+5)=-6n+25$$
$$-21n-35=-6n+25$$
$$-15n=60$$
$$n=-4$$

QUANTITATIVE REASONING
ANSWER KEY : SECTION 3

15. D.
The triangle is a 30-60-90 triangle and have standard proportions for its sides.

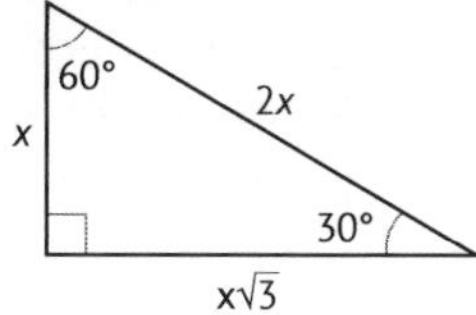

The hypotenuse is $4\sqrt{3}$. The shortest leg, b, is always half that, so $2\sqrt{3}$. The longest leg, a, is found using $\frac{1}{2}(hypotenuse)(\sqrt{3})$. When you solve, you end up with $(2\sqrt{3})(\sqrt{3}) = 2\sqrt{9} = 6$.

16. $\mathbf{\frac{1}{8}}$ **or** $\mathbf{\frac{7}{56}}$

$g \boxtimes k = \frac{g}{2k}$. Substitute 7 for g and 28 for k and solve.

$$\frac{g}{2k} = \frac{7}{2(28)} = \frac{7}{56} = \frac{1}{8}$$

17. D.
Create an equation: $100 + .025x = 900$. $x = 32000$.

18. B.
To solve this problem, understand that the product of all three terms is equal to 0. To make that possible, and make sure a is greater than 0, you need to find an answer choice that would make one of the terms equal zero. When either of terms are 0, the value of the entire equation will be 0 since you are looking for the product. So, your possible values are −2, 3, or −4. Only 3 is an answer choice.

19. D.
Distribute and combine like terms.

$$5a(3a+7)+3(-4+2a)$$

$$15a^2 + 35a - 12 + 6a = 15a^2 + 41a - 12$$

20. B.

$$\frac{10 \cdot 9 \cdot \cancel{8} \cdot \cancel{7} \cdot \cancel{6} \cdot \cancel{5} \cdot \cancel{4} \cdot \cancel{3} \cdot \cancel{2} \cdot \cancel{1}}{\cancel{8} \cdot \cancel{7} \cdot \cancel{6} \cdot \cancel{5} \cdot \cancel{4} \cdot \cancel{3} \cdot \cancel{2} \cdot \cancel{1}}$$

Cancel out like terms and you are left with (10)(9) = 90.

VERBAL REASONING
ANSWER KEY : SECTION 4

1. **D.**
   If everyone is admitted, the group looses its exclusivity.

2. **C.**
   Ennui is a sense of weariness and boredom.

3. **B.**
   While abrupt does mean quickly, you must consider that the technique was not only sudden but also effective. Deft is skillful or adroit.

4. **A, D.**
   Jodie did not have the qualifications for the position but applied any way. Requisite is required or necessary. So, Jodie did not have the requisite skills. In spite of that, she refused to relent and withdraw her application. "Because of her stubborn personality" is a context clue for the second blank. Mulish means stubborn, so it is a match for the missing word.

5. **B, F.**
   Those in the courtroom knew the defendant was guilty and was shocked to hear the verdict, meaning the verdict was not in agreement with what they believed to be true. So, the victim was vindicated, or found blameless. The courtroom erupted or burst into a shocked uproar.

6. **C, D.**
   At first glance, it might appear that both vet and appraise can fit into the first blank. But, the city council wants to assess the effect the decrease will have on learning outcomes. So, appraise, which means to evaluate, is the best fit. Vet is typically used to mean validate or affirm. The plan the city council decided on in the interim was temporary or provisional.

7. **C, D, H.**
   The researchers were only looking for mushrooms but happened upon a lost city. Their discovery was auspicious or lucky. Though the word myth is used to describe how historian began to think about the city, that does not mean the city itself was mythical. The context clues indicate it was well-hidden or clandestine. Their find landed them enough cash to retire. Boon is a windfall or gain.

8. **A, E, G.**
   The hiring process seems to be merely a smokescreen or a charade. Be careful with the shell-game answer choice D, despotism, which sounds similar to the correct answer, nepotism. Given the nepotism, people are ostensibly given jobs whether or not they are qualified for the job.

9. **A, C, D.**
   Eye shape is mentioned but not eye color.

10. **B.**
    The author explicitly states that more research needs to be done on the impact western beauty standards have on acculturation.

11. **C.**
    This question is closely linked to the previous question. The passage primarily focuses on the impact of western beauty standards on those from non-western cultures and the need for more research to explore the scope of those effects.

12. **B.**
    Several of the answers could be true in theory but are not supported by the passage. The passage makes explicit mention of the fact that some of the outcomes possible in mediation are not possible in a legal proceeding.

13. **A.**
    The author is supportive of mediation as an alternative to legal proceedings.

14. **C.**
    The passage suggests that the wage gap is a result of the increased need businesses have for tech-savvy employees. But if high school graduates were trained in the latest technology skills as part of their requirements for graduation, then something else must be driving the wage gap.

15. **D.**
    The passage incorrectly assumes that college graduates possess the requisite skills to fill the needs of companies and that college graduates are the only people who can fill the needs of the companies.

16. A, D.
The intern committed what appeared to be a minor infraction and was disciplined by the Director. Censured and admonished both mean to punish or to scorn.

17. A, C.
The transition "even though" steers you in the opposite direction of skepticism and disdain. Lauded and extolled both mean praised or acclaimed.

18. A, C.
You are looking for words related to recovery. After her surgery, Hannah didn't necessarily want to spend time recovering but knew she needed to in order to be ready for her season. Recuperate and convalesce mean to recover or to heal.

19. C, E.
After the argument the other founding members cut off all ties with John and terminated his access to company records. Ostracize and spurn mean to expel, rebuke, or reject.

20. A, D.
Paul went to break bad news to his team and took a moment to take in the collegial interactions among the members of the team. Mirthful and jovial both mean upbeat and pleasant. Be careful not to conflate the mood of Paul with that of the team. While Paul may have been melancholy, the blank corresponds to the mood of the team.

QUANTITATIVE REASONING
ANSWER KEY : SECTION 5

1. **D.**
Plugging in positive numbers of various values (1, ¼, for example) yields different results in terms of which column is greater. The relationship cannot be determined.

2. **B.**
Both the radicals are perfect roots, so column A is equal to 7 and column B is equal to 8. Column B is greater.

3. **B.**
The surface area of a sphere is found using $A = \pi r^2$ and the area of a circle is found using $A = \pi r^2$.

4. **B.**
The sum of the number is (36)(4) = 144. So, quantity B is greater.

5. **C.**
On a cube, any one face shares an edge with 4 other faces, which is equal to the number of sides of a square.

6. **A.**
70% of 90 is 67.5 and 30% of 80 is 56. Column A is greater.

7. **C.**
The statements are equivalent; landing on tails all three times is the same as never landing on heads.

8. **B.**
The triangle has all equal angles, so it is an equilateral triangle. So, all the sides are equal. You are given one side, so x = 10 which is less than 12. Column B is greater.

9. **E.**
Bob makes $1.20 in profit per cake. He needs to sell 30 cakes to make $36 in **profit**.

Total to make a cake:	1.20
Sale price:	3.00
Profit per cake:	1.20

To find the amount of cakes he needs to sell to make 36.00 in profit, divide 36 by the total profit per cake 1.20. $\frac{36}{1.2} = 30$.

10. **B.**
Cross-multiply to solve for a.

$$\frac{8}{a} = \frac{9}{6}$$

$$48 = 9a$$

Simply: $$a = \frac{48}{9} = \frac{16}{3}$$

11. **D.**
Plug in the given values and solve.

$$2(-1)^3 - 3(-1)(2) = -2 - (6-) = 4$$

12. **D.**
First solve for the slope by plugging the points into the slope equation $m = \frac{y_2 - y_1}{x_2 - x_1}$. m = −1. Put the equation in slope-intercept form, plug in the coordinates, and solve for b. b = 4.

13. **C.**
Take the sum of the AB and JK and divide by 2 to find ML. 36 + 32 = 68/2 = 34.

14. **E.**
Since the two sides are equal, the angle in the bottom right corner must also be 38 degrees. Together, those two angles measure 76 degrees. Since triangles always have 180 degrees, the remaining angle is 104 degrees.

15. **67**
Create an equation to solve for x:

$$\frac{76 + 42 + 55 + x}{4} = 60$$

$$\frac{173 + x}{4} = 60$$

$$240 = 173 + x$$

$$x = 67$$

16. **D.**
The loan is 5% of the total tuition, so $4200. (.05)(84000)=$4200.

17. A.
She received 50% from a fellowship grant and 10% from the NIH grant.

18. C.
If tuition is now 12% higher than the year before, tuition was \$75000. So, Freda's loan would have been 5% of \$75000 or \$3750.

19. C.
Using the rules of exponents, create a new expression, multiplying the exponents.

So, $4^6 = 4096$.

20. 8736.
Each radical is a perfect square (12, 8, 7, 13).

VERBAL REASONING
ANSWER KEY : SECTION 6

1. **A.**
Multi-level marketing companies try to entice potential contractors with attractive offers. Beguile means to lure or enthrall and best fits in the blank.

2. **B.**
Scandals mar or ruin a reputation; Mr. Barton, students believe, will work to help the school move past previous scandals and restore their reputation.

3. **C.**
Mr. Trent is carefree unlike the other teachers who are more serious. His demeanor can best be described as rollicking, which means carefree of boisterous.

4. **B, F.**
Deb is not fond of softening the truth for children and believes it will only hurt them in the future. Blank one is tricky. Repudiated means to denounce or retract and decried means denounced or criticized. Repudiated is typically used in the context of rejecting something that was previously accepted. As you are unsure of what Deb's previous stance on using euphemisms, or understatements, decried would be the best fit in the blank since it requires making fewer assumptions.

5. **A, E.**
Devotion and intention could both fit in the blank, in theory. However, the training is done alongside experts in the fields, making specialized training.

6. **C, D.**
Digital content has nearly rendered print material obsolescent or outdated and useless. In spite of that, however, major publications still have a committed loyal readership of their print materials.

7. **B, F, G.**
Robert moped or sulked for days before his wife confronted him some firm choices, or an ultimatum. Once he realized the impact his behavior had on his wife, he adjusted, or revamped his attitude.

8. **A, E, G.**
The treasure hunters ignored or flouted the warnings to steer clear of the mountains. Not until the storm started swirling did they realize how serious the situation was. They in essence, became aware of the gravity of the impending danger. Turning back was a more difficult or baleful task than they envisioned and they were forced to take cover until the storm passed.

9. **A, B.**
The location of the islands was a draw for several world powers as was its natural resources. James Cook is discussed in the passage, but answer choice C offers an inaccurate portrayal of the reasons the U.S became involved in the acquisition of Hawaii.

10. **C.**
The passage primarily discusses the reasons Hawaii was an interest to many world powers and how the U.S eventually came to acquire it.

11. Its population was made up of mostly natives who ascribed to the established culture and structure.

12. **D.**
The passage does not make a distinction between female and male monkeys and their ability to be higher up on the hierarchy. The passage also does not indicate how long a monkey has to be with a group to be high-ranking so you cannot assume new monkeys automatically start at the bottom.

13. **C.**
The fear grimace is expressed by a lower-ranking monkey in response to feeling intimidated by a higher ranking monkey. The passage offers no discussion on how social order among monkeys is determined so answer choices dealing with which monkeys can and cannot hold social rank are incorrect. You can infer, however, that the established hierarchy is accepted within a group of monkeys.

14. **A.**
The passage discusses the reasons behind chanting om including its transcendental effects.

15. **C.**
A metronome is a device often used by musicians to help them maintain the proper pacing when playing. The device has a pendulum that swings from side to side. The author discusses how one who chants om alternates between silence and vibration, much like the pendulum moves from one side to the other.

16. C, D.
Penchant and predilection mean an inclination or liking. In this case, those who tend to enjoy silence sometimes find the noisy world too much for them and need a retreat.

17. B, E.
The marathoners were close in pace until the champion widened the gap making him the probable winner and dashing the hopes of the challenger. Stymied and thwarted both mean to cut short or curtail. The challenger's hopes of winning were curtailed.

18. B, D.
In spite of things going wrong, the turkey burning and the cake being dropped, Martha was still in a good mood because her family was all together. Martha's disposition can best be described as genial or jocund, which both mean jovial or pleasant.

19. B, E.
The pile of gym socks and pizza boxes certainly did not produce a pleasant odor. Thus, the smell was pungent or putrid since both words mean foul-smelling or musty.

20. E, F.
Although the young politician had an excellent understanding of politics, he still had room for growth with regards to his interpersonal and organizational skills, which were undeveloped. Immature and unfledged both mean underdeveloped.

Raw Score	Scaled Score
40	170
39	169
38	168
37	167
36	166
35	165
34	164
33	163
32	162
31	161
30	160
29	159
28	158
27	157
26	156
25	155
24	154
23	153
22	152
21	151

Raw Score	Scaled Score
20	150
19	149
18	148
17	147
16	146
15	145
14	144
13	143
12	142
11	141
10	140
9	139
8	138
7	137
6	136
5	135
4	134
3	133
2	132
1	131

These practice tests are designed to simulate actual testing conditions as closely as possible. While the questions are similar to those you will encounter on the GRE, the sections are not adaptive for Verbal and Quantitative Reasoning like they will be if you sit for the computer-adaptive exam. The scale above gives you an **idea** of your projected score and can help you monitor your progress as you become more familiar with the material. The scale above is a rough guide to predict your score. **As a reminder**, the PowerPrep II software distributed by ETS offers two free computer-adaptive exams to supplement your study plan. Be sure to include those exams in your study plan in addition to the exams in this section; this will help you get an idea of the areas you need to study more closely in order to reach your scoring goals.

ARGO
BROTHERS

PRACTICE TEST 4

GRE®

Graduate Record Examinations

- This exam is 3 hours and 45 minutes long. Try to take this full exam in one sitting to simulate real test conditions.
- While taking this exam, refrain from listening to music or watching TV.
- When writing your response for Analyze an Issue & Analyze an Argument prompt, use a computer, and turn off the spell-check feature to simulate real testing conditions.
- Use a basic calculator, do not use a graphic or scientific calculator. On the real exam, you will have an on-screen calculator with only basic operation functions and a square root key.
- Concentrate and GOOD LUCK!

To calculate your score visit our web site and download excel calculator:

www.einstein-academy.com/GRE

ANALYTICAL WRITING
ANALYZE AN ISSUE

ESSAY 1
30 MINUTES

Participation awards, where everyone is recognized for simply participating, foster a sense of entitlement and encourages children early on to expect success to be handed to them instead of having to work for it.

Discuss the extent to which you agree or disagree with the claim and cite the most compelling reasons someone could use to dispute your stance.

ANALYTICAL WRITING | ESSAY 2
ANALYZE AN ARGUMENT | 30 MINUTES

The homeless shelter in Fizer Square has always been primarily staffed by student volunteers from the local high school. Without their consistent help, the shelter's operational capacity would be significantly reduced. This past year, the number of students helping at the shelter declined significantly. Because the shelter plays an integral role in the community and serves mainly local residents, the local high school should take steps to ensure that the shelter continues to receive enough student volunteers to operate. A preliminary survey concluded that teachers and parents think community engagement is important, so the school should require all students to volunteer at least 5 hours a week at the homeless shelter.

After reviewing the author's argument, examine any alternate explanations that could reasonably compete with the proposed explanation. In your response, explain how you might challenge the assertions provided in the argument.

VERBAL REASONING | 20 QUESTIONS
SECTION 3 | 30 MINUTES

DIRECTIONS: Answer each question according to the directions given.

For questions 1 to 8, you are to choose one answer for each blank from the corresponding column of choices.

1. The thunderstorm was ______________; it started up all of a sudden then fizzled out rather quickly.

Ⓐ absconding
Ⓑ ephemeral
Ⓒ amiable
Ⓓ wretched
Ⓔ abjure

2. After David forgot his anniversary, he tried to ______________ the situation by buying his wife the diamond necklace she wanted.

Ⓐ propitiate
Ⓑ exacerbate
Ⓒ negate
Ⓓ effulge
Ⓔ clear

3. In the early 1800's, the two royal families decided to stop the ______________ war started by their ancestors half a century before.

Ⓐ pointless
Ⓑ atavistic
Ⓒ palpable
Ⓓ degrading
Ⓔ opulent

4. The storm had a (i) ______________ effect on the city's water supply, leaving residents without clean water for weeks while the city worked to (ii) ______________ the water source.

Blank i	Blank ii
Ⓐ jovial	Ⓓ decontaminate
Ⓑ muted	Ⓔ obliterate
Ⓒ detrimental	Ⓕ pulsate

5. After four hours at the buffet Mark and John were so (i) ______________ that they sat on the porch for hours with not even an (ii) ______________ of interest in moving or doing anything productive.

Blank i	Blank ii
Ⓐ satiated	Ⓓ inchoate
Ⓑ invigorated	Ⓔ inkling
Ⓒ exhausted	Ⓕ iota

6. Her boss was impressed with Meg's (i) ______________ to help onboard new employees even though it was not part of her job. She often took the initiative to organize welcome events and prepare training manuals to best (ii) ______________ the new employees for success.

Blank i	Blank ii
Ⓐ obligation	Ⓓ situate
Ⓑ alacrity	Ⓔ direct
Ⓒ reluctance	Ⓕ appreciate

GO TO THE NEXT PAGE

7. The obstacle course proved more (i) ________ than he initially imagined. He soon discovered he had not adequately prepared and decided to accept the offered (ii) ________ for some of the obstacles. This allowed his to complete the course but disqualified him from consideration for awards, since in order to be recognized, the rules stated a competitor must have finished all the obstacles as they were (iii) ________ .

Blank i
Ⓐ onerous
Ⓑ wieldy
Ⓒ meek

Blank ii
Ⓓ enhancements
Ⓔ appropriations
Ⓕ modifications

Blank iii
Ⓖ conceived
Ⓗ disarrayed
Ⓘ prefixed

8. The fire department deployed its community outreach program after an increase in deaths from carbon monoxide poisoning. The aim of the program was to (i) ________ residents about the dangers of carbon monoxide and some of its causes. The fire department also distributed monitors for residents to (ii) ________ in their homes to (iii) ________ them of the presence of carbon monoxide before it reaches deadly levels.

Blank i
Ⓐ usher
Ⓑ caution
Ⓒ ruminate

Blank ii
Ⓓ gestate
Ⓔ obscure
Ⓕ install

Blank iii
Ⓖ alert
Ⓗ lull
Ⓘ convince

VERBAL REASONING

Questions 9-11 are based on the passage below. Select one answer unless otherwise indicated.

Efficient and environmentally conscious innovation is essential to softening the blow environmental damage and long-term economic destruction. As climate change, global warming, and resource depletion become ever-important concerns, it is necessary to be thoughtful and strategic when developing and refining how we use resources, what processes we employ, and what impacts these decisions have on not only the environment but also the economy. How can we meet our current needs without preventing future generations from meeting theirs? How can we properly shepherd resources and continue to innovate without causing irreparable harm to the environment or severely impacting the economy and availability of viable employment? The future of our society will be impacted by the decisions we make today. And, unless we can figure out how to balance social, economic, and environmental considerations in a productive and efficient manner, we are in doomed to fail.

Economic considerations have long been primary considerations when developing new technologies and processes. Investors and stakeholders want to know how economically viable it is to make environmentally conscious decisions and create new efficiencies. But, stakeholders also want to see their investment grow along with efficiencies and innovation. But, if we aim to foster a sustainable environment that delivers essential services and goods to its people, it is important to shift our understanding of development. Instead of characterizing development as a system of constant growth characterized by increased output and short-term gains, we must reframe development as the creation of innovative, efficacious processes that promote responsible stewardship of resources and decreases reliance on non-renewable sources all while providing economic stability.

9. The author suggests that in order to help create a sustainable environment, we must:

Ⓐ Eliminate economic incentives for development
Ⓑ Shift our understanding of development and focus primarily on renewable energy sources
Ⓒ Expand how we define development and seek to create systems that are financially stable and promote responsible use of resources
Ⓓ Engage stakeholders in the conversation about what is most advantageous for them
Ⓔ Halt the use of non-renewable energy sources

10. The passage is likely to appear in which one of the following publications?

Ⓐ A pop culture magazine
Ⓑ A text book for a course on creating sustainable artwork
Ⓒ An investor report for a top exporter of crude oil
Ⓓ A university journal published by environmental scholars
Ⓔ A school newspaper

11. What is the primary purpose of the passage?

Ⓐ To discuss the deleterious impact investors and stakeholders have on the environment
Ⓑ To outline the considerations that need to be taken into account when developing strategies to develop a sustainable environment
Ⓒ To criticize the continued use of renewable resources
Ⓓ To prompt immediate action against companies who fail to implement sustainable practices
Ⓔ To warn of the imminent decline of non-renewable resources.

Questions 12 and 13 are based on the passage below. Select one answer unless otherwise indicated.

Drinking too much coffee can have long-term effects on the brain. Caffeine directly impacts serotonin receptors by over-stimulating them to produce too much serotonin. Frequent over-production of serotonin causes structural damage to the brain in areas responsible for controlling speech and vision. So, if college students don't want to go blind or lose their speech prematurely, they should avoid caffeine.

12. The author's argument is flawed because it:

- (A) Fails to consider that there may be other causes for premature vison and speech loss
- (B) Assumes that college students would want to give up caffeine
- (C) Does not properly cite the information in the argument
- (D) Confuses serotonin with norepinephrine
- (E) Focuses only on college students when a majority of coffee drinkers are working adults

---

13. Which one of the following would weaken the author's claims? Select all that apply.

- [A] Serotonin controls the emotional center of the brain that sits in the hippocampus, far away from the structures that control vision and speech
- [B] Scientists recently established a link between too much serotonin and blindness
- [C] Serotonin over-production causes other systems to over-produce other hormones that can lead to lots of complications.

Questions 14 is based on the passage below. Select one answer unless otherwise indicated.

Last year, a special task force was commissioned to address the rampant corruption plaguing the city. The task force was commissioned and hand-picked by the city's mayor, who himself had been subject to accusations of impropriety. When citizens raised concerns, the mayor retorted saying that people should not question the integrity of the people he handpicked because they are honest people.

14. The mayor's response to the criticism was:

- (A) Justified because the people he chose were indeed honest
- (B) Circularly flawed in that it conflated the premise and the conclusion of the argument.
- (C) A reasonable objection to the unfair criticism levied by the citizens
- (D) Overzealous and boastful
- (E) Inappropriate given the history of some of the members of the task force.

For questions 15-20, select two answers that best complete the blank and produces two sentences that are alike in meaning.

15. Cecilia's ______________ behavior often shocked her classmates who tended to generally be polite and well-behaved.

- [A] indolent
- [B] torpid
- [C] impertinent
- [D] heretical
- [E] brazen
- [F] diplomatic

GO TO THE NEXT PAGE

VERBAL REASONING

16. It is important to examine the motives of individuals who make large donations to political campaigns. While their actions are sometimes purely ____________, more often than not, they are looking for something in return from the candidate if elected.

Ⓐ venal
Ⓑ veritable
Ⓒ altruistic
Ⓓ miserly
Ⓔ philanthropic
Ⓕ sanctioned

17. Greg's ____________ is what made him a strong candidate for the union leader position since the members felt he would be able to go toe-to-toe with the corporate officials trying to block their contract negotiations.

Ⓐ passivity
Ⓑ gregariousness
Ⓒ bellicosity
Ⓓ culpability
Ⓔ pugnacity
Ⓕ demureness

18. Technology is outpacing the laws of our country. It is increasingly unclear what rights exist and to what extent those rights are or should be protected. The ____________ leads to many legal debates, some making their way up to the Supreme Court and still being unclear.

Ⓐ vagueness
Ⓑ curtailment
Ⓒ ambiguity
Ⓓ faultlessness
Ⓔ rancor
Ⓕ docility

19. Dogs have been domesticated for thousands of years and throughout that time have preserved their reputation as man's best friend and a symbol of ____________.

Ⓐ existence
Ⓑ perpetuity
Ⓒ fidelity
Ⓓ honor
Ⓔ tarnish
Ⓕ allegiance

20. The young designer was honored at the annual fashion conference for her ____________ designs that were unlike anything the committee had seen before.

Ⓐ eccentric
Ⓑ distinctive
Ⓒ stellar
Ⓓ unique
Ⓔ morose
Ⓕ haughty

STOP

QUANTITATIVE REASONING *SECTION 4*	20 QUESTIONS 35 MINUTES

DIRECTIONS: For questions 1-8, use any provided centered information to help you compare Column A and Column B. Select the answer that describes the relationship between the two quantities, noting that the same answer choices are presented for each Quantitative Comparison question:

- A **Quantity A is greater.**
- B **Quantity B is greater.**
- C **The two quantities are equal.**
- D **The relationship cannot be determined from the information given.**

---

1. A data set has a mean of 0

Column A	Column B
Total numbers in the data set less than 0	Total numbers in the data set greater than 0

Ⓐ Ⓑ Ⓒ Ⓓ

2.

Column A	Column B
The sum of the coordinates of a point located in quadrant IV on the coordinate plane	The product of the coordinates located in quadrant I on the coordinate plane

Ⓐ Ⓑ Ⓒ Ⓓ

---

3. 420 high school juniors represent 30% of the student body.

Column A	Column B
1200	The total number of students in the school

Ⓐ Ⓑ Ⓒ Ⓓ

---

4. x is a positive integer
When x is divided by 36, the remainder is 30

Column A	Column B
The remainder when $\frac{x}{3}$ is divided by 6	4

Ⓐ Ⓑ Ⓒ Ⓓ

---

5. $2 \leq a \leq 10$
$b > 3$

Column A	Column B
ab	$a - b$

Ⓐ Ⓑ Ⓒ Ⓓ

---

6. The radius of cylinder A is twice that of cylinder B. The height of cylinder A is half the height of cylinder B.

Column A	Column B
The volume of right cylinder A	The volume of right cylinder B

Ⓐ Ⓑ Ⓒ Ⓓ

GO TO THE NEXT PAGE

QUANTITATIVE REASONING

7.

Column A	Column B
3569	$3(10^3) + 5(10^2) + 6(10^1) + 9(10^0)$

Ⓐ Ⓑ Ⓒ Ⓓ

8. $a = \frac{b+1}{2}$

Column A	Column B
$2a + 1$	b

Ⓐ Ⓑ Ⓒ Ⓓ

9. If you roll a six-sided die once, what is the probability of rolling a 2 or a 4?

Ⓐ $\frac{2}{3}$
Ⓑ $\frac{4}{5}$
Ⓒ $\frac{1}{3}$
Ⓓ $\frac{1}{6}$
Ⓔ $\frac{5}{6}$

10. For his new workout regimen, Ian runs or walks each day for a total of 4 hours. If he runs at a rate of of 6 miles per hour and walks at a rate of 3 miles per hour, select all of the possible distances Ian can cover in a single workout.

Ⓐ 4
Ⓑ 7
Ⓒ 12
Ⓓ 26
Ⓔ 17
Ⓕ 28

11. 20! has how many distinct prime factors? Enter your answer in the text box below.

12. What is the slope of the line that contains the points (1,3) and (4,–3)?

Ⓐ –2
Ⓑ 3
Ⓒ 4.5
Ⓓ 4
Ⓔ –3

13. After the new president was caught embezzling money, the largest members-only philanthropy organization in the country experienced a 6% decline in their membership, leaving only 22,278 members. What was the size of the membership before the decline?

Ⓐ 22,000
Ⓑ 23,200
Ⓒ 23,700
Ⓓ 24,644
Ⓔ 37,100

14. Find the value of x in the diagram below.

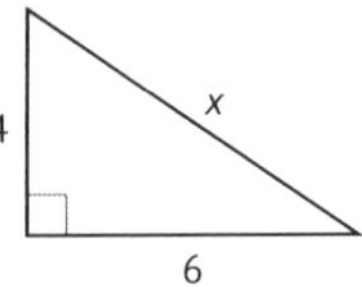

Ⓐ $13\sqrt{2}$
Ⓑ $2\sqrt{13}$
Ⓒ $4\sqrt{13}$
Ⓓ $2\sqrt{5}$
Ⓔ $3\sqrt{5}$

GO TO THE NEXT PAGE

QUANTITATIVE REASONING

Use the graph below to answer questions 15 and 16. Select one answer unless otherwise indicated.

Age of Presidents at Inauguration

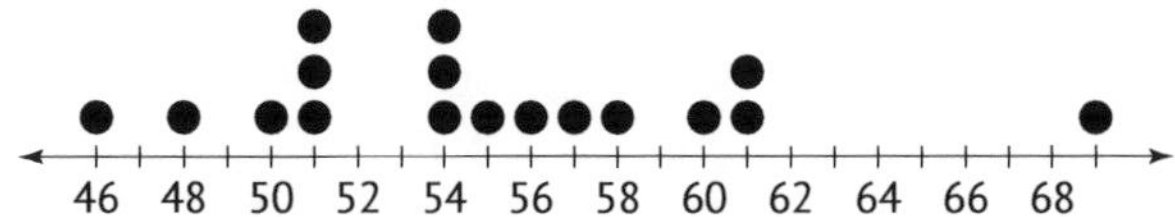

15. According to the graph below, what is the median age of U.S. Presidents at their inauguration? Enter your answer in the text box below.

16. What is the approximate mean age of Presidents at inauguration?

Ⓐ 54
Ⓑ 55
Ⓒ 44
Ⓓ 33
Ⓔ 50

17. Which of the following is a factor of x^2 - 5x - 6?

Ⓐ (x + 2)
Ⓑ (x – 6)
Ⓒ (x – 3)
Ⓓ (x – 2)
Ⓔ (x – 1)

18. Simply $(2b^4)^3$

Ⓐ $8b^{12}$
Ⓑ $8b^3$
Ⓒ $27b^3$
Ⓓ $343b^3$
Ⓔ 86

19. A fair coin is to be flipped 5 times. The first 4 flips land heads up. What is the probability of the coin landing o heads on the next (5th) flip of the coin?

Ⓐ $\frac{1}{2}$
Ⓑ $\frac{4}{5}$
Ⓒ $\frac{1}{3}$
Ⓓ $\frac{1}{6}$
Ⓔ $\frac{5}{6}$

20. Which of the following points is the greatest distance from the *y*-axis?

Ⓐ (1, 10)
Ⓑ (2, 7)
Ⓒ (2, 8)
Ⓓ (3, 5)
Ⓔ (5, 1)

STOP

QUANTITATIVE REASONING | 20 QUESTIONS
SECTION 5 | 35 MINUTES

DIRECTIONS: For questions 1-8, use any provided centered information to help you compare Column A and Column B. Select the answer that describes the relationship between the two quantities, noting that the same answer choices are presented for each Quantitative Comparison question:

- **A** **Quantity A is greater.**
- **B** **Quantity B is greater.**
- **C** **The two quantities are equal.**
- **D** **The relationship cannot be determined from the information given.**

---

1. $x \neq 1$

Column A	Column B
x	x^3

Ⓐ Ⓑ Ⓒ Ⓓ

---

2. $3a + 2 = 4 - b$

Column A	Column B
ab	b

Ⓐ Ⓑ Ⓒ Ⓓ

3.

Column A	Column B
The greatest prime factor of 21	The greatest prime factor of 36

Ⓐ Ⓑ Ⓒ Ⓓ

4.

Column A	Column B
70% of 100	30% of 500

Ⓐ Ⓑ Ⓒ Ⓓ

---

5. Set 1: {1, 2, 4, 8, 16, 32}
Set 2: {all prime numbers less than 10}

Column A	Column B
Mean of Set 1	Mean of Set 2

Ⓐ Ⓑ Ⓒ Ⓓ

6.

Column A	Column B
The measure of the interior angles of a four-sided polygon	The measure of the interior angle of an isosceles triangle

Ⓐ Ⓑ Ⓒ Ⓓ

7.

Column A	Column B
The probability of rolling a 6-sided die once and getting an odd number	$\frac{1}{4}$

Ⓐ Ⓑ Ⓒ Ⓓ

QUANTITATIVE REASONING

8.

Column A	Column B
$\lvert x \rvert$	x

Ⓐ Ⓑ Ⓒ Ⓓ

Use the graph below to answer questions 9-11. Select one answer choice unless otherwise indicated.

Weather-Related Car Accidents

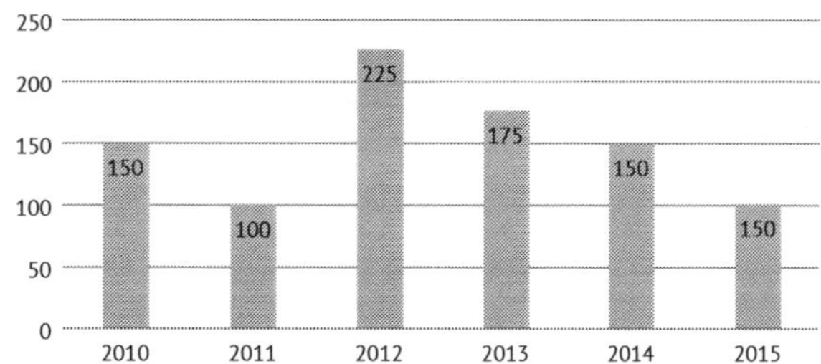

9. In 2013, county police responded to 305 car accidents. What percentage of the total number of accidents police responded was not weather-related?

Ⓐ 75%
Ⓑ 65%
Ⓒ 65.5%
Ⓓ 42.6%.
Ⓔ 47.6%

10. One year between 2010 and 2015, the number of total car accidents was 500 and 45% were weather-related. What year was that?

Ⓐ 2010
Ⓑ 2011
Ⓒ 2012
Ⓓ 2013
Ⓔ 2014

11. A report indicated that police responded to 800 car accidents between 2010 and 2012. How many were weather-related?

Ⓐ 400
Ⓑ 475
Ⓒ 500
Ⓓ 350
Ⓔ 600

12. Candace can put together 100 wedding trinkets in 1 hour and 15 minutes. Selena can put together 75 wedding trinkets in 50 minutes. If Candace and Selena worked together, how many trinkets can they complete in an hour?

13. What is the value of x when $6(x - 2) = x + 8$?

Ⓐ -2
Ⓑ 3
Ⓒ 4.5
Ⓓ 4
Ⓔ -3

14. Find the slope of the line on the graph below.

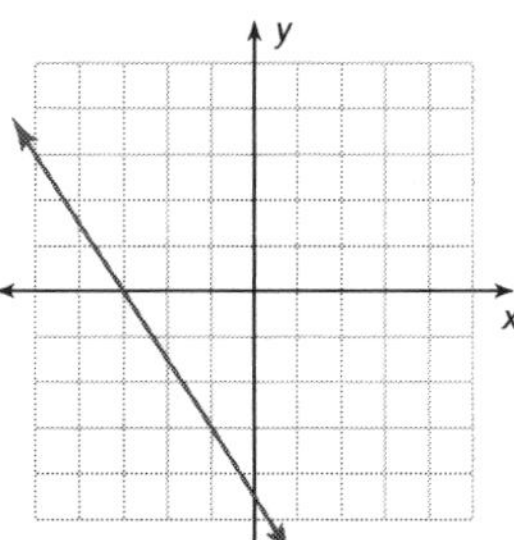

Ⓐ $\frac{2}{3}$
Ⓑ $-\frac{2}{3}$
Ⓒ $\frac{3}{2}$
Ⓓ $-\frac{3}{2}$
Ⓔ 3

GO TO THE NEXT PAGE

QUANTITATIVE REASONING

15. For the equation $\frac{|4x+6|}{4}=5$, solve for x.

Ⓐ (−5, 0)
Ⓑ (−5, 15)
Ⓒ $\left(\frac{7}{2}, -\frac{13}{2}\right)$
Ⓓ $\left(\frac{1}{2}, -\frac{1}{2}\right)$
Ⓔ (−2 ,3)

16. What is the length of a rectangle with a perimeter of 90 where $w = 20$?

17. Simplify $5a(3a + 7) + 3(-4 + 2a)$.

Ⓐ $15a^2 + 41a - 12$
Ⓑ $19a - 5 + 8a^2$
Ⓒ $50a - 16a^2 + 12$
Ⓓ $9a - 16a + 12$
Ⓔ $50a - 16a^2 - 12$

18. What is the range of following data?

32, 41, 28, 54, 35, 26, 33, 23, 38, 40

Ⓐ 25
Ⓑ 23
Ⓒ 31
Ⓓ 54
Ⓔ 62

19. What is the distance between (5,6) and (2, 4)?

Ⓐ $\sqrt{23}$
Ⓑ $2\sqrt{5}$
Ⓒ $\sqrt{13}$
Ⓓ $\sqrt{34}$
Ⓔ 6

20. If x is not equal to 0, select all of that following that must be positive:

Ⓐ x^3
Ⓑ x^0
Ⓒ x^{-4}
Ⓓ $|x - 2|$
Ⓔ $2x$
Ⓕ $-x$

STOP

VERBAL REASONING | 20 QUESTIONS
SECTION 6 | 30 MINUTES

DIRECTIONS: Answer each question according to the directions given.

For questions 1 to 8, you are to choose one answer for each blank from the corresponding column of choices.

1. Because opposing counsel filed so many ______________ motions the trial was delayed for two years.

Ⓐ germane
Ⓑ accusatory
Ⓒ dilatory
Ⓓ apposite
Ⓔ extemporaneous

2. The Dali Lama is endeared as a(n) ______________ leader; many trust his judgment and aspire to follow his teachings.

Ⓐ astute
Ⓑ tedious
Ⓒ debased
Ⓓ uncouth
Ⓔ popular

3. Although the young TV actress had earned millions portraying a precocious banker on the hit TV show, she still needed a ______________ of her own to manage her affairs.

Ⓐ confidante
Ⓑ fiduciary
Ⓒ exemplar
Ⓓ sage
Ⓔ wanton

4. Many wounded veterans who have suffered amputations experience phantom limb syndrome where they experience pain in the limb that is no longer attached to their body. The syndrome (i) ______________ in the nervous system and sparks sensations in the nerve endings throughout the body. No treatment options are available for the condition; patients are often (ii) ______________ to a life of frustration and misery.

Blank i	Blank ii
Ⓐ originates	Ⓓ effused
Ⓑ stalls	Ⓔ indoctrinated
Ⓒ excretes	Ⓕ fated

5. The airline had strict rules for its employees to follow outside of work. The slightest (i) ______________ could result in suspension with more (ii) ______________ transgressions resulting in termination.

Blank i	Blank ii
Ⓐ adherence	Ⓓ riotous
Ⓑ infraction	Ⓔ inconsequential
Ⓒ dilettante	Ⓕ egregious

6. The hospital administrator carefully reviewed the complaint from the patient who (i) ______________ that he was treated unfairly during his last visit to the emergency room. The documents showed that the patient had a history of filing complaints against emergency rooms that (ii) ______________ his repeated requests for narcotics.

Blank i	Blank ii
Ⓐ averred	Ⓓ disregarded
Ⓑ retracted	Ⓔ conceded
Ⓒ bemused	Ⓕ prolonged

7. George received top honors at the film fest for his film *Lord of the Oreos*, a (i) ________ film that mocks the popular *Lord of the Rings* trilogy. Instead of searching for middle earth, the main character in George's film is in search of "middle O" and goes on a mission to find out how to best get to the center of an Oreo. George's long-time fans and critics alike appreciated the (ii) ________ plot and (iii) ________ the film as one of the funniest of the year.

Blank i	Blank ii
Ⓐ emotive	Ⓓ droll
Ⓑ atirical	Ⓔ staid
Ⓒ documentary	Ⓕ atrocious

Blank iii
Ⓖ extolled
Ⓗ escalated
Ⓘ enumerated

---

8. John and Jake missed their final exams and (i) ________ a story to convince their professor to allow them to take a make-up exam. They told the professor they were driving to the exam and got a flat tire and didn't have a spare. Because roadside assistance took so long to come, they missed the exam. The professor allowed them to take the exam though he was skeptical about the (ii) ________ of their story. John and Jake thought they had gotten away with their (iii) ________ plan until they got to that last question on the exam that asked which tire went flat. That was one detail they had failed to corroborate.

Blank i	Blank ii
Ⓐ canoodled	Ⓓ veracity
Ⓑ concocted	Ⓔ ingenuity
Ⓒ derided	Ⓕ dispute

Blank iii
Ⓖ salacious
Ⓗ wily
Ⓘ febrile

GO TO THE NEXT PAGE

Questions 9-11 are based on the following passage. Select one answer unless otherwise indicated.

Vaccines are a hotly debated topic lately; but regardless of the schism of public opinion, significant scientific research supports their effectiveness in controlling infectious diseases in a cost-effective manner. Access to vaccines is largely unequal, especially in developing countries; and, lack of infrastructure supporting the storage, transportation, and administration of the vaccines that are available, further exacerbates the threat of complications and lower efficacy.

What makes vaccine access and administration such a complicated issue? The short answer is that vaccines require many *critical* moving pieces to be in coordination in order to ensure safe delivery of a viable product from laboratory to recipient. In fact, the steps are so complex, even developed countries have a hard time managing them in some regards. The general idea of what a vaccine is, a syringe filled with liquid, is largely incomplete and prevents many from understanding the full complexity of vaccine issues.

Originally, vaccines were developed as a powder (usually derived from the carcass of an infected animal) that contained a form of a specified disease and were administered to breed immunity. As science evolved, so did the manufacture of vaccines and similar powders were created in a sterile environment and mass-produced. Vaccines that are manufactured as powders must be reconstituted with diluent. The diluent is a major complicating factor and threatens the sterility of vaccines. The World Health Organization outlined some of the issues related to the diluent including a strict time window for administering the vaccine after it is reconstituted. Administering the vaccine after this time frame carries the risk of potentially fatal staphylococcus.

Diluents are also not universal; each one is specific to the vaccine it accompanies and it modulates pH and directly impacts the final chemical composition of the vaccine. When diluents are mixed up and used with the wrong vaccine, the recipient is vulnerable to unpleasant side events that can be as severe as toxic shock. The mix-up can also render the vaccine useless. Other modalities for vaccine administration include freeze-dried vaccines that require strict temperature controls, conditions that also present challenges for developing countries. The administration of the vaccine itself also creates challenges as it requires knowledge of how to use the diluent and sterile needles for each interaction with the diluent, among other critical considerations.

9. What is the primary purpose of the passage?

- Ⓐ To discuss the dangers of vaccines when administered to children at too young of an age
- Ⓑ To discuss some of the factors that contribute to the disparity in vaccine availability especially in the developing world
- Ⓒ To analyze the World Health Organization's response to challenges associated with vaccine administration
- Ⓓ To discuss new technology available to make diluents less confusing
- Ⓔ To advocate for clearer instructions on the labels of vaccines

---

10. The passage mentions which of the following possible problems that can arise when dealing with vaccines? Select all that apply.

- [A] Diluents can be mixed up and create an adverse reaction or render the vaccine ineffective
- [B] Vaccines not stored at the proper temperatures can be deadly
- [C] Lack of sterile needles can present various dangers

---

11. The author would most likely agree with which one of the following efforts to make vaccines more accessible in developing countries?

- Ⓐ Clear and large-print labeling of diluents that correspond to a particular vaccine
- Ⓑ The creation of a streamlined vaccine that is temperature stable and does not require a diluent
- Ⓒ A non-profit dedicated to providing sterile needles to developing countries
- Ⓓ A multi-level vaccine refrigeration unit that allows different vaccines to be kept in the same space but at different temperatures
- Ⓔ A non-toxic color solution that turns the vaccine pink when it has expired

---

VERBAL REASONING

Question 12 is based on the following passage. Select one answer unless otherwise indicated.

The City Council is debating a bill that would mandate all hospitals to require that nurses have a 20-minute break for every 3 hours that they work. If the bill passes, hospitals will likely need to hire more staff to cover nurses who are on break. This bill is being supported by members of the Nurse's Union who were recently disciplined for social media posts that violated HIPPA regulations regarding patient privacy. These supporters should not be trusted and the bill should not be passed.

12. The author's argument is flawed because it:

Ⓐ fails to outline the nature of the disciplinary actions levied against the nurses
Ⓑ attacks the the supporters of the legislation rather than the legislation itself
Ⓒ assumes that nurses would actually want a 20-minute break
Ⓓ presupposes the legislation will not add additional costs to the hospital budget
Ⓔ fails to provide an alternative if the bill does not pass

Question 13 and 14 are based on the following passage. Select one answer unless otherwise indicated.

Salmonella is a food-borne microorganism that attacks the intestinal track. The illness, if not identified and treated quickly, can be fatal. Conventional tests to detect the presence of salmonella often take too long and lack the ability to identity unusual strains of the microorganism. Researchers have been working to develop a new method to test for the presence of the one piece of genetic material that all strains of salmonella share. Public health officials should not hesitate to replace their current tests with this new method.

13. Which one of the following would strengthen the author's argument?

Ⓐ The new test requires two test panels instead of one like previous tests
Ⓑ The new test has a quick turn-around time for getting results back
Ⓒ A new treatment for salmonella has been found to be effective for other intestinal disorders
Ⓓ The incidence of salmonella poisoning is on the decline
Ⓔ The test is non-invasive

---

14. Which one of the following would most weaken the argument?

Ⓐ The test only identifies salmonella microorganisms
Ⓑ Doctors often misdiagnose patients as having salmonella poisoning when they in fact have something else
Ⓒ The new test was designed in a lab funded by the Health Department
Ⓓ New strains of salmonella have been discovered that share no common traits with previous strains of the microorganism
Ⓔ The new test has the potential to be used to detect other diseases

GO TO THE NEXT PAGE

VERBAL REASONING

For questions 15-20, select two answers that best complete the blank and produces two sentences that are alike in meaning.

15. Saul's ______________ appearance was hardly appreciated by the hosts of the black-tie gala. He was promptly asked to leave and return only if he was dressed appropriately.

- Ⓐ conservative
- Ⓑ slapdash
- Ⓒ regal
- Ⓓ slipshod
- Ⓔ suave
- Ⓕ glitzy

---

16. The Lohman medal was awarded to the rescue team that exhibited outstanding courage and ______________ in the face of arduous circumstances. After rescuing 70 people during one of the worst storms of the century, Team Bravo was certainly deserving.

- Ⓐ tenacity
- Ⓑ pliability
- Ⓒ adamancy
- Ⓓ paucity
- Ⓔ aloofness
- Ⓕ bravado

---

17. The Manitowoc county police department interrogated the young suspect without permission from his parents. As a result, his defense team argued that the confession should be ______________.

- Ⓐ barred
- Ⓑ sanctioned
- Ⓒ auspicious
- Ⓓ inadmissible
- Ⓔ censured
- Ⓕ redacted

18. The flash mob was a complete ______________. Not only had people not practiced and learned the movements, the content was also not properly vetted and ended up offending some of those in the crowd.

- Ⓐ feat
- Ⓑ fiasco
- Ⓒ apropos
- Ⓓ stalemate
- Ⓔ impasse
- Ⓕ debacle

---

19. The rain was ______________. It seemed to only get worse as the night went on.

- Ⓐ arcane
- Ⓑ unrelenting
- Ⓒ amiable
- Ⓓ affable
- Ⓔ unremitting
- Ⓕ dowse

---

20. The school bus drivers decided to go on strike starting the first day of the new school year. When news of the plan reached the school board, who had recently stalled negotiations with the drivers after a disagreement over a pay increase, they immediately reached out to the strike organizers to try to identify a(n) ______________ solution for all parties involved.

- Ⓐ feudal
- Ⓑ inequitable
- Ⓒ viable
- Ⓓ practical
- Ⓔ just
- Ⓕ gusseted

STOP

VERBAL REASONING
ANSWER KEY : SECTION 3

1. **B.**
The storm was fleeting, so ephemeral, which means passing or short-lived.

2. **A.**
David wanted to fix or soothe the situation. Propitiate means to placate or soothe.

3. **B.**
While the war may be pointless, the point here is that the war was started by their ancestors. Atavistic means ancestral and is the most appropriate term for the blank.

4. **C, D.**
The impact of the storm was severe or detrimental. The residents were without clean water, meaning the water supply was contaminated and needed to be decontaminated before the residents could have access to water again.

5. **A, F.**
Mark and John were full, or satiated. They had little interest in doing anything. They had not an iota, or the tiniest inclination, to move or be productive.

6. **B, D.**
Meg took initiative to welcome and orient new employees. Alacrity means a sense of willingness and matches Meg's actions, that best situated or positioned the new employees for success.

7. **A, F, G.**
The obstacle course, which was more difficult or onerous than imagined, was not completed as it was designed since he accepted the modifications offered.

8. **B, F, H.**
After the number of death for CO poisoning increased, the fire department wanted to warn or caution residents about the dangers and possible causes. The fire department gave residents monitors to place or install in their homes to detect the presence of CO and alert or notify residents of its presence before the levels became deadly.

9. **C.**
The author discusses the need for an expanded definition and understanding of development to be woven in the sustainability conversation.

10. **D.**
The passage provides an informed perspective and offers insight on how to address current and projected issues. A university journal of environmental scholars would be the most likely originators of this line of thought.

11. **B.**
The passage outlines useful elements of an expanded understanding of development. The purpose of the passage is to address ways to better approach the sustainability conversation and outline comprehensive and viable actions to build a more sustainable environment.

12. **A.**
The author asserts that if college students don't want to go blind or lose their speech, they should avoid caffeine. Speech and vision loss are still possible for a number of other reasons.

13. **A.**
Answer choice B strengthens the argument while answer choice C has no impact on the argument. If answer choice A were true, it would cast serious doubt on the notion that excess serotonin is responsible for damaging areas of the brain that control vision and speech.

14. **B.**
The mayor's argument is essentially that the citizens should not question if the people who he selected are honest because they are indeed honest. The mayor offers no support for his claim.

15. **C, E.**
You are looking for words that stand opposite of polite and well-behaved. Impertinent and brazen are synonyms brash or rude.

16. **C, E.**
More often than not, the donors are looking for something in return for their donations. The blank requires a word that describes the times when the donors are actually not looking for something in return contribute out of pure generosity. Altruistic and philanthropic mean unconditional generosity.

17. **C, E.**
Greg was capable for being a force against the corporate officials meaning he likely had the aggressive personality needed to do so. You can conclude the Greg possessed the bellicosity or pugnacity, both synonymous with aggression and fervor, to represent the union.

18. **A, C.**
The context clues (making it all the way up to the Supreme court and still being unclear) indicate that you are looking for words that express ambiguity or opaqueness.

19. **D, F.**
Dogs, over the course of thousands of years have "maintained" a reputation as man's best friend. The words you are looking for will be positive and likely address the longevity of dog's relationship to man. Fidelity and allegiance both fit the bill.

20. **B, D.**
Just because the clothing was unique does not mean that it was odd as eccentric implies. Distinctive and unique best fit here.

QUANTITATIVE REASONING
ANSWER KEY : SECTION 4

1. **D.**
It is not possible to determine the relationship. Even if you had the size of the data, there are many possibilities that could result in *a* or *b* having a greater value.

2. **D.**
This question requires knowledge of the coordinate plane and the types of values you can expect from a point in a particular quadrant. Plugging in different coordinates will yield different outcomes with either *a* or *b* being greater. The relationship cannot be determined.

3. **B.**
Let x = total number of students. Since 420 is 30% of the total student body, you find the total number of juniors by solving the expression $\frac{420}{.30x}$. There are 1400 students. So, column b is the greater quantity.

4. **C.**
From the centered information you know that whenever you divide x by 36 you have a remainder of 30. So, create an equation to represent this: $x = 36y + 30$. In this equation, y is a positive integer as dictated by the centered information. Plug in x to solve and compare the quantities. $36y + \frac{30}{3} = 12n + 10$ when simplified. Dividing 6 by the simplified expression will leave a remainder of 4. So, the quantities are equal.

5. **A.**
Plugging in a variety of numbers, you can figure out that A will always be greater than B.

6. **A.**
The formula to find the volume for a right cylinder is area of the base * height. The volume of cylinder *a* is twice that of cylinder *b*.

7. **C.**
Simply and solve.

$$3(1000) \square 5(100) + 6(10) + 9 =$$
$$3000 + 500 + 60 + 9 = 3569$$

8. **A.**
Solve for *b*.

$$a = \frac{b+1}{2}$$
$$2a = b + 1$$
$$2a \square 1 = b$$

If $2a \square 1 = b$ then $2a + 1$ will always be 1 greater than b.

9. **C.**
There is a 2 in 6 chance of rolling a 2 or 4. Reduce to $\frac{1}{3}$.

10. **C, E.**
Calculate the minimum and maximum where the minimum mileage is when Ian walks all four hours and the maximum is when Ian runs all six hours. Any values that fall with those values (12 and 24) are possible mileages he could achieve in a 4-hour workout.

11. **8.**
The are 8 prime factors that are less than 20: 2, 3, 5, 7, 11, 13, 17, 19

12. **A.**
Plug the coordinates in to the slope equation.

$$m = \frac{(y_1 \square y_2)}{(x_1 \square x_2)} = \frac{3 \square (\square 3)}{1 \square 4} = \square\frac{6}{3} = \square 2$$

13. **C.**
22,278 presents 94% of the previous membership. Create an equation and solve.

$$\textit{Previous membership} = \frac{22278}{.94} = 23700$$

14. **B.**
x is the hypotenuse of the triangle. Use the Pythagorean Theorem to solve.

$$a^2 + b = c^2$$
$$16 + 36 = c^2$$

52 is equal to c^2. Take the square root of 52 to find c.

$$\sqrt{52} = \sqrt{4} \bullet \sqrt{13} = 2\sqrt{13}$$

15. 54
The graph gives you the number of Presidents inaugurated at each age. The median is 54.

16. B.
The sum of the 17 data points is 936. To find the mean, divide 936 by 17 to get 55.05 or ~55.

17. B.
In order to arrive at the answer, you must consider what both factors are even though the question only asks for one. Because you have $-5x$, none of the terms adding or subtracting 2 or 3 from x will work because, while they solve to include $-5x$, you will not be able to also get -6, only 6. When $(x - 6)$ is a factor, the other factor is $(x + 1)$.

18. A.
Using exponent rules, multiply the exponents together to get $8b^{12}$.

19. A.
The probability of the coin landing on heads is not affected by the previous coin flips. The is always a 50/50 chance.

20. E.
The coordinate indicates the distance from the y-axis, which is the vertical axis on a coordinate plane. You need to consider the x-coordinate to determine how far a point is from the y-axis. (5,1) is 5 units away from the y-axis, a greater distance than any of the other points.

QUANTITATIVE REASONING
ANSWER KEY : SECTION 5

1. **D.**
It is not possible to determine the relationship with the information provided.

2. **D.**
Plugging in a variety of numbers favors quantity *a* in some instances and quantity *b* in others. The relationship cannot be determined.

3. **A.**
The greatest prime factor of 21 is 7. The greatest prime factor of 36 is 3. Column A is greater.

4. **B.**
70% of 100 is 70 and 30% of 500 is 150. Column B is greater.

5. **A.**
The mean of set 1 is 10.5 and the mean of set 2 is 4.25.

6. **A.**
The interior angles of a 4-sided polygon add up to 360 degrees while the measure of any triangle will always be 180 degrees.

7. **A.**
The probability of getting an odd number is $\frac{1}{2}$, which is greater than column B.

8. **D.**
Since column A can be negative or positive, the relationship cannot be determined.

9. **D.**
Out of 305 accidents, 175 were weather-related, so 130 were not. The percentage of those that were not weather-related is found by calculating $\frac{130}{305} = 42.6\%$.

10. **C.**
The question is asking during what year where the total number of accidents was 500, would weather-related accidents have been 45% of those. 45% is pretty close to 50% so look for the value that is closest to 50% of 500. 225 is 45% of 500.

11. **B.**
Add the number of weather-related accidents in 2010, 2011, and 2012.

12. **170.**
First determine how many trinkets each person can produce in an hour at their own work rate. Candace produces 100 widgets in 75 mins. Set up an equation to solve for her hourly rate:

$$\frac{100\ trinkets}{75\ mins} = \frac{x\ trinkets}{60.}$$

Cross-multiply. Candace can make 80 wedding trinkets per hour. Do the same to figure out the number of trinkets Selena can produce in an hour. Selena can produce 90 trinkets in an hour. So working together, they can produce 170 trinkets in an hour.

13. **D.**

$$6(x-2) = x+8$$
$$6x-12 = x+8$$
$$5x = 20$$
$$x = 4$$

14. **D.**
The points on the line are (−3, 0) and (−1, −3). Plug them into the equation $m = \frac{y_1 - y_2}{x_1 - x_2}$ to solve.

$$m = \frac{0-(-3)}{-3-(-1)} = -\frac{3}{2}$$

15. **C.**

$$\frac{|4x+6|}{4} = 5$$
$$20 = 4x+6$$
$$4x = 14,\ so\ x = \frac{14}{4} = \frac{7}{2}$$

Since you are taking the absolute value of 4*x* + 6, you must also solve the equation assuming the outcome is negative.

$$4x+6 = -20$$
$$4x = -26,\ so\ x = -\frac{26}{4} = -\frac{13}{2}$$

QUANTITATIVE REASONING
ANSWER KEY : SECTION 5

16. 25

The perimeter of a rectangle is 2(*l* + *w*). Create an equation with the given information to solve for the length.

$$p = 2(l \cdot 20)$$
$$p = 2l + 40$$
$$p = 25$$

17. A.

$$5a(3a+7)+3(-4+2a)$$
$$15a^2+35a-12+6a=15a^2+41a-12$$

18. C.

The range is the difference of the largest and smallest numbers in the data set. 54 – 23 = 31.

19. C.

Plug the points in to distance formula and solve.

$$d=\sqrt{(x_2-x_1)^2+(y_2-y_1)^2}$$
$$\sqrt{9+4}$$
$$\sqrt{13}$$

20. B, C, D

Since you don't know if x is positive or negative, your answer choices must yield a positive number regardless if x is positive or not. It is possible that A can be negative if x is negative, so you can eliminate it. Any number to the power of zero is 1, so B must be positive. Any number raised to an even power is positive so C must be true. The absolute value of any number will be positive so D must be true. E and F can be negative so they can be eliminated.

VERBAL REASONING
ANSWER KEY : SECTION 6

1. **C.**
The motions delayed the trial for whatever reason. Dilatory means to cause delay or to stall.

2. **A.**
The Dali Lama is respected and people value his opinion. He is viewed as an astute or wise leader.

3. **B.**
A fiduciary is a person who manages someone's financial or personal affairs.

4. **A, F.**
The syndrome originates or starts in the nervous system and afflicts patients with life-long suffering. So, patients are fated or destined to a life of frustration and misery.

5. **B, F.**
The airline has strict rules that it expects its employees to adhere to. Any deviation from those rules, which is the definition of an infraction, could land them in trouble. The mention of slightest gives you a context clue for the second blank. You know that it will be more than a slight infraction, or more egregious.

6. **A, D.**
The patient filed a complaint against the emergency department. He averred or claimed that he was treated unfairly. The patient seemed to have a history of filing complaints against emergency rooms that disregarded or ignored his repeated requests for narcotics.

7. **B, D, G.**
The film mocked the original version, so it was farcical or satirical. Fans and critics appreciated the merits of the film and found the plot funny or droll. Droll is a synonym for humorous. As a result, the fans and critics lauded or extolled the film as one of the funniest.

8. **B, D, H.**
John and Jake came up with or concocted a story to convince their professor to allow them to make-up the final exam. The professor agreed even though he was not convinced their story was true. He questioned the veracity or truth of what the students told him. The students thought they had put together a wily or clever plan but failed to seal up the most critical detail.

9. **B.**
While several of the answer choices are discussed in the passage, the main point of the passage is to discuss challenges associated with securing and administering vaccines.

10. **A, C.**
The passage mentions that administering a vaccine too long after it has been reconstituted can be deadly, but makes no such mention with regards to vaccines not stored at the proper temperatures.

11. **B.**
Many of the problems listed in the passage have to do with the ability for developing countries to transport and maintain the proper temperature of vaccines. (D) proposes a complex temperature refrigeration system that would likely be useless in the developing world. Having a streamlined vaccine that does not require diluents and is temperature stable addresses both the issues in developing countries: temperature maintenance and confusion over and availability of multiple diluents

12. **B.**
The argument is a classic example of a source argument. The author attacks the past transgressions of the nurses and suggests the bill should not be passed not based on its merit but because of its supporters' past.

13. **B.**
One of the issues with the current test is that it takes too long to process. So, adding the fact that the new method reduces the wait time for result would only add to the argument.

14. **D.**
If D were true, it would negate the entire premise on which the new test, and thus the argument is based upon.

15. **B, D.**
Saul's attire was not appropriate for the black tie gala and he was asked to leave. Slapdash and slipshod mean messy or casual, which would accurately describe Saul's attire.

VERBAL REASONING
ANSWER KEY : SECTION 6

16. A, C.
The team was honored for their courage and perseverance under tough circumstances. The team exhibited courage and tenacity, which is synonymous with dedication.

17. A, D.
The police department did not get parental permission before interrogating the suspect. The defense team argued that the confession should not be permitted. Barred or inadmissible both mean disallowed. Be careful with the distractor answer *redacted* which means allowed only in an edited form. While this could fit in the sentence, there is not a word in the answer choice set that would pair with redacted to create two similar sentences.

18. B, F.
The flash mob was poorly put together. In essence it was a fiasco or a debacle. Both mean a flop or a mess.

19. B, E.
The rain seemed to not let up. Unrelenting and unremitting both mean persistent.

20. C, D.
The school board, in an effort to avoid a strike, reached out to the bus drivers to try to reach a decision that would work for both of them. They were looking for a viable or practical option.

Raw Score	Scaled Score
40	170
39	169
38	168
37	167
36	166
35	165
34	164
33	163
32	162
31	161
30	160
29	159
28	158
27	157
26	156
25	155
24	154
23	153
22	152
21	151

Raw Score	Scaled Score
20	150
19	149
18	148
17	147
16	146
15	145
14	144
13	143
12	142
11	141
10	140
9	139
8	138
7	137
6	136
5	135
4	134
3	133
2	132
1	131

These practice tests are designed to simulate actual testing conditions as closely as possible. While the questions are similar to those you will encounter on the GRE, the sections are not adaptive for Verbal and Quantitative Reasoning like they will be if you sit for the computer-adaptive exam.The scale above gives you an **idea** of your projected score and can help you monitor your progress as you become more familiar with the material. The scale above is a rough guide to predict your score. **As a reminder**, the PowerPrep II software distributed by ETS offers two free computer-adaptive exams to supplement your study plan. Be sure to include those exams in your study plan in addition to the exams in this section; this will help you get an idea of the areas you need to study more closely in order to reach your scoring goals.

ARGO
BROTHERS

PRACTICE TEST 5

GRE®

Graduate Record Examinations

- This exam is 3 hours and 45 minutes long. Try to take this full exam in one sitting to simulate real test conditions.
- While taking this exam, refrain from listening to music or watching TV.
- When writing your response for Analyze an Issue & Analyze an Argument prompt, use a computer, and turn off the spell-check feature to simulate real testing conditions.
- Use a basic calculator, do not use a graphic or scientific calculator. On the real exam, you will have an on-screen calculator with only basic operation functions and a square root key.
- Concentrate and GOOD LUCK!

To calculate your score visit our web site and download excel calculator:

www.einstein-academy.com/GRE

ANALYTICAL WRITING | ESSAY 1
ANALYZE AN ISSUE | 30 MINUTES

Consenting adults should not be forced to wear seatbelts when riding in or operating a vehicle or safety helmets while on a bike or motorcycle.

Discuss your viewpoint on the proposed plan and the reasons for your perspective. Consider potential consequences of implementing the policy and the extent to which these consequences influence your stance.

ANALYTICAL WRITING | ESSAY 2
ANALYZE AN ARGUMENT | 30 MINUTES

The following appeared in a memorandum from the advertising department of a new fruit energy drink prior to its launch:

The JuiceSpruce brand leads the pack when it comes to energy fruit juice sales. Consumers young and old recognize the brand and are loyal to it. They equate the brand with high quality, great taste, and a guaranteed rush of energy. JuiceSpruce has outperformed all major juice and energy drink producers for the past five years. So, as we launch our product, it makes sense to develop branding very close in nature to JuiceSpruce in order to capitalize on their brand recognition and strong customer base. By doing so, we can get consumers to try our product and, even when they realize they have not purchased JuiceSpruce, become loyal customers based on taste, low-sugar content, and a rush of energy. We are excited about this move and cannot wait to see our sales soar.

Discuss the stated and unstated assumptions in the argument and discuss what the consequences might be if those assumptions are shown to be unwarranted.

VERBAL REASONING | 20 QUESTIONS
SECTION 3 | 30 MINUTES

DIRECTIONS: Answer each question according to the directions given.

For questions 1 to 8, you are to choose one answer for each blank from the corresponding column of choices.

1. The Dali Lama is endeared as a __________ leader; many trust his judgment and aspire to follow his teachings.

Ⓐ sagacious
Ⓑ aloof
Ⓒ sanguine
Ⓓ gracious
Ⓔ imperceptive

2. The __________ of warm and cold weather systems created the perfect conditions for the powerful thunderstorm.

Ⓐ consummate
Ⓑ confluence
Ⓒ coagulate
Ⓓ preceptor
Ⓔ laconic

3. Nate was __________ by the contradictory diagnoses he received and decided to solicit a third opinion.

Ⓐ perplexed
Ⓑ uncouth
Ⓒ bequeathed
Ⓓ ablaze
Ⓔ clear

4. Determined to place in the top three at this year's gymnastics championship, Simone practiced (i) __________ and frequently asked he coach to (ii)__________ her performance and offer constructive criticism on how to improve her overall routine.

Blank i	Blank ii
Ⓐ assiduously	Ⓓ peruse
Ⓑ haphazardly	Ⓔ critique
Ⓒ copiously	Ⓕ uproot

5. After they lost everything in the fire, they were pleasantly surprised and (i) __________ when the entire neighborhood (ii) __________ to help them replace what they lost and get back on their feet.

Blank i	Blank ii
Ⓐ beholden	Ⓓ rallied
Ⓑ befuddled	Ⓔ refaced
Ⓒ laden	Ⓕ harried

6. Kenna so full of energy and (i) __________ that she filled the entire room with positivity and (ii) __________.

Blank i	Blank ii
Ⓐ antipathy	Ⓓ exuberance
Ⓑ vivacity	Ⓔ lethargy
Ⓒ languidness	Ⓕ garrulousness

GO TO THE NEXT PAGE

7. As a(n) (i)____________ of the Iceland's (ii) ____________ climate, the temperature of the water at the Silfra rift, where the Eurasian and North American plates meet, is below freezing. Since very few organisms can survive in such temperatures, the water is so (iii)____________ you can drink it without any type of filtration.

Blank i
(A) upshot
(B) precursor
(C) misnomer

Blank ii
(D) glacial
(E) searing
(F) ambivalent

Blank iii
(G) loused
(H) unsullied
(I) magnetic

8. The Romer home was a large and regal (i) ____________ that had been exquisitely maintained since the late 1800's. The landscaping was in pristine condition and the inside of the home was decorated with furnishings that reflected its rich history. Though there were many expensive treasures in the home, the designers were careful to ensure the décor was not too (ii) ____________. Even with their efforts, it was hard to hide the (iii) ____________ of the place.

Blank i
(A) aperture
(B) tome
(C) edifice

Blank ii
(D) garish
(E) unpretentious
(F) mown

Blank iii
(G) sparseness
(H) opulence
(I) idiosyncrasies

VERBAL REASONING

Questions 9 and 10 are based on the following passage. Select one answer unless otherwise indicated.

Ozone gas is comprised of three bound oxygen atoms and is formed when methane and nitrogen in the atmosphere are tempered by the sun. Ozone has long been the subject of the global warming debate as many scientists believe that pollutants like CFCs are slowly destroying the protective ozone layer the protects the earth from the sun's harmful rays. However, ozone gas found in the air is quite different from the protective ozone layer in both composition and function. Ozone gas can cause health concerns for humans and animals who are in an area where there is a high concentration of ozone gas in the air. Unlike the ozone gas that comprises the ozone layer, ozone gas in the atmosphere can precipitate respiratory problems and skin conditions; prolonged exposure can elevate one's risk for certain cancers.

9. What is the primary purpose of the passage?

- Ⓐ Discuss the impact ozone gas has on the depletion of the ozone layer
- Ⓑ Highlight the critical role atmospheric ozone plays in the development of cancer in humans and animals
- Ⓒ Explain the difference between the ozone layer and atmospheric ozone gas and expound on the harmful effects of the latter
- Ⓓ Criticize the notion that the ozone layer provides a protective shield
- Ⓔ Offer advice on how to be avoid prolonged contact with ozone gas

10. Which of the following are probable outcomes of prolonged exposure to non-atmospheric ozone? Select all that apply.

- Ⓐ Elevated risk for certain cancers
- Ⓑ Respiratory and skin conditions
- Ⓒ None of these

Questions 11 and 12 are based on the following passage. Select one answer unless otherwise indicated.

Mental disorders manifest in a variety of different ways. Those suffering from mental disorders may experience behavioral, emotional, or cognitive issues that can affect their ability to function properly. Some patients see a therapist to help manage their symptoms, but some clinicians argue that therapy is not effective in addressing the chemical imbalance that is often at the root of mental disorders. So, it is safe to say that patients should avoid therapy since taking medications to address their chemical imbalance is the only effective treatment for reducing the symptoms experienced as a result of mental disorders.

11. The author makes which one of the following assumptions in the passage?

- Ⓐ Patients who take medication to treat their mental illness will cease to experience any symptoms
- Ⓑ Therapy has a deleterious effect on patients diagnosed with mental disorders
- Ⓒ Most mental disorders stem from causes other than chemical imbalances
- Ⓓ Therapy cannot lessen the symptoms experienced by someone suffering from a mental disorder
- Ⓔ Insurance does not typically cover therapy so patients should not waste money on an ineffective treatment

12. The passage most strongly supports which one of the following assertions?

- Ⓐ If choosing between two treatments, one that provides some relief and one that effectively addresses the root of the problem, one should completely avoid the treatment that does not address the root of the problem.
- Ⓑ Selecting a therapist who understands the intricacies of chemical imbalance is a critical component to addressing mental disorders.
- Ⓒ Mental disorders that are not caused by a chemical imbalance are best addressed through psychotherapy.
- Ⓓ Mental disorders are life-long afflictions that cannot be cured regardless of the treatment.
- Ⓔ Those who suffer from mental disorders are less likely to seek help for their problems.

GO TO THE NEXT PAGE

Questions 13-15 are based on the following passage. Select one answer unless otherwise indicated.

Even though significantly more women now choose to pursue engineering as a career, there is a still a long way to go in terms of making women feel comfortable in their male-dominated work environments. Even when they have the same credentials as their male colleagues, female engineers are given less demanding work, make less money, and have fewer opportunities for advancement. Furthermore, women have to contend with micro-aggressions from their male colleagues who often subtly comment on the veracity of their qualifications; in some cases, women are even subjected to crude and inappropriate language and advances. As a result, many either tend to become withdrawn or eventually leave their job or the field all together.

As more women enter the engineering workforce, cultural changes need to be made to ensure that women are just as valued as their male counterparts. Not only does the disparity in pay and and task allocation need to be addressed, but companies also need to be intentional about creating an environment that is welcoming and comfortable for all of its employees. Without these changes, the growth rate of women in the engineering feel will most certainly see a downturn in the near future.

13. The passage mentions which of the following issues that women encounter in the engineering workforce. Select all that apply.

- [A] Lower wages than their male counterparts
- [B] Fewer opportunities for continuing education
- [C] Less challenging work than they are qualified to perform.

---

14. The author is concerned that without cultural changes in the engineering industry:

- (A) Women will grow tired of the inequitable treatment and start their own engineering firms
- (B) The number of women who choose to enter and remain in the engineering field will decline
- (C) Male engineers will recognize the need to create more hospitable environments for their female colleagues
- (D) The engineering industry will suffer a great loss of talent that will hinder the rate of innovation
- (E) The industry will experience a shortage of properly trained professionals

---

15. Select the sentence in the passage that highlights some of the non-professional, more personal challenges women engineers may encounter in the workplace.

VERBAL REASONING

For questions 16-20, select two answers that best complete the blank and produces two sentences that are alike in meaning.

16. After the long and uncomfortable bus ride, the backpackers were thrilled to finally reach their beach destination and enjoyed a much needed ____________ before having to make the return trip.

Ⓐ anecdote
Ⓑ respite
Ⓒ hajj
Ⓓ sojourn
Ⓔ panegyric

---

17. Seeing an opportunity to cool off, the tourists jumped into the reservoir for a swim. The security guard immediately pulled them out and ____________ them for possibly contaminating the city's water supply.

Ⓐ solaced
Ⓑ harangued
Ⓒ gerrymandered
Ⓓ admonished
Ⓔ flouted
Ⓕ denigrated

---

18. Tom was not excited about accompanying his wife to the ballet, but he ____________ his feelings and pretended to be enthused so as not to offend his wife.

Ⓐ suppressed
Ⓑ promulgated
Ⓒ lambasted
Ⓓ muted
Ⓔ parlayed
Ⓕ posited

---

19. After their first date, Nicole was smitten and looking forward to meeting Brad again. But, when she saw him light a cigarette after he dropped her off, she was repulsed and her interest in seeing him again ____________ immediately.

Ⓐ ceased
Ⓑ waned
Ⓒ halted
Ⓓ progressed
Ⓔ irrigated
Ⓕ absconded

---

20. Since her parents were famous musicians, it's no surprise that Hannah has a ____________ for listening to and playing music.

Ⓐ prolixity
Ⓑ proclivity
Ⓒ penchant
Ⓓ prerogative
Ⓔ premonition
Ⓕ pejorative

QUANTITATIVE REASONING
SECTION 4

20 QUESTIONS
35 MINUTES

DIRECTIONS: For questions 1-8, use any provided centered information to help you compare Quantity A and Quantity B. Select the answer that describes the relationship between the two quantities, noting that the same answer choices are presented for each Quantitative Comparison question:

- A **Quantity A is greater.**
- B **Quantity B is greater.**
- C **The two quantities are equal.**
- D **The relationship cannot be determined from the information given.**

1. $a > 0$ and $a + b = 0$

Column A	Column B
a	b

Ⓐ Ⓑ Ⓒ Ⓓ

2. The average of $2x + 3x + 10x + 9 + 27 = 210$

Column A	Column B
60	x

Ⓐ Ⓑ Ⓒ Ⓓ

3.

Column A	Column B
$2(3+6)^2 + 20$	$2 + (3+6)^2 + 20$

Ⓐ Ⓑ Ⓒ Ⓓ

4.

Column A	Column B
$\sqrt{4+64}$	10

Ⓐ Ⓑ Ⓒ Ⓓ

5.

Column A	Column B
Area of a square that has a perimeter of 320	Area of a rectangle that has a perimeter of 320

Ⓐ Ⓑ Ⓒ Ⓓ

6. $x < 0 < y$

Column A	Column B
$x + y$	$\frac{y - x}{8}$

Ⓐ Ⓑ Ⓒ Ⓓ

GO TO THE NEXT PAGE

QUANTITATIVE REASONING

7.

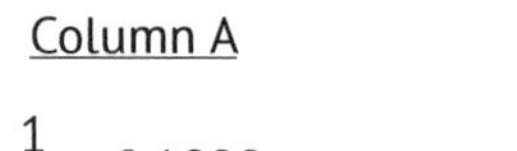

Column A	Column B
$\frac{1}{20}$ *of* 1000	5% of 1000

Ⓐ Ⓑ Ⓒ Ⓓ

8.

Column A	Column B
The sum of two acute angles	180°

Ⓐ Ⓑ Ⓒ Ⓓ

9. Suppose a is the smallest prime number that is greater than 109 and b is the largest prime number that is less than 89. What is $a+b$?

Ⓐ 198
Ⓑ 102
Ⓒ 196
Ⓓ 120
Ⓔ 145

10. If the product and the sum of six integers are even, which of the following could be the total number of even integers in the group? Select all that apply.

Ⓐ 1
Ⓑ 2
Ⓒ 4
Ⓓ 0

11. If you roll a die and flip a coin, what is the probability of rolling a 3 and having the coin land on tails?

Ⓐ $\frac{1}{6}$
Ⓑ $\frac{1}{2}$
Ⓒ $\frac{5}{24}$
Ⓓ $\frac{1}{12}$
Ⓔ $\frac{2}{3}$

Use the information below to answer questions 12 and 13.

Ashu recently added 14 new books to his home library. The addition increased the size of his collection by 35%.

12. How many books are currently in his collection?

Ⓐ 40
Ⓑ 52
Ⓒ 36
Ⓓ 54
Ⓔ 50

13. If Ashu increased the current number of books in his library by 50%, how many books does he have? Write your answer in the text box below.

14. If $5x = -10$, then $6x + 7x - 10 =$

Ⓐ 36
Ⓑ 24
Ⓒ −36
Ⓓ 23
Ⓔ 45

QUANTITATIVE REASONING

15. Last Monday, Gretchen sent x text messages each hour for 5 hours. Tony sent y text messages each hour for 4 hours. Which equation represents the total number of messages sent by Gretchen and Tony?

Ⓐ $9xy$
Ⓑ $20xy$
Ⓒ $4x+5y$
Ⓓ $24xy$
Ⓔ $5x+4y$

---

16. If $\frac{x}{y}=2$, what is the value of $\frac{4y}{x}$?

Ⓐ 1
Ⓑ 0
Ⓒ 2
Ⓓ 4
Ⓔ 8

---

17. For the figure below, find b.

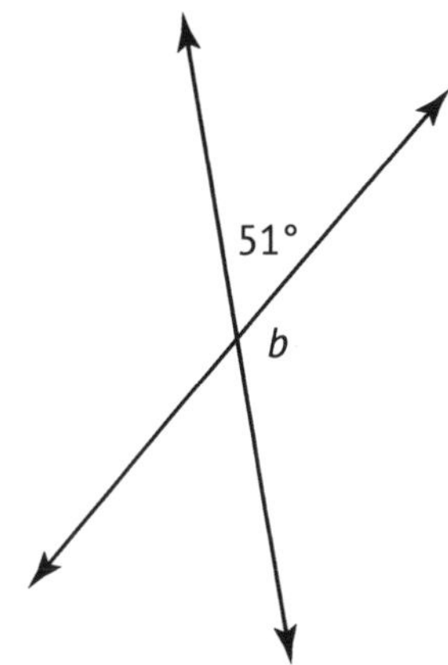

Ⓐ 62°
Ⓑ 51°
Ⓒ 39°
Ⓓ 141°
Ⓔ 129°

---

18. Find the distance between the points (1, 8), (6, 3).

Ⓐ $\sqrt{170}$
Ⓑ $6\sqrt{2}$
Ⓒ $\sqrt{10}$
Ⓓ $5\sqrt{2}$
Ⓔ $2\sqrt{5}$

Use the graph below to answer questions 19 and 20. Select one answer unless otherwise indicated.

European Spacecraft Launches

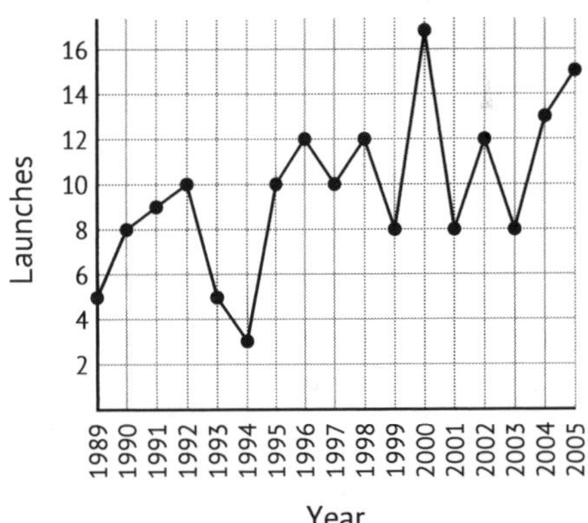

The graph represents the number of spacecraft launches by Europe from 1989-2005.

19. What is the difference of the number of spacecraft launched in the last three years from the number launched in the first three years?

Ⓐ 58
Ⓑ 14
Ⓒ 21
Ⓓ 19
Ⓔ 18

---

20. What is the median number of launches for the last five years?

Ⓐ 14
Ⓑ 10
Ⓒ 12
Ⓓ 8
Ⓔ 15

STOP

VERBAL REASONING — SECTION 5 | 20 QUESTIONS 30 MINUTES

DIRECTIONS: Answer each question according to the directions given.

For questions 1 to 8, you are to choose one answer for each blank from the corresponding column of choices.

1. Many of her friends considered Amber a ____________ since she was often loud, boisterous, and domineering.

- (A) prelude
- (B) filibuster
- (C) recluse
- (D) maverick
- (E) virago

2. The ex-convict found it difficult to move beyond his past once he was released from prison. He lived in a constant state of ____________.

- (A) attrition
- (B) banality
- (C) perdition
- (D) principality
- (E) restraint

3. While his wife Tia typically seems depressed and disinterested, Rolan is generally ____________.

- (A) vexed
- (B) uncouth
- (C) ebullient
- (D) agitated
- (E) haughty

4. As far as Denin was concerned, the bakery's cake was (i)____________; not a single bakery in the world could produce something so amazingly (ii) ____________.

Blank i	Blank ii
(A) fusty	(D) scrumptious
(B) middling	(E) redundant
(C) nonpareil	(F) mawkish

5. Myron couldn't seem to shake his intense (i) ____________; he spent hours every day researching places he wanted to travel and (ii) ____________ about all the wonderful things he could see and do if only he had the time.

Blank i	Blank ii
(A) disquiet	(D) fanaticizing
(B) wanderlust	(E) contravening
(C) compunction	(F) fantasizing

6. With a great deal of (i) ____________, the stranded campers gingerly crossed the dilapidated and (ii) ____________ bridge to get to the rescue crew on the other side.

Blank i	Blank ii
(A) perdition	(D) decrepit
(B) trepidation	(E) everted
(C) assurance	(F) callow

7. The level of service at Ma Belle's was (i) ______________. The servers were attentive without being invasive, the food was tasty, and the live music created a relaxing (ii) ______________ that made for an overall great afternoon. It's not surprising that so many people (ii)______________ the restaurant. The experience is definitely worth repeating.

Blank i	Blank ii
Ⓐ superlative	Ⓓ paramour
Ⓑ frenzied	Ⓔ milieu
Ⓒ extorted	Ⓕ séance

Blank iii
Ⓖ frequent
Ⓗ compliment
Ⓘ extol

8. The national treasures were stored in an (i) ______________ concrete safe. Even if someone were able to (ii)______________ the safe, the other highly tactical security measures would make it nearly impossible for someone to (iii) ______________ with the jewels.

Blank i	Blank ii
Ⓐ imbecilic	Ⓓ penetrate
Ⓑ deriver	Ⓔ prostrate
Ⓒ impervious	Ⓕ tensile

Blank iii
Ⓖ fraternize
Ⓗ abscond
Ⓘ callow

VERBAL REASONING

Questions 9 and 10 are based on the following passage. Select one answer unless otherwise indicated.

The cicada, a large insect with long transparent wings, communicate using vibrations to produce several distinctive sounds; these sounds are critical to the mating process of cicadas and consequentially, their survival. Cicadas make three distinct ticking and buzzing noises to announce their location to other cicadas and to engage in mating. Cicadas are able to distinguish between calls announcing location, called congregation calls, and those for the purpose of mating based on the number of times a cicada ticks of buzzes. The congregation call consists of 12 to 40 ticks, delivered rapidly, followed by a two-second buzz. Males use the mating call but it attracts cicadas of both sexes.

Once they are all together, the males use courtship calls. The preliminary call, a prolonged, slow ticking, is used when the male notices a female near him. The advanced call, a prolonged series of short buzzes at the same slow rate, is given when a female is almost within grasp. The preliminary call almost invariably occurs before the advanced call, although the latter is given without the preliminary call occurring first if a female is suddenly discovered near by. During typical courtship, though, the two calls together result in ticking followed by a buzzing in the same pattern which comprises the congregation call but delivered at a slower rate. In this way, cicadas show efficient use of their minimal sound producing ability, organizing two sounds delivered at a high rate as one call and the same sounds delivered at a slow rate as two more calls.

9. What is the primary purpose of the passage?

Ⓐ To discuss the dominance of male cicadas in colonies of cicadas
Ⓑ To discuss the nuances of the communication mechanisms of cicadas
Ⓒ To discuss the mating rituals of cicadas
Ⓓ To expand on current theories about the importance of communication in cicada colonies
Ⓔ To explain the threats to cicada colonies if pesticides were to impact their ability to communicate with potential mates

10. Based on the passage, which of the following is true about the call a male cicada might emit during courtship call? Select all that apply.

[A] It has 12-40 ticks followed by a slow 2-second buzz
[B] It is a series of short buzzes
[C] It is prolonged with short ticks.

Questions 11 and 12 are based on the following passage. Select one answer unless otherwise indicated.

Activist: As electronic surveillance of public places becomes more common and pervasive, the government gets more creative in its explanations of the need for the technology and invasion of privacy. According to the government, surveillance is an asset to our quality of life as it keeps people in line. Such explanations are obviously self-serving and meritless and should not be believed as valid justifications for the government's gross invasion of privacy rights.

11. A questionable technique used in the activist's argument is to:

Ⓐ Attack an argument different from that actually offered by government officials
Ⓑ Presume that members of the public will modify their behavior based on the presence of technology
Ⓒ Insist that government surveillance practices violate specific legal codes
Ⓓ Attack the government's motives instead of addressing its arguments
Ⓔ Make a generalization based on a sample that may be biased

---

12. The passage is primarily concerned with:

Ⓐ The rights of citizens to be free from surveillance
Ⓑ The rights of the government to keep citizens safe
Ⓒ The responsibility of technology companies to safeguard information
Ⓓ The responsibility of private citizens to report unauthorized surveillance
Ⓔ Exploring alternatives to unchecked surveillance

Questions 13-15 are based on the following passage. Select one answer unless otherwise indicated.

The following is an excerpt from Francis Bacon's *Of Youth and Age.*

On the other side, heat and vivacity in age is an excellent composition for business. Young men are fitter to invent than to judge, fitter for execution than for counsel, and fitter for new projects than for settled business. For the experience of age, in things that fall within the compass of it, direct them, but in new things abuse them. The errors of young men are the ruin of business; but the errors of aged men amount but to this, that more might have been done, or sooner. Young men, in their conduct and manage of actions, embrace more than they can hold; stir more than they can quiet; fly to the end, without consideration of the means and degrees; pursue some few principles which they have chanced upon absurdly; care not to innovate, which draws inconveniences; use extreme remedies at first; and, that which double all errors, will not acknowledge or retract them; like an unready horse that will neither stop nor turn.

13. What is the main point of the passage?

Ⓐ There is a sharpness and business acumen that comes with time and age.
Ⓑ Young men are generally better for the overall health of a business.
Ⓒ Older businessmen hinder progress within the company.
Ⓓ Keeping more mature businessmen in the company is a symbolic gesture of respect.
Ⓔ Young businessmen have a greater ability to execute innovative ideas.

---

14. Based on the passage, which of the following pairs of words would best characterize young businessmen in comparison to older businessmen, respectively?

Ⓐ methodical; hardened
Ⓑ stately; slipshod
Ⓒ attentive; harried
Ⓓ aggressive; meek
Ⓔ brash; seasoned

VERBAL REASONING

15. Which of the following best describes the tone of the author towards younger businessmen?

Ⓐ critical
Ⓑ encouraging
Ⓒ vitriolic
Ⓓ bemused
Ⓔ perturbed

For questions 16-20, select two answers that best complete the blank and produces two sentences that are alike in meaning.

16. Ben ______________ denied his involvement in the scandal, passionately asserting that he would never do something so contrary to the organization's mission.

Ⓐ vehemently
Ⓑ docilely
Ⓒ fervently
Ⓓ adjured
Ⓔ stoically
Ⓕ pompously

17. Submitting documents to a government office that contain false information is ______________ to perjury; both are crimes with equally severe punishments.

Ⓐ essential
Ⓑ tantamount
Ⓒ apropos
Ⓓ equivalent
Ⓔ incomparable
Ⓕ jocund

18. Tonya's neighbors thought she was quite ______________; she often yelled at other residents walking down the street and rejected cordial greetings from well-meaning visitors.

Ⓐ surly
Ⓑ sordid
Ⓒ truculent
Ⓓ defiant
Ⓔ coniferous
Ⓕ deluged

19. Everyone questioned the mayoral candidate's motives for supporting the charity. While his actions seemed ______________, many believe he had ulterior motives.

Ⓐ asinine
Ⓑ altruistic
Ⓒ magnanimous
Ⓓ abject
Ⓔ renitent
Ⓕ guffaw

20. Red wine typically has a lot of tannins in it; tannins largely account for the ______________ taste of the wine, not bitter or sour grapes like most people suspect.

Ⓐ tepid
Ⓑ smooth
Ⓒ acrid
Ⓓ saccharine
Ⓔ putrid
Ⓕ acerbic

STOP

QUANTITATIVE REASONING | 20 QUESTIONS
SECTION 6 | 35 MINUTES

DIRECTIONS: For questions 1-8, use any provided centered information to help you compare Column A and Column B. Select the answer that describes the relationship between the two quantities, noting that the same answer choices are presented for each Quantitative Comparison question:

- A **Quantity A is greater.**
- B **Quantity B is greater.**
- C **The two quantities are equal.**
- D **The relationship cannot be determined from the information given.**

1.

Column A	Column B
The *y*-intercept of a line that is parallel to the *y*-axis	1

Ⓐ Ⓑ Ⓒ Ⓓ

Use the figure below to answer questions 2 and 3.

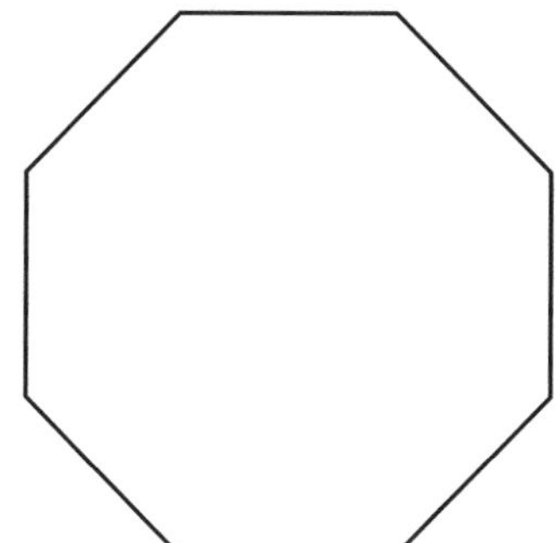

2.

Column A	Column B
Sum of the interior angles of the pictured polygon	Sum of degrees in two circles

Ⓐ Ⓑ Ⓒ Ⓓ

3.

Column A	Column B
The perimeter of the polygon if all sides are 9	The perimeter of a right triangle with sides 25 and 20

Ⓐ Ⓑ Ⓒ Ⓓ

---

4. $x < 1$

Column A	Column B
$\frac{1}{x}$	$\frac{x}{1}$

Ⓐ Ⓑ Ⓒ Ⓓ

---

5. Each concert ticket costs x dollars

Column A	Column B
50% of the cost of 6 tickets	$100

Ⓐ Ⓑ Ⓒ Ⓓ

GO TO THE NEXT PAGE

QUANTITATIVE REASONING

6.

Column A	Column B
$(5x+5y)^2$	$25x^2+25y^2$

Ⓐ Ⓑ Ⓒ Ⓓ

7. In a triangle, one angle is equal to 60° and one side is equal to 12

Column A	Column B
The sum of the other two angles	The area of the triangle

Ⓐ Ⓑ Ⓒ Ⓓ

8. Madge breaks open her piggy bank and has exactly \$1.15 in dimes and quarters.

Column A	Column B
The number of dimes	The number of quarters

Ⓐ Ⓑ Ⓒ Ⓓ

9. Find the distance between the points on the graph below:

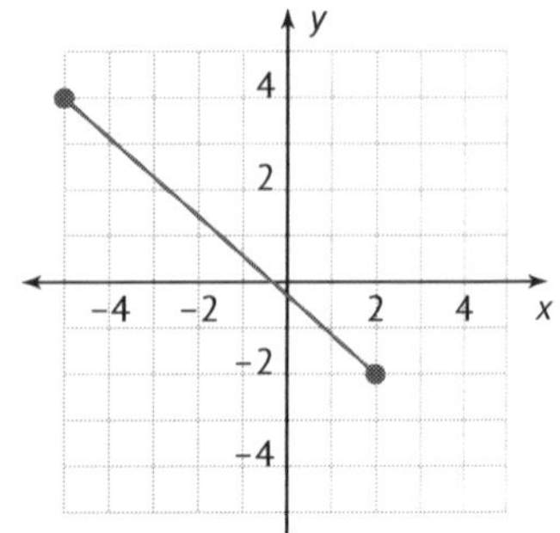

Ⓐ 3
Ⓑ $2\sqrt{10}$
Ⓒ $\sqrt{85}$
Ⓓ $\sqrt{13}$
Ⓔ $4\sqrt{2}$

10. Simplify $-(3k + 1) + 6(-8 - 3k)$.

Ⓐ $-38k + 2$
Ⓑ $-36k + 2$
Ⓒ $-21k - 49$
Ⓓ $-28k - 49$
Ⓔ $-26k - 4$

11. If the measure of angle P of triangle PQR is $3x$, the measure of angle Q is $5x$, and the measure of angle R is $4x$, what is the value of x?

Ⓐ 30°
Ⓑ 45°
Ⓒ 120°
Ⓓ 15°
Ⓔ 18°

12. Two complementary angles have measures that are in a ratio of 7:8 to each other. Find the measure of the smallest angle.

Ⓐ 90°
Ⓑ 70°
Ⓒ 42°
Ⓓ 58°
Ⓔ 71°

13. Suppose a circle has a circumference of 196π. What is the radius?

Ⓐ 320
Ⓑ 105
Ⓒ 98
Ⓓ 90
Ⓔ 78

QUANTITATIVE REASONING

14. Solve the inequality $-7(x+3) < -4x$.

Ⓐ $x \geq -12$
Ⓑ $x < -7$
Ⓒ $x > -7$
Ⓓ $x < -15$
Ⓔ $x < 8$

Use the following graph to answer questions 15 and 16.

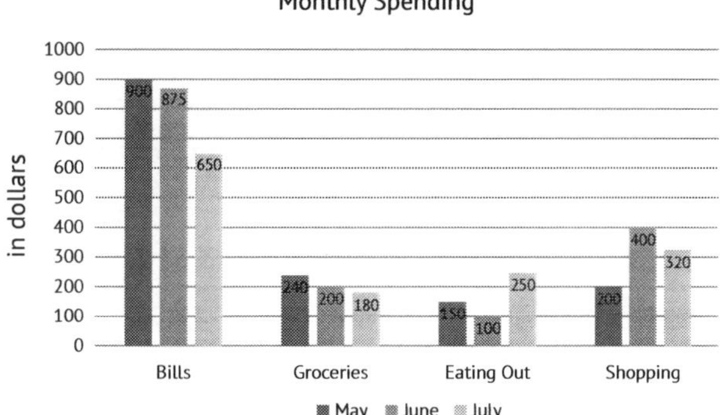

Michelle tracked her spending for three months to help determine where she could cut spending in order to save for her big trip.

15. If Michelle's earned \$4000 in June, what percentage of her earnings that month did she spend on groceries?

Ⓐ 20%
Ⓑ 10%
Ⓒ 15%
Ⓓ 5%
Ⓔ 8%

16. Which value is the greatest?

Ⓐ The amount Michelle spent on all food for all three months
Ⓑ The difference of what Michelle spent on bills for all three months and what she spent shopping for all three months
Ⓒ The median amount Michelle spent on bills for May, June, and July
Ⓓ The median total expenses for all three months
Ⓔ \$1200

17. If $8(x+3)-10=4x+20$, solve for x.

Ⓐ 2
Ⓑ 3
Ⓒ 5
Ⓓ $\frac{1}{2}$
Ⓔ $\frac{3}{2}$

18. If Tom draws two poker chips randomly from a bag containing six poker chips where three are red and three are blue, what is the probability that he will draw two blue poker chips from the bag? Write your answer in the text box below as a fraction.

19. Which of the following could be an interior angle of a right triangle? Select all that apply.

Ⓐ 90
Ⓑ 45
Ⓒ 30
Ⓓ 100
Ⓔ 110

20. If $\left|\frac{x}{5}\right| > 1$, which one of the following must be true?

Ⓐ $x > 5$
Ⓑ $x \leq 5$
Ⓒ $x \neq 5$
Ⓓ $x < -5$
Ⓔ $x = 5$

STOP

VERBAL REASONING
ANSWER KEY : SECTION 3

1. **A.**
   Sagacious means wise.

2. **B.**
   Confluence meets a meeting or convergence.

3. **A.**
   Nate was unclear or unconvinced. Because he was perplexed, he wanted to seek another opinion.

4. **A, E.**
   Simone was determined, so she likely worked assiduously, or diligently. Her coach offered her criticism to help her improve, so he critiqued her performance.

5. **A, D.**
   Beholden means grateful. The entire neighborhood came together, or rallied, to help.

6. **B, D.**
   You are looking for positive words that means energetic; vivacious means bubbly and energetic, and vivacity is a derivative of the word vivacious. The same applies for the second blank; exuberance means enthusiasm or energy.

7. **A, D, H.**
   The context clues let you know that Iceland's temperature is responsible for the freezing temperatures of the water at Silfra. Use those context clues to help you with the first two blanks. An upshot is a consequence of something, in this case, the climate. If the climate is responsible for the freezing temps, the climate must be cold, or glacial. Unsullied means pure.

8. **C, D, H.**
   An edifice is a building or structure. With all the expensive items in the home, designers wanted to make sure those things did not dominate the focus of the decor. Garish means gaudy or flashy, so that works in this instance. Opulence means wealth or richness.

9. **C.**
   The passage discusses the two types of ozone and gas and then goes more in-depth about atmospheric ozone.

10. **C.**
    The passage gives no information about the harmful effects of prolonged exposure to ozone gas in the ozone layer, only atmospheric ozone.

11. **D.**
    The author claims that patients should avoid therapy since only medication is effective. The author assumes not other helpful benefits can be obtained from therapy.

12. **A.**
    Choice A restates the arguments main claim in general terms.

13. **A, C.**
    There is no explicit mention of continuing education, only opportunities for advancement.

14. **B.**
    The author mentions that fewer women in the field is an inevitable consequence if the culture does not change.

15. Furthermore, women have to contend with micro-aggressions from their male colleagues who often subtly comment on the veracity of their qualifications; in some cases, women are even subjected to crude and inappropriate language and advances.

16. **B, D.**
    Both respite and sojourn mean a break or a rest.

17. **B, D.**
    Both mean to scold or to reprimand. Denigrated means to belittle or degrade, which does not fit in this sentence as it is too over-the-top and does not have a word that matches that would create a similar sentence.

18. **A, D.**
    Tom did not want his wife to know how he really felt, so he suppressed or muted his feelings, both meaning that he did not allow them to show.

19. **A, C.**
    Nicole's interest ended immediately, so ceased or halted. It is not possible to wane immediately, since waning indicates a gradual decline.

20. **B, C.**
    No one is surprised about Hannah's inclinations based on her upbringing. Context clues lead you to believe she has an interest in music; proclivity and penchant both mean liking or interest in.

QUANTITATIVE REASONING
ANSWER KEY : SECTION 4

1. **A.**
Since a must always be positive and $a+b=0$, b must be negative. So a will always be greater.

2. **B.**
Add the like terms and create an equation to solve for the sum since you are only given the average.

$$210=\frac{15x+36}{5}$$

$$15x+36=1050$$

$15x=1014$, so $x = 67.6$.

3. **A.**
Remember PEMDAS. Solve the parentheses first. The quantity of column A is 182 while column B is 103.

4. **B.**
Be careful not to assume that $\sqrt{4+64}=\sqrt{4}+\sqrt{64}$. It is equal to $\sqrt{68}$ which when solved is ~8.2. Column B is greater.

5. **D.**
We cannot determine the area given only the perimeter for Column B. Column A, we know squares have equal sides, and therefore $s = 80$, and area is equal to 6,400.

6. **D.**
x will always be negative and y will always be positive. When you plug in various numbers for each variable, they yield different results where it is possible for column A and column B to be the larger value in a given instance. Therefore, the relationship cannot be determined.

7. **C.**
1/20 and 5% are equivalent so the quantities are the same.

8. **B.**
Acute angles measure less than 90°. So, even at their maximum measurement, it is not possible for their sum to exceed 180°. So, column B will always be greater.

9. **C.**
The smallest prime number greater than 109 is 113 and the largest prime number less than 89 is 83. So, the sum is 196.

10. **B, C.**
If the product and the sum are even, you need an even number of even terms. 1 even number will not allow you to have both an even sum and product.

11. **D.**
Isolate each event and find the probability separately and then multiply to find the probability of both events happening. So, $\frac{1}{2}\bullet\frac{1}{6}=\frac{1}{12}$.

12. **D.**
Divide the increase by the percentage change to find the original number of books. In this case, $\frac{14}{.35}=40$. 40 represents the original value. But, the question asks how many books Ashu currently has. So, $40+14=54$.

13. **81.**

Set up an equation to solve for the missing value:

$.5=\frac{x}{54}=27$. A 50% increase is 27 books. But, the question asks what Ashu's new number of books is and that is $27+54=81$.

14. **C.**
$x=-2$. So, $-12-14-10=-36$

15. **E.**
The total number of text messages sent is the sum of the message sent by Gretchen and the messages sent by Tony.

16. **C.**
If $\frac{x}{y}=2$ then $\frac{y}{x}=\frac{1}{2}$. Multiply each side of the equation to solve.

17. **E.**
The sum of the angles should be 180°, so subtract the given angle from 180° to find b.

18. **D.**
Plug in the coordinates of the points into the distance formula.

$$d=\sqrt{(x_2-x_1)^2+(y_2-y_1)^2}$$

$$d=\sqrt{(6-1)^2+(3-9)^2}$$

QUANTITATIVE REASONING
ANSWER KEY : SECTION 4

$$d = \sqrt{50} \text{ or } \sqrt{2} \bullet \sqrt{25} = 5\sqrt{2}$$

19. B.

In the last three years, the number of launches was 15, 13, and 8, so 36. In the first three years, the number of launches was 5, 8, and 9, so 22. The difference of 39 and 22 is 14.

20. C.

You already know the values of the last three years from the previous question. Add the number of launches in 2001 and 2002 to get the data set: 8, 12, 15, 13, 8. The median of the set is 12.

VERBAL REASONING

ANSWER KEY : SECTION 5

1. **E.**
A virago is a loud and boisterous woman.

2. **C.**
A state of perdition is one of guilt or purgatory.

3. **C.**
Rolan is the opposite of is depressed and disinterested wife. Ebullient means cheery and jovial.

4. **C, D.**
The sentence suggests that Denin believes the bakery's cakes are second to none or unparalleled, nonpareil means unmatched, or elite. The second blank is a continuation of Denin's positive thoughts about the cakes. Mawkish is overly sweet or sappy in an emotional sense and is not correct; the cakes were scrumptious, or overly delicious.

5. **B, F.**
Myron has a great desire to travel, which is the definition of wanderlust. Blank two is tricky as it has a distractor answer, D, that looks similar to the correct answer. Choice D means to be fanatical or overly zealous while F means to daydream or imagine.

6. **B, D.**
Gingerly means cautiously, so the stranded campers were likely unsure about the bridge. Trepidation means a sense of caution, so it matches with the rest of the sentence. Decrepit is broken or rundown.

7. **A, E, G.**
Superlative means particularly notable. Milieu is typically used to refer to a type of environment or scenery that is set, in this case, with the live music. The third blank is tricky in that all three of the words fit into the sentence. However, you must use the context clues in the last sentence for reference. The experience is worth repeating so the previous sentence must make some mention of customers returning to the restaurant.

8. **C, D, H.**
The safe is concrete which would make it hard to access. Impervious means impenetrable or protected. The opposite of that would fill blank two given the transition "even if", so penetrate. Abscond means to escape or flee.

9. **B.**
The passages discusses the various calls cicadas use to communicate.

10. **A.**
During typical courtship, though, the two calls together result in ticking followed by a buzzing in the same pattern which comprises the congregation call but delivered at a slower rate.

11. **D.**
The author bases the argument on the premise that government arguments for surveillance are self-centered and should not entertained as a result.

12. **A.**
The activist is addressing the rights of citizens to not have their privacy violated.

13. **A.**
The passages focuses on the need and benefit of older more experienced businessmen.

14. **E.**
Young men, "fly to the end, without consideration of the means and degrees" while older men whose, "heat and vivacity in age is an excellent composition."

15. **A.**
The author repeatedly highlights the shortcomings of younger businessmen in the passage.

16. **A, C.**
Ben's denial is passionate, so you can eliminate E and B which are the opposite. Vehemently and fervently are both synonymous with passionately.

17. **B, D.**
The second part of the sentence tells you that you are looking for a word that means two things are equal. Tantamount and equivalent both mean equal. Be careful not to fall for the opposite answer, E.

18. **A, C.**
Tonya's behavior is confrontational and unpleasant. Both surly and truculent mean confrontational or hostile.

VERBAL REASONING
ANSWER KEY : SECTION 5

19. B, C.

"While" signals a transition, so you are looking for words that signify the opposite of giving with ulterior motives, so, generous. Magnanimous and altruistic both mean selfless and generous.

20. C, F.

According to the sentence, people incorrectly presume bitter or sour grapes give red wine its taste, which you can infer is bitter or sour. So, you are looking for a word similar to bitter or sour. Acerbic and acrid, both mean bitter or sour. Putrid means moldy or decaying, which is outside of the scope of what the sentence is discussing.

QUANTITATIVE REASONING
ANSWER KEY : SECTION 6

1. B.
A lines parallel to the y-axis have a y-intercept of 0. So, column B is greater.

2. A.
The sum of the interior angles of the 8-sided polygon is 1080° and the sum of the degrees in two circles is 720°.

3. A.
The perimeter of the octagon is 72 while the perimeter of the triangle, a 3:4:5 triangle is 60 (20 + 25 + 15).

4. D.
The relationship cannot be determined since plugging in various values less than 1 yields different results in terms of which column is greater.

5. D.
The relationship cannot be determined without knowing the cost of the tickets. Be careful not to make assumptions about tickets prices that are not supported by the information provided.

6. D.
$(5x + 5y)^2$ is not equal to $25x^2 + 25y^2$. You must square the expression in column A. So, $(5x + 5y)(5x + 5y)$. When you factor, you are unable to determine the relationship because there are no other restrictions on the variables. Either column could end up being greater.

7. D.
The calculations are not comparable. You cannot compare area to the measure of internal angles as area is not measure in degrees.

8. A.
You must have at least one quarter since the total amount of $1.15 is not possible with just dimes. That being said, you can have at most 3 quarters. There are number possibilities but you will always have more dimes than quarters.

9. C.
Plug in the coordinates of the points into the distance formula to solve. (2, −2) and (−5, 4) are the coordinates.

$$d = \sqrt{(x_2 - x_1)^2 + (y_2 - y_1)^2}$$

$$d = \sqrt{49 + 36}$$

$$d = \sqrt{85}$$

10. C.
Distribute and combine like terms:

$$-(3k + 1) + 6(-8 - 3k)$$

$$-3k - 1 - 48 - 18k$$

$$-21k - 49$$

11. D.
The measure of the interior angles for any triangle is 180°. Create an equation to solve for x.

$$3x + 5x + 4x = 180$$

$$12x = 18$$

$$x = 15$$

12. C.
Complementary angles add up to 90°. Since you are given the ratio 7:8, you can create an equation to solve for x.

$$7x + 8x = 90$$

$$15x = 90$$

$$x = 6$$

The smallest angle given is $7x$. So, substitute the value of x in the expression to solve. The smallest angle is 7(6) or 42°.

13. C.
The circumference is twice the radius, so the radius is $\frac{196}{2} = 98$.

QUANTITATIVE REASONING
ANSWER KEY : SECTION 6

14. C.
Distribute and then solve.

$$-7x - 21 < -4x$$

$$-3x < 21$$

$$x > -7$$

Remember that when you divide both sides by a negative number in an inequality, you must reverse the sign. Be careful not to fall for B which fails to account for the sign flip.

15. D.

Create an equation and solve: $\frac{200}{4000} = .05 = 5\%$.

16. B.
Answer choice A asks for the total Michelle spent on all food, so that includes groceries and eating out. The total is $1120. For answer choice B, find the difference of Michelle's shopping and bills expenses: 2425 – 920 = 1505. The median of what Michelle spent on bills is 875, since it is the center term when the bills are placed in numerical order. For D, to find the median total expenses for each month, add the expenses for each month and find the median: 1490 (May) + 1575 (June) + 1400 (July). The median is 1490.

17. E.
Distribute and solve.

$$8x + 24 - 10 = 4x + 20$$

$$8x + 14 = 4x + 20$$

$$4x = 6$$

$$x = \frac{6}{4} = \frac{3}{2}$$

18. $\frac{1}{5}$ **or** $\frac{3}{15}$.

First, find the probability of each event happening.

The probability of him drawing one blue chip is $\frac{3}{6}$ and the probability of him drawing a second blue chip is $\frac{2}{5}$. Multiply the probabilities to get

$$\frac{6}{30} = \frac{3}{15} = \frac{1}{5}.$$

19. A, B, C.
A right triangle has one angle equal to 90° and only has a total of 180°. So, D and E are too large to be just one angle of a right triangle.

20. C.
Make sure you understand the implications of absolute value. Choice A is an attractive answer but fails to consider that x can be a negative number, -20 for example, can be greater than 1 because of the absolute value notation. The only statement that must be true is that $x \neq 5$ since plugging in 5 for x will make the sides of the inequality equal.

Raw Score	Scaled Score	Raw Score	Scaled Score
40	170	20	150
39	169	19	149
38	168	18	148
37	167	17	147
36	166	16	146
35	165	15	145
34	164	14	144
33	163	13	143
32	162	12	142
31	161	11	141
30	160	10	140
29	159	9	139
28	158	8	138
27	157	7	137
26	156	6	136
25	155	5	135
24	154	4	134
23	153	3	133
22	152	2	132
21	151	1	131

These practice tests are designed to simulate actual testing conditions as closely as possible. While the questions are similar to those you will encounter on the GRE, the sections are not adaptive for Verbal and Quantitative Reasoning like they will be if you sit for the computer-adaptive exam. The scale above gives you an **idea** of your projected score and can help you monitor your progress as you become more familiar with the material. The scale above is a rough guide to predict your score. **As a reminder**, the PowerPrep II software distributed by ETS offers two free computer-adaptive exams to supplement your study plan. Be sure to include those exams in your study plan in addition to the exams in this section; this will help you get an idea of the areas you need to study more closely in order to reach your scoring goals.

ARGO
BROTHERS

PRACTICE TEST 6

GRE®

Graduate Record Examinations

- This exam is 3 hours and 45 minutes long. Try to take this full exam in one sitting to simulate real test conditions.
- While taking this exam, refrain from listening to music or watching TV.
- When writing your response for Analyze an Issue & Analyze an Argument prompt, use a computer, and turn off the spell-check feature to simulate real testing conditions.
- Use a basic calculator, do not use a graphic or scientific calculator. On the real exam, you will have an on-screen calculator with only basic operation functions and a square root key.
- Concentrate and GOOD LUCK!

To calculate your score visit our web site and download excel calculator:

www.einstein-academy.com/GRE

ANALYTICAL WRITING
ANALYZE AN ISSUE

ESSAY 1
30 MINUTES

The proliferation of technology is crippling the ability of humans to do and think for themselves. At this rate, before long humans will be unable to care for themselves without the assistance of technology.

Discuss the extent to which you agree or disagree with the statement and explain your position. Also discuss instances when the statement may or may not be true and how these instances impact your viewpoint.

GO TO THE NEXT PAGE

ANALYTICAL WRITING | ESSAY 2
ANALYZE AN ARGUMENT | 30 MINUTES

The following appeared in a conference document presented at an education law symposium focused on discussing the parameters of free speech at private universities.

The parameters of free speech are something campuses have long grappled with in terms of the creation and enforcement of policies. As perhaps the most disputed constitutional directive, free speech presents a myriad of challenges related to the interpretation of what exactly constitutes free speech and what, if any, restrictions can be levied against it. Although First Amendment rights are guaranteed for constituents of public institutions, private institutions possess the right to regulate speech as it sees fit. One of the most compelling arguments against censoring speech is its potential to quell students' free expression. While private institutions are certainly within their rights to impose such censorship, they should consider that such censorship has the potential to rob students of formidable growth that is be borne out of difficult interactions and conversation where one's values and attitudes may be critically challenged. Even without bearing the obligation of free and unregulated campus speech, private universities must be careful to not adopt policies that impede upon the free expression of ideas, regardless of how controversial they may be.

Discuss the stated and unstated assumptions in the argument and discuss what the consequences might be if those assumptions are shown to be unwarranted.

QUANTITATIVE REASONING | 20 QUESTIONS
SECTION 3 | 35 MINUTES

DIRECTIONS: For questions 1-8, use any provided centered information to help you compare Column A and Column B. Select the answer that describes the relationship between the two quantities, noting that the same answer choices are presented for each Quantitative Comparison question:

A Quantity A is greater.
B Quantity B is greater.
C The two quantities are equal.
D The relationship cannot be determined from the information given.

Use the following centered information to answer questions 1 and 2.

1. A coin is tossed three times

Column A	Column B
6	The total number of possible outcomes

Ⓐ Ⓑ Ⓒ Ⓓ

2.

Column A	Column B
The probability that the coin will land on heads on the second toss	$\frac{1}{3}$

Ⓐ Ⓑ Ⓒ Ⓓ

---

3. $x^2 \square 6 = 19$
$x > 0$

Column A	Column B
$-x$	-5

Ⓐ Ⓑ Ⓒ Ⓓ

---

4. The discount of x% dropped the price of the backpack from \$60 to \$56.

Column A	Column B
x	11

Ⓐ Ⓑ Ⓒ Ⓓ

---

5. $x > 0$

Column A	Column B
$x+1$	$\lvert x \rvert$

Ⓐ Ⓑ Ⓒ Ⓓ

Use the following centered information to answer questions 6 and 7.

Half of a standard deck of 52 cards is made up of 26 black cards. The other half is made up of red cards. You select one card.

6.

Column A	Column B
Probability of drawing a red card	Probability of drawing a non-red card

Ⓐ Ⓑ Ⓒ Ⓓ

QUANTITATIVE REASONING

7.

Column A	Column B
$\frac{1}{2}$	The probability of drawing a red card after discarding 5 black cards from the deck

Ⓐ Ⓑ Ⓒ Ⓓ

8. $x > 0$

Column A	Column B
$\frac{\frac{1}{x}}{\frac{x}{1}}$	1

Ⓐ Ⓑ Ⓒ Ⓓ

9. Which of the following two integers have a sum greater than 1?

Ⓐ -3
Ⓑ -7
Ⓒ -6
Ⓓ 5

10. A colored pebble is chosen at random from a sack of pebbles. The probability that the pebble chosen will be green is $\frac{4}{9}$. Which of the following could not be the total number of pebbles in the sack?

Ⓐ 81
Ⓑ 72
Ⓒ 108
Ⓓ 90
Ⓔ 74

11. Using the figure below, find the missing value.

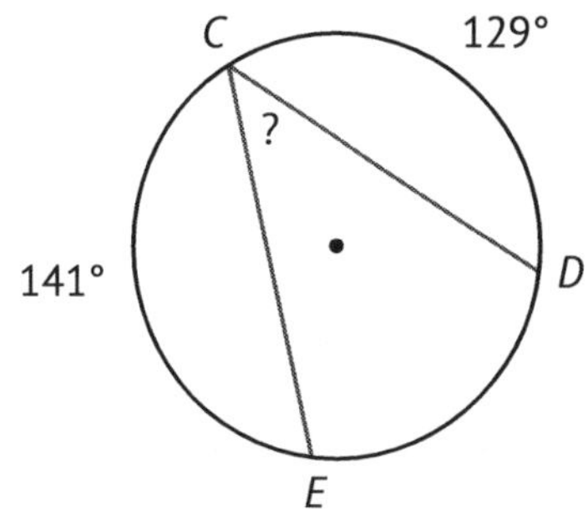

Ⓐ 90°
Ⓑ 120°
Ⓒ 60°
Ⓓ 45°
Ⓔ 95°

Use the graph below to answers questions 12 and 13. Select one answer unless otherwise indicated.

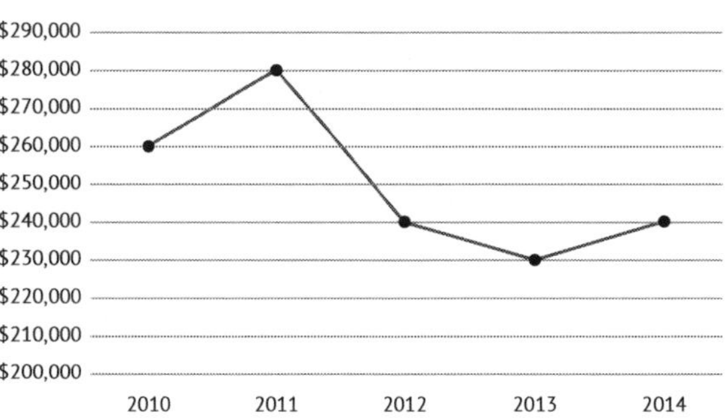

QUANTITATIVE REASONING

12. What was the approximate percentage decrease in average annual salary from 2011 to 2012?

Ⓐ 14.3%
Ⓑ 15.2%
Ⓒ 50%
Ⓓ 25%
Ⓔ 18.5%

13. What was the average salary in 2015 if it was 10% greater than the median salary for the previous five years?

A $250,000
B $240,000
C $274,000
D $264,000
E $282,000

14. If you toss a coin 8 times, what is the total number of possible outcomes? Write your answer in the text box below.

15. Factor $n^2 + 2n + 1$

Ⓐ $(4n+1)(4n-1)$
Ⓑ $(n-1)(n+1)$
Ⓒ $(n+1)^2$
Ⓓ $(n-1)^2$
Ⓔ $(3n+1)(3n-1)$

16. Four 3ft legs are attached at a right angle to a 5ft long table. What is the distance from the bottom of one leg to the opposite end of the table?

Ⓐ 4ft
Ⓑ 5ft
Ⓒ 15ft
Ⓓ 15.5ft
Ⓔ 8ft

17. The surface area of a cube with side length $x+3$ is 486. Solve for x.

Ⓐ $x=5$
Ⓑ $x=6$
Ⓒ $x=9$
Ⓓ $x=4$
Ⓔ $x=3$

18. Solve $\frac{8!}{6!}$. Enter your answer in the text box below.

19. If x is an even integer and y is an odd integer, which of the following must be odd? Select all that apply.

Ⓐ $x-y$
Ⓑ $x+y$
Ⓒ $x+2y$
Ⓓ $4x+y$
Ⓔ $5x+3y$

20. How many degrees does a minute hand on a clock move in 20 minutes?

Ⓐ 90°
Ⓑ 120°
Ⓒ 180°
Ⓓ 45°
Ⓔ 110°

STOP

QUANTITATIVE REASONING | 20 QUESTIONS
SECTION 4 | 35 MINUTES

DIRECTIONS: For questions 1-8, use any provided centered information to help you compare Column A and Column B. Select the answer that describes the relationship between the two quantities, noting that the same answer choices are presented for each Quantitative Comparison question:

- A **Quantity A is greater.**
- B **Quantity B is greater.**
- C **The two quantities are equal.**
- D **The relationship cannot be determined from the information given.**

Use the following centered information to answer questions 1 and 2.

1. $x = 5$

Column A	Column B
60	$2x^2 + x + 5$

Ⓐ Ⓑ Ⓒ Ⓓ

2.

Column A	Column B
$26x$	$28x$

Ⓐ Ⓑ Ⓒ Ⓓ

3.

Column A	Column B
The sum of integers from −7 to 5	The sum of integers from 5 to −7

Ⓐ Ⓑ Ⓒ Ⓓ

---

4. The frozen yogurt bar costs $.50 for the first ounce and .20 for each additional ounce. Tom's yogurt was $2.50

Column A	Column B
The number of ounces of Tom's yogurt	10

Ⓐ Ⓑ Ⓒ Ⓓ

---

5. One angle in a right triangle measures 65°

Column A	Column B
The measure of the angle that is not the right angle	30°

Ⓐ Ⓑ Ⓒ Ⓓ

6.

Column A	Column B
The greatest prime factor of 41	The greatest prime factor of 68

Ⓐ Ⓑ Ⓒ Ⓓ

GO TO THE NEXT PAGE

QUANTITATIVE REASONING

7.

$$x^5 = 32$$
$$y^4 = 16$$

Column A	Column B
x	y

Ⓐ Ⓑ Ⓒ Ⓓ

---

8. Point (x, y) is found in quadrant four on a coordinate plane

Column A	Column B
x	y

Ⓐ Ⓑ Ⓒ Ⓓ

---

9. If 18 + 6x is 20 percent larger than y, what is y?

Ⓐ $\frac{10+4x}{5}$
Ⓑ $20+5x$
Ⓒ $15+5x$
Ⓓ 20+18x
Ⓔ $\frac{6(12+6x)}{5}$

---

10. If $f(x) = x^2 + \sqrt[3]{x}$, solve for $f(-8)$. Write your answer in the text box below.

[ ]

---

11. Evaluate 1! + 2! + 5!

Ⓐ 8
Ⓑ 10
Ⓒ 75
Ⓓ 123
Ⓔ 178

---

12. Keith spent \$60 on a new pair of ski pants for his upcoming ski weekend. The pants were on sale and he saved 5%. If there was a 5% sales tax, how much did Keith pay for the ski pants?

Ⓐ \$60.00
Ⓑ \$59.00
Ⓒ \$63.00
Ⓓ \$59.85
Ⓔ \$57.75

---

13. What is the ratio of the radius of a circle to its circumference?

Ⓐ 1
Ⓑ □
Ⓒ □²
Ⓓ $\frac{1}{2}\pi$
Ⓔ 2□

---

14. Solve: $\frac{8\sqrt{12}}{2\sqrt{3}}$.

Ⓐ 4
Ⓑ $16\sqrt{6}$
Ⓒ 96
Ⓓ 64
Ⓔ 8

---

15. Find the value of b using the diagram below.

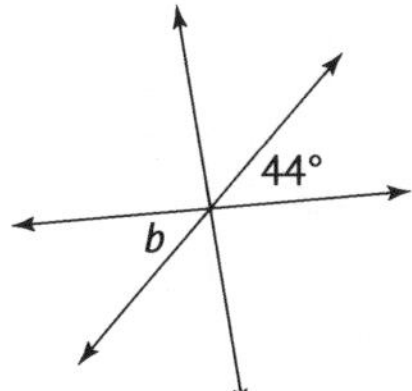

Ⓐ 46°
Ⓑ 73°
Ⓒ 44°
Ⓓ 136°
Ⓔ 124°

---

16. What is the slope of the parallel a line with the equation $4y = -9$?

Ⓐ $-\frac{4}{9}$
Ⓑ $-\frac{9}{4}$
Ⓒ 4
Ⓓ 0
Ⓔ −9

Environmental Action Committee Budget Allocations

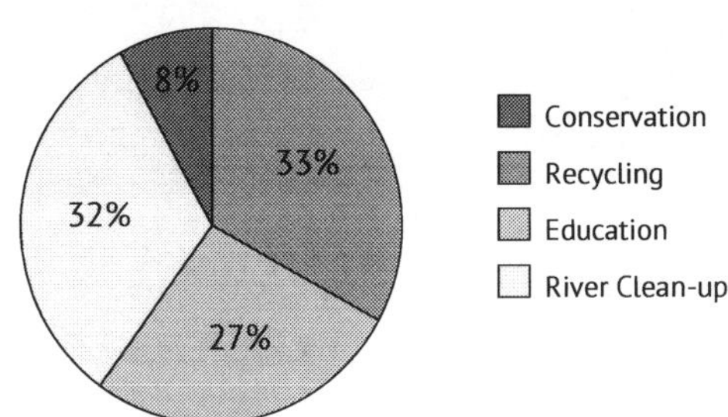

The graph represents this year's budget allocation for the Environmental Action Committee. The total amount of funds allocated this year was $150,000.

17. What was the total dollar amount spent on Education and River Clean-up?

Ⓐ $50,000
Ⓑ $55,000
Ⓒ $60,000
Ⓓ $62,000
Ⓔ $64,000

18. Suppose after the allocation the committee received an unexpected grant of $5000. If the committee decided to spread the grant over each of the four areas while keeping percentage of the total allocation the same, what would be the new dollar amount allocated to conservation?

Ⓐ $51,150
Ⓑ $52,350
Ⓒ $55,000
Ⓓ $53,500
Ⓔ $41,000

---

19. Calculate the distance of point (-3,-4) from the origin on a coordinate plane.

Ⓐ −3
Ⓑ −4
Ⓒ 2
Ⓓ −7
Ⓔ 5

---

20. What is the volume of a cube whose surface area is 96? Write your answer in the text box below.

STOP

VERBAL REASONING | 20 QUESTIONS
SECTION 5 | 30 MINUTES

DIRECTIONS: Answer each question according to the directions given.

For questions 1 to 8, you are to choose one answer for each blank from the corresponding column of choices.

1. Keith slid the cash to Emily ______________ hoping no one would notice the exchange.

Ⓐ precipitously
Ⓑ clandestinely
Ⓒ scrupulously
Ⓓ shyly
Ⓔ coyly

2. The blind date was a total failure in terms of conversation since Justin found Beth's obsession with talking about reality television and fashion to be ______________ at best.

Ⓐ alight
Ⓑ banal
Ⓒ grotesque
Ⓓ agape
Ⓔ parched

3. Walt was a ______________ of integrity and kindness; his family and community looked up to him, respected his judgment, and admired his devotion to others.

Ⓐ paragon
Ⓑ profiteer
Ⓒ cleric
Ⓓ prophet
Ⓔ propitiate

4. This recently published biography provides a gripping account of the adventures of Peter Kohls, one of the most (i) ______________ explorers of our time. The book was (ii)______________researched and gave readers even more insight into his courageous and daring journeys and harrowing experiences.

Blank i	Blank ii
Ⓐ intrepid	Ⓓ superlatively
Ⓑ insipid	Ⓔ entrenched
Ⓒ specious	Ⓕ sparsely

5. Contrary to what is widely believed, the detrimental effects of the stock market crash and the Great Depression were (i)______________, worsening over the course of several years until eventually unemployment rose, resources waned, and millions of Americans were left (ii)______________ as a result.

Blank i	Blank ii
Ⓐ abrupt	Ⓓ enervated
Ⓑ gradual	Ⓔ destitute
Ⓒ fulsome	Ⓕ fuddled

6. The judges of the cooking show were not quite sure what to make of the (i)______________ garnish that accompanied the already over-the-top dessert. To them, it seemed (ii)______________ and added nothing to the dessert overall.

Blank i	Blank ii
Ⓐ unswerving	Ⓓ juxtaposing
Ⓑ rigid	Ⓔ cultivating
Ⓒ aspic	Ⓕ fermenting

7. The new policy (i) ______________ the control the investors over the operation of the company. The change was well-received by the company's employees who felt the investors' involvement was a conflict of interest and that they often inappropriately (ii)______________ their authority to advance policy decisions that catered to their financial needs instead of the needs of the company. The investors on the other hand (iii)______________ the change and threatened to withdraw their financial support.

Blank i
Ⓐ augmented
Ⓑ attenuated
Ⓒ assayed

Blank ii
Ⓓ brandished
Ⓔ teetered
Ⓕ expiated

Blank iii
Ⓖ equivocated
Ⓗ lambasted
Ⓘ reproofed

---

8. After the guilty verdict was read, the convicted attacker sat (i) ______________ as the family read their victim impact statements. The victim's father was so (ii) ______________ by the lack of remorse shown by the attacker that he lunged towards him and tried to strike him. Luckily for the attacker, the quick-thinking District Attorney (iii) ______________ the father's path, preventing the attack.

Blank i
Ⓐ prodigally
Ⓑ credulously
Ⓒ stolidly

Blank ii
Ⓓ incensed
Ⓔ dismantled
Ⓕ malingered

Blank iii
Ⓖ dilated
Ⓗ obstructed
Ⓘ fomented

VERBAL REASONING

Questions 9-11 are based on the following passage. Select one answer unless otherwise indicated.

What right have I to write on Prudence, whereof I have little, and that of the negative sort? My prudence consists in avoiding and going without, not in the inventing of means and methods, not in adroit steering, not in gentle repairing. I have no skill to make money spend well, no genius in my economy, and whoever sees my garden discovers that I must have some other garden. Yet I love facts, and hate lubricity, and people without perception. Then I have the same title to write on prudence, that I have to write on poetry or holiness. We write from aspiration and antagonism, as well as from experience. We paint those qualities which we do not possess. The poet admires the man of energy and tactics; the merchant breeds his son for the church or the bar: and where a man is not vain and egotistic, you shall find what he has not by his praise. Moreover, it would be hardly honest in me not to balance these fine lyric words of Love and Friendship with words of coarser sound, and, whilst my debt to my senses is real and constant, not to own it in passing. Prudence is the virtue of the senses. It is the science of appearances. It is the outmost action of the inward life. It is God taking thought for oxen. It moves matter after the laws of matter. It is content to seek health of body by complying with physical conditions, and health of mind by the laws of the intellect.

The world of the senses is a world of shows; it does not exist for itself, but has a symbolic character; and a true prudence or law of shows recognizes the co-presence of other laws, and knows that its own office is subaltern; knows that it is surface and not center where it works. Prudence is false when detached. It is legitimate when it is the Natural History of the soul incarnate; when it unfolds the beauty of laws within the narrow scope of the senses.

There are all degrees of proficiency in knowledge of the world. It is sufficient, to our present purpose, to indicate three. One class live to the utility of the symbol; esteeming health and wealth a final good. Another class live above this mark to the beauty of the symbol; as the poet, and artist, and the naturalist, and man of science. A third class live above the beauty of the symbol to the beauty of the thing signified; these are wise men. The first class have common sense; the second, taste; and the third, spiritual perception. Once in a long time, a man traverses the whole scale, and sees and enjoys the symbol solidly; then also has a clear eye for its beauty, and, lastly, whilst he pitches his tent on this sacred volcanic isle of nature, does not offer to build houses and barns thereon, reverencing the splendor of the God which he sees bursting through each chink and cranny.

The world is filled with the proverbs and acts and winkings of a base prudence, which is a devotion to matter, as if we possessed no other faculties than the palate, the nose, the touch, the eye and ear; a prudence which adores the Rule of Three, which never subscribes, which never gives, which seldom lends, and asks but one question of any project--Will it bake bread? This is a disease like a thickening of the skin until the vital organs are destroyed. But culture, revealing the high origin of the apparent world, and aiming at the perfection of the man as the end, degrades every thing else, as health and bodily life, into means. It sees prudence not to be a separate faculty, but a name for wisdom and virtue conversing with the body and its wants. Cultivated men always feel and speak so, as if a great fortune, the achievement of a civil or social measure, great personal influence, a graceful and commanding address, had their value as proofs of the energy of the spirit. If a man lost his balance, and immerse himself in any trades or pleasures for their own sake, he may be a good wheel or pin, but he is not a cultivated man.

9. The author mentions 'disease' in the third paragraph, most likely referring to what?

Ⓐ ensuousness
Ⓑ egotism
Ⓒ antipathy
Ⓓ shame
Ⓔ depression

---

10. The author's tone in the first paragraph is best described as:

Ⓐ modest
Ⓑ heretical
Ⓒ rudimentary
Ⓓ laconic
Ⓔ austere

11. Throughout the passage, the author constructs an over-arching definition of prudence as:

Ⓐ the steadfast pursuit of wealth and notoriety
Ⓑ the confluence of education and practical skills
Ⓒ a commitment to the acquisition of practical skills and sensory experiences
Ⓓ a deep spiritual connection to a higher power
Ⓔ a commitment to service and noble deeds

Questions 12 and 13 are based on the following passage. Select one answer unless otherwise indicated.

Eyjafjallajökull is an active volcano in Iceland. It gained worldwide notoriety in 2010 when its eruptions caused massive damage throughout the country and delayed flights to and from Europe for weeks. The volcano lies just west of another volcano, Katla. Katla is a complicated geological wonder. The volcano is covered by the Mýrdalsjökull ice cap and has as massive magma chamber prone to frequent seismic activity. Though Katla did not erupt following the 2010 eruption of Eyjafjallajökull, all of Eyjafjallajökull's previous eruptions have been followed by an eruption of Katla. Scientists contend that the next big eruption of Katla will be an eruption of epic proportions; they have continued to keep a watchful eye on the sleeping giant. Scientists believe that the eruption will prompt the rapid melting of the ice sheet and cause major flooding and large plumes of blinding ash. The eruption of Katla will obviously be a major geological event with far-reaching consequences. It would be in the best interest of neighboring countries to start developing a plan to manage to fall-out of the inevitable eruption.

12. What is the main point of the passage?

Ⓐ The eruption of Eyjafjallajökull is imminent and neighboring countries should start preparing now for it.
Ⓑ The ice sheet melting is the most dangerous threat if Katla were to erupt.
Ⓒ Scientist believe that the eruption of Katla is inevitable and have started taking steps to brace for the likely huge impact.
Ⓓ The 2010 eruption of Eyjafjallajökull caused Iceland and many European countries to lose millions to clean-up efforts.
Ⓔ Both Katla and Eyjafjallajökull pose major threats to Iceland and the rest of Europe.

13. The author would like agree with which of the following statements? Select all that apply.

[A] Katla's lack of activity following the 2010 Eyjafjallajökull eruption was uncharacteristic.
[B] The rapid melting of the ice cap is likely to cause major flooding.
[C] Neighboring European countries should wait until Katla registers activity to start planning a contingency plan.

GO TO THE NEXT PAGE

VERBAL REASONING

Questions 14-16 are based on the following passage. Select one answer unless otherwise indicated.

Jean Piaget was a prominent developmental psychologist whose research on cognitive development became the foundation for developmental psychology as we know it today. Piaget grew up during a time when Sigmund Freud's psychological theories were percolating through mainstream consciousness and were the subject of much intrigue. Piaget was largely influenced by Freud's work and later went on to study under the tutelage of Alfred Binet who was a pioneer in the field of intelligence testing. While working with Binet, Piaget became increasingly aware of the differences in the levels of cognitive processing between younger children and that of older children and adults. These observations lead Piaget to investigate the development of cognition further and eventually outline the stages of cognitive development. Many of his writings are critical inclusions in the seminal texts for developmental psychologists and educators.

Piaget had three children of his own and observed and chronicled their development throughout their childhood; he used his observations to expand his theories on development that detailed how children learn through exploration and constructed their understanding of reality by interpreting their thoughts and experiences. This ideology later became known more formally as constructivism. In more ways than one, Piaget was a pioneer in the field of developmental psychology and contributed significantly to our understanding of how children learn and develop at various stages of their childhood.

14. What is the main point the passage?

Ⓐ Piaget's theories are largely based on the work of Freud and Binet.
Ⓑ Piaget was a pioneer in the field of developmental psychology and his theories still remain relevant.
Ⓒ Piaget's work was largely based on observation.
Ⓓ Piaget is responsible for our current understanding of intelligence and how it develops.
Ⓔ Cognition is an important field of study.

15. Piaget's hypothesis that children develop their understanding of the world around them through exploration and interpreting their own thoughts and experiences became known as:

Ⓐ Conservatism
Ⓑ Constructivism
Ⓒ Cognition
Ⓓ Child development
Ⓔ Intelligence

16. While working with Binet, Piaget's observations led him to believe that:

Ⓐ Children and adults developed at roughly the same rate.
Ⓑ Adults developed more rapidly than children.
Ⓒ There are observable differences in the cognitive processing of younger children and older children.
Ⓓ Intelligence testing is not effective in younger children.
Ⓔ Intelligence testing is only effective for adults.

VERBAL REASONING

For questions 17-20, select two answers that best complete the blank and produces two sentences that are alike in meaning.

17. After she raided the free sample bin at the expo, Asha had amassed a ______________ of pre-packaged noodles to stock her dorm room pantry.

- (A) dearth
- (B) paucity
- (C) surfeit
- (D) wok
- (E) surplus
- (F) allocation

18. The report contained some strong recommendations on how to improve the current product line. However, the assignment was to explore products that were not previously implemented and the ideas in the report were hardly ______________.

- (A) perfunctory
- (B) pioneering
- (C) conventional
- (D) naïve
- (E) novel
- (F) extant

19. Once the company installed the new fiber optic internet network, their ability to transfer their large files to their counterparts throughout the world led to ______________ advances in their business flow and skyrocketed overall productivity.

- (A) miniscule
- (B) mammoth
- (C) primordial
- (D) revolutionary
- (E) quotidian
- (F) fillip

20. Elephant conservation camps often are the subject of ______________ from animal activists who insist that even the conservation efforts are harmful to the animals and deprive them of their freedom.

- (A) protest
- (B) affirmation
- (C) indignation
- (D) remonstration
- (E) sedition
- (F) agape

STOP

VERBAL REASONING | 20 QUESTIONS
SECTION 6 | 30 MINUTES

DIRECTIONS: Answer each question according to the directions given.

For questions 1 to 8, you are to choose one answer for each blank from the corresponding column of choices.

1. Even the most experienced hikers were intimidated by the ______________ trail that winded scarily up the mountain and led to the Tiger's Nest monastery.

Ⓐ incendiary
Ⓑ sinuous
Ⓒ sacred
Ⓓ decrepit
Ⓔ ancient

2. It was important for the family to adopt a dog with a calm ______________ since their youngest son was autistic and often agitated by sudden and frantic movements.

Ⓐ disposition
Ⓑ opposition
Ⓒ frankness
Ⓓ etiquette
Ⓔ restraint

3. Since the novelist would often ______________ the stories of others by adding just a few of his own words, the critics did not view him as real writer.

Ⓐ alight
Ⓑ abscess
Ⓒ reattribute
Ⓓ attribute
Ⓔ rearticulate

4. The school decided to name the library after Mrs. Leham because of her nearly three decades of (i) ______________ service to the student body, and her impactful role in (ii) ______________ a love of reading in hundreds of young scholars.

Blank i	Blank ii
Ⓐ unswerving	Ⓓ juxtaposing
Ⓑ rigid	Ⓔ cultivating
Ⓒ aspic	Ⓕ fermenting

5. After extinguishing the devastating five-alarm fire and examining the scene, the fire chief was certain that the (i) ______________ was probably started by some sort of ______________ device.

Blank i	Blank ii
Ⓐ burnish	Ⓓ incendiary
Ⓑ coup	Ⓔ infantile
Ⓒ conflagration	Ⓕ incensed

6. Most U.S states partner with the Department of Motor Vehicles to administer a point system for drivers who violate traffic laws. After a driver (i) ______________ a certain number of points in a defined time period, they may be subject to having their licenses (ii)______________ and being unable to legally operate a vehicle during the suspension.

Blank i	Blank ii
Ⓐ accrues	Ⓓ revered
Ⓑ assesses	Ⓔ revoked
Ⓒ abstains	Ⓕ reissued

7. Introverts sometimes find it difficult to work in an environment with lots of (i) ______________ people. Introverts need time to process their thoughts and recharge, and being around people who talk all the time (ii)______________ their ability to do so. To preserve their sanity, introverts often (iii) ______________ to whatever quiet place they can find to enjoy a few minutes of silence.

Blank i
Ⓐ lethargic
Ⓑ loquacious
Ⓒ specious

Blank ii
Ⓓ curtails
Ⓔ propitiates
Ⓕ satiates

Blank iii
Ⓖ corroborate
Ⓗ abscond
Ⓘ squander

8. It was a welcomed change to read a book from an author who discussed the merits of veganism without letting the facts be (i) ______________ by his personal feelings. While the author has been a vegan for over 20 years and has strong feelings about the (ii)______________ effects eating meat and dairy has on the body, he instead wanted to ensure the book had a more positive (iii) ______________, discussing the healthful benefits of a vegan lifestyle.

Blank i
Ⓐ obscured
Ⓑ expunged
Ⓒ occult

Blank ii
Ⓓ legit
Ⓔ deleterious
Ⓕ beleaguered

Blank iii
Ⓖ trajectory
Ⓗ repass
Ⓘ impulse

Questions 9-10 are based on the following passage. Select one answer unless otherwise indicated.

Hillman College is one the most prestigious universities in the South and relies heavily on alumni donations to support its wide-range of student programming and academic offerings. Some of the institution's most notable alumni, such as legends Debbie Allen and Alvin Ailey, are huge benefactors of the school's world-renowned dance program that turns out highly-celebrated dancers each year who go on the prestigious companies like the American Ballet Company and the Royal Academy of the Arts. This year, none of the dancers expected to join a major company received invitations to do so. As a result, Hillman can expect to see a decline in alumni contributions next year.

9. The above argument relies on which of the following assumptions about Hillman College?

Ⓐ Hillman's academic offerings take a backseat to its dance program.
Ⓑ Alumni contributions are critical if the dance program wants to continue to attract top talent.
Ⓒ Hillman alumni contributions depend to an extent on the success of the dancers in the dance program.
Ⓓ No donors will make contributions since no dancers went on to top companies this year.
Ⓔ Debbie Allen and Alvin Ailey will withdraw their financial support.

10. Select the sentence in the passage that most supports the notion that loss of alumni support could be detrimental to Hillman College.

VERBAL REASONING

Questions 11 and 12 are based on the following passage. Select one answer unless otherwise indicated.

In 1934, the U.S was reeling from the effects of the Great Depression, facing rampant unemployment, a nearly dismantled stock market, and a dearth of food and essential resources. The rise of the Third Reich was well under way under the command of Adolf Hitler in 1933; the movement gave rise to the fascist ideas that started to seep into the America rhetoric, being touted by many American supporters of the regime as the only way to address America's state of economic shambles. President Roosevelt was deeply concerned by the proliferation of fascist ideology on American soil as he had already seen the fallout said ideas were having in Germany and worried the same would happen in the U.S.

The Third Reich had begun ignoring democratic safeguards, abrogating certain international treaties, and decisively asserting their need for more land, which they used as justification for their eastward expansion and appropriation of neighboring countries. Roosevelt certainly did not want the U.S, already in a fragile position, to began teeming with the notion that fascism was the answer to mitigate the grim effects of the Great Depression.

11. The author uses the word "abrogating" in the first sentence of the second paragraph, most likely to mean:

Ⓐ disregarding
Ⓑ revising
Ⓒ acknowledging
Ⓓ adjusting
Ⓔ approbating

---

12. President Roosevelt was concerned about fascism causing which of the following in the U.S? Select all the apply.

[A] Democracy would be challenged
[B] The Depression would deepen
[C] Food and resources would be more readily available

Questions 13-15 are based on the following passage. Select one answer unless otherwise indicated.

American author Henry Miller once asserted, "True strength lies in submission which permits one to dedicate his life, through devotion, to something beyond himself." The concept of devotion takes many forms, but none seem to be more powerful than the devotion to one's god or spiritual being. Such a notion is abundantly exemplified in many Hindi texts and not only permeates throughout Hindi culture, but also seems to be the thread weaving throughout the complex and diverse loom of religion that is Hinduism.

Perhaps one of the most demonstrative texts highlighting both the plight and rewards of devotion is the Mahabharata, a smrti text and Sanskrit poem believed to have been a mystical poem that boasts nearly 100,000 verses dissecting and exploring the highs and lows of human nature. The text explores the depths of devotion and invokes a cascade of inflection on what it means to truly capitulate our stakes in the material and mortal world and succumb instead to the relentless worship and devotion to the Supreme, something much larger than our personal selves.

13. The author would most likely agree that the Mahabharata can be characterized as:

- Ⓐ A balanced portrayal of the human experience
- Ⓑ A cynical retort to agnosticisms
- Ⓒ The sine qua non of Hinduism
- Ⓓ A guide to becoming more spiritual
- Ⓔ An in-depth explanation of the complex and diverse loom of religion that is Hinduism

---

14. Which of the following is, according the author, the main premise of Hinduism and the texts mentioned in the passage?

- Ⓐ penance
- Ⓑ devotion
- Ⓒ spirituality
- Ⓓ poetry
- Ⓔ reflection

---

15. Select the sentence in the passage that best describes how one might achieve full devotion to the Supreme.

For questions 16-20, select two answers that best complete the blank and produces two sentences that are alike in meaning.

16. Dr. Lightman is an expert on deception and can tell if a person is lying by studying the ______________ changes in their facial expression that would be unnoticeable to the untrained eye.

- Ⓐ infinitesimal
- Ⓑ imposed
- Ⓒ diminutive
- Ⓓ conspicuous
- Ⓔ examinable
- Ⓕ secondary

---

17. Gary was uncertain of his future with the company after they announced that employees with fewer than 5 years of service were not safe from the next round of layoffs. He ______________ began exploring his options so he could have a plan in the event he was laid off.

- Ⓐ collectively
- Ⓑ proactively
- Ⓒ preemptively
- Ⓓ protractedly
- Ⓔ despondently
- Ⓕ earnestly

VERBAL REASONING

18. Greta often went on endlessly about her religious beliefs and openly expressed her disdain towards those who made lifestyle choices she did not support. Her friends eventually grew tired of her fanatic ______________ and started to avoid her.

- (A) piety
- (B) devotedness
- (C) garrulousness
- (D) dimity
- (E) prudishness
- (F) haughtiness

---

19. In keeping with tradition of showing respect to visiting dignitaries, the guards wore their formal attire and stood at attention while the ______________ processed to the dais.

- (A) granary
- (B) delegation
- (C) pulpit
- (D) entourage
- (E) drumlin
- (F) morula

---

20. Although Jethro wanted to stay outside and work on his car in the garage, when his wife asked him to come in and help prepare for the dinner party, he ______________ to her request, leaving his car project for another day.

- (A) assented
- (B) objected
- (C) acquiesced
- (D) ushered
- (E) abstained
- (F) opposed

STOP

QUANTITATIVE REASONING
ANSWER KEY : SECTION 3

1. **C.**
There are six possible outcomes so the quantities are equal.

2. **A.**
Regardless of how many flips you complete, the chance of the coin landing on heads is always 1/2.

3. **C.**
$x = 5$. So the quantities are the same.

4. **B.**
Solve for x: $\frac{60-56}{60} \bullet 100 = 6.66\%$. So, Column B is greater.

5. **D.**
You do not have enough information to determine the relationship.

6. **C.**
The statements are equivalents since the only option you have is a red card or a non-red card (black) card.

7. **B.**
The probability of drawing a red card after removing 5 black card from the deck is $\frac{26}{47}$ or 55.3%. So, column B is greater.

8. **D.**
Plugging in different positive numbers of x yields various results. The relationship cannot be determined.

9. **A, D.**
$5-3=2$. For the sum to be greater than 1, at least one of the numbers must be positive. Once you select 5, determine which number, when added to 5, will give you are positive number greater than 1. In this case, -3.

10. **E.**
The probability of the selecting a green marble is $\frac{4}{9}$. Since the given probability is in its simplest form, you know that the denominator, which represents the total number of pebbles, must be a multiple of 9. 74 is not a multiple of 9.

11. **D.**
To find the missing angle, you need to first find the value of the missing arc $\widehat{DE}$. Since a circle has 360°, you can find the measure of $\widehat{DE}$ by subtracting the given measurements from 360°. $\widehat{DE}$ is 90°. The measure of the inscribed angle is $\frac{1}{2}$ of the corresponding, so the angle measures 45°.

12. **A.**
To calculate the percentage decrease, find the difference in the annual salaries, which is $40,000. Then divide the original value by the amount change to find the percentage change:

$$\frac{\$40,000}{\$280,000} = .1428 = 14.28\%$$

13. **D.**
First, you must find the median of the original data set {260,000, 280,000, 240,000, 230,000, 240,000}. The median is $240,000. If the increase was ten percent, solve for the amount of increase by multiplying your original value by the percentage increase:

$$(.10)(240000) = 24,000$$

A 10% increase would be $24,000. So, the average annual salary in 2015 was $240,000+$24,000=$264,000.

14. **256.**

There are two possible outcomes for each toss, so the total of possibilities from 8 tosses can be determined by $2^8 = 256$.

15. **C.**
This is a classic quadratic problem. Since you have no coefficient on the first term, you can eliminate A and E. Since the remaining two terms are positive, you can eliminate B as it will yield a negative middle term. The same goes for D.

QUANTITATIVE REASONING
ANSWER KEY : SECTION 3

16. A.

If you draw a diagram to visualize the elements of the table, you will end up with a right triangle. If the table top is 5ft long and the leg is 3ft long, you have two elements of a Pythagorean triple 3:4:5, so the remaining side is 4ft.

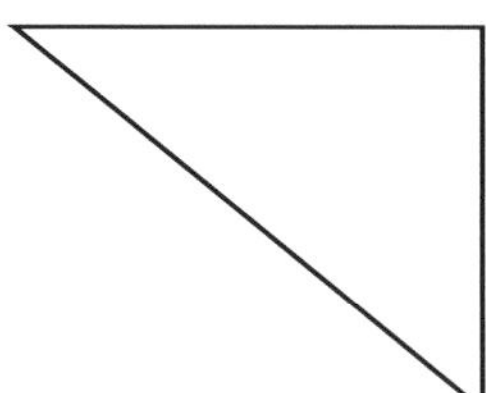

17. B.

To find the surface area of a cube, use the formula $A = 6a^2$ where a is equal to the length of the side. All the sides of a cube are equal and you are given the side with the expression $x+3$. Since you already know that surface area, you can work backwards to find the length of the side. Since the surface area is 6 times the squared value of each side, divide the surface area by 6 to find the length of one side.

$$\frac{486}{6} = 81$$

Next, solve for the length of the side.

$$(x+3)^2 = 81$$

If the value of $(x+3)^2 = 81$, then $x = 3 = 9$. Solve the simplified equation.

$$x + 3 = 9$$
$$x = 6$$

Be careful with the distractor answer choice C. 9 is length of the side but you are only looking for x.

18. 56.

The factorials 8 and 6 contains several similar elements that cancel out each other:

$$\frac{8!}{6!} = \frac{8 \bullet 7 \bullet \cancel{6} \bullet \cancel{5} \bullet \cancel{4} \bullet \cancel{3} \bullet \cancel{2} \bullet \cancel{1}}{\cancel{6} \bullet \cancel{5} \bullet \cancel{4} \bullet \cancel{3} \bullet \cancel{2} \bullet \cancel{1}} = 8 \bullet 7 = 56$$

19. A, B, C, D, E.

This question relies on your understanding of number theory. The product of two even numbers is even, and the product of two odd numbers is always odd. The sum of two odd numbers is always even, as is the sum of two even numbers. The sum of an even and odd number is always odd. All of the answers choices conform to one or more of these rules.

20. B.

There are 360° in a circle. 20 minutes is $\frac{1}{3}$ of an hour, so divide 360 by 3 to determine to degrees the hand moves.

$$\frac{360}{3} = 120$$

QUANTITATIVE REASONING
ANSWER KEY : SECTION 4

1. **C.**
The quantities are equal.

2. **D.**
Plugging in 0 would make the quantities equal while negative and positive numbers would yield different results in terms of which quantity is larger.

3. **C.**
The expressions are equivalent.

4. **A.**
The first ounce is \$.50, so Tom purchases an additional \$2.00 worth of yogurt at \$.20 per ounce. So, his yogurt was 11 ounces.

5. **B.**
If you have a right triangle, one of the angles will measure 90°. The centered information tells you that another angle measures 65°. To find the unknown angle, subtract the know angles from 180°. The angle measurement is 25°.

6. **A.**
41 is a prime number so its greatest prime factor is itself. The greatest prime factor of 68 is 17. So column A is greater.

7. **D.**
Both values are equal to 2. Since *x* could be a negative number, it is not possible to determine the relationship.

8. **A.**
x values in quadrant four are positive while *y* values in quadrant four are negative. So, Column A will always be greater.

9. **B.**
Set up an equation to solve for y.

$$18+6x=\left(y+\frac{1}{5}y\right)=\frac{6}{5}y$$

$\frac{1}{5}$ is the fraction equivalent to 20%.

$$y=\frac{5(18+6x)}{6}=\frac{90+30x}{6}=15+5x$$

10. **62**

$$f(-8)=-8^2+\sqrt[3]{-8}=64+(-2)=62$$

11. **D.**
$1+(2\bullet 1)+(5\bullet 4\bullet 3\bullet 2\bullet 1)=1+2+120=123$

12. **D.**
Do not assume that the discount and the tax cancel each other out and that the ski pants are still \$60.00. \$60.00 being the first answer choice is likely not a coincidence here. Carry out each calculation separately. If the \$60.00 pants were 5% off, then the sale price of the pants was (60)(.05) = 3. So the sale price is \$57.00 Next, add 5% sales tax to the *sale* price, so: (57)(.05) = 2.85, 2.85 + 57 = \$59.85.

13. **D.**
The formula for the circumference of a circle is $C=2\pi r$. So, the circumference is twice the radius. The question asks you for the ratio of the radius to the circumference, however. If the circumference is twice the radius, the radius is half the circumference. So, the ratio of the radius to the circumference is $\frac{1}{2}\pi$.

14. **E.**
When dividing radicals, simply divide values on both sides of the radical sign.

$$\frac{8\sqrt{12}}{2\sqrt{3}}=\frac{4\sqrt{12}}{\sqrt{3}}=4\sqrt{4}=4\bullet 2=8$$

15. **C.**
The angles are vertical angles and are always congruent. So, the measurement of angle b is the same as the measurement for the given angle.

16. **D.**
When you put the equation in slope-intercept form, you have $y=-\frac{9}{4}$. The line is horizontal and has no slope.

QUANTITATIVE REASONING
ANSWER KEY : SECTION 4

17. C.

$$(150000)(.32)+(150000)(.08)=\$60,000$$

18. A.

The new total budget amount after the grant is $155,000. If the allocations are to remain the same percentage wise, find the dollar amount allocated to conservation by: $(155000)(.33)=\$51,150$

19. E.

This is a classic distance problem, though the question only gives you the coordinates of one point explicitly. However, the origin is always (0, 0), so that is your second coordinate that you will plug into the distance formula.

$$d=\sqrt{(0-(-3))^2+(0-(-4))^2}$$

$$d=\sqrt{9+16}$$

$$d=\sqrt{25}=5$$

20. 64.

Each face of a cube is a square. There are six faces on a cube. So, divide the surface area by 6 to find the area of each square.

$$\frac{96}{2}=16$$

16 is the area of each square, and the area of a square is found by calculating the value of s^2. So, $s=4$. The volume of a cube is found by calculating the value of s^3, so $4^3=64$.

VERBAL REASONING

ANSWER KEY : SECTION 5

1. **B.**
Keith tried the conceal the exchange. Clandestine means secret or hidden.

2. **B.**
Banal means trivial or trite.

3. **A.**
Walt is the paragon or epitome of integrity and kindness.

4. **A, D.**
Peter Kohls was known for his courageous and daring journeys and harrowing experiences, according to the second sentence. The tone of the sentence is positive, so the first blank should be positive and reflect back on Kohl's adventures. Intrepid means fearless, bold, or courageous and fits blank one. The book provided even more insight into Kohl's life as a result of the author's research. Superlative means outstanding or exceptional and can accurately characterize the author's research.

5. **B, E.**
The impact of the Great Depression worsened over the years, so they were not abrupt or all of a sudden. The had a more gradual progression. After unemployment rose and the availability of resources declined, Americans faced destitute, or impoverished conditions.

6. **A, E.**
The dessert was already over-the-top and the garnish only added to that. It was unnecessary or gratuitous. The words for the second blank is closely related in meaning as it explains that the garnish was superfluous or unessential, and added nothing to the dish.

7. **B, D, H.**
The policy reduced control of the investors. Attenuated means to decrease or weaken. The investors asserted or brandished their power inappropriately. The investors were not in support of the policy change and threatened action. Lambasted means criticized or condemned, so it fits in this instance.

8. **C, D, H.**
The context clue for the first blank is located in the second sentence. The father was upset by the lack of remorse shown. Stolidly means unemotional or lacking sensitivity. Incensed means angry or enraged which explains why the father lunged towards the attacker. The DA blocked the path, so she obstructed it.

9. **C.**
Emerson describes the problem of devotion and the lack of reliance on our sense by saying "this is a disease like a thickening of the skin until the vital organs are destroyed" Emerson believes the *disease* is the problem of sensuousness.

10. **A.**
The author starts the passage by disclosing that he himself if not prudent and lacks many of the skills he discussed in the passage.

11. **C.**
The passage focuses heavily on the need for understanding of prudence and the prioritization of sensory experiences.

12. **C.**
The passage primarily focuses on the imminent eruption of Katla.

13. **A, B.**
Katla did not erupt following the eruption of Eyjafjallajökull as it had historically done. The ice cap sits atop the volcano and is likely to melt rapidly and cause major flooding. Answer choice C contradicts information in the passage.

14. **B.**
The passage focuses primarily on Piaget's contributions to the field of developmental psychology.

15. **B.**
The passage explicitly mentions constructivism as the formal name assigned to Piaget's hypothesis.

16. **C.**
While working with Binet, Piaget observed noticeable differences in the cognitive processing of young children and older children and adults.

VERBAL REASONING
ANSWER KEY : SECTION 5

17. C, E.
Amassed means stockpiled or hoarded. After she raided the free sample bin, you can infer that she had a considerable amount of samples. Surfeit and surplus are synonyms for oversupply or excess.

18. B, E.
The report offered suggestions on enhancements to existing products but the assignment asked for ideas about new products. Because the report addressed existing products, the products were not original; novel and pioneering both mean original or innovative.

19. B, D.
The upgrades to the internet network positively impacted the business flow and led to large increases in overall productivity as indicated by the use of the word skyrocketed. You are looking for words that reflect a largely positive change. Mammoth and revolutionary both fit the bill.

20. A, D.
Conservations have a negative perception of elephant camps as evidenced by their beliefs that they deprive animals of their freedom. You are looking for words that reflect their inclination to speak out against the conservation camps. To be subject to protest or remonstration is to be subject to objection or disapproval, which accurately characterizes how animal activists feel about conservation camps.

VERBAL REASONING
ANSWER KEY : SECTION 6

1. **B.**
The trail was scarily windy. Sinuous means winding of twisting.

2. **A.**
Disposition is temperament or personality.

3. **E.**
The novelist simply reworked others' writing and peppered a few of his own ideas in the mix. He reshaped or recalculated to make them appear to be news works.

4. **A, E.**
As Mrs. Lehman has been honored by having a building named after her, it can be inferred that she had a positive impact throughout her 30 years of unswerving, or dedicated service to the student body. In her role, she fostered or cultivated a love of reading in hundreds of young scholars.

5. **C, D.**
A conflagration is another word for fire. The fire chief believe an incendiary or flammable device was responsible for the fire.

6. **A, E.**
Violators accumulate or accrue points, they may get their licenses revoked or suspended.

7. **B, D, H.**
The context clue for the first blank is found in the second sentence. The blank refers to people who talk all the time. Loquacious means overly talkative, so it fits in the blank. When introverts are around loquacious people, their ability to recharge is hindered or curtailed and they sometimes need to find a place to go to enjoy silence. Abscond means to escape and fits in the blank here.

8. **A, E, G.**
The author's personal feelings did not conceal or obscure his discussion of the merits of veganism. Whatever the effects are for the second blank, they are the opposite of positive as indicated by the transition words "while" and "instead". Trajectory is a direction or arc.

9. **C.**
The author assumes that at least some Hillman alumni will reconsider their donations based on the lack of dancers who went on the major companies.

10.
Hillman College is one the most prestigious universities in the South and relies heavily on alumni donations to support its wide-range of student programming and academic offerings.

11. **A.**
The Third Reich was abrogating or disregarding established treaties.

12. **A.**
Roosevelt feared that fascism in the U.S would have similar consequences as it did in Germany. Only threatened democracy is listed as a consequence in the passage.

13. **A.**
The text explored the plight and rewards of devotion and dissected the high and lows of human nature.

14. **B.**
"The concept of devotion takes many forms, but none seem to be more powerful than the devotion to one's god or spiritual being." The passage mentions devotion several times throughout the passage.

15.
The text explores the depths of devotion and invokes a cascade of inflection on what it means to truly capitulate our stakes in the material and mortal world and succumb instead to the relentless worship and devotion to the Supreme, something much larger than our personal selves.

16. **A, C.**
The changes in facial expression are unnoticeable to the untrained eye. It can be inferred that the changes are not obvious, but rather more obscure changes that alert Dr. Lightman to deception. Infinitesimal and diminutive are synonyms and both mean minute or tiny.

VERBAL REASONING
ANSWER KEY : SECTION 6

17. B, C.
Gary started to explore his other options before learning whether or not he would be laid off. To do something proactively or preemptively mean to initiate it before it needs to be done usually in anticipation of a particular outcome. Earnest could reasonably fit in the blank if not for the last sentence which alludes to the proactive nature of his intentions. To pursue something earnestly means to pursue it seriously or intently. While Gary may have also been serious on intentional about his search, the context clues and the fact that there is no word to match earnestly make answer choice F incorrect.

18. A, B.
The sentence refers to Greta's expression of her religious views are fanatic. Piety and devotedness both have religious connotations and mean a steadfast commitment to beliefs. Her piety and devotedness, or her belief in and commitment to her religious beliefs were fanatic.

19. B, D.
The context clues tell you that visiting dignitaries are processing to the dais, or podium. A delegation or entourage is a group of representatives.

20. A, C.
Jethro gave into or agreed to his wife's request. Acquiesced and assented both mean to agree or conceded.

Raw Score	Scaled Score
40	170
39	169
38	168
37	167
36	166
35	165
34	164
33	163
32	162
31	161
30	160
29	159
28	158
27	157
26	156
25	155
24	154
23	153
22	152
21	151

Raw Score	Scaled Score
20	150
19	149
18	148
17	147
16	146
15	145
14	144
13	143
12	142
11	141
10	140
9	139
8	138
7	137
6	136
5	135
4	134
3	133
2	132
1	131

These practice tests are designed to simulate actual testing conditions as closely as possible. While the questions are similar to those you will encounter on the GRE, the sections are not adaptive for Verbal and Quantitative Reasoning like they will be if you sit for the computer-adaptive exam. The scale above gives you an **idea** of your projected score and can help you monitor your progress as you become more familiar with the material. The scale above is a rough guide to predict your score. **As a reminder**, the PowerPrep II software distributed by ETS offers two free computer-adaptive exams to supplement your study plan. Be sure to include those exams in your study plan in addition to the exams in this section; this will help you get an idea of the areas you need to study more closely in order to reach your scoring goals.

FOR ACCESS TO PRACTICE
TESTS 7 AND 8 PLEASE VISIT:
www.einstein-academy.com/GRE

ARGO
BROTHERS

VOCABULARY

aberration: noun – deviating from the right path or usual course of action; a mental disorder, especially of a minor or temporary nature. *Everyone was sure that Yoo's poor race performance was an aberration, and that he would run faster at the championship meet.*

abstinence: noun – the giving up of certain pleasures such as food or drink. *During Lent, many people believe that abstinence from indulgences helps them be more reflective and open to spiritual guidance.*

abstract: adjective – theoretical, not applied or practical; not concrete; hard to understand. *The artwork was a bit too abstract for Janna to understand; all she saw was dots and lines, not the masterpiece everyone else claimed to see.*

acclaim: noun – loud applause; approval. *Gina's discovery of the gene mutation earned her great acclaim in the science community.*

acquiesce: verb – to accept the conclusions or arrangements of others; to accede; to give consent by keeping silent. *The teacher refused to acquiesce to the student's request for an extension on the assignment since ample time had already been allotted.*

admonish: verb – to advise against something; to warn; to scold gently; to urge strongly. *Andrew admonished Doug for failing to turn on the alarm after he left.*

advocate: verb – to support; to be in favor of. *David failed to advocate for his employees' needs; as a result, they all left and found better positions in another department.*

aesthetic; adjective – showing an appreciation of beauty in nature or art; artistic. *The designer's fresh aesthetic won over the judges at the fashion show.*

affinity: noun – natural attraction to a person or liking for a thing; relation; connection. *Emily has an affinity for unique craft beers and single-malt whiskey.*

aggrandizement: noun – to increase in rank or wealth; growth in power. *I attributed the lieutenant's aggressiveness towards his subordinates to his need for aggrandizement and validation.*

alienate: verb – to turn away the normal feelings of fondness toward anyone; to estrange. *Jess felt alienated by her peers after they discovered she she had inadvertently gotten them in trouble for skipping school.*

alleviate: verb – to make easier to endure; to relieve; to diminish. *Serena asked for an ice pack in hopes that it would alleviate her pain.*

altruistic: adjective – thoughtful of the welfare of others. *Father Merchant was known for his altruistic deeds; he gave freely to those in need and encouraged others to do the same.*

ambiguous: adjective – permitting more than one interpretation; not clearly defined. *Based on the union rep's ambiguous remarks, the workers were not sure whose side he was actually on.*

ambivalence: noun – condition of having conflicting attitudes. *The director's ambivalence toward his cast made way for lots of confusion and uncomfortable interactions.*

ameliorate: verb – to make better or more tolerable; to improve. *Seeing that tensions were flying, Berry stepped in and tried to ameliorate the situation by asking everyone to take a break and reconvene later.*

analogous: adjective – similar in certain qualities; comparable. *The engineer said that the new machine was analogous to the human heart.*

anonymity: noun- condition of being nameless or unknown. *The witness agreed to speak only under the condition of anonymity because he feared for his life.*

antithesis: noun – direct opposite. *While most people believe twins are exactly alike, Laura is the antithesis of her twin Kate in every way.*

apocryphal: adjective – of doubtful authenticity; counterfeit. *The Easter Bunny is one of the most recognizable apocryphal symbols in the world.*

arduous: adjective – hard to do; strenuous. *The marathon was more arduous than Victor anticipated, especially since it started to rain as soon as he started the hilly part of the course.*

articulate: adjective – able to put one's thoughts into words easily and clearly. *The attorney was able to clearly articulate the facts of his client's self-defense case and convince the jury of his client's innocence.*

augment: verb – to increase or enlarge; to become greater in size. *Ryan suggested to his manager that they augment the amount budgeted for the main event in order to make sure enough funds were available for adequate security.*

belittle: verb – to make something seem less important. *The candidate tried to belittle her competitor by repeatedly mentioning that she only had a community college degree.*

bequeath: verb – to leave money or property by a will; to pass along. *Dawn bequeathed her estate to her daughters to split evenly.*

bizarre: adjective – strikingly odd in appearance or style; grotesque. *The zombie movie had too many bizarre and gory scenes for Taylor; he turned it off before it was finished.*

blithe: adjective – happy and cheerful; gay. *Despite the unfortunate circumstances, Linda remained blithe and positive and tried to encourage those around her to see the silver lining.*

bombastic: adjective – high-sounding; marked by use of language without much real meaning. *The review board was not impressed with the doctor's bombastic plea and proceeded with the hearing to review whether or not he should keep his medical license.*

buffoon: noun – a clown; someone who amuses with tricks and jokes. *Sila often acted like a buffoon to make her friends and family laugh.*

cache: noun – a hiding place; something hidden in a hiding place. *The battle took a turn for the worse when the enemy bombers destroyed the cache of weapons the squadron had stored away for later use.*

cacophony: noun- discord; harsh sound. *Her thoughts were interrupted by a cacophony of construction noises from the nearby building site.*

cajole: verb – to persuade by pleasant words or false promises. *The private investigator tried to cajole the neighbor into lying for his client by offering him part of the insurance settlement his client stood to receive.*

callous: adjective – unfeeling; insensitive. *Cynthia was not expecting her husband's callous response to her suggestion that they see a therapist.*

capitulate: verb – to surrender; to cease resisting. *The rebels finally decide to capitulate when they realized they were surrounded and had no where to run or hide.*

capricious: adjective – changeable, fickle. *The weather in Chiang Mai has been so capricious lately that it has been nearly impossible to make outdoor plans based on the weather reports.*

carping: adjective – complaining. *Carl spent most of the trip carping about how uncomfortable his train seat was and how awful the food tasted.*

catalyst: noun – someone or something that brings about a change. *The conference was just the catalyst Evita needed to kick-start her new business venture.*

catharsis: noun – an emotional purification or relief. *The movie provoked more of a catharsis than even the directors imagined.*

caustic: adjective – stinging, biting. *The caustic environment caused Pamela to seek another place of employment.*

celestial: adjective – having to do with the heavens; divine. *The clouds and setting sun treated onlookers to a celestial display of colors and natural beauty.*

chimerical: adjective – absurd; wildly fanciful. *The chimerical effigies in the haunted house were hardly scary; more people laughed at them than were afraid of them.*

clairvoyant: adjective –having exceptional insight. *The fortune-teller claimed to be clairvoyant and insisted that the police take her vision of the impending threat seriously.*

clandestine: adjective – secret or hidden. *The clandestine passageway led to a secret garden full of poppies and intricate topiaries.*

colloquial: adjective – conversational; used in an informal speech or writing. *Wanting to better relate to his constituents, Robert abandoned his formal tone and spoke in a more colloquial manner during the town hall.*

commiserate: verb – to sympathize with; to feel sorrow for another's suffering. *Jack and his co-worker met up after work to eat ice cream and commiserate about their demanding boss.*

composure: noun – calmness. *Everyone was surprised by how well the bank teller was able to maintain her composure during the bank robbery.*

copious: adjective – abundant. *Reese drank copious amounts of coffee while trying to finish writing her book.*

dearth: noun – shortage. *The dearth of resources led to the quick demise of the colony.*

debilitate: verb – to weaken. *The spike strips debilitated the vehicle by deflating its tires.*

deference: noun – great respect. *The squadron always showed deference towards older, more decorated officers.*

deprecate: verb – to express strong disapproval of. *Mark grew tired of his mother-in-law constantly deprecating him and his profession.*

derogatory: adjective- tending to lower in estimation; degrading. *Bill neglected to pay his outstanding bill, so a derogatory mark was placed on his credit report.*

desecrate: verb – to treat with disrespect. *The tourists were arrested for desecrating the ancient temples of Angkor Wat.*

deter: verb – to discourage; to keep someone from doing something. *Laura did not let the slim possibility of success deter her from entering the competition.*

devoid: adjective – entirely without; lacking. *The campsite was devoid of any possible water source, and the rangers were forced to relocate.*

diatribe: noun – a denunciation; bitter verbal attack. *The politician's insult-laden diatribe angered many of the citizens and caused them to seriously reconsider whether or not to re-elect him.*

didactic: adjective – intended to instruct. *Once Sarah finished the didactic portion of the course, she enrolled in the practicum to gain hands-on experience treating patients.*

diffuse: adjective – spread out; wordy. *The hall monitor tried to diffuse the situation before it escalated and required the involvement of formal sanctions.*

disdain: noun – a feeling of contempt for anything that is regarded as unworthy; scorn. *The Queen looked on in disdain as the prisoner was escorted into the court to face charges of treason.*

dismantle: verb – to pull down; to take apart. *The sharp student used well-known facts to quickly dismantle the teacher's circumstantial argument.*

disparage: verb – to discredit; to belittle. *Sue grew tired of the disparaging remarks from her coach and decided to quit the team.*

ebb: verb – to decline. *The lottery winnings continued to ebb and Gretchen carelessly purchased big-ticket items and fancy trips.*

eclectic: adjective – consisting of selections from various sources. *Bryce was known for his eclectic sense of style and his quirky personality.*

efface: verb – to wipe out; to erase. *The thief attempted to efface the evidence of his crime to no avail; the police quickly captured him.*

effervescent: adjective – lively; giving off bubbles. *Corey's effervescent personality rubbed off on all those around him; it's no wonder he was always invited to parties.*

egregious: adjective – extraordinarily bad. *Sam's egregious error was hard to overlook no matter how unintentional it was.*

elucidate: verb – to make clear. *The event this weekend elucidated the need for better crowd management policies.*

embellish: verb – to decorate; to elaborate upon. *Katniss loved sparkly things and would often use glitter and crystals to embellish her shoes and accessories.*

emulate: verb – to try to equal or surpass. *Tina was committed to becoming the best ballerina around and often emulated Misty Copland's style and choreography to try to push herself to the next level.*

enigma: noun – a puzzle; a baffling situation. *The stone was a real enigma to the archeologists since they had never seen anything like it and nothing similar had been found on the entire continent.*

ephemeral: adjective – lasting for only a short time. *Rick had an ephemeral feeling of nostalgia every time he drove past his old house.*

equivocate: verb – to use ambiguous or unclear expressions in order to mislead; to be shifty; to hedge. *Unlike his competitor who was very clear about his stance on the matter, Harold preferred instead to equivocate on the issue.*

esoteric: adjective – understood by only a few; little known; obscure. *The once esoteric band became a national sensation after being featured on a popular online music blog.*

exacerbate: verb – to make a situation worse; to irritate. *William tried to help, but his involvement only exacerbated the situation.*

exemplary: adjective – serving as a model. *Justin was an exemplary mentor for the internal medicine residents.*

expedite: verb – to make easy and quick; to speed up. *The mail-forwarding service had several options available for those who wanted to expedite the delivery of their orders.*

expunge: verb – to erase; to remove completely. *The law student asked for his record to be expunged since his arrest was found to be unjustified.*

extol: verb – to praise highly. *The convent was extolled for having the best egg tarts in all of Portugal.*

fastidious: adjective – hard to please; dainty in taste. *Jasmine was so fastidious that no one knew what to get her for her birthday.*

fervor: noun – intense emotion; great warmth of feeling. *His fervor when discussing current events was a shock to the generally calm group.*

flagrant: adjective – outrageous; glaringly offensive. *The coach argued that the foul was flagrant and deserved a stiffer penalty.*

fledgling: adjective - newly developed; little known. *The fledgling start-up secured a large grant from an angle investor.*

forlorn: adjective - deserted; left alone and neglected; unhappy. *The forlorn gazelle grazed aimlessly hoping to stumble upon his herd.*

formidable: adjective - hard to overcome; to be dreaded. *The warped wall proved to be a formidable challenge for the competitive skate boarder.*

galvanize: verb - to arouse suddenly; to startle. *The massive oil spill quickly galvanized efforts to prevent the transport of crude via boats and barges.*

garbled: adjective - confused; mixed up. *The formatting was garbled making the document hard to read.*

garner: verb - to gather and store away; to collect. *Fanny was able to garner the support of her family to help her train for the obstacle course race.*

garrulous: adjective - talkative. *Wendy's garrulous nature was annoying to her roommate who preferred to be left alone in silence.*

gratuitous: adjective - freely given; unnecessary; uncalled-for. *The gratuitous violence in the movie was a distraction from the main storyline.*

gullible: adjective - easily deceived. *The con man took advantage of Austin's gullible nature and swindled him out of thousands of dollars.*

hackneyed: adjective - used too often; trite; commonplace. *The hackneyed décor made the café seem more like a chain restaurant rather than the trendy hotspot it purported to be.*

hedonist: noun - one who lives solely for pleasure. *Pai is a haven for hedonists given its remote location and rampant availability of drugs and alcohol.*

heretic: noun - a person who upholds religious doctrines contrary to the established beliefs of his church. *Joan of Arc was considered a heretic because she supposedly saw visions that contradicted the monarchy.*

homogeneous: adjective - similar; uniform in nature. *The rabbits had been carefully breed to ensure they all had homogenous phenotypes.*

hyperbole: noun - an exaggerated statement used as a figure of speech for rhetorical effect. *Although they were well aware that the motivational speaker's speech was full of hyperbole, they were motivated by the deeper implications of the speaker's rhetoric.*

iconoclast: noun - a person who attacks cherished beliefs or established institutions. *Gerald was proud of being labeled an iconoclast and stood by his decision to promulgate the hypocrisy of the well-respected university.*

imminent: adjective - about to occur. *Everyone knew the storm was imminent and prepared their houses by boarding up windows and placing sandbags around the perimeter.*

impassive: adjective - without feelings or emotion; insensible. *Greg sat looking impassively out the window, unable to feel anything after losing his beloved dog, Jake.*

incongruous: adjective - inappropriate; out of place. *The sale of alcohol was incongruous with the family-oriented nature of the event.*

incorrigible: adjective - too firmly fixed to be reformed or changed. *Helsa's behavior was incorrigible; after several intervention programs and various therapeutic approaches, it was clear nothing could assuage her aggression or limit her violent outbursts.*

indefatigable: adjective - tireless. *Pim's indefatigable efforts as a medical volunteer with the Peace Corps earned her national recognition and a scholarship from a local university.*

indigent: adjective - poverty stricken. *The government made a special effort to ensure the indigent population in the city had adequate housing and clothing during the brutally cold winter.*

ingratiate: verb - to make oneself acceptable. *Amy was constantly trying to ingratiate herself in hopes that her boss would notice and give her the promotion she desperately wanted.*

innocuous: adjective - harmless. *The bug looked big and scary, but in reality, it was rather innocuous.*

insurgent: noun - one who rises in revolt. *The insurgents launched a debilitating assault on the capital.*

intemperate: adjective - lacking in self-control. *John was intemperate when it came to chocolate; he just could not seem to stop eating it.*

jargon: noun - the specialized vocabulary of members of a group. *Most of the document was in the local jargon and was not easily understood by outsiders.*

judicious: adjective - wise; careful; showing sound judgment; prudent. *The principal handled the complaint judiciously, ensuring all parties had a chance to share their version of the story and that all facts were considered carefully.*

kindle: verb – to ignite; to arouse or inspire; to catch fire; to become aroused. *With the wind blowing furiously, Answar found it difficult to kindle the fire.*

lackluster: adjective – lacking brightness; dull; lacking liveliness, vitality, or enthusiasm. *Clint's lackluster response signaled that he might no longer be interested in serving as chair of the commission.*

laconic: adjective – brief or terse in speech; using few words. *Aldridge delivered a laconic but impactful speech after securing a win in the primary.*

lassitude: noun – state or feeling of being tired and listless; weariness. *The lassitude of the team was understandable given the arduous conditions they were forced to work under for several months.*

laudable: adjective – worthy of praise. *The board rewarded Ellen's laudable achievements by promoting her to project lead.*

lethargic: adjective – drowsy; dull; sluggish; indifferent. *The medication caused Dillon to be lethargic and foggy; he stayed home on the couch until he made a full recovery.*

levity: noun – lightness; lack of seriousness; fickleness. *Graham's sense of humor injected some much needed levity into the once tense atmosphere.*

listless: adjective – indifferent; marked by a lack of energy or enthusiasm. *The dog sat listlessly in the corner, not wanting to even go for a walk.*

lucid: adjective – easily understood; rational; clear; clear-minded. *It takes Tina about four cups of coffee to become lucid in the mornings.*

malicious: adjective- spiteful; intentionally mischievous or harmful. *Though he had no malicious intent, his negligence still caused a great deal of harm to those involved.*

marred: verb – injured; spoiled; damaged; disfigured. *The graffiti artist marred the newly erected statute in the square, covering it with spray paint and decals.*

meager: adjective – thin; lean; of poor quality or small amount. *Though he came from a meager background, Fred managed to make the most of what he had.*

meandering: verb – winding back and forth; rambling. *Meandering the streets and alley ways of a new city is one of the best ways to tap into the local culture.*

mitigate: verb – to make or to become milder or less severe; to moderate. *John hoped that drinking coffee would help mitigate the drowsiness caused by the medicine.*

nomenclature: noun – a systematic naming in an art or science. *The nomenclature of the chemical compound was more complicated than scientists originally suspected.*

nonchalance: noun – carelessness; lack of interest or concern. *Bert's nonchalance did little to help him convince his manager that he was ready for a promotion.*

obliterate: verb – to blot out leaving no traces; to destroy. *The nuclear bomb obliterated the old camp site, leaving nothing but charred and barren land behind.*

obscure: adjective – not clear or distinct; hidden; remote; not well known. *The obscure metal was once used by the ancient Romans to make swords and drinking vats.*

officious: adjective – meddling; giving unnecessary or unwanted advice or services. *Baxter's officious manner helped her gain friends, but once they discovered her true nature, they strayed away from her.*

opulent: adjective – wealthy; abundant. *The opulent stateroom was full of unique treasures and artifacts.*

overt: adjective – not hidden; open. *The overt sexism of the sportscaster did not go unnoticed; several people filed complaints with the network and the sportscaster was relieved of his duties.*

pariah: noun – an outcast. *Because of his shady past, the old man was treated like a pariah by a majority of the townspeople.*

parsimonious: adjective – too thrifty; stingy. *The parsimonious businessman amassed a small fortune as as a result of his frugality but rarely enjoyed the fruits of his labor because he was so focused on saving.*

paucity: noun – scarcity; smallness in number or amount. *The city was deeply impacted by the paucity of teacher's; they had to bring in teachers from a neighboring city to ensure they were able to staff all their classrooms at the start of the school year.*

peerless: adjective – having no equal; better than the rest. *Jasper's peerless athleticism made him the envy of football players throughout the state.*

perfidy: noun- treachery; betrayal of trust. *Pierce found it hard to grapple with the perfidy of his long-time training partner and friend.*

peruse: verb – to study; to read. *The director asked the panel to peruse the material before the interview started so that they could formulate specific questions about the candidate's credentials.*

philistine: adjective – narrow-minded; smugly conventional. *Heidi's philistine views were not warmly received by the stanchly liberal crowd.*

piety: noun – devotion and reverence, especially to god and family. *In addition to the pastor's piety, the congregation appreciated his sense of duty to the youth of the church and to the community.*

pique: verb – to hurt the feelings of or make resentful; to arouse; to excite. *The commercial piqued Jenna's curiosity about the new video game and prompted her to do some more research on its features.*

placate: verb – to soothe; to pacify. *Jade tried to placate the upset child with ice cream and candy to no avail.*

plagiarize: verb – to take ideas or writings from someone else and present them as one's own; to use without giving credit. *The thesis committee failed to approve the dissertation once they realized that a significant portion of it was plagiarized.*

ponderous: adjective – very heavy; bulky; labored and dull or tiresome. *Matt spent months in a ponderous state after his company failed; he hashed over every single business decision and transaction that could have made a difference in the outcome.*

pragmatic: adjective – practical; opinionated; concerned with actual practice rather than with theory or speculation. *The city council appointed Gerard to chair the budget committee because of his pragmatic approach to financial management.*

quandary: noun – condition of being doubtful or confused. *Weighing the benefits and potential drawbacks of the underwater pump left the environmentalists in a quandary.*

querulous: adjective – peevish; faultfinding; expressing or suggestive of complaint. *The camp staff became adept at ignoring the camper's querulous demands for attention.*

quixotic: adjective – idealistic and utterly impractical. *It is quixotic to think that we can ignore the inevitable consequences of climate change.*

rancor: noun – deep spite or malice; strong hate or bitter feeling. *His rancor towards his in-laws did little to ease the tensions between the families.*

rebuff: verb – to refuse in a sharp or due way; to snub; to drive or beat back. *The actress felt like she was rebuffed by the Academy for the third consecutive year.*

recalcitrant: adjective – refusing to obey or follow orders; unmanageably resistant. *Colin was expelled from the military academy for his recalcitrant attitude and his unwillingness to follow the rules.*

recluse: noun- a person who lives alone, away from others. *The kid in the neighborhood considered the old woman a recluse since she never came outside.*

redundant: adjective – wordy; exceeding what is necessary or normal; lavish; overflowing. *The newsletter was redundant; each article shared the same facts using different words and phrasing.*

refurbish: verb – to freshen or polish again; to make like new. *Although the laptop was refurbished, it looked and worked like new.*

rejuvenate: verb – to make young or fresh again. *Angela felt rejuvenated after spending the day at the spa.*

relic: noun – a thing or part that remains from the past; something kept as sacred because it belonged to a saint. *The pilgrims made the journey to Vezelay where the relics of Mary Magdalene were supposedly buried.*

repugnant: adjective – disgusting; loathsome; objectionable; incompatible. *The Ambassador held nothing back in his speech that condemned the repugnant actions of the opposition party.*

rescind: verb – to cancel; to repeal; to set aside. *The committee discovered that Stephen lied about his credentials and decided to rescind his offer of admission.*

residual: adjective – left over, remaining. *The residual crumbs on his mouth gave Oscar away when he tried to deny that he was the one who took the cookies from the jar.*

resilient: adjective – getting back strength or spirits quickly; springing back into shape or position. *The garden was resilient and bounced back quickly after being nearly destroyed by the storm.*

respite: noun – a temporary cessation or postponement, usually of something disagreeable; interval of rest. *After a long day wrangling unruly children at the slumber party, Kate treated herself to wine and a bubble bath, a much needed respite before the children woke up again.*

sagacious: adjective – very wise or shrewd. *The Dali Lama is a sagacious and unbiased leader revered for his wisdom and his commitment to fairness and equality.*

salutary: adjective – healthful; useful or helpful; remedial. *Esther acknowledged that although her father's lecture was hard to swallow, it was salutary and helped her refocus her behavior.*

sanction: noun – authorized approval or permission; support or encouragement; something that gives binding force to a law. *The Olympic Committee sanctioned the cyclers, stripping those who tested positive for doping of their medals.*

saturate: verb – to soak through and through; to fill completely. *The cloth was saturated with the dye in order to create a vibrant print.*

scapegoat: noun – one taking the blame for the mistake and crimes of others. *Dean Smith, wanting to avoid being held responsible for the email scandal, made Dean Hammonds the scapegoat and she took the fall instead.*

scoff: verb – to mock or jeer at; to make fun of. *The fans scoffed at the other team and mocked their odd looking mascot.*

scrupulous: adjective – very honest and conscientious; careful about claimed expense. *To avoid an unfavorable audit, the businessman kept scrupulous records of all his expenses.*

scrutinize: verb – to look at very carefully; to inspect minutely. *Every move the account administrator made was scrutinized since he was good friends with the bank manager who was recently indicted on fraud charges.*

sectarian: adjective – pertaining to a group within a larger group that is limited by common beliefs or interests; narrow-minded. *The small group of priests drew ire from religious leaders for perpetuating sectarian ideas that were not aligned with the larger mission of the faith.*

sequester: verb – to hide or keep away from others; to withdraw into seclusion; to confiscate; to segregate. *The judges were sequestered in a room so that they could deliberate without influence from outside sources.*

serene: adjective – unruffled; tranquil; unclouded. *The house was perched on the side of the hill and offered unobstructed views of the blue serene sea.*

skeptical: adjective – not easily persuaded or convinced. *Kim was skeptical of the sudden increase in test scores and asked the school board to launch an investigation.*

sobriety: noun – seriousness, gravity, or solemnity; absence of alcoholic intoxication. *Calvin celebrated 20 years of sobriety with cake and alcohol-free sparkling cider.*

taciturn: adjective –laconic; uncommunicative. *Discontent with her job, Sophia became withdrawn and taciturn; she spent most of her time in her office and barely returned calls or emails.*

tangential: adjective – diverging or digressing. *The conversation was tangential at best, barely focusing on the main point for more than a few seconds.*

tawdry: adjective – gaudy and cheap; vulgarly ornamental. *The display was tawdry and salacious and solicited much admonishment from offended customers.*

tedious: adjective – long or verbose and wearisome; tiresome; boring. *The problem sets were tedious and time-consuming; everyone complained that they were just busy work with no real value.*

temerity: noun – rashness; foolish or reckless boldness. *AJ's temerity in constantly challenging his manager cost him his promotion and landed him on probation.*

tenet: noun – a principle, doctrine, or belief held as a truth by a group. *The disciples worked hard to practice the tenets of their faith in all their endeavors.*

terse: adjective – using only a few words but clear to the point; polished. *Theresa was often terse when delivering her opening statement, believing that the jury only needed to hear a clear presentation of the facts.*

threadbare: adjective – frayed or shabby; used so often that it is stale. *The children played so much in their playroom that patches of the carpet had become threadbare.*

thwart: verb – to oppose directly; to baffle; to block; to frustrate. *The construction project was thwarted by activists who contented building the new bridge would destroy protected greenspace.*

tirade: noun – a long, angry, or scolding speech; a harangue. *The public was disappointed in the candidate's insult-laden tirade about the judge assigned to his case.*

trepidation: noun – a trembling; apprehension; a state of alarm and dread. *The team moved forward with trepidation, not sure what was ahead in the dense forest.*

unassailable: adjective – undeniable; unquestionable; not able to attack. *Erica's version of the story was unassailable; video evidence confirmed all the details she shared.*

undermine: verb – to dig or to make a tunnel under; to wear away and weaken the support of; to injure or to weaken in a slow or sneaky way. *Shannon hoped that her injuries were not going to undermine her ability to perform in the track meet.*

unequivocal: adjective – plain; very clear in meaning. T*he professor was impressed by the student's unequivocal explanation of the complex theorem.*

ungainly: adjective – clumsy; awkward; hard to handle. *Tim had trouble maneuvering his way down the steps with the ungainly air cast on his ankle.*

unimpeachable: adjective – beyond doubt or reproach; unquestionable. *The prosecution believed their witness was unimpeachable; they were sure the jury would have no issues believing everything in his statement.*

unobtrusive: adjective – not readily noticeable; inconspicuous. *Given his height and large stature, it was nearly impossible for Tony to make an unobtrusive entrance into a room.*

unscathed: adjective – undamaged; unharmed. *The car was completely totaled in the accident leaving many shocked that the race car driver escaped the accident unscathed.*

untenable: adjective – that which cannot be maintained or occupied; incapable of being defended or held. *The social worker determined that the home was untenable for the children; there was no running water, no electricity, and only one bedroom.*

urbane: adjective – courteous suave; polished. *Jimmy was the epitome of urbane with his tailored suits, debonair personality, and fine taste in wine.*

utopian: adjective – excellent, but existing only in fancy or theory; given to dreams or schemes of perfection. *For Fran, the island was her own utopian escape from the stress of her job and her family.*

vacillate: verb – to say unsteadily; to totter; to waver; to fluctuate. *The vacillating fan provided intermittent relief to the hot and exhausted campers.*

validate: verb- to declare or make legally sound; to substantiate; to verify. *The results of the contest were unofficial until they were validated.*

venerate: verb – to regard with respect and reverence; to honor. *Pope John Paul II is venerated as one of the most influential Pope's in modern history.*

verbose: adjective – wordy; tedious. *The reporter was overly verbose and took an inordinate amount of time to get past the unnecessary details and to the point.*

viable: adjective – able to live or exist; practicable. *Many couples opt not to share news that they are expecting until after 12 weeks when they are certain that the fetus is viable.*

vicarious: adjective – taking the place of another; experienced through sympathetic participation in the experience of another. *Many people are afraid to travel or feel like they don't have the time, so they instead live vicariously through those who do travel.*

vindictive: adjective – revengeful; unforgiving; bitter; spiteful. *The small claims court judge admonished Sharon for bringing what he considered a clearly vindictive lawsuit; he cited her husband's recent filing of divorce papers as the only justification for the frivolous legal action.*

virtuoso: noun – one interested in the pursuit of knowledge; one with mastery skill or technique in any field. *BK Jackson's saxophone rendition of Prince's Purple Rain was considered a virtuoso performance by many.*

vitriolic: adjective - extremely biting or caustic; sharp and bitter. *Jackson's vitriolic management style created a hostile environment for his employees who did not respond well to his biting and unconstructive feedback and generally surly disposition.*

volatile: adjective – evaporating readily at normal temperatures; changeable; explosive. *The situation in Pattani is quite volatile at the moment, and government officials have warned citizens not to travel there.*

voluminous: adjective – large, bulky; enough to fill volumes. *The hairdresser used lots of hair spray and mousse to make her normally flat and stringy hair appear more voluminous.*

whet: verb – to sharpen; to make stronger; to stimulate. *The executive gave the investors just enough information to whet their curiosities.*

wither: verb – to dry; to shrivel; to cause to lose courage or to be ashamed. *After not being watered for a month, the plants started to wither and die.*

writhe: verb – to twist or squirm, as in pain; to suffer from shame or shyness. *Following his surgery, Antonio spent a week in bed writhing in pain since he refused to take any pain medication.*

zany: adjective – clownish; foolish; funny; absurd. *Jennifer's friends often commented on her zany and eccentric personality since she loves to entertain and tell corny jokes.*

zenith: noun – the point in the sky directly above one; the highest point. *The Shaman Dynasty reached its zenith at the end of the 15th century.*

ARGO
BROTHERS

PREFIXES & SUFFIXES

Prefix	Definition	Example
a	in, on, of, up, to	aloof
an	without, lacking	anaerobic
ad	to, toward	advance
am	friend, love	amiable
ante	before, previous	antebellum
anti	against, opposing	antithetical
auto	self	autonomy
belli	war, warlike	belligerent
bene	well, good	benefit
bi	two	bilateral
chron	time	chronological
circum	around	circumspect
com	with, together, very	communion
contra	against, opposing	contradiction
cred	belief, trust	credible
dem	people	demographic
dia	through, across, apart	diameter
dis	away, off, down, not	disparate
equi	equal, equally	equidistant
ex	out	extract
fore	before, previous	forecast
homo	same, equal	homogenous
hyper	excessive, over	hyperventilate
hypo	under, beneath	hypothermia
in	in, into	invade
in	not, opposing	ineligible
inter	among, between	interconnected
intra	within	intranet
mal	bad, poorly, not	malware

Prefix	Definition	Example
mis	bad, poorly, not	mistake
mono	one, single	monogamy
mor	die, death	morbid
neo	new	neoclassical
non	not	nonsense
ob	against, opposing	obstruct
omni	all, everywhere	omniscient
over	above	overhead
pan	all, entire	panorama
para	beside, beyond	parallel
per	through	permit
peri	around	perimeter
phil	love, like	philosophy
poly	many	polygon
post	after, following	postscript
pre	before, previous	preface
prim	first, early	primary
pro	forward, in place of	propel
re	back, backward, again	revert
retro	back, backward	retrospect
semi	half, partly	semicircle
sub	under, beneath	subterranean
super	above, extra	supersede
sym	with, together	symbiotic
trans	across, beyond, over	transmit
un	not, reverse of	unfit
uni	one	uniform
vis	to see	visible

Suffix	Definition	Example
able	able to, likely	palpable
age	process, state, rank	passage
ance	act, condition, fact	forbearance
ate	having, showing	isolate
ation	action, state, result	occupation
cy	state, condition	clemency
dom	state, rank, condition	kingdom
en	cause to be, become	enliven
esque	in the style of, like	picturesque
ess	feminine	empress
ful	full of, marked by	grateful
fy	make, cause, cause to have	exemplify
hood	state, condition	manhood
ible	able, likely, fit	possible
ion	action, result, state	union
ish	suggesting, like	sluggish
ism	act, manner, doctrine	Buddhism
ist	doer, believer	philanthropist
ition	action, state, result	contrition
ity	state, quality, condition	equality
ize	make, cause to be, treat with	ostracize
less	lacking, without	fearless
like	like, similar	childlike
logue	type of speaking or writing	prologue
ly	like, of the nature of	aptly
ment	means, result, action	engagement
ness	quality, state	eagerness
or	doer, office, action	editor
ous	marked by, given to	momentous

Suffix	Definition	Example
ship	the art or skill of	statesmanship
some	apt to, showing	fulsome
th	act, state, quality	warmth
tude	quality, state, result	magnitude
ward	in the direction of	toward

ARGO
BROTHERS

Made in the USA
Lexington, KY
08 July 2016